New Inside Out

Sue Kay, Vaughan Jones,

Helena Gomm, Peter Maggs

& Chris Dawson

Intermediate

Teacher's Book

 MACMILLAN

Macmillan Education
Between Towns Road, Oxford OX4 3PP
A division of Macmillan Publishers Limited
Companies and representatives throughout the world

ISBN 978-0-230-00910-3

Text © Sue Kay and Vaughan Jones 2009
Text by Helena Gomm
Photocopiable resource materials and language and cultural notes by Peter Maggs.
Design and illustration © Macmillan Publishers Limited 2009

First published 2009

All rights reserved; no part of this publication may be reproduced, stored in a retrieval system, transmitted in any form, or by any means, electronic, mechanical, photocopying, recording, or otherwise, without the prior written permission of the publishers.

Note to Teachers
Photocopies may be made, for classroom use, of pages xxxvii–xlvi, and 151–190 without the prior written permission of Macmillan Publishers Limited. However, please note that the copyright law, which does not normally permit multiple copying of published material, applies to the rest of this book.

Designed by 320 Design Limited
Page layout by Carolyn Gibson
Illustrated by Beach, Angus Cameron, Peter Campbell, Celia Canning, Paul Collicut, Ivan Gillet, Peter Harper, Ben Hasler, Ed McLachlan, Colin Meir and Gary Rees
Cover design by Andrew Oliver

The authors and publishers would like to thank the following for permission to reproduce their material: Quotation from *Language and Problems of Knowledge* by Noam Chomsky copyright © Noam Chomsky 1988 Massachusetts Institute of Technology, reprinted by permission of The MIT Press, Cambridge, Massachusetts. Quotation from *Understanding Second Language Acquisition* by Rod Ellis copyright © Rod Ellis 1985, reproduced by permission of Oxford University Press.

The authors and publisher are grateful for permission to reprint the following copyright material:
You've Got A Friend - Words and Music by Carole King copyright © Screen Gems-EMI Music Inc/Screen Gems-Music Limited 1971, reprinted by permission of International Music Publications Ltd (a trading name of Faber Music Ltd). All Rights Reserved;
It's My Party – Words and Music by Wiener Herb, Gottlieb Seymour, John, Jr. Gluck and Wally Gold, © 1963 (Renewed) Chappell & Co., Inc (ASCAP);
Somewhere Only We Know - Words & Music by Tim Rice-Oxley, Tom Chaplin & Richard Hughes © copyright 2004 Universal Music Publishing MGB Limited. Used by permission of Music Sales Limited. All Rights Reserved. International Copyright Secured;
Dedicated Follower of Fashion - Words and Music by Ray Davies copyright © Davray Music Limited and Carlin Music Corporation, London, NW1 8BD, 1966, reprinted by permission of the publisher. All Rights Reserved.
Quotation from *Language and Problems of Knowledge* by Noam Chomsky, copyright © Noam Chomsky 1988 Massachusetts Institute of Technology, reprinted by permission of The MIT Press, Cambridge, Massachusetts.
Quotation - Reproduced by permission of Oxford University Press. From *Oxford Applied Linguistics: Understanding Second Language Acquisition* by Rod Ellis © Rod Ellis 1985. New Edition *OAL: A Study of Second Language Acquisition* published 2008.

These materials may contain links for third party websites. We have no control over, and are not responsible for, the contents of such third party websites. Please use care when accessing them.

Although we have tried to trace and contact copyright holders before publication, in some cases this has not been possible. If contacted, we will be pleased to rectify any errors or omissions at the earliest opportunity.
Printed in Thailand

2014   2013   2012   2011

11 10 9 8 7 6 5 4

428.2 K

00051066

Contents

Student's Book contents map

WB = **Workbook**. Each unit of the Workbook contains a one-page section which develops practical writing skills.

Introduction

Welcome to *New Inside Out!*

New Inside Out is the fruit of many years' teaching, writing and developing material. Everything we write is informed by the reactions we get from our students. Our aim is simply to produce a set of materials that will help you create optimum conditions in your classroom for learning to take place.

Sue Kay   *Vaughan Jones*

Engaging content

The American linguist and philosopher Noam Chomsky once said:

'The truth of the matter is that about 99% of teaching is making the students feel interested in the material. Then the other 1% has to do with your methods'.

While we might want to quibble with the percentages, we would nevertheless agree whole-heartedly with the central message in Professor Chomsky's assertion: namely, students learn best when they're interested in the material. It's as simple as that. A text might contain six beautifully-crafted examples of the past simple, a good spread of high frequency lexical items and exemplify some useful functional language, but if it doesn't engage the students, if they can't relate to it, if it feels alien to them, then the most important ingredient for successful learning is missing. In *New Inside Out*, we've drawn on our own classroom experience, and that of our colleagues around the world, to select topics, texts and tasks that engage students both emotionally and intellectually. Students are our richest resource. They come to class with their own knowledge of the world, their own tastes, feelings and opinions. It's up to us to exploit this rich resource by organising learning around topics that they can relate to – topics that are part of their life experience.

Structured support

We all know that learning a language is a messy, non-linear business. We're dismayed when there seems to be little correlation between what is taught and what is learned! However, there is plenty of evidence to suggest that 'instructed' learners (those who attend classes or follow a course of study) learn faster, and ultimately attain a higher level of proficiency than 'non-instructed' learners.

In *New Inside Out*, new language input is carefully controlled: we aim to maximise exposure to high frequency language appropriate to this level. Students are encouraged to notice new grammar and new vocabulary in contexts where the meaning is clear. They are then given opportunities to manipulate the new language and try it out in different situations. They discover why using one particular form rather than another one actually matters: not just because it's right or wrong, but because it does or doesn't communicate a meaning successfully. The emphasis is always on what students can do with the language rather than what they know about the language. The new language is systematically reviewed and recycled until finally the students feel confident enough to use it to make their own meanings. It becomes part of their available repertoire. It has been 'learned'.

Real world tasks

We're strong believers in the old adage: 'practice makes perfect'. *New Inside Out* emphasizes output, particularly speaking, and there are a huge number of tasks that are designed to develop fluency. Students practise functional language in sections entitled *Useful phrases*. But for the most part, the speaking tasks simply encourage the students to talk about things that actually matter to them, rather than playing roles or exchanging invented information. One of our main objectives is to ensure that the language our students spend time rehearsing in the classroom is transferable to the real world. By orchestrating tasks that require the students to use grammar and vocabulary to make meaningful utterances, this objective becomes obtainable. As the linguist and academic Rod Ellis reminds us:

'It is the need to get meanings across and the pleasure experienced when this is achieved that motivates second language acquisition.'

www.insideout.net
'the art of communication'

Components of the course

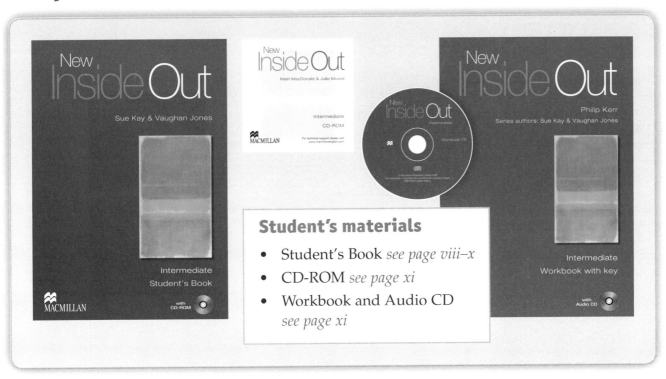

Student's materials

- Student's Book *see page viii–x*
- CD-ROM *see page xi*
- Workbook and Audio CD
  see page xi

Teacher's materials

- Teacher's Book
  see page xii
- Test CD *see page xii*
- Class Audio CDs
  see page xii
- DVD *see page xiii*
- DVD Teacher's Book
  see page xiii
- Website *see page xiii*

Student's materials A typical Student's Book unit (Unit 5)

Student's Book page 40

A language menu at the beginning of each unit summarises the main teaching points.

Headings throughout the units provide clear information about what the students are studying.

Language is presented in context with engaging material taken from modern authentic sources.

Students are encouraged to engage with the material on a personal level by relating topics to their own lives, views and feelings.

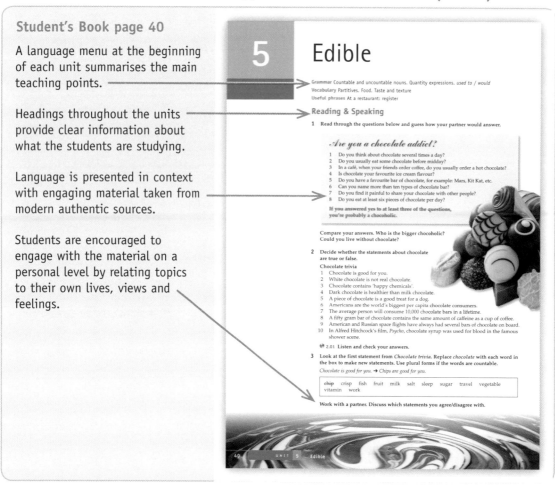

Student's Book page 41

New Inside Out Intermediate includes an average of two grammar sections in every unit. Typically, these follow a three-stage approach.

1 Students explore new grammatical structures that have been contextualized in the previous section. They focus on the way the new language works.

   A brief summary of the grammar point is provided in the margin.

2 Language practice is designed to be realistic and meaningful.

3 Students use target language for controlled, personalised practice.

In addition, students are referred to the Grammar *Extra* pages at the back of the Student's Book for extended explanations and further practice.

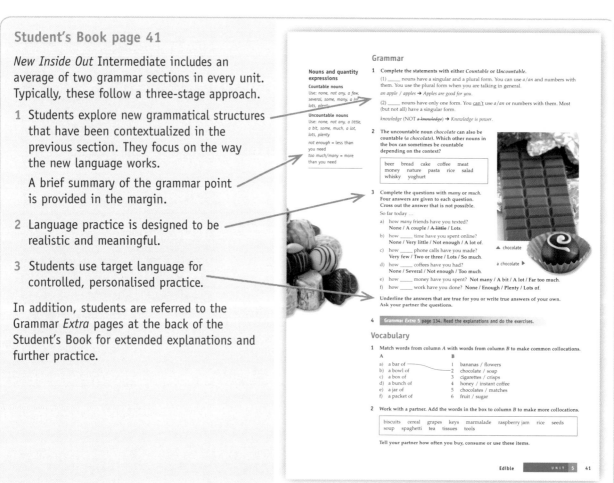

Student's Book page 42

Students are encouraged to exchange meaningful utterances in personalised speaking tasks.

Pronunciation work on particular areas of sound, stress and intonation is integrated into every unit.

Opportunities to explore important lexical areas such as collocation are integrated into vocabulary sections.

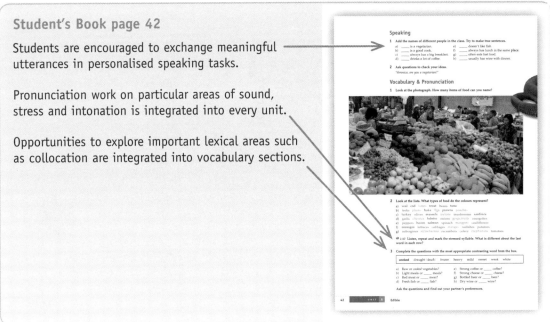

Student's Book page 43

The listenings include texts specially written for language learning. There are dialogues, conversations and monologues. There is a variety of English accents and the tasks are designed to develop real-life listening skills.

Vocabulary is presented in context and is related to the themes and topics in the unit. Practice activities expand the students' knowledge of particular lexical sets and give them opportunities to use the new vocabulary in meaningful exchanges.

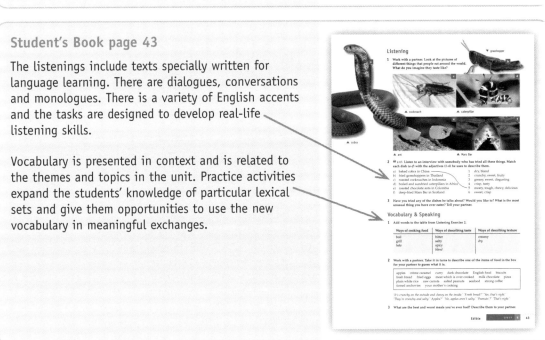

Student's Book page 44

Motivating reading texts have been adapted and graded to suit the Intermediate level student. They have been selected not only for their language content, but also for their interest and appropriacy.

Student's Book page 45

Here is another example of a typical grammar section. The students are required to 'notice' the way the target language is used in the reading text on the previous page. This is followed by meaningful, personalised practice.

For every unit, there is one pairwork which offers further speaking practice. These are clearly labelled for the student.

Anecdotes give students a chance to tackle a longer piece of discourse.

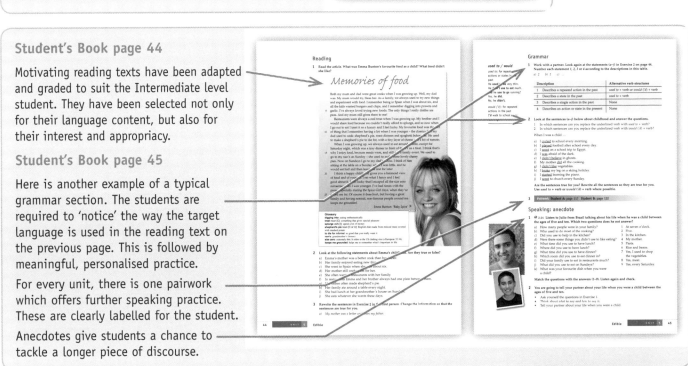

Student's Book page 46

Useful phrases gives students a portable toolkit of functional language. These sections are designed to be fun and engaging and the phrases are recorded on the Audio CD.

Student's Book page 47

The *Vocabulary Extra* pages at the end of every unit explore twelve key lexical areas such as collocation, verb patterns and word formation. They provide students with detailed practice activities and help promote useful dictionary skills.

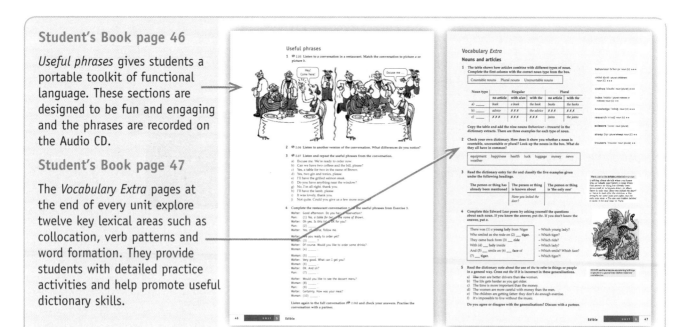

Student's Book page 56

There are four Review units in *New Inside Out* Intermediate Student's Book. Each Review unit revises the new structures taught in the previous three teaching units.

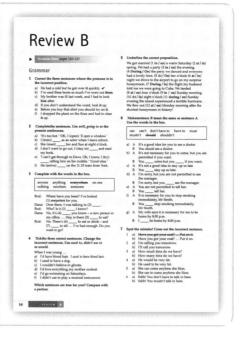

Student's Book pages 134 and 135

The *Grammar Extra* pages at the back of the Student's Book provide a summary of the new grammatical structures as well as extra practice.

Each unit has one full page of explanations and exercises.

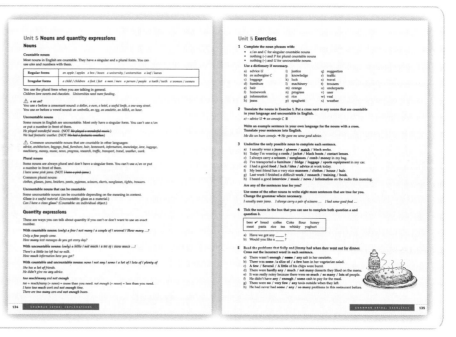

CD-ROM

The CD-ROM in the back of every Student's Book provides a wealth of interactive practice activities along with integrated listening material and video clips contextualising the *Useful phrases*.

Workbook pages 28 and 29

The Workbook provides revision of all the main points in the Student's Book, plus extra listening practice, pronunciation work and a complete self-contained writing course. There are *with* and *without key* versions, and an extract from the *Bernice bobs her hair* and *Gretchen's forty winks* (Macmillan Graded Reader) is included in the back of the Workbook.

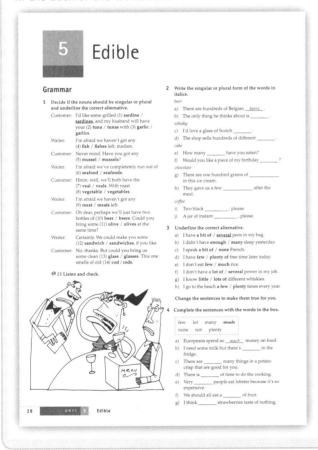

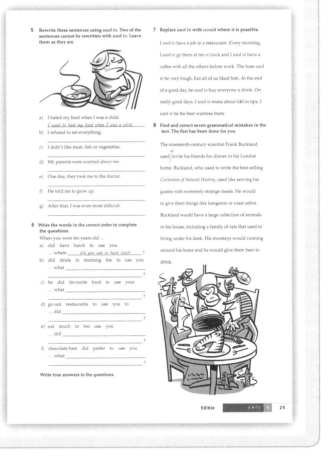

Teacher's materials

Teacher's Book

The 6-in-1 Teacher's Book contains:

- an Introduction
- Practical methodology
- Council of Europe (CEF) checklists
- complete teaching notes with answer keys
- a bank of extra photocopiable grammar, vocabulary and communicative activities
- a Test CD with word files that you can edit and the recordings of the listening test activities

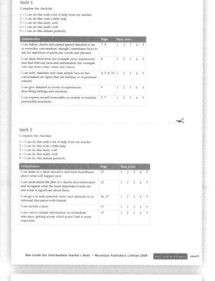

Class CD set

The Class CDs contain:

- the dialogues and listening activities from the Student's Book
- recordings of the songs
- recordings of the reading texts

DVD and DVD Teacher's Book

The DVD contains programmes which complement the topics in the Student's Book. There is a wide variety of formats including interviews, profiles, documentaries and video diaries. The DVD Teacher's Book contains related teaching notes and photocopiable worksheets.

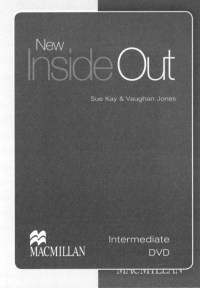

Website

www.insideout.net

Visit www.insideout.net to find out more details about the course and its authors. The new magazine-style website provides downloadable resources and more information about *New Inside Out*.

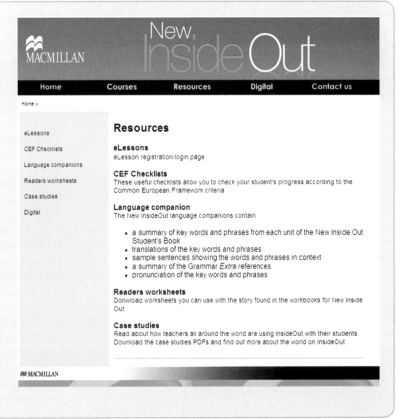

Practical methodology

Teaching intermediate students

Many teachers will be familiar with the term 'intermediate plateau'. It refers to a point in a student's language learning curve where, having made relatively quick and effortless progress from beginner to intermediate, they seem to get stuck and find it very difficult to progress onto more advanced levels. It's not difficult to understand why this might be so.

Intermediate students have already come across most of the basic grammar structures and, while their use of the present perfect might by wildly inaccurate, they can lose motivation if the teacher insists on going over what for them is 'learned' language. Coupled with this, their vocabulary probably extends to a passive knowledge of 2000–2500 of the most frequent words. Research tells us that 'knowing' the 2500 most frequent words means you can understand over 80% of everything you read – which is sufficient for many students. In other words, being familiar with most of the grammar and knowing enough vocabulary to 'get by' in most situations the intermediate student is already a fairly competent language learner. Breaking through to the next level requires considerable time, energy and dedication.

In *New Inside Out* Intermediate we've tried to get the balance right between challenging students with new grammar and vocabulary and providing important recycling and consolidation work in more familiar areas. In particular, there is a clear emphasis on learning new vocabulary – the key to breaking through the intermediate ceiling. A relentless focus on meaning, and in particular how students can make their own meanings with the language, is built into every stage of the learning process. It's this core feature of *Inside Out* which helps students maintain their enthusiasm and motivation.

Right from the start

Every teacher has their own way of setting up their classroom, interacting with their students and conducting their lessons. Here are a few things that we have found useful to bear in mind.

The right atmosphere

It's important to do everything you can to creating a supportive learning environment. Start by memorising every student's name and learn as much information as you can about them. Make sure students learn each other's names too and that they all get to know things about each other early on in the course. Think of appropriate ways you could help foster good classroom dynamics.

Pay attention to how you respond to students both individually and collectively. Make sure you find time to 'chat' to individual students or small informal groups of students before or after class. More formally, it's a good idea to devote at least one lesson per term to counsel your students individually and discuss their progress.

Even at intermediate level students are often shy and under-confident about speaking in class. It takes a great deal of courage to open your mouth and say something in the very early stages of a course. For this reason, students are encouraged to work in pairs and groups so they can rehearse the language 'in private' rather then be immediately required to speak in the more intimidating arena of the class.

Always give your students time to think. It's perfectly normal to have moments of silence while students absorb and process new information, write down new vocabulary from the board, or think about their answers. Don't be afraid of the 'pregnant pause'!

The right environment

Your classroom might be the only exposure to English that students get. Make that exposure as rich as you can by decorating the walls with maps and posters. Have several monolingual dictionaries available to refer to – a class set if possible. Also, try to have a selection of English books, newspapers and magazines lying around that students can pick up and browse before and after lessons. Here are some further ideas:

*   Keep a 'wordbox' on your table where words or phrases that come up in the lesson are recorded on strips of paper and put in the box. Invite the students to record the words for you. They can then be used in a variety of quick revision games in subsequent lessons. Alternatively, you could institute the 'Class Scribe' idea. One student in the class is given the role of recording any new language that comes up during the lesson that isn't necessarily the target language of that lesson. This unique record is then kept in a folder in the class and provides the teacher with valuable data for revision activities. The role of class scribe is rotated so that each student gets a turn at being responsible for recording the lesson. This shared responsibility can help promote positive group dynamics.

- Promote simplified graded readers. There is a huge selection of readers available at the intermediate level: both simplified classics and original stories. Many of them now come as 'talking books' with CDs. Ask the students to always bring their reader to the lesson and occasionally set aside a ten-minute slot for them to talk about what they are reading. Alternatively, just devote ten minutes to silent reading. This is invaluable input. Most intermediate students will be best suited to readers where the basic vocabulary is in the range 1600–2000 words. Make sure the students understand that it is better to read and enjoy ten easy books than struggle through one difficult one. Get your students hooked on books!

- Use English in the classroom. It's very tempting to slip into the students' language – particularly if you are teaching in a monolingual situation. Try only to use L1 as an absolute last resort: an occasional quick translation or brief explanation.

The right learning skills

Students will always benefit from help with learning strategies. Here are some thoughts:

- Encourage students to ask questions about language. If you have created the right atmosphere in your classroom then students will be more likely to take an active approach in their own learning and this is important. Students should never feel intimidated about asking questions.

- Spend time encouraging students to experiment with how they record words and phrases from the lesson. Get them to draw the word rather than translate it. They're then associating the word with the concept rather than with another word. Make sure they note the part of speech – verb, noun, adjective, etc. Tell them to find a way of noting the pronunciation of the word, either using phonemic script (in the back of the Student's Book) or by developing their own system. Ask them to write complete personalised sentences putting the new word or phrase in a real context and thereby making it more memorable.

- A dictionary is a very important language learning tool and most students will buy one. Usually students prefer a bilingual dictionary as this provides them with a quick translation of the word they need. However, at the intermediate level they need to think seriously about investing in a good monolingual dictionary. The Vocabulary Extra pages at the end of each unit in New Inside Out Intermediate have been designed to give students valuable dictionary practice and make them aware of all the useful 'extra' information that is available in a good monolingual dictionary.

The right amount of practice

In our experience, the most successful lessons consist of a manageable amount of new input, and then a lot of meaningful practice. For this reason, we've tried to provide maximum practice activities in New Inside Out, both in the Student's Book and in the other supporting components. But there is never enough time in the lessons alone. Always set homework, even if it's just reading a chapter from a reader, and make homework feedback or correction an integral part of the lesson.

The top 10 activities for intermediate students

These tried and trusted activities can be used as lead-ins, warmers, fillers, pair-forming activities, or for revision and recycling. Most of them require very little or no preparation and can be adapted to cover a wide variety of different language points. The emphasis is on vocabulary revision as we all know that it's only through repeated exposure to new words and expressions that students are likely to transform 'input' into 'intake'. You may be familiar with some of the ideas and others may be new. In any event, we hope they provide a useful extension to your teaching repertoire. They certainly get used and re-used in our own classrooms!

It's always useful to have a stock of small white cards and access to a collection of pictures. Magazine pictures are ideal, and can be filed in alphabetical order according to topics.

1 Board bingo

Aim

This activity is good for revising any type of vocabulary.

Preparation

Write down twelve to fifteen words you want to revise on the board. They could be words from the last lesson, words from the unit you've just finished or a random selection of words covering the whole term.

Procedure

- Ask the students to choose five of the words and write them down. When they've done that, tell the students that you're going to read out dictionary definitions of the words in random order and that they should cross out their words if they think they hear the definition. When they've crossed out all five words, they shout *Bingo!* Make sure you keep a record of the word definitions you call out so that you can check the students' answers.

- If you teach a monolingual class, you could read out a translation of each word rather than an English definition. Alternatively, you could turn it into a pronunciation exercise by working on the recognition of phonemic script. Hold up cards with phonemic transcriptions of the words in random order. Students cross out their words if they think they've seen the corresponding phonemic transcription.

2 My criteria

Aim

This activity can be used to review almost any vocabulary.

Preparation

Choose up to ten words that you want to revise. You might want to start with recognisable lexical sets and then move onto groups of random words.

Procedure

- Write the words on the board in no particular order. Put the students in pairs or small groups. The activity consists of writing out the words in a specific order according to a particular criteria of the students' choosing. Each pair or group keeps their criteria secret. They then give their list to another pair or group who have to work out what they think the criteria is.

- For example, let's say you want to revise words for clothes from Unit 12. You write eight items on the board, e.g. *pinstripe suit, leather belt, woolly jumper, cotton hoody, silk blouse, fur hat, stripy top, snakeskin boots*. The students then rearrange the list according to a criteria that they have thought of. The criteria can be anything from 'alphabetical order': i.e. 1) *leather <u>belt</u>*, 2) *silk <u>blouse</u>*, 3) *snakeskin <u>boots</u>*, etc. to 'warm': i.e. 1) *fur hat*, 2) *woolly jumper*, 3) *pinstripe suit*, etc.

- Sometimes the criterion clearly suggests only one possible order (i.e. 'alphabetical order'). If the criterion is 'warm', then the order of items might be open to debate. This is fine and can lead to some interesting discussion. To get the students used to this activity, in the first instance you might want to give them different criteria to choose from. Here are some more possible criteria for clothes: *comfortable, smart, expensive, useful, things I wear*. Alternatively, you might want to give them just one criterion – one where the order is not obvious – and see if each group comes up with the same order.

- Here are some more ideas for lexical sets and criteria:

  1 Extreme sports (Unit 2)
  Possible criteria: *dangerous, expensive, healthy, sociable, weather-dependant.*

  2 Food (Unit 5)
  Possible criteria: *sweet, salty, luxury, essential to life, fattening, cheap.*

  3 Jobs (Unit 6)
  Possible criteria: *creative, well-paid, useful to society, easy, fun.*

3 Category dictation

Aim

This activity can be adapted to review almost any vocabulary. It can also be used to review certain pronunciation and grammar points.

Preparation

Choose the language you want to review and devise a way of categorising it into two or more categories.

Procedure

- Write the category headings on the board and ask the students to copy them onto a piece of paper. Two simple categories is usually best. More than three can get complicated. Then dictate the words (10–12 maximum) slowly and clearly, and ask the students to write them down in the correct category.

- For example, you might want to revise the names for different jobs as a lead-in to the Listening on page 52 in Unit 6. Your categories might be jobs you do inside and jobs you do outside. So, write the following on the board and ask the students to copy it down.

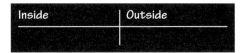

Inside	Outside

- Then dictate the words: e.g. an archaeologist, a journalist, a train driver, a lawyer, a vet, etc. The students write down the words in the correct category. When you've dictated 10 or 12 words, ask students to compare their lists. When they've done this, ask them to call out their answers and write them on the board in the correct category, so that they can check the spelling. Alternatively, you could ask the students to take it in turns to write the answers on the board.

- Here are some more ideas for categories:

  1 Revise adjectives. (Unit 2)
  Suggested categories: *'gradable'* or *'non-gradable'*, *I feel …* or *It is …* (e.g. *I feel <u>bored</u>* but *It is <u>boring</u>*).

  2 Revise sports. (Unit 2)
  Suggested categories: *Sports with a ball* and *Sports without a ball; Sports you play in teams* and *Sports you play individually; Sports you use 'go' with* or *Sports you use 'play' with.*

  3 Revise family words. (Unit 3)
  Suggested categories: *Male or Female, Have or Don't have.*

  4 Revise more adjectives. (Unit 3)
  Suggested categories: *Positive or Negative; Adjectives that take the prefix 'un-'* or *Adjectives that don't take the prefix 'un-'.*

  5 Revise food (Unit 5)
  Suggested categories: *Countable nouns or Uncountable nouns; Can freeze or Can't freeze; Can buy in tins* or *Can't buy in tins; Have in my fridge or Never have in my fridge.*

4 Whose dialogue?

Aim

To imagine what people in pictures are saying to one another and to write a short dialogue.

Preparation

You will need a selection of eight to ten magazine pictures. Each picture should show two people who could be talking to one another. Try to get pictures of as widely varying contexts as possible.

Procedure

- Divide the students into pairs or small groups. Display the pictures on the board, on the wall or on the floor where everybody can see them. Ask each pair or group to secretly choose a picture, but without pointing or touching it. The students then write a short dialogue between the people in the picture they've chosen. When they've finished, ask them to act out their dialogue to the other members of the class without indicating which picture it's based on. The other students guess which picture the dialogue goes with.

- This activity is particularly suited to revising some of the functional language from the Useful phrases sections in the Student's book. You could write six or more useful phrases on the board and tell the students that their dialogues must include at least one (or two, or three) of them. The Useful phrases could be part of a recognisable set (e.g. Unit 5: *Do you have a reservation? A table for two, please, Two gin and tonics, please, I'll have the steak*, etc.) Alternatively, they could just be random (e.g. *You'd better put a bag of ice on it, She can be a bit talkative, We're making good time, Oh, I'm sorry to hear that*, etc.)

- Alternatively, you could choose any ten to twelve words you want to revise and put them on the board. Then tell the students that they must include at least three (or four, or five) of the words in their dialogues.

5 Random letters

Aim

This activity is good for revising any type of vocabulary.

Preparation

None

Procedure

- Ask the students to call out any seven letters from the alphabet. (It doesn't have to be seven letters: anything between seven and twelve is fine.) Write the letters scattered on the board.

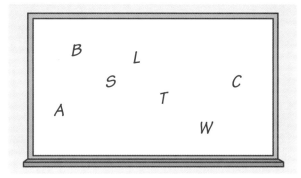

- Then ask the students in pairs to think of a word beginning with each letter on the board. The most obvious criteria is to revise words from a specific lexical set that you have taught recently. Alternatively, you could simply ask them for words they've noted down in lessons over the past two weeks.

- Another possibility would be to find the most interesting words they can from the Student Book unit that you've just finished. If the lexical set you want them to revise is particularly rich, you could ask the students to think of as many words for each letter as they can in say three minutes: make it into a contest to find the most words.

- There are lots of possible variations using different criteria for words from the letters on the board. Here are a few:

1 Use the same criteria as above but ask the students to think of words ending with the letter on the board.

2 Ask the students to write only nouns, or adjectives or irregular verbs or some other part of speech.

3 Ask the students to write only words with three syllables or words with the same vowel sounds.

4 Ask students to write only words that start with the same letter in their own language or only words that start with a different letter.

6 Five favourites

Aim

This activity is good for revising any words learned recently.

Preparation

None

Procedure

- Students look back through their lesson notes for the last two weeks and select from the words they've recorded five words that they think are particularly useful. They compare their list with a partner and together they produce a common list of five words from the combined list of ten. To do this they'll have to argue for and against words on the combined list until they are both satisfied that they have the most useful five.

- If you wanted to continue the activity, you could then have each pair join up with another pair as a group of four and repeat the procedure. Depending on the size of your class, you might continue until you had established a list of 'five favourites' for the whole class.

- The value of this activity lies in the students looking back through their notes, choosing the words and then arguing for them to be part of the combined list. The whole procedure gives them valuable repeat exposure to words recently learned.

- A possible extension activity after each pair has formed their common list of five words is to collect the lists and redistribute them so that each pair has a different list. The pairs then write a dialogue or short story incorporating the five words they have on the list they've just received. You could then ask them to read out their dialogues or stories and the other students guess what the five listed words were.

7 Crosswords

Aim

This activity is good for revising lexical sets and can help with spelling.

Preparation

Choose a lexical set you want to revise. For example, *sports* (Unit 2*)*, nouns that collocate with '*do*' (or '*make*') (Unit 4), *food* (Unit 5), *clothes* (Unit 12), etc.

Procedure

- Students work in pairs. They'll need a piece of paper, preferably graph paper with squares on.

- Choose a topic, for example, *Food*.

- Student A writes 'Across' words, and Student B writes 'Down' words.

- It's a good idea to provide the first word across, and make sure that it's a long one (e.g. *vegetables*). Student B then adds another food word down the paper from top to bottom. This word must intersect with the food word written across the page.

- Student A then writes another food word across that intersects with the word Student B has written down. Students continue taking it in turns to write in their words.

- Students build up a crossword until they can't think of any more food words. (You could make it into a game by saying that the last person to write a food word is the winner.) Note that students must leave one square between each word – this is why it's better and clearer to use squared paper.

- At this level, with a topic as big as 'food', it might be advisable to narrow the category, e.g. *fruit and vegetables*, *meat and fish*, or *food you put in the fridge*, etc.

8 Odd one out

Aim

This activity can be used to revise almost any language.

Preparation

Think of the vocabulary, pronunciation or grammar point you want to revise.

Procedure

- Write five words on the board and ask students which one is the odd one out. The students then explain why. This usually relates to the meaning of the word.

> milk   cheese   cream   butter   sugar

- Here *sugar* is the odd one out because the other words are all dairy products.

- Note that it doesn't matter if the students can't explain in perfect English why *sugar* is the odd one out. The important thing is that they're looking at and thinking about the words you want them to revise.

- You can use this format to practise and revise all sorts of things. Here are some examples:

  1 For meaning:
    sister / nephew / daughter / wife / mother
    nephew is the odd one out because he's a man. The other words describe women.

  2 For spelling:
    pen / book / bag / phone / diary
    diary is the odd one out because you spell the plural *ies*. The other words you just add *s*.

  3 For pronunciation: sounds
    A / I / H / J / K
    I is the odd one out because the vowel sound is different.

  4 For pronunciation: stress
    hospital / banana / potato / Italian / computer
    hospital is the odd one out because the stress is on the first syllable. The other words have the stress on the second syllable.

  5 For collocation: *do* or *make*
    your homework / the washing / an appointment / a training course / the shopping
    an appointment is the odd one out because you use *make*. For the others you use *do*.

  6 For grammar:
    agree / promise / want / can't stand / offer
    can't stand is the odd one out because it is followed by a gerund – the other words are followed by the *to*-infinitive.

- You should tell the students what the criteria is, for example, 'think about meaning' or 'think about the sounds'. To make the activity a little more challenging, instead of writing the words on the board, you can dictate them. As a follow-up, ask the students to write their own odd ones out.

9 Making sentences

Aim

This activity is good for revising any type of vocabulary. It works best if the words are a fairly random selection and not part of a tight lexical set.

Preparation

Choose 12 words you want to revise and write them in a circle (like a clockface) on the board.

Procedure

- Students work in pairs. They choose two or more of the words and try to make a sentence with them.

  Example sentences:

  My brother is doing yoga *in the* park *.*

  The snowboarder *eats* organic vegetables *on* Friday *.*

  I saw *an* ambitious puppy *in the* canal *with a* blue neck *.*

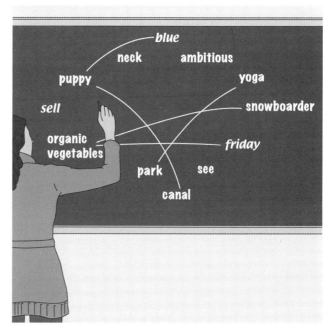

- The students then read out their sentences and you connect the words they have used on the board. You can correct the grammar as necessary or you can make it more difficult for the students by only accepting grammatically correct sentences. (You could make it into a game by saying that the pair who form the sentence including the highest number of words on the board is the winner.) It doesn't matter how bizarre the sentences are, the important thing is that students spend time looking at and remembering the vocabulary.

10 Spell check

Aim

To revise any vocabulary and focus particularly on spelling.

Preparation

Choose the words you want to review. They can be lexical sets or words at random. Eight to ten words is best.

Procedure

- There are various different ways you can approach this, but the following four ways seem to work best:

  1 The missing letter
  Student work in pairs. Write up the words with a letter missing from each one, e.g. *samon*, *courgete*, *rasberry*, etc. The students have to decide which is the missing letter in each case and rewrite the word correctly. Then give a definition.

  2 The extra letter
  Students work in pairs. Write up the words with an extra letter in each one, e.g. *unfaithfull*, *sosciable*, *tollerant*, etc. The students have to decide which is the extra letter in each case and rewrite the word correctly. Then give a definition.

  3 The wrong letter
  Students work in pairs. Write up the words with a wrong letter in each one, e.g. *nefhew*, *cousen*, *neece*, etc. The students have to decide which is the wrong letter in each case and rewrite the word correctly. Then give a definition.

  4 Anagrams
  Students work in pairs. Write up the words as anagrams. The students have to unscramble the anagram and rewrite the word correctly. This is the most challenging version of 'Spell check', so it's best to give the students a clue, for example: 'these are all ways of describing hair', e.g. *lurcy*, *ssemy*, *cidenger*, etc. (*curly*, *messy*, *receding*). Then give a definition.

Anecdote tasks

New Inside Out Intermediate includes a number of extended speaking tasks, where students tackle a longer piece of discourse. We've called these 'Anecdotes'. They are based on personal issues, for instance, memories, stories, people you know. When you learn a musical instrument, you can't spend all your time playing scales and exercises: you also need to learn whole pieces in order to see how music is organised. Anecdotes give students a chance to get to grips with how discourse is organised. We have found the following strategies helpful in getting our students to tell their Anecdotes.

1 Choose global topics that everybody can relate to

One of the main objectives of an Anecdote is to encourage students to experiment with and hopefully grow more competent at using language at the more demanding end of their range. It therefore seems only fair to ask them to talk about subjects they know something about. With familiar subject matter students can concentrate on how they're speaking as well as what they're speaking about. The eight Anecdote topics in *New Inside Out* Intermediate have been carefully selected to appeal to the widest range of students, whilst at the same time, fitting in to the context of the unit.

Unit 1	A friend who is different from you
Unit 2	A time you were in a dangerous/exciting situation
Unit 4	A party you've been to
Unit 5	Your childhood memories
Unit 8	A journey you've been on
Unit 9	A film you enjoyed
Unit 10	An activity you did as a child
Unit 12	Somebody you met for the first time recently

As soon as you have got to know your students well enough, you'll be able to choose other Anecdote topics suited to their particular interests and experiences.

2 Allow sufficient preparation time

Students need time to assemble their thoughts and think about the language they'll need. The Anecdotes are set up through evocative questions. Students read or listen to a planned series of questions and choose what specifically they'll talk about; shyer students can avoid matters they feel are too personal. This student preparation is a key stage and should not be rushed. Research, by Peter Skehan and Pauline Foster among others, has shown that learners who plan for tasks attempt more ambitious and complex language, hesitate less and make fewer basic errors.

The simplest way to prepare students for an Anecdote is to ask them to read the list of questions in the book and decide which they want to talk about. This could be done during class time or as homework preparation for the following lesson. Ask them to think about the language they'll need. Sample answers are provided in the Student's Book to give the students some extra help. Encourage them to use dictionaries and make notes – but not to write out what they'll actually say. Finally, put them into pairs to exchange Anecdotes.

A variation is to ask the students to read the questions in the book while, at the same time, listening to you read them aloud. Then ask them to prepare in detail for the task, as above.

Alternatively, ask the students to close their books – and then to close their eyes. Ask them to listen to the questions as you read them aloud and think about what they evoke. Some classes will find this a more involving process. It also allows you to adapt the questions to your class: adding new ones or missing out ones you think inappropriate. After the reading, give them enough time to finalise their preparation before starting the speaking task.

3   Monitor students and give feedback

It's important for students to feel that their efforts are being monitored by the teacher. Realistically, it's probably only possible for a teacher to monitor and give feedback to one or two pairs of students during each Anecdote activity. It's therefore vital that the teacher adopts a strict rota system, and makes sure that everyone in the class is monitored over the course of a term. Constructive feedback helps students improve their delivery.

4   Provide a 'model anecdote'

It's always useful for the students to hear a model Anecdote at some stage during the Anecdote task cycle. The most obvious model is you, the teacher. Alternatively, you might ask a teaching colleague or friend to talk to the students. For every Anecdote activity in *New Inside Out* Intermediate there's a model listening on the CD with an accompanying task in the student's book.

5   Repeat the same anecdote with a new partner at regular intervals

Consider going back to Anecdotes and repeating them in later classes. Let the students know that you're going to do this. This will reassure them that you're doing it on purpose, but more importantly, it will mean that they'll be more motivated to dedicate some time and thought to preparation. When you repeat the task, mix the class so that each student works with a new partner, i.e. one who has not previously heard the Anecdote.

In our experience, most students are happy to listen to their partner's Anecdotes. If, however, any of your students are reluctant listeners, you might think about giving them some sort of 'listening task'. Here are three examples:

*   Ask the listener to tick the prompt questions that the 'Anecdote teller' answers while telling the Anecdote.

*   Ask the listener to time the 'Anecdote teller'. In *Teaching Collocations* (page 91) Michael Lewis suggests reducing the time allowed to deliver the Anecdote each time it's repeated: for example, in the first instance the student has five minutes; for the second telling they have four minutes; and the third three minutes.

*   Ask the listener to take brief notes about the Anecdote and write them up as a summary for homework. Then give the summary to the 'Anecdote teller' to check.

The pedagogic value of getting students to re-tell Anecdotes – repeat a 'big chunk' of spoken discourse – cannot be over-stated. Repeating complex tasks reflects real interactions. We all have our set pieces: jokes, stories, and we tend to refine and improve them as we retell them. Many students will appreciate the opportunity to do the same thing in their second language. Research by Martin Bygate among others has shown that given this opportunity students become more adventurous and at the same time more precise in the language they use.

You can also use the Anecdotes to test oral proficiency and thereby add a speaking component to accompany the tests in the Teacher's Book.

Key concepts in *New Inside Out*

The following excerpts are from *An A–Z of ELT* by Scott Thornbury (Macmillan Books for Teachers, 2006). They give clear authoritive definitions and explanations of some of the most important concepts in *New Inside Out*.

Scott Thornbury

Contents

Note: SLA = Second Language Acquisition

classroom interaction METHODOLOGY

Classroom interaction is the general term for what goes on between the people in the classroom, particularly when it involves language. In traditional classrooms, most interaction is initiated by the teacher, and learners either respond individually, or in unison. Teacher-centred interaction of this kind is associated with *transmissive* teaching, such as a lecture or presentation, where the teacher *transmits* the content of the lesson to the learners. In order to increase the amount of student involvement and interaction, teacher–learner interaction is often combined with **pairwork** and **groupwork**, where learners interact among themselves in pairs or small groups. Other kinds of interaction include *mingling* or *milling*. Pairwork and groupwork are associated with a more **learner-centred** approach. Rather than passively receiving the lesson content, the learners are actively engaged in using language and discovering things for themselves. The value of pairwork and groupwork has been reinforced by the belief that **interaction** facilitates language learning. Some would go as far as to say that it is *all* that is required.

The potential for classroom interaction is obviously constrained by such factors as the number of students, the size of the room, the furniture, and the purpose or type of activity. Not all activities lend themselves to pairwork or groupwork. Some activities, such as reading, are best done as *individual work*. On the other hand, listening activities (such as listening to an audio recording, or to the teacher) favour a *whole class* format, as do grammar presentations. The whole class is also an appropriate form of organization when reviewing the results of an activity, as, for example, when spokespersons from each group are reporting on the results of a discussion or survey.

The success of any classroom interaction will also depend on the extent to which the learners know what they are meant to be doing and why, which in turn depends on how clearly and efficiently the interaction has been set up. Pair- and groupwork can be a complete waste of time if learners are neither properly prepared for it, nor sure of its purpose or outcome.

Finally, the success of pair- and groupwork will depend on the kind of group **dynamics** that have been established. Do the students know one another? Are they happy working together? Do they mind working without constant teacher supervision? Establishing a productive classroom dynamic may involve making decisions as to who works with whom. It may also mean deliberately staging the introduction of different kinds of interactions, starting off with the more controlled, teacher-led interactions before, over time, allowing learners to work in pairs and finally in groups.

collocation VOCABULARY

If two words *collocate*, they frequently occur together. The relation between the words may be grammatical, as when certain verbs collocate with particular prepositions, such as *depend on, account for, abstain from*, or when a verb, like *make, take*, or *do*, collocates with a noun, as in *make an arrangement, take advantage, do the shopping*. The collocation may also be lexical, as when two **content words** regularly co-occur, as in *a* broad hint, *a* narrow escape (but not **a* wide hint* or **a* tight escape*). The strength of the collocation can vary: *a broad street* or *a narrow path* are weak collocations, since both elements can co-occur with lots of other words: *a broad river, a busy street*, etc. *Broad hint* and *narrow escape* are stronger. Stronger still are combinations where one element rarely occurs without the other, as in *moot point, slim pickings* and *scot free*. Strongest of all are those where both elements never or rarely occur without the other, such as *dire straits* and *spick and span*. These have acquired the frozen status of *fixed expressions*.

Unsurprisingly, learners lack intuitions as to which words go with which, and this accounts for many errors, such as *You can* completely *enjoy it* (instead of *thoroughly*), *On Saturday we* made *shopping* (instead of *went*), and *We went the* incorrect *way* (for *wrong*). Using texts to highlight particular collocations, and teaching new words in association with their most frequent collocations are two ways of approaching the problem. Nowadays learners' dictionaries also include useful collocational information, such as this entry from the *Macmillan English Dictionary for Advanced Learners*:

communicative activity METHODOLOGY

A communicative activity is one in which real communication occurs. Communicative activities belong to that generation of classroom **activities** that emerged in response to the need for a more **communicative approach** in the teaching of second languages. (In their more evolved form as **tasks**, communicative activities are central to **task-based learning**). They attempt to import into a practice activity the key features of 'real-life' communication. These are

- *purposefulness*: speakers are motivated by a communicative goal (such as getting information, making a request, giving instructions) and not simply by the need to display the correct use of language for its own sake
- *reciprocity*: to achieve a purpose, speakers need to interact, and there is as much need to listen as to speak

- *negotiation*: following from the above, they may need to check and **repair** the communication in order to be understood by each other
- *unpredictability*: neither the process, nor the outcome, nor the language used in the exchange, is entirely predictable
- *heterogeneity*: participants can use any communicative means at their disposal; in other words, they are not restricted to the use of a pre-specified grammar item.

And, in the case of spoken language in particular:

- *synchronicity*: the exchange takes place in real time

The best known communicative activity is the *information gap* activity. Here, the information necessary to complete the task is either in the possession of just one of the participants, or distributed among them. In order to achieve the goal of the task, therefore, the learners have to share the information that they have. For example, in a *describe-and-draw* activity, one student has a picture which is hidden from his or her partner. The task is for that student to describe the picture so that the partner can accurately draw it. In a *spot-the-difference* task, both students of a pair have pictures (or texts) that are the same apart from some minor details. The goal is to identify these differences. In a *jigsaw activity*, each member of a group has different information. One might have a bus timetable, another a map, and another a list of hotels. They have to share this information in order to plan a weekend break together.

Information gap activities have been criticized on the grounds that they lack **authenticity**. Nor are information gap activities always as productive as might be wished: unsupervised, learners may resort to **communication strategies** in order to simplify the task. A more exploitable information gap, arguably, is the one that exists between the learners themselves, ie, what they don't know – but might like to know – about one another (→ **personalization**).

context LINGUISTICS

The context of a language item is its adjacent language items. In the absence of context, it is often impossible to assign exact meaning to an item. A sentence like *Ben takes the bus to work*, for example, could have past, present, or future reference, depending on the context:

I know this chap called Ben. One day *Ben takes the bus to work*, and just as …
Most days *Ben takes the bus to work*, but sometimes he rides his bike …
If *Ben takes the bus to work* tomorrow, he'll be late, because there's a strike …

Likewise, a sentence like *You use it like this* is meaningless in the absence of a context. By the same token, a word or sentence in one context can have a very different meaning in another. The sign *NO BICYCLES* in a public park means something different to *NO BICYCLES* outside a bicycle rental shop. It is sometimes necessary to distinguish between different kinds of context. On the one hand, there is the context of the accompanying **text**, sometimes called the *co-text*. The co-text of this sentence, for example, includes the sentences that precede and follow it, as well as the paragraph of which it forms a part. It is the co-text that offers clues as to the meaning of unfamiliar vocabulary in a text. The *situational* context (also *context of situation*, *context of use*), on the other hand, is the physical and temporal setting in which an instance of language use occurs. The typical context for the spoken question *Are you being served?* is in a shop, for example. Both co-text and context influence the production and interpretation of language. **Discourse analysis** studies the relationship between language and co-text, including the way that sentences or utterances are connected. **Pragmatics** studies the relationship between language and its contexts of use, including the way meaning can be inferred by reference to context factors.

Various theories have been proposed in order to account for the ways that language choices are determined by contextual factors. One of the best known of these is Michael Halliday's **systemic functional linguistics**. Halliday distinguishes three variables in any context that systematically impact on language choices and which, together, determine a text's **register**:

- the *field*: what the language is being used to talk about, and for what purposes
- the *tenor*: the participants in the language event, and their relationship
- the *mode*: how language is being used in the exchange, eg is it written or spoken?

For example, this short text shows the influence of all three factors:

> Do u fancy film either 2nite or 2moro? Call me.

The field is 'making arrangements about leisure activities', hence the use of words like *film*, *2nite* (*tonight*), *2moro* (*tomorrow*). The tenor is one of familiarity and equality (accounting for the informal *fancy* and the imperative: *call me*); and the mode is that of a written text message, which explains its brevity, its use of abbreviated forms (*u*, *2nite*) and the absence of salutations. A change in any of these contextual factors is likely to have a significant effect on the text.

Language learners, it is argued, need to know how these contextual factors correlate with language choices in order to produce language that is appropriate to the context. One way of doing this is to ask them to make changes to a text (such as the text message above) that take into account adjustments to the field, tenor, or mode.

drill METHODOLOGY

A drill is repetitive oral practice of a language item, whether a sound, a word, a phrase or a sentence structure. Drills that are targeted at sentence structures are sometimes called *pattern practice drills*.

Drills follow a prompt–response sequence, where the prompt usually comes from the teacher, and the students respond, either in chorus (a *choral drill*) or individually. An *imitation drill* simply involves repeating the prompt, as in:

Teacher	They have been watching TV.
Student	They have been watching TV.

A *substitution drill* requires the students to substitute one element of the pattern with the prompt, making any necessary adjustments:

Teacher	They have been watching TV.
Student	They have been watching TV.
Teacher	She
Student	She has been watching TV.
Teacher	I
Student	I have been watching TV.

etc.

A *variable substitution drill* is the same, but the prompts are not restricted to one element of the pattern:

Teacher	They have been watching TV.
Student	They have been watching TV.
Teacher	She
Student	She has been watching TV.
Teacher	radio
Student	She has been listening to the radio.
Teacher	We
Student	We have been listening to the radio.

etc.

Drills were a defining feature of the **audiolingual** method, and were designed to reinforce good language 'habits'. The invention of language laboratories allowed sustained drilling without the need for a teacher to supply the prompts. With the demise of audiolingualism, drilling fell from favour. However, many teachers – even those who subscribe to a **communicative approach** – feel the need for some form of repetition practice of the kind that drills provide. This may be for the purpose of developing **accuracy**, or as a form of **fluency** training, ie, in order to develop **automaticity**. Hence, communicative drills were developed. A communicative drill is still essentially repetitive, and focuses on a particular structure or pattern, but it has an *information gap* element built in. Learners can perform the drill in pairs, or as a *milling activity* (→ **classroom interaction**) and they are required to attend to what they hear as much as what they say. The milling activity popularly known as *Find someone who …* is one such activity. Students are set the task of finding other students in the class who, for example, can ride a horse, can speak French, can play the guitar, etc. They mill around, asking questions of the type *Can you …?* until they have asked all the other students their questions, and then they report their findings.

dynamics: group, classroom METHODOLOGY

Dynamics are the actions and interactions, both conscious and unconscious, that take place between members of a group, whether the whole class or sub-groups. Group dynamics are instrumental in forging a productive and motivating classroom environment. They are determined by such factors as: the composition of the group (including the age, sex, and relative status of the members, as well as their different attitudes, beliefs, learning styles and abilities); the patterns of relationships between members of the group, including how well they know each other, and the roles they each assume, such as group leader, spokesperson, etc; physical factors such as the size of the group and the way it is seated; and the tasks that the group are set, eg: Does the task require everyone to contribute? Does it encourage co-operation or competition? Are the goals of the task clear to the group members?

Ways that the teacher can promote a positive group (and class) dynamic include:

- ensuring all class or group members can see and hear one another, and that they know (and use) each other's names
- keeping groups from getting too big – three to six members is optimal
- setting – or negotiating – clear rules for groupwork, such as using only the target language, giving everyone a turn to speak, allowing individuals to 'pass' if they don't want to say anything too personal
- using 'ice-breaking' activities to encourage interaction, laughter, and relaxation
- ensuring that group tasks are purposeful, interactive, and collaborative
- personalizing tasks, ie, setting tasks that involve the sharing of personal experiences and opinions
- defining the roles and responsibilities within the group, and varying these regularly, eg by appointing a different spokesperson each time
- monitoring groupwork in progress, and being alert to any possible conflicts or tensions between members, and reconstituting groups, if necessary
- discussing the importance of groupwork with learners, and getting feedback on group processes

fluency SLA

If someone is said to be fluent in a language, or to speak a language fluently, it is generally understood that they are able to speak the language idiomatically and accurately, without undue pausing, without an intrusive accent, and in a manner appropriate to the context. In fact, research into listeners' perceptions of fluency suggests that fluency is primarily the ability to produce and maintain speech in *real time*. To do this, fluent speakers are capable of:

- appropriate pausing, ie:
  - their pauses may be long but are not frequent
  - their pauses are usually filled, eg with **pause fillers** like *erm*, *you know*, *sort of*
  - their pauses occur at meaningful transition points, eg at the intersections of clauses or phrases, rather than midway in a phrase
- long runs, ie, there are many syllables and words between pauses

All of the above factors depend on the speaker having a well-developed grammar, an extensive vocabulary, and, crucially, a store of memorized *chunks*. Being able to draw on this store of chunks means not having to depend on grammar to construct each utterance from scratch. This allows the speaker to devote **attention** to other aspects of the interaction, such as planning ahead. Speakers also use a number of 'tricks' or *production strategies* to convey the illusion of fluency. One such strategy is disguising pauses by filling them, or by repeating a word or phrase.

Some proponents of the **communicative approach** re-defined fluency so as to distinguish it from **accuracy**. Fluency came to mean 'communicative effectiveness', regardless of formal accuracy or speed of delivery. Activities that are communicative, such as information-gap activities, are said to be *fluency-focused*. This is the case even for activities that produce short, halting utterances. Separating accuracy and fluency, and defining the latter as *communicative* language use, is misleading, though. There are many speech events whose communicativeness depends on their accuracy. Air traffic control talk is just one. Moreover, many learners aspire to being more than merely communicative.

Classroom activities that target fluency need to prepare the learner for real-time speech production. Learning and memorizing lexical chunks, including useful conversational gambits, is one approach. **Drills** may help here, as will some types of **communicative activity** that involve repetition. Research has also shown that fluency improves the more times a **task** is repeated. Fluency may also benefit from activities that manage to distract learners' attention away from formal accuracy so that they are not tempted to slow down. (This has been called 'parking their attention'). Some interactive and competitive language **games** have this effect. **Drama** activities, such as roleplays, recreate conditions of real-time language use, and are therefore good for developing fluency. Finally, learners can achieve greater fluency from learning a repertoire of **communication strategies**, ie, techniques for getting around potential problems caused by a lack of the relevant words or structures.

focus on form SLA

When learners focus on form, they direct conscious attention to some formal feature of the language **input**. The feature may be the fact that the past of *has* is *had*, or that *enjoy* is followed by verb forms ending in *-ing*, or that adjectives do not have plural forms in English. The learners' attention may be self-directed, or it may be directed by the teacher or by another learner. Either way, it has been argued that a focus on **form** is a necessary condition for language learning. Simply focusing on the **meaning** of the input is not enough. Focusing on form is, of course, not a new idea: most teaching methods devote a great deal of time to the forms of the language, eg when new grammar items are presented. But the term *focus on form* captures the fact that this focus can, theoretically, occur at any stage in classroom instruction. Thus, **correction**, especially in the form of negative **feedback**, is a kind of focus on form. In fact, some researchers argue that the most effective form focus is that which arises incidentally, in the context of communication, as when the teacher quickly elicits a correction during a classroom discussion. This incidental approach contrasts with the more traditional and deliberate approach, where teaching is based on a **syllabus** of graded structures (or *forms*), and these are pre-taught in advance of activities designed to practise them. This traditional approach is called – by some researchers – a *focus on formS*.

function LINGUISTICS

The function of a language item is its communicative purpose. Language is more than simply **forms** and their associated meanings (ie, **usage**). It is also the communicative **uses** to which these forms and meanings are put. These two sentences, for example, share the same forms, but function quite differently:

> [in an email] *Thank you for sending me the disk.*
> [a notice in a taxi] *Thank you for not smoking.*

The function of the first is *expressing thanks*, while the second is more like a *prohibition*. Likewise, the same function can be expressed by different forms:

> [a notice in a taxi] *Thank you for not smoking.*
> [a sign in a classroom] *No smoking.*

Thus, there is no one-to-one match between form and function. Assigning a function to a text or an utterance usually requires knowledge of the **context** in which the text is used. The study of how context and function are interrelated is called **pragmatics**.

Communicative functions can be categorized very broadly and also at increasing levels of detail. The 'big' functions, or macrofunctions, describe the way language is used in very general terms. These include the use of language for *expressive* purposes (eg poetry), for *regulatory* purposes (eg for getting people to do things), for *interpersonal* purposes (eg for socializing), and for *representational* purposes (eg to inform). More useful, from the point of view of designing language syllabuses, are microfunctions. These are usually expressed as **speech acts**, such as *agreeing and disagreeing, reporting, warning, apologizing, thanking, greeting*, etc. Such categories form the basis of **functional syllabuses**, a development associated with the **communicative approach**. They often appear as one strand of a coursebook **syllabus**. Functions differ from notions in that the latter describe areas of meaning – such as *ability, duration, quantity, frequency*, etc – rather than the uses to which these meanings are put.

One way to teach functions is to adopt a 'phrasebook' approach, and teach useful ways of expressing common functions (what are called *functional exponents*), such as *Would you like …?* (*inviting*) and *Could you …, please?* (*requesting*). More memorable, though, is to teach these expressions in the contexts of **dialogues**, so that the functional exponents are associated not only with common situations in which

they are used, but with related functions (such as *accepting* and *refusing*). The term *function*, in contrast to **form**, is also used in linguistics, specifically with regard to the functions of the different elements of a **clause** (such as subject and object).

grammar teaching METHODOLOGY

Like the word **grammar** itself, the topic of grammar teaching is a controversial one, and teachers often take opposing views. Historically, language teaching methods have positioned themselves along a scale from 'zero grammar' to 'total grammar', according to their approach to grammar teaching. Proponents of *natural methods*, who model their approach to teaching second languages on the way that first languages are acquired, reject any explicit teaching of grammar at all. (They may, however, teach according to a grammar **syllabus**, even if no mention of grammar as such is made in the classroom). This implicit approach is common both to the **direct method** and to **audiolingualism**. Through exposure to demonstrations, situations or examples, learners are expected to pick up the rules of grammar by **inductive learning**. At the other end of the spectrum, there are approaches, such as **grammar-translation**, that adopt an explicit and **deductive learning** approach. From the outset, learners are presented with rules which they study and then practise. Occupying a midway point between zero grammar and total grammar is the approach called **consciousness-raising**. Instead of being given rules, learners are presented with language data which challenge them to re-think (and *restructure*) their existing mental grammar. This data might take the form of **input** that has been manipulated in some way. For example, pairs of sentences, such as the following, have to be matched to pictures, forcing learners to discriminate between them, and, in theory, **notice** the difference (→ **noticing**):

> The Queen drove to the airport.
> The Queen was driven to the airport.

(This is sometimes called a *grammar interpretation task*, or *structured input*.) In order to do the task, learners have to process not just the individual words, but also their grammatical form. That is why this approach to teaching grammar is sometimes called *processing instruction*. There are other researchers who argue that it is by means of manipulating the learner's output, eg through productive practice, that mental restructuring is best effected.

The **communicative approach** accommodates different approaches to grammar teaching. Proponents of **task-based learning**, for example, argue that, if the learner is engaged in solving problems using language, then the mental grammar will develop of its own accord. However, advocates of the weaker version of the communicative approach (and the version that is most widespread) justify a role for the pre-teaching of grammar in advance of production. This view finds support in **cognitive learning theory**, which suggests that conscious attention to grammatical form (called **focus on form**) speeds up language learning, and is a necessary corrective against premature **fossilization**. There is some debate, though, as to whether this form focus should be planned or incidental. Incidental grammar teaching occurs when the teacher deals with grammar issues as and when they come up, eg in the form of **correction**, or task **feedback**. In this way (it is argued) grammar teaching follows the learners' own 'syllabus'. Such an approach attempts to address one of the dilemmas of grammar teaching: the fact that the learner's mental grammar, and the way it develops, bears only an accidental relation to a formal grammar syllabus.

Nevertheless, the research into these different choices is still inconclusive. It may be the case that some items of grammar respond better to explicit teaching, while others are more easily picked up through exposure. There are also different learner types: some prefer learning and applying rules, while others are happier with a more 'deep-end' approach (→ **learning style**). Most current teaching materials hedge their bets on these issues. They offer both deductive and inductive grammar presentations, and opportunities for incidental as well as for planned learning.

learner-centred instruction, learner-centredness
METHODOLOGY

Learner-centred instruction aims to give learners more say in areas that are traditionally considered the domain of the teacher or of the institution. Learner-centred instruction is true to the spirit of progressive education, including the movement towards providing learners with greater **autonomy**. For example, a learner-centred **curriculum** would involve learners in negotiating decisions relating to the choice of syllabus content, of materials, of activity-types, and of assessment procedures. Learner-centredness also describes ways of organizing **classroom interaction** so that the focus is directed away from the teacher, and on to the learners, who perform tasks in pairs or small groups. This contrasts with traditional, teacher-centred, classroom interaction. Some writers believe that the dichotomy between learner-centred (= good) and teacher-centred (= bad) is a false one. It might be more useful to talk about *learning-centred instruction*, ie, instruction which prioritizes sound learning principles. In a learning-centred approach there would be room for both learner-centred *and* teacher-centred interactions.

learning style PSYCHOLOGY

Your learning style is your preferred way of learning. This style may be influenced by biographical factors (such as how you were taught as a child) or by innately endowed factors (such as whether you have a 'good ear' for different sounds). Types of learning style are often presented in the form of polarities (some of which may overlap), such as:

- analytic versus global (or holistic) thinkers, ie, learners who tend to focus on the details, versus learners who tend to see 'the big picture'

- rule-users versus data-gatherers, ie, learners who learn and apply rules, versus those who prefer exposure to lots of examples
- reflective versus impulsive learners
- group-oriented versus solitary learners
- extrovert versus introverted learners
- verbal versus visual learners
- passive versus active learners

Attempts have been made to group these polarities and relate them to brain lateralization. So, a bias towards left-brain processing correlates with analytic, rule-forming and verbal learners, while a bias towards right-brain processing correlates with their opposite. A less binary view of learning style is that proposed by the psychologist Howard Gardner. He identified at least seven distinct intelligences that all individuals possess but to different degrees. These include the *logical/mathematical*, the *verbal/linguistic*, and the *visual/spatial*. Similarly, proponents of **neuro-linguistic programming** distinguish between different sensory orientations, including the *visual*, *aural* and *kinesthetic* (ie, related to movement, touch). So far, though, there is no convincing evidence that any of these dispositions correlates with specific learning behaviours. Nor has it been shown that a preference in one area predicts success in language learning. In fact, it is very difficult to separate learning style from other potentially influential factors, such as personality, intelligence, and previous learning experience. Nor is it clear to what extent learning style can be manipulated, eg through **learner training**. The best that can be said is that, if the learner's preferred learning style is out of synch with the type of instruction on offer, then success is much less likely than if the two are well matched. This supports the case for an **eclectic** approach, on the one hand, and the individualization of learning, on the other.

listening METHODOLOGY

Listening is the skill of understanding spoken language. It is also the name given to classroom activities that are designed to develop this skill – what are also called *listening comprehension* activities – as in 'today we're going to do a listening'. Listening is one of the four language **skills**, and, along with **reading**, was once thought of as being a 'passive' skill. In fact, although receptive, listening is anything but passive. It is a goal-oriented activity, involving not only processing of the incoming speech signals (called *bottom-up processing*) but also the use of prior knowledge, contextual clues, and expectations (*top-down processing*) in order to create meaning. Among the sub-skills of listening are:

- perceiving and discriminating individual sounds
- segmenting the stream of speech into recognizable units such as words and phrases
- using **stress** and **intonation** cues to distinguish given information from new information
- attending to **discourse markers** and using these to predict changes in the direction of the talk

- guessing the meaning of unfamiliar words
- using clues in the text (such as vocabulary) and context clues to predict what is coming
- making inferences about what is not stated
- selecting key information relevant to the purpose for listening
- integrating incoming information into the mental 'picture' (or **schema**) of the speech event so far

Also, since listening is normally interactive, listeners need to be capable of:

- recognizing when speakers have finished their turns, or when it is appropriate to interrupt
- providing ongoing signals of understanding, interest, etc. (*backchannelling*)
- asking for clarification, asking someone to repeat what they have just said, and repairing misunderstandings

These sub-skills exist across languages, so, in theory, learners should be able to transfer them from their first language into their second. In fact, there are a number of reasons why this does not always happen. One is that speakers of different languages process speech signals differently, depending on the phonetic characteristics of the language they are used to. This means that speakers of some languages will find it harder than others to match the spoken word to the way that the word is represented in their mind. They simply do not recognize the word. Another problem is lack of sufficient L2 knowledge, such as vocabulary or grammar. A third problem is that learners may lack the means (and the confidence) to negotiate breakdowns in understanding. Finally, many learners simply lack exposure to spoken language, and therefore have not had sufficient opportunities to experience listening. These problems can be compounded in classrooms because:

- Listening to audio recordings deprives the learners of useful visual information, and allows the learners no opportunity to interact and repair misunderstandings.
- Classroom acoustics are seldom ideal.
- If learners do not know what they are listening for (in the absence, for example, of some pre-set listening task) they may try to process as much information as possible, rather than being selective in their listening. This can lead to listening overload, which in turn can cause inhibiting anxiety.
- Listening texts that have been specially written for classroom use are often simplified. But if this simplification means eliminating a lot of redundant language, such as speaker repetitions, pause fillers and vague language, the density of information that results may make it harder – not easier – to process.

For this reason, the use of audio recordings to develop listening skills needs to be balanced against the advantages of using other media, such as video, and face-to-face interaction with the teacher or another speaker.

Nevertheless, the use of audio recordings is an established part of classroom practice, so it is important to know how to use them to best advantage. The following approach is one that is often recommended:

- Provide some minimum contextual information, eg who is talking to whom about what, and why. This helps to compensate for lack of visual information, and allows learners to activate the relevant mental **schema**, which in turn helps top-down processing, including the sub-skill of prediction.
- Pre-teach key vocabulary: this helps with bottom-up processing, although too much help may mean that learners don't get sufficient practice in guessing from context.
- Set some 'while-listening' questions. Initially, these should focus on the overall *gist* of the text. For example: true/false questions, selecting, ordering or matching pictures, ticking items on a list, following a map
- Play a small section of the recording first, to give learners an opportunity to familiarize themselves with the different voices, and to trigger accurate expectations as to what they will hear.
- Play the recording right through, and then allow learners to consult on the answers to the pre-set task. Check these answers. If necessary, re-play the recording until satisfied that learners have 'got the gist'.
- Set a more demanding task, requiring more intensive listening, such as listening for detail, or inferring speakers' attitudes, intentions, etc. If the recording is a long one, it may pay to stage the intensive listening in sections. Again, allow learners to consult in pairs, before checking the task in open class.
- On the basis of the learners' success with these tasks, identify problem sections of the recording and return to these, playing and re-playing them, and perhaps eliciting a word-by-word transcription and writing this on the board.
- Distribute copies of the transcript of the recording (if available) and re-play the recording while learners read the transcript. This allows the learners to clear up any remaining problems, and also to match what they hear to what they see.

The above approach can be adapted to suit different kinds of recorded texts and different classroom needs. For higher level learners, for example, it may be counter-productive to make listening *too* easy. The approach can also be adapted to the use of video, and even to *live listenings*, such as listening to the teacher or a guest.

motivation PSYCHOLOGY

Motivation is what drives learners to achieve a goal, and is a key factor determining success or failure in language learning. The learner's goal may be a short-term one, such as successfully performing a classroom task, or a long-term one, such as achieving native-like proficiency in the language. With regard to long-term goals, a distinction is often made between *instrumental motivation* and *integrative motivation*. Instrumental motivation is when the learner has a functional objective, such as passing an exam or getting a job. Integrative motivation, on the other hand, is when the learner wants to be identified with the target language community. Intersecting with these two motivational *orientations* are two different *sources* of motivation: *intrinsic* (eg the pleasure of doing a task for its own sake) and *extrinsic* (eg the 'carrot and stick' approach). Another motivational source that has been identified is success: experience of succeeding can result in increased motivation (called *resultative motivation*), which raises the question as to whether motivation is as much a result as a cause of learning.

Various theories of motivation have been proposed. Most of these identify a variety of factors that, in combination, contribute to overall motivation, such as:

- *attitudes*, eg to the target language and to speakers of the language
- *goals*, both long-term and short-term, and the learners' *orientation* to these goals
- how much *value* the learner attaches to achieving the goals, especially as weighed against *expectancy of success*; expectancy of success may come from the learner's assessment of their own abilities, and how they account for previous successes or failures
- *self-esteem*, and the need to achieve and maintain it
- *intrinsic interest*, *pleasure*, *relevance* or *challenge* of the task
- *group dynamic*: is it competitive, collaborative, or individualistic?
- *teacher's attitudes*, eg what expectations does the teacher project about the learners' likelihood of success?

As the last point suggests, teachers can play a key role in motivating learners, not just in terms of choosing activities that are intrinsically motivating, but in the attitudes they project. Two researchers on motivation offer the following advice for teachers:

Ten commandments for motivating language learners

1. Set a personal example with your own behaviour
2. Create a pleasant, relaxed atmosphere in the classroom.
3. Present the tasks properly.
4. Develop a good relationship with the learners.
5. Increase the learner's linguistic self-confidence.
6. Make the language classes interesting.
7. Promote learner autonomy.
8. Personalise the learning process.
9. Increase the learners' goal-orientedness.
10. Familiarise learners with the target language culture.

noticing SLA

If you notice a feature of the language that you are exposed to, it attracts your attention and you make a mental note of it. For example, a learner might notice (without necessarily understanding) the sign *Mind the gap*, repeated several times on a railway station platform. That same day, the learner hears the teacher say *would you mind* in the context of making a request in class. A day or two later, the same learner hears someone else say *I don't mind*. Each successive 'noticing' both primes the learner to notice new occurrences of *mind*, and at the same time contributes to a growing understanding of the use and meaning of *mind*. Proponents of **cognitive learning theory** believe that noticing is a prerequisite for learning: without it input would remain as mere 'noise'. The *noticing hypothesis*, then, claims that noticing is a necessary condition for acquisition, although not the only one. Some kind of mental processing of what has been noticed is also necessary before the **input** becomes *intake*, ie before it is moved into long-term **memory**.

Teachers obviously play an important role in helping learners to notice features of the language. They do this when they repeat words or structures, write them on the board, or even drill them. One way of increasing the chance of learners' noticing an item is to include it lots of times in a text, a technique called *input flood*. For example, learners read a text with the word *mind* included several times. They then categorize these examples according to their meaning. A set of **concordance** lines for a particular word can be used in the same way.

There is another type of noticing, called *noticing the gap*. This is when learners are made aware of a gap in their language knowledge. This might happen when they do a **dictation**, for example. When they compare their version with the correct version, they may notice certain differences, such as the lack of past tense endings, that represent a gap in their **interlanguage**. It has been argued that noticing the gap can trigger the **restructuring** of interlanguage. That is, 'minding the gap' leads learners to 'fill the gap'.

personalization METHODOLOGY

When you personalize language you use it to talk about your knowledge, experience and feelings. Personalization of the type *Now write five true sentences about yourself using 'used to'* is often motivated by the need to provide further practice of pre-taught grammar structures. But it is also good preparation for the kinds of situations of genuine language use that learners might encounter outside the classroom. These advantages are lost, though, if the teacher's response is to treat the exercise as *only* an exercise, and correct the learners' errors without responding to the content. The influence of **humanistic approaches** has given a fresh impetus to personalization, both in terms of providing a more coherent rationale and suggesting a broader range of activity types. For a start (it is argued), personalization creates better classroom **dynamics**. This is because groups are more likely to form and bond if the individuals in them know more about one another. And the mental and emotional effort that is involved in finding personal associations with a language item is likely to make that item more memorable. This quality is called cognitive and affective *depth*. Finally, lessons are likely to be more interesting, and hence more motivating, if at least some of the content concerns the people in the room, rather than the characters in coursebooks. On these grounds, some writers have suggested that personalization should not be considered simply as an 'add-on', but should be the principle on which most, if not all, classroom content should be based. One teaching approach that is committed to this view is **community language learning**. In this approach, all the content of the lesson comes from the learners themselves. Personalization is not without risks, though. Teachers need to be sensitive to learner resistance: learners should have the right to 'pass' on questions that they consider too intrusive. And teachers should be authentic in the way that they respond to learners' personalizations. This means that they should respond to *what* their learners are saying, not just how they say it.

practice METHODOLOGY

If you practise a skill, you experience doing it a number of times in order to gain control of it. The idea that 'practice makes perfect' is fundamental to **cognitive learning theory**. It is through practice that the skill becomes automatic. **Sociocultural learning theory** finds room for practice too. Performing a skill with the assistance of someone who is good at it can help in the **appropriation** of the skill. At issue, then, is not so much whether practice is beneficial, but what form it should take, when, and how much of it is necessary. In addressing these questions, it is customary to distinguish between different kinds of practice, such as *controlled practice* vs *free practice*, *mechanical practice* vs *meaningful/communicative practice*, and *receptive practice* vs *productive practice*.

Controlled practice is associated with the second P of the **PPP** instructional model. Practice can be controlled in at least two senses: *language control* and *interactional control*. In the first, the language that is being practised is restricted to what has just been presented (hence it is also called *restricted practice*). For example, if the first **conditional** has been presented, learners practise this, and only this, structure, and in a repetitive way, eg through a sequence of **drills**. Practice is also said to be controlled if the learners' participation is overtly managed and monitored by the teacher, such as in open-class work, as opposed to closed **pairwork** or **groupwork**. One reason for this degree of control is that it maintains a focus on accuracy, and pre-empts or corrects errors. *Free practice*, on the other hand, allows learners a measure of creativity, and the opportunity to integrate the new item into their existing language 'pool'. It is also less controlled in terms of the interactions, with pairwork and groupwork being favoured. Typical free practice activities might be **games**, **discussions** or **drama**-based activities.

Mechanical practice is a form of controlled practice, where the focus is less on the meaning of an item than on manipulating its component parts. Mechanical practice can be either oral or written: many traditional **exercises** are mechanical in this sense, such as when learners transform sentences from active into passive, or from direct speech into reported speech. The arguments in favour of controlled and mechanical practice have lost their force since the decline of **behaviourism** and its belief that learning is simply habit-formation.

Meaningful practice requires learners to display some understanding of what the item that they are practising actually means. One way of doing this is through **personalization**. *Communicative practice* involves the learners interacting in order to complete some kind of task, such as in an *information gap* activity (→ **communicative activity**). Proponents of a communicative approach argue that it is only this kind of practice that is truly effective. This is because learners are not simply practising language, but are practising the behaviours associated with the language, and this is a pre-condition for long-term behavioural change.

Finally, some practice activities are purely *receptive*. They involve the learners in identifying, selecting, or discriminating between language items, but not actually producing them. Many **consciousness-raising** activities are receptive, on the grounds that learners first need to understand a new structure before they can properly internalize it. Receptive practice is also associated with comprehension-based approaches to teaching. *Productive practice*, on the other hand, requires learners to produce the targeted items (either orally or in writing), and is associated with output-based models of learning.

There is fairly general agreement nowadays that the most effective practice activity combines at least some of the following features:

- It is meaningful, which may mean that is personalized.
- It is communicative, thus it will require learners to interact.
- It involves a degree of repetition – not of the mindless type associated with imitation drills, but of the type associated with many games.
- It is language-rich, ie, learners have to interpret or produce a lot of language.
- Learners can be creative and take risks, but support is at hand if they need it.
- Learners are pushed, at least some of the time, to the limits of their competence
- Learners get **feedback**.

pronunciation teaching PHONOLOGY

Pronunciation is the general term for that part of language classes and courses that deals with aspects of the **phonology** of English. This includes the individual sounds (**phonemes**) of English, sounds in **connected speech**, word and sentence **stress, rhythm** and **intonation**. These components are customarily divided into two groups: the *segmental* features of pronunciation, ie, the individual sounds and the way they combine, and the *suprasegmental* features, ie, stress, rhythm and intonation. **Paralinguistic** features of speech production such as voice quality, tempo and loudness, are also classed as suprasegmental.

Effective pronunciation teaching needs to consider what goals, course design and methodology are most appropriate for the learners in question. The goal of acquiring a native-like **accent** is generally thought to be unachievable for most learners (and perhaps even undesirable). Instead, the goal of **intelligibility** is nowadays considered more realistic, if less easily measurable. It is often claimed that suprasegmental features play a greater role in intelligibility than do segmental ones. Unfortunately, however, some of these suprasegmental features, such as intonation, are considered by many teachers to be unteachable. Moreover, learners intending to interact with native speakers may need to set different goals from those learners whose purpose is to learn **English as an international language (EIL)**. For this latter group, the so-called **phonological core** is a checklist of those pronunciation features considered critical for intelligibility in EIL.

In terms of the design of course content, a basic choice is whether the pronunciation focus is *integrated* or *segregated*. In an integrated approach, pronunciation is dealt with as part of the teaching of grammar and vocabulary, or of speaking and listening. In a segregated approach it is treated in isolation. A classical segregated exercise is the **minimal pairs** task, in which learners are taught to discriminate and produce two contrasted phonemes (as in *hit* and *heat*). There are doubts as to whether this item-by-item approach to pronunciation reflects the way that the features of pronunciation are interconnected. Nor does it reflect the way that they jointly emerge over time ('as a photo emerges in the darkroom'). A related issue is whether pronunciation teaching should be *pre-emptive* or *reactive*. That is to say, should pronunciation teaching be planned around a syllabus of pre-selected items, or should the focus on pronunciation emerge *out of* practice activities, in the form, for example, of **correction**? There is evidence that the latter approach is more effective than the former.

In 1964 the writer (and former language teacher) Anthony Burgess wrote, 'Nothing is more important than to acquire a set of foreign phonemes that shall be entirely acceptable to your hosts'. However, there is generally less emphasis given to pronunciation teaching nowadays. Indeed, some teachers are sceptical as to the value of teaching pronunciation at all. This view is reinforced by research that suggests that the best predictors of intelligible pronunciation are 'having a good ear' and prolonged residence in an English-speaking country. On the other hand, faulty pronunciation is one of the most common causes of misunderstandings. This is an argument for demanding higher standards than the learners can realistically achieve, in the hope that they will meet you 'halfway'.

reading METHODOLOGY

Reading is a receptive **skill**. But the fact that it is receptive does not mean that it is passive: reading is an active, even interactive, process. Readers bring their own questions to the text, which are based on their background knowledge, and they use these to interrogate the text, modifying their questions and coming up with new ones according to the answers they get. In order to do this, they draw on a range of knowledge bases. They need to be able to decode the letters, words and grammatical structures of the individual sentences – what is called *bottom-up processing*. But they also enlist *top-down processes*, such as drawing on **discourse** and schematic knowledge, as well as on immediate contextual information. Discourse knowledge is knowing how different text-types – such as news reports, recipes or academic papers – are organized. Schematic knowledge is the reader's existing knowledge of the topic. Reading involves an interaction between these different 'levels' of knowledge, where knowledge at one 'level' can compensate for lack of knowledge at another.

Readers also bring their own *purposes* to texts, and these in turn determine the way they go about reading a text. The two main purposes for reading are for *information* (such as when consulting a directory), and for *pleasure* (such as when reading a novel), although these purposes may overlap. Different ways of reading include:

- *skimming* (*skim-reading, reading for gist*): rapidly reading a text in order to get the *gist*, or the main ideas or sense of a text. For example, a reader might skim a film review in order to see if the reviewer liked the film or not.
- *scanning*: reading a text in search of specific information, and ignoring everything else, such as when consulting a bus timetable for a particular time and destination.
- *detailed reading*: reading a text in order to extract the maximum detail from it, such as when following the instructions for installing a household appliance.
- *reading aloud*: such as when reading a prepared speech or lecture, or reading a story aloud, or an extract from the newspaper.

A reader's purpose usually matches the writer's intentions for the text. Readers seldom read telephone books from cover to cover, for example. Nor do they normally skim through a novel looking for names beginning with *Vron* .... In classrooms, however, texts are frequently used for purposes other than those for which they were originally intended. They are often used not so much as vehicles of information or of pleasure, but as 'linguistic objects', that is, as contexts for the study of features of the language. A distinction needs to be made, therefore, between two types of classroom reading: reading as *skills development*, and reading as *language study*. There is no reason why the same text cannot be used for both purposes.

Another distinction that is often made is between *intensive reading* and *extensive reading*. The former applies to the way short texts are subject to close and detailed classroom study. Extensive reading, on the other hand, means the more leisurely reading of longer texts, primarily for pleasure, or in order to accumulate vocabulary, or simply to develop sound habits of reading. This is typically done outside class, using graded **readers**, authentic texts, or literary texts.

A third important distinction is between testing reading and teaching reading. Traditional reading tasks usually involve reading a text and then answering **comprehension questions** about it. This is the testing approach. A teaching approach, on the other hand, aims to help learners to become more effective readers by training them in the *sub-skills* of reading, and by teaching them *reading strategies*. Some of the sub-skills of reading are:

- understanding words and identifying their grammatical function
- recognizing grammar features, such as word endings, and 'unpacking' (or **parsing**) the syntax of sentences
- identifying the topic of the text, and recognizing topic changes
- identifying text-type, text purpose, and text organization, and identifying and understanding **discourse markers** and other cohesive devices
- distinguishing key information from less important information
- identifying and understanding the gist
- inferring the writer's attitude
- following the development of an argument
- following the sequence of a narrative
- paraphrasing the text

Activities designed to develop these sub-skills include: underlining topic-related words; contrasting different text-types; comparing different examples of the same text type and identifying *generic* features; circling and categorizing discourse markers; identifying what the pronouns refer to; predicting the direction the text will take at each discourse marker; choosing the best summary of a text; putting a set of pictures in order; extracting key information on to a grid, writing a summary of the text, etc. *Strategy training* involves training learners in ways of overcoming problems when they are reading. Some useful strategies include:

- using contextual and extra-linguistic information (such as pictures, layout, headlines) to make predictions regarding what the text is about

- brainstorming background (or schematic) knowledge in advance of reading
- skimming a text in advance of a more detailed reading
- keeping the purpose of the text in mind
- guessing the meaning of words from context
- **dictionary** use

There is some argument, however, as to the value of a 'skills and strategies' approach to teaching reading. Most adult learners of English come to English texts with already well-developed reading skills in their own language. They already know how to skim, scan, use context clues, enlist background knowledge, and so on. Theoretically, at least, these skills are transferable. What makes reading difficult is not so much lack of reading skills as lack of *language knowledge*. That is, learners lack sufficient vocabulary and grammar to unpack sentences, and they cannot easily identify the ways that sentences are connected. This can result in 'tunnel vision', with readers becoming distracted by unfamiliar words, at the expense of working out meaning from context. On the other hand, it can also result in an over-reliance on guesswork, and on superficial 'text attack' strategies such as skimming. This suggests that texts needs to be chosen that do not over-stretch learners' ability to read them fluently. At the same time, texts should not be so easy that learners can process them simply by skimming. It also means that tasks need to be chosen that both match the original purpose of the text, and that encourage learners to transfer their first language reading skills. Such tasks are likely to be those that motivate learners to *want* to read the text. This might mean activating interest in the topic of the text, through, for example, a pre-reading quiz. At the same time, classroom reading texts should be exploited, not just for their potential in developing reading skills, but as sources of language input. This will involve, at some point, detailed study of the text's formal features, such as its linking devices, its collocations or its grammar.

speaking METHODOLOGY

Speaking is generally thought to be the most important of the four **skills**. The ability to speak a second language is often equated with proficiency in the language, as in *She speaks excellent French*. Indeed, one frustration commonly voiced by learners is that they have spent years studying English, but still can't speak it. One of the main difficulties, of course, is that speaking usually takes place spontaneously and in real time, which means that planning and production overlap. If too much **attention** is paid to planning, production suffers, and the effect is a loss of **fluency**. On the other hand, if the speaker's attention is directed solely on production, it is likely that **accuracy** will suffer, which could prejudice **intelligibility**. In order to free up attention, therefore, the speaker needs to have achieved a degree of **automaticity** in both planning and production. One way of doing this is to use memorized routines, such as **formulaic language**. Another is to use *production strategies*, such as the use of **pause fillers**, in order to 'buy' planning time. The situation is complicated by the fact that most speaking is interactive. Speakers are jointly having to manage the flow of talk. The management of interaction involves *turn-taking skills*, such as knowing how and when to take, keep, and relinquish speaker turns, and also knowing how to repair misunderstandings.

For language learners these processing demands are magnified through lack of basic knowledge of grammar and vocabulary. For the purposes of most day-to-day talk, however, the grammar that is required is not as complex nor need be as accurate as the grammar that is required for writing. Nor do speakers need an enormous vocabulary, especially if they have developed some **communication strategies** for getting round gaps in their knowledge. A core vocabulary of 1000–1500 high-frequency words and expressions will provide most learners with a solid basis for speaking.

Activating this knowledge, though, requires **practice**. This in turn suggests that the more speaking practice opportunities that learners are given, and the sooner, the easier speaking will become. Speaking practice means more than simply answering the teacher's questions, or repeating sentences, as in grammar practice activities. It means interacting with other speakers, sustaining long turns of talk, speaking spontaneously, and speaking about topics of the learners' choice.

Approaches to teaching speaking vary. Traditionally, speaking was considered to be a by-product of teaching grammar and vocabulary, reinforced with work on **pronunciation**. This view has been replaced by approaches that treat speaking as a skill in its own right. One such approach is to break down the speaking skill into a number of discrete sub-skills, such as *opening and closing conversations, turn-taking, repairing, paraphrasing, interrupting*, etc. Another approach is to focus on the different *purposes* of speaking and their associated **genres**, such as *narrating, obtaining service, giving a presentation, making small talk*, etc. This approach is particularly well suited to learners who have a specific purpose for learning English. A third is to adopt a topic-based approach, where learners are encouraged to speak freely on a range of topics, at least some of which they have chosen themselves. This is the format used in many conversation classes. Typical activity types for the teaching of speaking include: **dialogues, drama** activities (including *roleplays* and *simulations*), many **games, discussions** and debates, as well as informal classroom chat.

task METHODOLOGY

A task is a classroom activity whose focus is on communicating meaning. The objective of a task may be to reach some consensus on an issue, to solve a problem, to draft a plan, to design something, or to persuade someone to do something. In contrast, practising a pre-selected item of language (such as the present perfect) for its own sake would not be a valid task objective. In the performance of the task, learners are expected to make use of their own language resources. In theory, tasks may be receptive or productive, and may be done individually or in pairs or small groups. However, in practice, most activities that are labelled 'tasks' in coursebooks involve production (either speaking or writing, or both) and require learners to interact with one another.

Tasks are the organizing principle in **task-based learning**. In order to devise a syllabus of tasks it is necessary both to classify tasks, and to identify the factors that make one task more difficult than another. Different criteria for classifying tasks have been suggested. For example, tasks can be *open-ended* or *closed*. An open-ended task is one in which learners know there is no predetermined solution. It might be planning an excursion, or debating a topical issue. A closed task, on the other hand, requires learners to discover the solution to a problem, such as identifying the differences in a *spot-the-difference* task (→ **communicative activity**). Tasks can also be classified according to the kinds of operations they involve, such as *ranking, selecting, sorting, comparing, surveying* and *problem-solving*.

Factors which influence the degree of difficulty of the task, and hence which affect the grading of tasks, include:

- *linguistic factors*: How complex is the language that learners will need to draw on, in order to do the task? How much help, either before, or during the task, will they get with their language needs?
- *cognitive factors*: Does the task require the processing of complex data? Is the task type familiar to learners?
- *performance factors*: Do the learners have to interact in real time in order to do the task? Do they have time to rehearse? Do they have to 'go public'?

The term *task* is now widely accepted as a useful way of labelling certain types of classroom activity, including many which have a thinly disguised grammar agenda. But the concept of task is not without its critics. Some writers feel that the associations of task with 'work' undervalues the more playful – and possibly less authentic or communicative – types of classroom activity, such as games, songs and drama.

vocabulary teaching METHODOLOGY

Vocabulary describes that area of language learning that is concerned with word knowledge. Vocabulary learning is a major goal in most teaching programmes. It hasn't always been so. In methods such as **audiolingualism**, vocabulary was subordinated to the teaching of grammar structures. Words were simply there to fill the slots in the sentence patterns. The move towards *semantic* (ie, meaning-based) **syllabuses** in the 1970s, along with the use of **authentic** materials, saw a revival of interest in vocabulary teaching. Subsequently, developments in **corpus** linguistics and **discourse analysis** started to blur the distinction between vocabulary and grammar. In the 1990s the **lexical approach** ushered in a major re-think regarding the role of vocabulary. This concerned both the *selection* of items (**frequency** being a deciding factor) and the *type* of items: **formulaic language** (or lexical chunks) were recognized as being essential for both **fluency** and **idiomaticity**. These developments have influenced the design of teaching materials. Most contemporary coursebooks incorporate a lexical syllabus alongside the grammar one. Recent developments in lexicography have complemented this trend. There is now a wide range of **dictionaries** available for learners, many of which come with sophisticated software for accessing databases of examples and collocations.

It is now generally agreed that, in terms of goals, learners need a receptive vocabulary of around 3000 high-frequency words (or, better, **word families**) in order to achieve independent user status. This will give them around ninety per cent coverage of normal text. For a productive vocabulary, especially for speaking, they may only need half this number.

Classroom approaches to achieving these goals include dedicated vocabulary lessons. Typically these take the form of teaching *lexical sets* of words (ie, groups of thematically linked words) using a variety of means, including visual **aids**, demonstration, situations, texts and dictionary work. As well as the **meaning** of the items, the **form**, both spoken (ie, **pronunciation**) and written (ie, **spelling**), needs to be dealt with, especially if the words are being taught for productive use. Other aspects of word knowledge that may need to be highlighted include **connotation** and **style**, **collocation**, derived forms, and grammatical features, such as the word's **word class**. Vocabulary is also taught as preparation for listening or reading (*pre-teaching vocabulary*) or as a by-product of these skills.

It would be impossible, in class, to teach all the words that learners need. Learners therefore need opportunities for *incidental* learning, eg through *extensive reading*. They may also benefit from training in how to make the most of these opportunities, eg by means of dictionary use, note-keeping, etc. Some strategies for deducing the meaning of unfamiliar words will also help.

Amassing a fully-functioning vocabulary is essentially a **memory** task, and techniques to help in the memorizing of words can be usefully taught, too. It also helps to provide learners with repeated encounters with new words, eg through the re-reading of texts, or by reading several texts about the same topic. Constant recycling of newly learned words is essential. One simple way of doing this is to have a *word box* (or word bag) in the classroom. New words are written on to small cards and added to the word box. At the beginning of the next lesson, these words can be used as the basis for a review activity. For example, the teacher can take words out of the box and ask learners to define them, provide a translation or put them into a sentence. The words can also form the basis for peer-testing activities, in which learners take a number of word cards and test each other in pairs or small groups.

writing METHODOLOGY

Like speaking, writing is a productive **skill**, and, like other skills, writing involves a hierarchy of *sub-skills*. These range from the most mechanical (such as handwriting or typing legibly) through to the ability to organize the written text and lay it out according to the conventions of the particular text type. Along the way, writers also need to be able to:

- produce grammatically accurate sentences
- connect and punctuate these sentences
- select and maintain an appropriate style
- signal the direction that the message is taking
- anticipate the reader's likely questions so as to be able to structure the message accordingly

In order to enable these skills, writers need an extensive knowledge base, not only at the level of vocabulary and grammar, but at the level of connected discourse. This includes familiarity with a range of different text types, such as *informal letters, instructions, product descriptions*, etc. It follows that if classroom writing is mainly spelling- or grammar-focused, many of the sub-skills of writing will be neglected.

Nevertheless, the teaching of writing has tended to focus on the 'lower-level' features of the skill, such as being able to write sentences that are both accurate and complex, that demonstrate internal cohesion, and that are connected to the sentences next to them. This language-based approach is justified on the grounds that stricter standards of accuracy are usually required in writing than in speaking. Also, writing demands a greater degree of explicitness than speaking, since writers and their readers are separated in time and space. They therefore can't rely on immediate feedback in order to clear up mis-understandings.

By contrast, a text-based approach to teaching writing takes a more 'top-down' view. This approach finds support in **discourse analysis**, which shows that a **text** is more than a series of sentences, however neatly linked. Instead, texts are organized according to larger *macrostructures*, such as problem-solution, or definition-examples. Hence, learners need explicit guidance in how texts are structured. This typically involves analysing and imitating models of particular text types. For example, a business letter might be analysed in terms of its overall layout, the purpose of each of its paragraphs, the grammatical and lexical choices within each paragraph, and the punctuation. Each of these features is then practised in isolation. They are then recombined in tasks aimed first at reproducing the original text and then at producing similar texts incorporating different content.

This approach is called a *product approach* to the teaching of writing, since the focus is exclusively on producing a text (the product) that reproduces the model. By contrast, a *process approach* argues that writers do not in fact start with a clear idea of the finished product. Rather, the text emerges out of a creative process. This process includes:

planning (*generating ideas*, *goal setting* and *organizing*), *drafting* and *re-drafting*; *reviewing*, including *editing* and *proofreading*, and, finally, '*publishing*'. Advocates of a process approach argue for a more organic sequence of classroom activities, beginning with the brainstorming of ideas, writing preliminary drafts, comparing drafts, re-drafting, and *conferencing*, that is, talking through their draft with the teacher, in order to fine-tune their ideas.

The process approach to writing has a lot in common with the **communicative approach** to language teaching, and each has drawn support from the other. The communicative approach views writing as an act of communication in which the writer interacts with a reader or readers for a particular purpose. The purpose might be to ask for information about a language course, to relay personal news, to complain about being overcharged at a hotel, or simply to entertain and amuse. Thus, advocates of a communicative approach argue that classroom writing tasks should be motivated by a clear purpose and that writers should have their reader(s) in mind at all stages of the writing process. Such principles are now reflected in the design of writing tasks in public examinations, such as this one, from the Cambridge ESOL First Certificate in English (FCE) paper:

> The school where you learn English has decided to buy some videos in English. You have been asked to write a report to the Principal, suggesting what kinds of videos the school should buy. In your report you should also explain why students at the school will like these videos.
>
> Write your report.

The social purposes of writing are also foregrounded by proponents of a *genre-based approach*. **Genre** analysis attempts to show how the structure of particular text-types are shaped by the purposes they serve in specific social and cultural contexts. Put simply, a business letter is the way it is because of what it does. Advocates of genre-based teaching reject a process approach to teaching writing. They argue that to emphasize self-expression at the expense of teaching the generic structures of texts may in fact disempower learners. Many learners, especially those who are learning English as a *second* language, need a command of those genres – such as writing a CV, or requesting a bank loan – that permit access to the host community. A genre approach to teaching writing is not unlike a product approach, therefore. It starts with model texts that are subjected to analysis and replication. The difference is that these models are closely associated with their contexts of use, and they are analysed in functional terms as much as in linguistic ones. The genre approach has been particularly influential in the teaching of academic writing.

In reality, none of these approaches is entirely incompatible with any other. Resourceful teachers tend to blend elements of each. For example, they may encourage learners to 'discover' what they want to write, using a process approach. They may then give them a model text, both as a source of useful language items, and as a template for the final product. They may also provide exercises in specific sub-skills, such as linking sentences, or using a formal style.

The Common European Framework and *New Inside Out*

The Common European Framework for language learning

Introduction

The Common European Framework (CEF) is a widely used standard created by the Council of Europe. In the classroom, familiarity with the CEF can be of great help to any teacher in identifying students' actual progress and helping them to set their learning priorities.

Students can use the descriptors (description of competences) at any point to get a detailed, articulated, and personal picture of their own individual progress. This is important, as no two language learners progress in the same way, and consequently it's always rather artificial to apply a 'framework level' to a class as a whole, or to a course or coursebook.

The European Language Portfolio is another Council of Europe project, designed to give every learner a structure for keeping a record of their language learning experiences and their progress as described in the CEF. Up-to-date information about developments with the CEF and Portfolio can be found on www.coe.int/portfolio.

The Swiss-based Eurocentres Foundation played a major role in the development of the levels and the descriptors for the CEF and the prototype Portfolio. The CEF descriptors, developed in a Swiss National Research Foundation project, were presented in clearer, simpler, self-assessment form in the prototype (Swiss) Portfolio. There are now dozens of different national versions of the Portfolio for different educational sectors, but the only version for adults is that developed from the Swiss version by EAQUALS (European Association for Quality Language Services) in collaboration with ALTE. The descriptors used in this guide are taken from the EAQUALS/ALTE Portfolio. An electronic version that can be completed on-line can be downloaded in English or French from www.eelp.org. The EAQUALS/ALTE portfolio descriptors have been used in this guide, as they're more concrete and practical than the original CEFR descriptors.

New Inside Out CEF checklists

New Inside Out Intermediate is appropriate for students who can already use basic English in a limited range of situations and are now facing the daunting task of expanding their language abilities towards more general competence. By the end of *New Inside Out* Intermediate, if the students have had access to English outside the classroom, and have had the opportunity to practise, they should feel able to accomplish the things described at the B1 level with a good degree of confidence.

In order to help the teacher and student assess their progress, we've provided a list of B1 descriptors for each unit of *New Inside Out* Intermediate. A good ability with the A2 descriptors is presupposed at the start of the book, and most students who have reached that level will already be able to make a fair attempt at some of the things described at B1. The intermediate level is about building confidence and expanding the range of situations in which the student can operate comfortably in English. The descriptors allow the teacher to see a typical pattern of language acquisition. It's important to remember that every student learns differently, and that the various abilities will be acquired in a different sequence and at a different pace by each individual.

At intermediate level students have reached a stage at which it's difficult to direct their learning effectively. Up to now there's been a clear set of basic grammar rules and essential vocabulary to learn, but now students begin to realise that there's a vast amount more information about the language that they need in order to use it well, and that that information is much more difficult to codify and organise. They can gain a real sense of achievement, however, from understanding the slightly technical descriptors and applying them to their own experience.

Suggested targets for the checklist are provided for each unit. They allow the teacher to see how a typical student's confidence might be building, to identify the key skills focused on in each unit, and so to select supplementary materials or change the emphasis as necessary. At the same time, they give the students a yardstick to measure themselves against, so that they can easily identify their own weak areas and take responsibility for their own learning. It's a good idea to include the students in the ongoing planning of the course at this level: they can now express their needs and preferences in English and so if they feel consulted about the course, it's possible to establish very productive feedback.

1 Schneider, Günther, & North, Brian (2000): "Fremdsprachen können – was heisst das?" Zürich, Rüegger
North, Brian (2000): "The Development of a Common Framework Scale of Language Proficiency", New York, Peter Lang

2 EAQUALS is a pan-European language school accreditation body with over 100 full members. ALTE is an association dedicated to raising standards in language testing and encompasses the major European examination providers. Eurocentres provides high quality language teaching in countries where the language concerned is spoken. EAQUALS, ALTE and Eurocentres are the three NGOS advisers for language learning to the Council of Europe and all three implement the CEFR.

CEF Student checklists

Unit 1

Complete the checklist.

1 = I can do this with a lot of help from my teacher
2 = I can do this with a little help
3 = I can do this fairly well
4 = I can do this really well
5 = I can do this almost perfectly

Competences	Page	Your score				
I can follow clearly articulated speech directed at me in everyday conversation, though I sometimes have to ask for repetition of particular words and phrases.	7, 9	1	2	3	4	5
I can skim short texts (for example news summaries) and find relevant facts and information (for example who has done what, when and where).	8	1	2	3	4	5
I can start, maintain and close simple face-to-face conversation on topics that are familiar or of personal interest.	4, 5, 8, 10	1	2	3	4	5
I can give detailed accounts of experiences, describing feelings and reactions.	9	1	2	3	4	5
I can express myself reasonably accurately in familiar, predictable situations.	5, 7	1	2	3	4	5

Unit 2

Complete the checklist.

1 = I can do this with a lot of help from my teacher
2 = I can do this with a little help
3 = I can do this fairly well
4 = I can do this really well
5 = I can do this almost perfectly

Competences	Page	Your score				
I can listen to a short narrative and form hypotheses about what will happen next.	15	1	2	3	4	5
I can understand the plot of a clearly structured story and recognise what the most important events are and what is significant about them.	12	1	2	3	4	5
I can give or seek personal views and opinions in an informal discussion with friends.	16, 17	1	2	3	4	5
I can narrate a story.	15	1	2	3	4	5
I can convey simple information on immediate relevance, getting across which point I feel is most important.	13	1	2	3	4	5

Unit 3

Complete the checklist.

1 = I can do this with a lot of help from my teacher
2 = I can do this with a little help
3 = I can do this fairly well
4 = I can do this really well
5 = I can do this almost perfectly

Competences	Page	Your score				
I can understand the main points of radio news bulletins and simpler recorded material on topics of personal interest delivered relatively slowly and clearly.	22, 24	1	2	3	4	5
I can read columns or interviews in newspapers and magazines in which someone takes a stand on a current topic or event and understand the overall meaning of the text.	22, 25	1	2	3	4	5
I can start, maintain and close simple face-to-face conversation on topics that are familiar or of personal interest.	24, 25	1	2	3	4	5
I can give or seek personal views and opinions in an informal discussion with friends.	22, 23	1	2	3	4	5
I can keep a conversation going comprehensibly, but have to pause to plan and correct what I am saying – especially when I talk freely for longer periods.	21	1	2	3	4	5

Unit 4

Complete the checklist.

1 = I can do this with a lot of help from my teacher
2 = I can do this with a little help
3 = I can do this fairly well
4 = I can do this really well
5 = I can do this almost perfectly

Competences	Page	Your score				
I can catch the main points in TV programmes on familiar topics when the delivery is relatively slow and clear.	34	1	2	3	4	5
I can guess the meaning of single unknown words from the context thus deducing the meaning of expressions if the topic is familiar.	36	1	2	3	4	5
I can understand the most important information in short simple everyday information brochures.	32	1	2	3	4	5
I can give detailed accounts of experiences, describing feelings and reactions.	34, 36, 37	1	2	3	4	5
I can write simple texts about experiences or events, for example about a trip, for a school newspaper or a club newsletter.	33, 34	1	2	3	4	5

 CEF: PHOTOCOPIABLE *New Inside Out* Intermediate Teacher's Book © Macmillan Publishers Limited 2009

Unit 5

Complete the checklist.

1 = I can do this with a lot of help from my teacher
2 = I can do this with a little help
3 = I can do this fairly well
4 = I can do this really well
5 = I can do this almost perfectly

Competences	Page	Your score				
I can understand the main points of radio news bulletins and simpler recorded material on topics of personal interest delivered relatively slow and clear.	40, 43	1	2	3	4	5
In private letters, I can understand those parts dealing with events, feelings and wishes well enough to correspond regularly with a pen friend.	44	1	2	3	4	5
I can deal with most situations likely to arise when making travel arrangements through an agent or when actually travelling.	46	1	2	3	4	5
I can give detailed accounts of experiences, describing feelings and reactions.	43, 45	1	2	3	4	5
I have a sufficient vocabulary to express myself with some circumlocutions on most topics pertinent to my everyday life such as family, hobbies and interests, work, travel and current events.	41, 42	1	2	3	4	5

Unit 6

Complete the checklist.

1 = I can do this with a lot of help from my teacher
2 = I can do this with a little help
3 = I can do this fairly well
4 = I can do this really well
5 = I can do this almost perfectly

Competences	Page	Your score				
I can read columns or interviews in newspapers and magazines in which someone takes a stand on a current topic or event and understand the overall meaning of the text.	50, 51	1	2	3	4	5
I can maintain a conversation or discussion but may sometimes be difficult to follow when trying to say exactly what I would like to.	50, 52, 54	1	2	3	4	5
I can deal with most situations likely to arise when making travel arrangements through an agent or when actually travelling.	49	1	2	3	4	5
I can express myself reasonably accurately in familiar, predictable situations.	49, 51	1	2	3	4	5
I can reply in written form to advertisements and ask for more complete or more specific information about products (for example a car or an academic course).	53	1	2	3	4	5

Unit 7

Complete the checklist.

1 = I can do this with a lot of help from my teacher
2 = I can do this with a little help
3 = I can do this fairly well
4 = I can do this really well
5 = I can do this almost perfectly

Competences	Page	Your score
I can understand the main points of radio news bulletins and simpler recorded material on topics of personal interest delivered relatively slowly and clearly.	60, 64	1 2 3 4 5
I can understand the main points in short newspaper articles about current and familiar topics.	62, 63, 64	1 2 3 4 5
I can guess the meaning of single unknown words from the context thus deducing the meaning of expressions if the topic is familiar.	62	1 2 3 4 5
I can express and respond to feelings such as happiness, sadness, interest and indifference.	66	1 2 3 4 5
In a letter, I can express feelings such as grief, happiness, interest, regret and sympathy.	65	1 2 3 4 5

Unit 8

Complete the checklist.

1 = I can do this with a lot of help from my teacher
2 = I can do this with a little help
3 = I can do this fairly well
4 = I can do this really well
5 = I can do this almost perfectly

Competences	Page	Your score
I can listen to a short narrative and form hypotheses about what will happen next.	72	1 2 3 4 5
I can understand the most important information in short simple everyday information brochures.	69, 70	1 2 3 4 5
I can understand the plot of a clearly structured story and recognise what the most important events are and what is significant about them.	68, 72	1 2 3 4 5
I can ask for and follow detailed directions.	68, 74	1 2 3 4 5
I can explain and give reasons for my plans, intentions and actions.	71	1 2 3 4 5

 CEF: PHOTOCOPIABLE *New Inside Out* Intermediate Teacher's Book © Macmillan Publishers Limited 2009

Unit 9

Complete the checklist.

1 = I can do this with a lot of help from my teacher
2 = I can do this with a little help
3 = I can do this fairly well
4 = I can do this really well
5 = I can do this almost perfectly

Competences	Page	Your score				
I can read columns or interviews in newspapers and magazines in which someone takes a stand on a current topic or event and understand the overall meaning of the text.	77, 79, 81	1	2	3	4	5
I can start, maintain and close simple face-to-face conversation on topics that are familiar or of personal interest.	76, 78	1	2	3	4	5
I can express and respond to feelings such as happiness, sadness, interest and indifference.	80, 81	1	2	3	4	5
I can relate to the plot of a book or film and describe my reactions.	79	1	2	3	4	5
I can describe in a personal letter the plot of a film or a book and give an account of a concert.	81	1	2	3	4	5

Unit 10

Complete the checklist.

1 = I can do this with a lot of help from my teacher
2 = I can do this with a little help
3 = I can do this fairly well
4 = I can do this really well
5 = I can do this almost perfectly

Competences	Page	Your score				
I can catch the main points in TV programmes on familiar topics when the delivery is relatively slow and clear.	92	1	2	3	4	5
I can understand simple technical information, such as operating instructions for everyday equipment.	94	1	2	3	4	5
I can maintain a conversation or discussion but may sometimes be difficult to follow when trying to say exactly what I would like to.	90, 91, 93, 94	1	2	3	4	5
I can narrate a story.	93	1	2	3	4	5
When I can't think of a word I want, I can use a simple word meaning something similar and invite 'correction'.	89	1	2	3	4	5

Unit 11

Complete the checklist.

1 = I can do this with a lot of help from my teacher
2 = I can do this with a little help
3 = I can do this fairly well
4 = I can do this really well
5 = I can do this almost perfectly

Competences	Page	Your score				
I can understand the main points of radio news bulletins and simpler recorded material on topics of personal interest delivered relatively slowly and clearly.	96	1	2	3	4	5
In private letters, I can understand those parts dealing with events, feelings and wishes well enough to correspond regularly with a pen friend.	98, 100	1	2	3	4	5
I can start, maintain and close simple face-to-face conversation on topics that are familiar or of personal interest.	100, 101	1	2	3	4	5
I can give or seek personal views and opinions in an informal discussion with friends.	96, 100, 101	1	2	3	4	5
In a letter, I can express feelings such as grief, happiness, interest, regret and sympathy.	99, 100	1	2	3	4	5

Unit 12

Complete the checklist.

1 = I can do this with a lot of help from my teacher
2 = I can do this with a little help
3 = I can do this fairly well
4 = I can do this really well
5 = I can do this almost perfectly

Competences	Page	Your score				
I have a sufficient vocabulary to express myself with some circumlocutions on most topics pertinent to my everyday life such as family, hobbies and interests, work, travel, and current events.	105, 111	1	2	3	4	5
I can understand the most important information in short simple everyday information brochures.	106	1	2	3	4	5
I can skim short texts (for example news summaries) and find relevant facts and information (for example who has done what and where).	106	1	2	3	4	5
I can express myself reasonably accurately in familiar, predictable situations.	107, 108, 110	1	2	3	4	5
I can describe dreams, hopes and ambitions.	109	1	2	3	4	5

CEF Student checklists: Answer key

Unit 1

Competences	Page	Your score
I can follow clearly articulated speech directed at me in everyday conversation, though I sometimes have to ask for repetition of particular words and phrases.	7, 9	① 2 3 4 5
I can skim short texts (for example news summaries) and find relevant facts and information (for example who has done what, when and where).	8	1 ② 3 4 5
I can start, maintain and close simple face-to-face conversation on topics that are familiar or of personal interest.	4, 5, 8, 10	① 2 3 4 5
I can give detailed accounts of experiences, describing feelings and reactions.	9	① 2 3 4 5
I can express myself reasonably accurately in familiar, predictable situations.	5, 7	1 ② 3 4 5

Unit 2

Competences	Page	Your score
I can listen to a short narrative and form hypotheses about what will happen next.	15	① 2 3 4 5
I can understand the plot of a clearly structured story and recognise what the most important events are and what is significant about them.	12	① 2 3 4 5
I can give or seek personal views and opinions in an informal discussion with friends.	16, 17	1 ② 3 4 5
I can narrate a story.	15	1 ② 3 4 5
I can convey simple information on immediate relevance, getting across which point I feel is most important.	13	① 2 3 4 5

Unit 3

Competences	Page	Your score
I can understand the main points of radio news bulletins and simpler recorded material on topics of personal interest delivered relatively slowly and clearly.	22, 24	1 ② 3 4 5
I can read columns or interviews in newspapers and magazines in which someone takes a stand on a current topic or event and understand the overall meaning of the text.	22, 25	1 ② 3 4 5
I can start, maintain and close simple face-to-face conversation on topics that are familiar or of personal interest.	24, 25	1 ② 3 4 5
I can give or seek personal views and opinions in an informal discussion with friends.	22, 23	1 2 ③ 4 5
I can keep a conversation going comprehensibly, but have to pause to plan and correct what I am saying – especially when I talk freely for longer periods.	21	1 ② 3 4 5

Unit 4

Competences	Page	Your score
I can catch the main points in TV programmes on familiar topics when the delivery is relatively slow and clear.	34	1 2 ③ 4 5
I can guess the meaning of single unknown words from the context thus deducing the meaning of expressions if the topic is familiar.	36	1 ② 3 4 5
I can understand the most important information in short simple everyday information brochures.	32	1 ② 3 4 5
I can give detailed accounts of experiences, describing feelings and reactions.	34, 36, 37	1 2 ③ 4 5
I can write simple texts about experiences or events, for example about a trip, for a school newspaper or a club newsletter.	33, 34	1 2 ③ 4 5

Unit 5

Competences	Page	Your score
I can understand the main points of radio news bulletins and simpler recorded material on topics of personal interest delivered relatively slow and clear.	40, 43	1 2 ③ 4 5
In private letters, I can understand those parts dealing with events, feelings and wishes well enough to correspond regularly with a pen friend.	44	1 ② 3 4 5
I can deal with most situations likely to arise when making travel arrangements through an agent or when actually travelling.	46	1 ② 3 4 5
I can give detailed accounts of experiences, describing feelings and reactions.	43, 45	1 2 ③ 4 5
I have a sufficient vocabulary to express myself with some circumlocutions on most topics pertinent to my everyday life such as family, hobbies and interests, work, travel and current events.	41, 42	1 2 ③ 4 5

Unit 6

Competences	Page	Your score
I can read columns or interviews in newspapers and magazines in which someone takes a stand on a current topic or event and understand the overall meaning of the text.	50, 51	1 2 ③ 4 5
I can maintain a conversation or discussion but may sometimes be difficult to follow when trying to say exactly what I would like to.	50, 52, 54	1 ② 3 4 5
I can deal with most situations likely to arise when making travel arrangements through an agent or when actually travelling.	49	1 2 ③ 4 5
I can express myself reasonably accurately in familiar, predictable situations.	49, 51	1 2 ③ 4 5
I can reply in written form to advertisements and ask for more complete or more specific information about products (for example a car or an academic course).	53	1 ② 3 4 5

Unit 7

Competences	Page	Your score
I can understand the main points of radio news bulletins and simpler recorded material on topics of personal interest delivered relatively slowly and clearly.	60, 64	1 2 3 ④ 5
I can understand the main points in short newspaper articles about current and familiar topics.	62, 63, 64	1 ② 3 4 5
I can guess the meaning of single unknown words from the context thus deducing the meaning of expressions if the topic is familiar.	62	1 ② 3 4 5
I can express and respond to feelings such as happiness, sadness, interest and indifference.	66	1 ② 3 4 5
In a letter, I can express feelings such as grief, happiness, interest, regret and sympathy.	65	① 2 3 4 5

Unit 8

Competences	Page	Your score				
I can listen to a short narrative and form hypotheses about what will happen next.	72	1	②	3	4	5
I can understand the most important information in short simple everyday information brochures.	69, 70	1	2	③	4	5
I can understand the plot of a clearly structured story and recognise what the most important events are and what is significant about them.	68, 72	1	2	③	4	5
I can ask for and follow detailed directions.	68, 74	1	2	③	4	5
I can explain and give reasons for my plans, intentions and actions.	71	1	②	3	4	5

Unit 9

Competences	Page	Your score				
I can read columns or interviews in newspapers and magazines in which someone takes a stand on a current topic or event and understand the overall meaning of the text.	77, 79, 81	1	2	3	④	5
I can start, maintain and close simple face-to-face conversation on topics that are familiar or of personal interest.	76, 78	1	2	③	4	5
I can express and respond to feelings such as happiness, sadness, interest and indifference.	80, 81	1	2	③	4	5
I can relate to the plot of a book or film and describe my reactions.	79	1	②	3	4	5
I can describe in a personal letter the plot of a film or a book and give an account of a concert.	81	1	②	3	4	5

Unit 10

Competences	Page	Your score				
I can catch the main points in TV programmes on familiar topics when the delivery is relatively slow and clear.	92	1	2	③	4	5
I can understand simple technical information, such as operating instructions for everyday equipment.	94	1	②	3	4	5
I can maintain a conversation or discussion but may sometimes be difficult to follow when trying to say exactly what I would like to.	90, 91, 93, 94	1	2	3	④	5
I can narrate a story.	93	1	2	3	④	5
When I can't think of a word I want, I can use a simple word meaning something similar and invite 'correction'.	89	1	②	3	4	5

Unit 11

Competences	Page	Your score				
I can understand the main points of radio news bulletins and simpler recorded material on topics of personal interest delivered relatively slowly and clearly.	96	1	2	3	4	⑤
In private letters, I can understand those parts dealing with events, feelings and wishes well enough to correspond regularly with a pen friend.	98, 100	1	2	3	④	5
I can start, maintain and close simple face-to-face conversation on topics that are familiar or of personal interest.	100, 101	1	2	3	4	⑤
I can give or seek personal views and opinions in an informal discussion with friends.	96, 100, 101	1	2	3	4	⑤
In a letter, I can express feelings such as grief, happiness, interest, regret and sympathy.	99, 100	1	2	③	4	5

Unit 12

Competences	Page	Your score				
I have a sufficient vocabulary to express myself with some circumlocutions on most topics pertinent to my everyday life such as family, hobbies and interests, work, travel, and current events.	105, 111	1	2	3	4	⑤
I can understand the most important information in short simple everyday information brochures.	106	1	2	3	4	⑤
I can skim short texts (for example news summaries) and find relevant facts and information (for example who has done what and where).	106	1	2	3	4	⑤
I can express myself reasonably accurately in familiar, predictable situations.	107, 108, 110	1	2	3	④	5
I can describe dreams, hopes and ambitions.	109	1	2	3	4	⑤

 CEF: PHOTOCOPIABLE *New Inside Out* Intermediate Teacher's Book © Macmillan Publishers Limited 2009

1 Friends *Overview*

Section & Aims	What the students are doing
Speaking & Reading SB page 4 Fluency work Reading for detail	Talking about friends, relatives and famous people. Reading a questionnaire about David Schwimmer. Answering the questionnaire for themselves.
Speaking & Grammar SB page 5 Asking questions Question forms	Matching beginnings and endings to form questions. Studying the structure of questions. Asking and answering questions about close friends.
Pronunciation SB page 6 Fractions	Listening and repeating fractions. Matching percentages and fractions.
Reading SB page 6 Reading for detail	Talking about ways of communicating with friends. Reading and choosing the correct alternative to complete a survey about keeping in touch.
Listening SB page 7 Listening for detail	Guessing what people will say about contacting friends and listening to check.
Grammar SB page 7 Adverbs of frequency	Adding adverbs of frequency to a table. Studying the position of adverbs of frequency. Writing sentences which are true for them.
Reading SB page 8 Reading for gist	Predicting the content of a text, then reading to check. Choosing names to complete sentences about the text.
Vocabulary SB page 9 Friendship expressions	Completing sentences about friendship. Putting a summary of the reading text in order. Talking about staying in touch with old friends.
Speaking: anecdote SB page 9 Fluency practice	Talking about a friend who is different from them.
Useful phrases SB page 10 Useful conversational phrases: meeting friends unexpectedly	Listening to conversations and saying whether statements are true or false. Choosing the best expressions to complete conversations. Completing a table with useful phrases, then listening and repeating the useful phrases. Practising conversations.
Vocabulary *Extra* SB page 11 Using a dictionary	Discussing information you can find in a dictionary. Matching dictionary abbreviations with their meanings. Answering questions about information from dictionary extracts.
Writing WB page 9	Writing emails.

1 Friends *Teacher's notes*

Warm up

Write on the board: *You can't choose your family, but fortunately you can choose your friends.* Students talk about whether they agree with the message of this sentence – that families are an obligation and friends a pleasure.

Speaking & Reading (SB page 4)

1

- Write on the board the names of three people who are important to you: a friend, a relative and somebody famous. Students ask you questions about the three people: *Who's Greg? How did you meet him? When did you meet him? How long have you known him?*, etc. Answer their questions and correct obvious or important errors.

- Students write the names of their three chosen people. They then show their lists to a partner and take turns to ask questions about the names their partner has chosen. Encourage them to ask as many questions as they can, and to find out as much about these people as possible.

2

- Focus attention on the photo of David Schwimmer and find out if any of the students have seen any TV programmes or films he's been in. Go through the list of famous people in the box with the class. Elicit any information they know about these people.

- Give the students time to read the questionnaire and decide which of the famous people in the box is the odd one out.

Michael Jackson – because he wouldn't be invited to his dream dinner party.

Cultural notes

David Schwimmer /ˈdeɪvɪd ˈʃwɪmə/ (born 1966)
David Schwimmer was one of the main actors in the American sitcom *Friends*. He played the role of Dr Ross Geller in the series. Since *Friends* finished, he has moved into directing.

Friends

Friends is an American sitcom about the lives of six friends living in Manhattan in New York City. It was originally broadcast between 1994 and 2004. The final episode of the show was watched by around 51 million people in the United States. The series won six Emmys and a Golden Globe.

Fyodor Dostoevsky /ˈfiːjədɔː dɒstɔrˈjevski/ (1821–1881)
Fyodor Dostoevsky was a Russian novelist whose works include *Crime and Punishment* (1866) and *The Brothers Karamazov* (1880).

Sophia Loren /səʊˈfɪə ləˈren/ (born 1934)
Sophia Loren was born in Rome and raised in Naples. She was one of the most popular big screen actresses of the 1950s and 1960s, starring in such classics as *The Millionairess* (1960) and *El Cid* (1961).

Mahatma Gandhi /məhætmə ˈgændiː/ (1869–1948)
Mahatma Gandhi was a political and spiritual leader in India, who helped his country, through peaceful resistance, to achieve independence in 1947 from the British Empire. Gandhi was committed to non-violence, and so his assassination at the hands of an extremist Hindu (Gandhi's own faith) gunman was all the more ironic.

Gene Kelly /dʒiːn ˈkeli/ (1912–1996)
Gene Kelly was an American dancer, singer and actor. Most famously known for his performance in *Singin' in the Rain* (1952), Kelly was a top star of Hollywood musicals throughout the 1940s and 50s.

Martin Luther King, Jr /mɑːtɪn luːθə kɪŋ/ (1929–1968)
One of the leaders of the American civil rights movement, Luther King was a Baptist minister who advocated civil disobedience to gain rights for the black citizens of the United States. Luther King was assassinated by a gunman's bullet, in 1968.

Leonardo da Vinci /lɪjɒnɑːdəʊ dæ vɪntʃi/ (1452–1519)
Leonardo da Vinci was an Italian Renaissance artist, famous for paintings such as the *Mona Lisa* and *The Last Supper*. He also made designs, some hundreds of years ahead of his time, for the helicopter, the armoured tank, the calculator and many others. He contributed greatly to the study of anatomy, astronomy and civil engineering.

Charlie Chaplin (Sir Charles Chaplin)
/'tʃɑːli: 'tʃæplɪn/ (1889–1977)
Charlie Chaplin was an English comedy actor
and director. He was best known as a star of
silent films between 1914 and 1936. He won three
Academy Awards over the course of his career
and in 1975 received a knighthood.

Cole Porter /kəʊl 'pɔːtə/ (1891–1964)
Cole Porter was an American composer and
songwriter. He produced the musicals *Anything
Goes* (1934) and *Kiss Me, Kate* (1948), and enjoyed
Hollywood success in films such as *High Society*
(1955).

Sade /ʃɑːdeɪ/ (born 1959)
Helen Folasade Adu, also known as Sade, was
born in Nigeria and moved to the UK when she
was four. In the early 1980s she found success as
a songwriter and soul/jazz recording artist with
songs like *Smooth Operator* and *Your Love is King*
(both 1984).

Michael Jackson /maɪkəl 'dʒæksən/ (born 1958)
American pop singer whose hits include *Beat it,
Billie Jean* and *Thriller*.

La Vie en Rose (2007)
La Vie en Rose is a film about the life of French
singer Edith Piaf, starring Marion Cotillard,
Gérard Depardieu and Silvie Testud. The film
won two Academy Awards and four BAFTAS.

Don't Stop 'Til You Get Enough (1979)
Don't Stop 'Til You Get Enough was written and
composed by Michael Jackson. It was the first hit
off his album *Off The Wall* (1979).

3

Pairwork. Students work in pairs to identify and discuss
what David Schwimmer says about the subjects listed.
Go round, offering help with vocabulary.

a) The theatre – It's the greatest love of his life.
   (However, forgetting what he's supposed to
   do on stage is also his greatest fear.)
b) The ocean – Being in the ocean alone is another
   fear: feeling something large brush against his leg.
   But it's also the place he'd most like to live near
   one day.
c) Gifts – He's happier giving rather than receiving
   a gift.
d) Pizza and television – They are his guiltiest
   pleasures.
e) *La Vie en Rose* – Watching this film was the last
   time he cried.
f) Love – It's wonderful to fall in love.

4

- Give the students time to choose the questions they'd
  like to answer from the questionnaire and to think
  about their answers. Go round giving any help they
  need with vocabulary

- Pairwork. Put the students in pairs to compare their
  questions and their answers to them. Encourage them
  to report back to the class on their discussions.

Speaking & Grammar (SB page 5)

1

- Pairwork. Ask the students to work in pairs to match
  the beginnings of the questions with the endings.
- Check answers with the class. Students then take
  turns asking and answering the questions. Encourage
  them to make notes of their answers so that they can
  compare them. You could then ask them to compare
  their answers with those of another pair.

a) 5   b) 8   c) 10   d) 7   e) 12   f) 1   g) 2   h) 11
i) 3   j) 6   k) 4   l) 9

Language note

Grammar: word order in questions

When making questions …
… the auxiliary comes before the subject, not after it
(as in statements).
… if there is no other auxiliary verb, use *do*.
… if there is another auxiliary verb, don't use *do*.
(~~Do you can swim?~~).
… *What, Who, Where, How*, etc. (question words)
come at the beginning.

Question forms

2

- Focus the students' attention on the question forms
  in the margin. Elicit or explain which tenses these
  questions are in (present simple, present perfect, past
  continuous, past simple).
- Ask the students to look at the table and focus
  attention on the examples, getting a student to read
  out the completed questions a) and b) and making
  sure they know why these belong in the present
  simple column of the table.
- Ask the students to work individually to classify the
  remaining questions from Exercise 1 according to
  tense. Go round, monitoring and giving help. Check
  answers with the class and then ask them which
  two tenses are not included in the questions. With
  strong classes, you could ask the students to think of
  example questions in these two tenses.

Present simple: a, b, c, e, f, g, l
Present continuous: d
Present perfect: i
Present perfect continuous: h
Past simple: j
Past continuous: k

Past perfect and past perfect continuous.

3

- Read out questions a) and g) from Exercise 1, or get a student to do it. Highlight the position of the prepositions: *Where do you come from? What kind of music do you listen to?* Focus attention on the example in the exercise and ask the students to identify the preposition (*for*).
- Ask the students to work individually to rewrite the remaining questions in the correct order. Go round, monitoring and giving help.
- Check answers with the whole class before getting the students to ask and answer the questions in pairs.

> a) What are you learning English for?
> b) What sort of things are you good at?
> c) What kind of things are you interested in?
> d) What do you spend most money on?
> e) What clubs or groups do you belong to?
> f) What kind of things do you worry about?
> g) Who do you usually have lunch with?
> h) Who do you confide in?

Language notes

Grammar: word order

- When a question word is the object of a preposition, the preposition often comes at the end of the clause, especially in informal spoken language.
  What are you interested in?
  Where did you get it from?

Vocabulary: *confide in*

- You may need to clarify the meaning of *confide in* (to talk freely to someone about personal matters), as this is a 'false friend' in some Romance languages. In Spanish, for example, a similar verb means 'to trust in', not 'to talk to'.

4

Do this with the whole class and make sure the students understand the difference between *Who* as a subject and *Who* as an object.

> *Who* is the subject in *b*.
> You don't use the auxiliary *do* when *Who*, *What* or *Which* is the subject.

Language note

Grammar: subject questions

If the question word *who* is the subject of the question, you don't use *do*, *does* or *did*. Compare:
Who went to the party? (*Who* is the subject)
Who did you go with? (*Who* is the object – *you* is the subject)
Who saw him? (*Who* is the subject)
Who did he see? (*Who* is the object – *he* is the subject)

5 Grammar *Extra* 1

Ask the students to turn to *Grammar Extra* 1 on page 126 of the Student's Book. Here they'll find an explanation of the grammar they've been studying and further exercises to practise it.

> **1**
> a) didn't study   e) enjoy
> b) 've been / never been   f) 'm reading
> c) was doing   g) haven't been doing
> d) hadn't used
>
> **2**
> 1 What   5 how many
> 2 Which   6 What
> 3 How old   7 Where
> 4 How long   8 why
>
> **3**
> a) What about?   d) Who with?
> b) Who to?   e) Who for?
> c) What for?   f) Who from?
>
> a) What does he/she like talking about?
> b) Who did you send a text to?
> c) What are you saving your money for?
> d) Who are you going out with?
> e) Who have you bought a present for?
> f) Who did you get it from?
>
> **4**
> a) What did you watch on TV last night?
> b) Who usually gets up the earliest in your house?
> c) What do you normally have for breakfast?
> d) Who texts you the most?
> e) How many people remembered your last birthday?
> f) Which bus (*or* What number) bus stops near your house?
> g) Who did you have dinner with last night?
> h) How many people phoned you yesterday?

6

- Go through the example with the class. Ask the students to identify that *Who* is the subject of this question.
- Ask the students to work individually to write the remaining questions, using *Who* as the subject each time. Check answers with the class before putting them in pairs to take turns asking and answering the questions.

> a) Who talks the most?
> b) Who always remembers your birthday?
> c) Who wears the best clothes?
> d) Who texts you the most?
> e) Who lives the closest to you?
> f) Who has known you the longest?

Pronunciation (SB page 6)

1 🌐 1.01

- Focus the students' attention on the fractions in the box. Play the recording and ask them to repeat them. After they've done this chorally, ask several students to repeat the fractions individually, and check that everyone is pronouncing them correctly. Some fractions with consonant clusters, e.g. *four fifths*, *an eighth* and *three tenths*, are harder to say than others. Pay particular attention to these and give the students plenty of practice.

> 🌐 **1.01**
>
> *a half   a third   a quarter   three quarters*
> *four fifths   an eighth   three tenths   a twentieth*

Language note
Pronunciation: fractions

It's usual to use *a/an* (/ə/ /ən/) rather than *one* when saying any fraction that has number '1' in the top half (⅛, ¼ , ⅓, ½, etc.) For example, *a third* is more common than *one third*.

Extra activity

Divide the class into two teams. Write various fractions on the board and ask the teams to compete to be the first to draw a circle around the correct one as you read them out.

2 🌐 1.02

- Focus the student's attention on the example. Point out that each fraction can also be expressed as a percentage. Then ask them to match the percentages with the fractions in Exercise 1.
- Play the recording for them to check their answers. Then play it again for them to listen and repeat.

> a) 5% – ¹⁄₂₀   e) 33.3% – ⅓
> b) 12.5% – ⅛   f) 50% – ½
> c) 25% – ¼   g) 75% – ¾
> d) 30% – ³⁄₁₀   h) 80% – ⅘

> 🌐 **1.02**
> a) *5% – a twentieth*
> b) *12.5% (twelve point five percent) – an eighth*
> c) *25% – a quarter*
> d) *30% – three tenths*
> e) *33.3% (thirty-three point three percent) – a third*
> f) *50% – a half*
> g) *75% – three quarters*
> h) *80% – four fifths*

Reading (SB page 6)

1

- Explain the expression *in touch*. Point out that it refers to any kind of communication with someone, it doesn't have to involve a face-to-face meeting. You can say *We keep in touch by phone / by letter / by email*, etc. Ask the students to write down their five names quickly. They should then think about the last time they were in touch with these people and decide how they communicated.
- Put the students into pairs to talk about their five people and how they last communicated.

2 🌐 1.03

- Pairwork. Read the introduction to the survey to the class or ask a student to do this. Then put the students into pairs and ask them to read the survey together and decide which alternative is most likely to be true.
- Play the recording for them to check their answers. Then have a class discussion on which were the most and least surprising results.

> a) 94   b) 53   c) boys   d) men
> e) they can talk about more things than
>   face-to-face
> f) gossip   g) more   h) improved
> i) happier   j) 59%

> 🌐 **1.03**
>
> *Keeping in touch*
> *A Global poll was conducted into how young people communicate with friends. 18,000 people between the ages of fourteen and twenty-four in sixteen countries were interviewed. These were some of the key results of the survey.*
>
> a) *The average young person has 94 numbers in their mobile phone.*
> b) *On average, young people communicate regularly online and face-to-face with 53 friends.*
> c) *The group who has the largest number of friends are boys 14–21.*
> d) *Of all the people surveyed, those who spend the most time online (31 hours per week) are men 22–24.*
> e) *Over half of young people said that they like messaging because they can talk about more things than face-to-face.*
> f) *The top messaging topic is gossip.*
> g) *Technology has resulted in young people having more close friendships.*
> h) *Technology has improved face-to-face interaction.*
> i) *Technology makes young people happier.*
> j) *59% of young people prefer television to their computer.*

Listening (SB page 7)

1

- Focus the students' attention on the pictures. Ask them to say how old they think the people are and what kind of people they are.

- Focus attention on the words in the box and make sure everyone understands them. Then ask them to look at the texts under the pictures and decide which word they think should go in each gap.

- Allow them to compare answers in pairs and discuss their guesses, but don't confirm or deny anything at this stage.

2 🔘 1.04–1.06

- Play the recording for the students to see if they guessed correctly in Exercise 1.

- Give the students a minute or two to think about whether or not the sentences are true for them. Then ask them to report back to the rest of the class.

Adam:
1 text   2 phone   3 emails

Carole:
4 emails   5 Skype   6 letters

Sharon:
7 emails   8 text   9 phone   10 online

🔘 **1.04–1.06** (I = Interviewer; A = Adam; S = Sharon; C = Carole)

🔘 **1.04 Adam**

I: *Hi, excuse me – we're doing some research into how people use technology to talk to their friends. Do you mind if we ask you a couple of questions?*

A: *Well, I'm in a bit of a hurry.*

I: *It'll only take a few minutes.*

A: *Well, OK then.*

I: *Right, how do you usually contact your friends – by phone, email, text, …?*

A: *Um, I use my phone.*

I: *Do you usually use it to speak to friends, or do you text them?*

A: *I text from time to time, but I usually speak on the phone. It's so much quicker, and I'm very bad at texting.*

I: *Do you ever use email?*

A: *Yes, I check my personal emails twice a day, before I go to work and when I get back home.*

I: *Do you use messaging?*

A: *No, never.*

🔘 **1.05 Carole**

I: *Hi, excuse me – can I ask you a question for some research we're doing?*

C: *Certainly.*

I: *How do you usually contact your friends?*

C: *Oh, I pick up the phone.*

I: *And do you ever use email?*

C: *Yes, of course. I check my emails once a week. Oh, and I use Skype now and again. One of my grandchildren lives in Australia and she calls me on Skype every weekend.*

I: *When was the last time you wrote a letter?*

C: *Oh dear, I love receiving letters. But I must admit, I rarely write letters nowadays. It's a shame really, don't you think?*

🔘 **1.06 Sharon**

I: *Hi, excuse me – we're doing some research into how people use technology to talk to their friends. Do you mind if we ask you a couple of questions?*

S: *OK.*

I: *How do you usually contact your friends – by phone, email, text …?*

S: *I never send emails. But I text all the time.*

I: *Do you speak on the phone?*

S: *Yes, but not very often – it's too expensive.*

I: *And what about when you're at home? Do you use your computer to communicate with friends?*

S: *Yeah, I use messaging. I'm always online so I chat with several friends every evening.*

I: *Do you use social networking?*

S: *What?*

I: *Facebook, MySpace, Bebo, …?*

S: *Oh yes, I've got 386 friends on Facebook. But I only contact about twenty of them regularly.*

Cultural notes

MySpace, Facebook, Bebo /ˈbiːbəʊ/ (launched 2003, 2004 and 2005 respectively)
MySpace, Facebook and Bebo are social networking websites in which groups of users submit and exchange photos, blogs, music and video.

Skype (released 2003)
Skype is a software system which allows users to call, message or video conference other users over the internet free of charge. In 2005, Skype became part of the eBay group.

Grammar (SB page 7)

Adverbs of frequency

1

- Focus the students' attention on the table and make sure they understand that the words in the table are adverbs of frequency, which tell us how often something happens. Point out that the table headings range in order of frequency from *Always* to *Never*.

- Ask the students to work individually to find more adverbs of frequency in the sentences in the listening in the previous section. When they've found them, they should put them in the correct place in the table according to how frequently the event they describe occurs. Allow them to compare with a partner before checking with the class.

- Point out that the position of the adverbs in a table such as this may be dependent on the nature of the action being described. So, for example, checking your emails once a week might be regarded as 'not often', whereas a weekly visit to the hairdresser's would be regarded as 'often'.

Always	Often	Sometimes	Not often	Never
all the time	normally	occasionally	hardly	never
always	regularly	from time to	ever	
	usually	time	now and	
	twice a	once a week	again	
	day		don't often	
			rarely	

Language notes

Grammar: adverbs of frequency

- Adverbs of frequency usually come before a main verb:
  She **always** has coffee for breakfast.
  Adverbs of frequency always come after *be*: *She's* **always** *happy*.

- While the rule states that the adverb comes between the subject and the main verb (and after the verb *be*), it's possible to use some adverbs at the beginning of the sentence, to emphasize the frequency. From the selection in the Student's Book, adverbs which can start a sentence are: *usually, normally, sometimes* and *occasionally*.
  Sometimes *I call her five times a day.* / *I* **sometimes** *call her five times a day.*
  Normally *they cost £25.* / *They* **normally** *cost £25.*
  It's probably as well not to mention this to your students at this stage, unless someone brings up the subject, as the rule in the Student's Book covers all adverbs of frequency.

- **Adverb phrases** usually come at the end of a sentence:
  He calls me **all the time**.
  I see them **now and again**.
  I go to the gym **once a week**.
  We get together for a meal **from time to time**.

2

When the students are deciding which adverbs go in which position, encourage them to say the potential sentences aloud so that they get a feel for what sounds right. When checking answers, encourage the students to read the whole sentence aloud so that they hear the words in context.

> Position A: always, often, normally, regularly, usually, occasionally, hardly ever, rarely, don't often, never
> Position B: all the time, twice a day, from time to time, now and again, once a week

3

- Put the students into pairs, but ask them to work individually to guess which adverbs would make the statements true for their partner. Do not allow them to consult.

- Go through the example questions with the class and ask for a few more examples of the sorts of questions they need to ask to find out the necessary information.

- Tell the students to take turns asking and answering questions. They should make a note of how many of their guesses were correct and then report back to the class.

4 Pairwork

- The pairwork exercise for this unit is on pages 116 and 121 of the Student's Book. Put the students in pairs and tell them who will be Student A, and who will be Student B.

- While they're doing the exercise, go round, monitoring and giving help. Take note of any errors which may need particular attention later, and also any examples of good language use, which you can praise in a feedback session.

Reading (SB page 8)

Warm up

Ask a few students how long they've known their oldest friends. Ask if anyone had a close friend at school that they no longer see. Ask them why some friendships last your whole life, while others die.

1

- Focus the students' attention on the pictures of Tina and Will. Go through the statements with the class and ask them to discuss in pairs or small groups whether they think they are true or false. Tell them they should try to guess and shouldn't look the answers up in the text at this stage.

- Ask them to report back to the class and see how much agreement there is. With strong classes, tell the students to give reasons for their opinions.

- Ask the students to read the article and check their answers.

> a) True.   b) False.   c) False.

2

Focus the students' attention on the example and point out that it was Tina, not Will, who was looking for someone to share the house with. Ask them to underline the correct name for each of the other sentences.

> a) Tina   b) Will   c) Tina   d) Will   e) Tina
> f) Will

Vocabulary (SB page 9)

1

Stronger students should be able to complete many of these expressions without looking back at the text. However, you may need to allow weaker students to find them in the text.

> a) we clicked straightaway / we hit it off immediately
> b) we had a lot in common
> c) we became close friends
> d) we fell out
> e) we went our separate ways / we've drifted apart
> f) we got on very well together
> g) we had our ups and downs
> h) I know she'll always be there for me

2

Students try to put the summary in the correct order. Encourage them to try to do this first without looking back at the text. They can then compare their answers in pairs before going back to the text to check.

> 3:   met. They became close
> 7:   separate ways and they've drifted
> 4:   friends and got on
> 1:   Tina and Will hit it
> 6:   in common. Now they have gone their
> 2:   off immediately when they first
> 9:   out and they say that they are still
> 10: there for each other.
> 8:   apart. They haven't fallen
> 5:   well together. They had a lot

3

- Give the students time to think of their answers. Then ask them to compare their answers with a partner.
- Encourage them to report back to the class on their discussions.

Speaking: anecdote (SB page 9)

Anecdotes are features that occur regularly in this series. They are extended speaking tasks, where the students tackle a longer piece of discourse on a personal topic. There are questions to guide them and a model to listen to. For more information about how to set up, monitor and repeat Anecdotes, see page xx in the Introduction.

1 🔘 1.07

- Focus the students' attention on the photos of Antonia and her friend. Explain that they're going to hear Antonia talking about her friend, who is very different from her.
- Go through the questions and the answers with the class. Explain any unknown vocabulary. Play the recording and ask the students to listen and find which two questions she doesn't answer.
- Ask the students to match the questions and answers. Then play the recording again for them to check their answers.

> Antonia doesn't answer questions *g* and *j*.
> a) 4   b) 7   c) 1   d) 8   e) 2   f) 3
> g) –   h) 5   i) 6   j) –

> 🔘 1.07
> *I suppose I've got five or six close friends, and most of them are really similar to me. But my friend, Jackie, is the exception. In many ways, we're opposites. We met about ten years ago in Paris. I was doing an intensive French language course, and she was doing a fashion course, but we were living in the same student accommodation. I arrived a few weeks after her, and she was really friendly. I guess we became friends because we were in the same situation and we were both from England. I'm amazed we got on so well, because we have nothing in common. For a start, we come from very different backgrounds. She grew up in the country on a farm with lots of brothers and sisters and dogs and horses. I grew up with my mother in a small apartment in the city with a pet hamster! We don't share the same taste in music, clothes, books, art, or anything really. Our personalities are very different – she's very artistic, and I'm not. I'm very tidy and organised, and she's not. We even look different – she's tall and dark, and I'm small and fair. But we do have one very important thing in common. We're both crazy about football, and we support the same team – Chelsea. We meet about three or four times a year and we usually go out for lunch and talk about football or the good old times in Paris.*

Cultural note

Chelsea /ˈtʃelsi/ **Football Club** (founded 1905)
Chelsea Football Club is an English Premier League
football club. In recent years the team have enjoyed
success at the top of the league and in Europe. It's
owned by Russian millionaire Roman Abramovitch.

2

- Give the students a minute or two to decide who
  they're going to talk about. Then ask them to look at
  the questions in Exercise 1 again. Allow them to make
  notes of what they're going to say about their friend
  and how they're going to say it, but discourage them
  from writing a paragraph that they can simply read
  out. Go round, monitoring and giving help.

- Pairwork. Put the students in pairs and ask them
  to take turns to tell their partner about their friend.
  Encourage them to ask each other follow-up
  questions to get further information.

- Ask some pairs to report back to the class about what
  they found out.

Useful phrases (SB page 10)

1 🌐 1.08

Focus the students' attention on the illustrations which
show Cathy meeting three of her friends. Go through
the statements with the class and tell them that they
should listen to the three conversations and decide if
these statements are true or false. Play the recording and
ask the students for their decisions.

> a) True.   b) True.   c) False.

> 🌐 1.08 (C = Cathy; H = Harry; J= Jim; E = Ed)
>
> a)
> C: *Hey! How's it going?*
> H: *Not bad.*
> C: *What have you been up to lately?*
> H: *Not a lot really. What about you?*
> C: *Oh, this and that.*
> H: *Look, I must dash – I'll give you a call.*
>
> b)
> C: *Hello, stranger!*
> J: *Cathy! How's life?*
> C: *Great! What are you up to these days?*
> J: *Oh, keeping busy, you know.*
> C: *You must come over for dinner some time.*
> J: *That would be lovely. Better get back to the office.*
>   *See you.*
>
> c)
> C: *Hi. How are things?*
> E: *Fine. What about you?*
> C: *Oh, pretty good. Are you doing anything special at*
>   *the weekend?*
> E: *No, just taking it easy.*
> C: *Me too.*
> E: *Look, I'm afraid I can't stop. Take care.*

2

- When the students have chosen the options they
  think are most natural sounding, ask them to identify
  the difference between the options in each case (the
  more natural options have words missed out) and say
  what effect they think this has (the conversations are
  less formal and, therefore, sound more friendly).

- Play the recording again for them to check their
  answers.

> 1 Not a lot, really.
> 2 Oh, this and that.
> 3 Oh, keeping busy, you know.
> 4 Oh, pretty good.
> 5 No, just taking it easy.

3 🌐 1.09

- Ask the students to complete the table with the useful
  phrases.

- Play the recording for them to listen and repeat the
  phrases.

> a) How's life?
> b) How are things?
> c) Great!
> d) Fine.
> e) What are you up to these days?
> f) Better get back to the office.
> g) I'm afraid I can't stop.
> h) See you.
> i) Take care.

> 🌐 1.09
> *Greetings*
> *How's it going?*
> *How's life?*
> *How are things?*
>
> ***Saying things are OK***
> *Not bad.*
> *Great!*
> *Fine.*
>
> ***Asking for news***
> *What have you been up to lately?*
> *What are you up to these days?*
>
> ***Saying you're in a hurry***
> *Look, I must dash.*
> *Better get back to the office.*
> *I'm afraid I can't stop.*
>
> ***Goodbyes***
> *I'll give you a call.*
> *See you.*
> *Take care.*

4

Pairwork. Ask the students to practise the conversation with a partner, taking turns to be Cathy and her friends. Go round, monitoring and giving help. Encourage the student playing the friends to use slightly exaggerated intonation at the end in order to convey the fact that they're in a hurry. Ask any particularly good pairs to perform their conversations for the class.

Vocabulary *Extra* (SB page 11)

Using a dictionary

1

- Pairwork. Ask the students to look at their own dictionaries as well as the one on the page and discuss in pairs what information they expect to find in a good dictionary. Then ask them to share their ideas with the class.

- Ask the students to discuss the questions about the dictionary page with their partner.

> *Possible answers:*
> Definitions, pronunciation, parts of speech, grammar information, grammar patterns, idioms, phrasal verbs, frequency, collocations, examples of use, synonyms and antonyms, British or American English, formal or informal usage, etc.
>
> a) 26
> b) The red words are more frequent.

2

Ask the students to work individually to match the dictionary abbreviations and symbols with their meanings. Allow them to check with a partner before they go on to find examples on the dictionary page.

> a) abbreviation   f) intransitive verb
> b) adjective   g) transitive verb
> c) adverb   h) somebody/something
> d) countable noun   i) synonym
> e) uncountable noun   j) opposite
>
> *Possible answers:*
> a) abbrev: Fri.
> b) adj: frightening
> c) adv: frighteningly
> d) noun [C]: friend
> e) noun [U]: fresh air
> f) verb [I]: fret
> g) verb [T]: freshen
> h) sb/sth: frighten / away
> i) =: frightened / scared
> j) ≠: friendly / unfriendly

3

Go through the questions with the class first to make sure they know what to do. Then ask the students to discuss the questions with their partner. Go round monitoring and giving help.

> a) Four: freshen up, freshen sth up;
>   frighten sb/sth away, frighten sb/sth off
> b) best, close, dear, good, great, lifelong, old, trusted
> c) I'm frightened with … is not possible.
> d) fried, friend, friendly, -friendly, friendship, fries, frieze
>   /aɪ/ as in fried; /e/ as in friend; /iː/ as in frieze
> e) *frightened* describes how you feel and *frightening* describes things or situations that make you feel frightened.

4

Ask the students to look at their own dictionaries and compare the information in it with the information on the dictionary page they've just looked at. Discuss any similarities and differences as a class.

> **Further practice material**
>
> **Need more writing practice?**
> → Workbook page 9
> • Writing emails.
>
> **Need more classroom practice activities?**
> → Photocopiable resource materials pages 151 to 153
>   **Grammar:** *Reasons to be famous*
>   **Vocabulary:** *You in pictures*
>   **Communication:** *Questions, questions, questions*
> → Top 10 activities pages xv to xx
>
> **Need DVD material?**
> → DVD – Programme 1: *Friends will be friends*
>
> **Need progress tests?**
> → Test CD – *Test Unit 1*
>
> **Need more on important teaching concepts?**
> → Key concepts in *New Inside Out* pages xxii to xxxv
>
> **Need student self-study practice?**
> → CD-ROM – Unit 1: *Friends*
>
> **Need student CEF self-evaluation?**
> → CEF Checklists pages xxxvii to xliv
>
> **Need more information and more ideas?**
> → www.insideout.net

2 Adrenalin *Overview*

Section & Aims	What the students are doing
Reading SB page 12 Reading for gist and detail	Reading a blog and determining the writer's attitude to skydiving. Correcting factual mistakes in sentences. Talking about doing a parachute jump.
Vocabulary SB page 13 Gradable adjectives	Studying the use of gradable and non-gradable adjectives. Matching pairs of adjectives and writing true sentences.
Pronunciation SB page 13 Intonation	Listening and copying exaggerated intonation. Listening and responding to prompts with exaggerated intonation.
Speaking SB page 13 Fluency practice	Discussing emotions in dramatic situations. Talking about exciting experiences.
Grammar SB page 14 Present perfect simple	Matching beginnings and endings of questions. Choosing possible responses to questions. Completing sentences about past experiences with time expressions.
Listening SB page 14 Listening for detail	Identifying key information from three stories. Studying the tenses used in narratives.
Grammar SB page 15 Past simple and continuous	Completing rules about the use of the past simple and past continuous. Completing sentences with appropriate tenses.
Speaking: anecdote SB page 15 Fluency practice	Talking about being in a dangerous or exciting situation.
Vocabulary & Speaking SB page 16 Vocabulary: sports; fluency practice	Categorising sports words. Talking about sports.
Listening & Vocabulary SB page 16 listening for gist; sports	Listening and identifying which sports are being talked about. Adding sports, locations and equipment to a table.
Grammar SB page 17 Comparative and superlative structures	Grouping words according to how their comparative and superlative forms are made and completing rules. Using statistics to complete sentences. Completing sentences about their own attitudes to sport.
Speaking SB page 17 Fluency practice	Discussing the town or city where they are studying.
Useful phrases SB page 18 Useful conversational phrases for giving advice about complaints or injuries	Reading conversations and identifying injuries or complaints. Matching phrases giving advice with the appropriate conversations. Listening and repeating useful phrases for giving advice. Discussing the advice they would give in certain situations. Writing a short conversation about an injury or complaint.
Vocabulary *Extra* SB page 19 Adjectives: exploring synonyms	Identifying synonyms for *important* and *nice*.
Writing WB page 15	Writing a story.

2 Adrenalin *Teacher's notes*

Warm up

Explain the meaning of *adrenalin* (a substance your body produces when you're angry, scared or excited, which makes your heart beat faster and gives you more energy). Ask the students to make a list of the subjects and activities that they think might be included in a unit entitled *Adrenalin*. Get feedback from the whole class and write any interesting ideas on the board. You could get the students to rank the activities in terms of how adrenalin-inducing they are.

Reading (SB page 12)

1

- Explain *skydiving* and ask if any of the students has ever done it. If anyone has, encourage them to talk about it to the class.

- Go through the three choices with the class, then ask them to read the text and decide which one best describes Mike's attitude to skydiving. Point out the collocation *the rush of adrenalin*.

> Sentence b

Language note

Pronunciation: *advertisement*
In British English the word *advertisement* is stressed on the second syllable whereas in American English it's stressed on the third syllable.

2

- Focus the students' attention on the example. Point out that each sentence contains one factual mistake. Ask them to correct the mistakes.

- Allow them to compare their answers in pairs before checking with the class.

> a) Mike was ~~reading a newspaper~~ watching the television …
> b) ~~A month later~~ The next day, …
> c) After a ~~week's~~ day's training …
> d) … It was a beautiful, cloudless ~~morning~~ evening.
> e) … ~~he was conscious of everything~~ his mind went blank.

> f) … ~~he stopped thinking about skydiving~~ he started to spend every free moment he had skydiving.
> g) … ~~his parachute didn't open~~ another skydiver collided with his parachute.
> h) … he could ~~see his family~~ go skydiving again.

3

Ask the students to discuss the questions in pairs and then to report back to the class on their discussion. Alternatively, have a class discussion and have a show of hands to find out how many people would choose each response.

Vocabulary (SB page 13)

1

- Do this exercise with the whole class. First, explain that some adjectives are gradable and some non-gradable. The difference lies in which adverbs you can use with them. Gradable adjectives are those where there can be many degrees of them, from weak to strong. Non-gradable adjectives tend to be more absolute.

- Focus the students' attention on the table and point out that *good* is a gradable adjective, i.e. there are many possible degrees of how good something is. *Incredible* is a non-gradable adjective; it has a stronger, more absolute meaning.

- Go through the questions with the class. As they work out their answers, encourage them to say the two sentences aloud so that they get a feel for what sounds right. Make sure everyone is clear on the answer to each question before moving on to the next.

> 1 extremely, fairly, really, very
> 2 absolutely, really
> 3 really
> 4 He said, 'This is absolutely incredible!'

2

- Go through the adjectives with the class and make sure that everyone understands them. Then ask them to work individually to match the pairs of adjectives with similar meanings. Explain that in each pair, one adjective will be gradable and the other non-gradable. Ask them to try to put them in the table in the appropriate columns. Allow them to compare in pairs before checking with the class.

Gradable	Non-gradable
angry	furious
surprised	astonished
hot	boiling
cold	freezing
dirty	filthy
exciting	thrilling
tired	exhausted
interesting	fascinating
frightened	terrified
funny	hilarious
pretty	gorgeous

Language note

Grammar: -ing and -ed adjectives

The difference between adjectives ending in -ing and those ending in -ed, such as *exciting/excited*, *boring/bored*, etc., is not made explicit in this unit (this is dealt with in Unit 9), but you might like to point out that *excited, bored, exhausted, terrified*, etc., describe how someone feels, whereas *exciting, boring, exhausting, terrifying*, etc. describe the thing or person that causes this feeling.

3

Go through the example with the class and make sure that everyone understands why it uses *absolutely* with *boiling*. Then ask them to work individually to write five more true sentences. Go round helping and checking that everyone understands the principle of gradable and non-gradable adjectives and is using them correctly.

Pronunciation (SB page 13)

1 🎧 1.10

- Focus the students' attention on the two exchanges and ask them to identify the gradable adjectives (*cold* and *funny*) and the non-gradable adjectives (*freezing* and *hilarious*).

- Play the recording and ask the students to listen carefully to the speakers' intonation. Ask them to say what they notice about it (they emphasize the adjectives to enhance their meaning and make what they're saying more dramatic and exciting). Try reading the dialogues to the class without emphasizing these words and allow them to see how flat and boring it sounds.

> 🎧 1.10
>
> a) 'It's very cold.'
>   'Cold? It's absolutely freezing!'
>
> b) 'She's very funny.'
>   'Funny? She's absolutely hilarious!'

2 🎧 1.11

- Go through the example with the class. Then play the recording and ask them to respond to the prompts with similar sentences. There's a gap on the recording after each prompt, but you may need to pause it to allow time for the students to respond.

- Students then make up similar short dialogues in pairs using gradable and non-gradable adjectives. Go round the class listening to them. Pick out any particularly good ones, which they can perform for the class. Encourage the students to use a range of adjectives from Exercise 2 as well as any of their own ideas, and not just those in the examples.

> a) 'It's very hot in here.' 'Hot? It's absolutely boiling!'
> b) 'He's very angry.' 'Angry? He's absolutely furious!'
> c) 'She's very pretty.' 'Pretty? She's absolutely gorgeous!'
> d) 'My car's very dirty.' 'Dirty? It's absolutely filthy!'
> e) 'They're very tired.' 'Tired? They're absolutely exhausted!'
> f) 'This lesson is really interesting.' 'Interesting? It's absolutely fascinating!'

> 🎧 1.11
>
> a) *It's very hot in here.*
> b) *He's very angry.*
> c) *She's very pretty.*
> d) *My car's very dirty.*
> e) *They're very tired.*
> f) *This lesson is really interesting.*

Speaking (SB page 13)

1

- Focus the students' attention on the photo and ask them to say how they think the people on the rollercoaster might be feeling.

- Go through the emotions in the box and the situations to make sure everyone understands them.

- Give the students time to decide how they'd feel in each situation. Also ask them to the tick the situations they've actually experienced. Remind them that they can use their own ideas if the words in the box don't describe exactly how they'd feel. Then put them in pairs and ask them to tell each other how they'd feel. Tell them they can add any more emotional situations that they can think of and would like to talk about.

Language note

Vocabulary: nervous

Note also that *nervous* is a 'false friend' for speakers of some languages in which the meaning is closer to excitable rather than anxious.

2

- Ask the students to compare the experiences in Exercise 1 with those that they've ticked of their partner to see which ones they have in common.

- They then discuss which experience was the most exciting for them and see if they agree. Encourage them to report back to the class on their discussion.

Grammar (SB page 14)

present perfect simple

1

- Focus the students' attention on the box in the margin, which gives examples of the use of the present perfect simple. Explain that this tense is often used to talk about experiences which have happened at some unspecified time in the past. It's formed with *have* + past participle, and questions about past experience often take the form: *Have you ever* + past participle? The short answer to such a question is either *Yes, I have* or *No, I haven't*.

- Read out the example question or ask a student to do so, choosing one of the options (either *ridden a horse* or *ridden a motorbike*). Then ask a student the question and make sure they structure their answer correctly. Then ask the students to match the remaining questions' beginnings and endings.

- Check answers and then ask the students to choose the correct meaning of *ever* in these questions.

> a) 3   b) 4   c) 1   d) 6   e) 2   f) 5
> *ever* means c) in your life

Language notes

Grammar: present perfect

- Many students have difficulty with the present perfect tense. To some students (e.g. French, Spanish, Italian, German) the tense may look similar to a composite tense (auxiliary *have/be* + past participle) they use in their own language. However, these students will find that the present perfect in English is used rather differently from the tense they know.

- The present perfect has many different usages. In Exercises 1–3 the focus is on questions about past experience (completed events in the past) using the adverb *ever* (*What's the best party you've ever been to?*). In this context, *ever* means *at any time* (*in your life up to now*). The present perfect used in this context is never used with precise past time references. Any answer requiring precise time references must revert to the past simple.

- In contrast with the present perfect, the past simple is used to describe completed events in the past where a precise time (e.g. *at 10.00 a.m., yesterday, two days ago*) is specified (*I visited New York in 2005*).

Grammar: past participle

The past participles of regular verbs are formed with *ed* (the same as the past simple). The verbs presented in Exercise 1 are irregular verbs. Note that as with the past simple, irregular verbs are not totally irregular, there are some patterns.

Cultural note

Alaska /əˈlæskə/
Alaska is a state within the United States of America, even though it's separated from the other states by a part of Canada.

2

- Ask the students to choose the possible responses. Encourage them to say the questions and answers aloud to get a feel for what sounds right.

- Check answers with the class before putting them into pairs to ask and answer the questions in Exercise 1.

> Yes, I have.
> No, I haven't but I'd like to.
> No, never, and I wouldn't like to.

3

- Do this exercise with the whole class. Use each time expression in the gap in each of sentences a)–d) and ask the students to say whether the sentence is correct or not.

- Check answers at the end, making sure that all the students have the time expressions in the correct places. Ask them what is different about the last sentence. If they are slow to answer, ask them what tense the verb is in (the past simple). Point out that the other sentences use the present perfect simple and explain that when you talk about specific times or dates in the past which have now finished, you use the present simple. When the time is less specific or continues into the present, you use the present perfect.

- Ask the students to say which of the possible sentences are true for them.

> a) already / just / never
> b) before / many times / twice
> c) for ages / lately / yet (also: before)
> d) in 2004 / last May / three weeks ago

Extra activity

Ask the students to choose three time expressions from Exercise 3 and write two true sentences and one false sentence about themselves. They then ask their partner to guess which is the false sentence.

Language notes

Grammar: *been* and *gone*

You may need to explain that *gone* is also a past participle of *go*. Write on the board:

John has gone to Egypt.
John has been to Egypt.

The first sentence means that John went to Egypt and he's still there. The second means that at some time in his life, John went to Egypt, but he isn't necessarily there at the moment.

Grammar: past simple time expressions

Some of the time expressions can be used in more than one position. The important point is that the time expressions for finished time are always used with the past simple.

Cultural note

Pyramids at Giza /giːzə/

The most famous pyramids in Egypt, at Giza, were built 4,500 years ago. The Great Pyramid is the only one of the Seven Wonders of the World still standing.

4 Pairwork

- The pairwork exercise for this unit is on pages 116 and 121 of the Student's Book. Put the students in pairs and tell them who will be Student A, and who will be Student B.

- While they're doing the exercise, go round monitoring and giving help. Take note of any errors which may need particular attention later, and also any examples of good language use, which you can praise in a feedback session.

Student A:	
1 Colombia	5 Gabriel Garcia Márquez
2 eight	6 her new album
3 performer	7 1997
4 2002	
Student B:	
1 1977	5 the Bahamas
2 four	6 Antonio de la Rúa
3 fifty million	7 five
4 one	

Cultural notes

Shakira Isabel Mebarak Ripoll (born in 1977)
Colombian singer-songwriter known as Shakira. She achieved great success in Latin America, then broke into the English speaking market in 2001 with her album *Laundry Service*. She mixes different sound styles in her songs and her dancing.

Gabriel García Márquez (born in 1927)
Colombian novelist García Márquez was awarded the Nobel Prize in Literature in 1982. He's regarded as one of the most influential authors of the last century. His works include *One Hundred Years of Solitude* (1967).

Listening (SB page 14)

1 1.12–1.14

- Focus the students' attention on the photos of the three people and the table. Explain that they'll hear these people being interviewed about their past experiences and the interviewer will ask about the topic, the background and the main events. Focus attention on the example and explain that Andy will answer the question *Have you ever had an injury?* and will talk about a time he was playing rugby. Play the first part of the recording and ask the students to listen and draw an arrow to complete the connection of Andy's story.

- Play the rest of the recording and ask the students to connect the key information from the other two stories.

- Check answers with the class. Then put the students into pairs and ask them to note down any other details they can remember from the three stories. Play the recording again for them to check their notes.

> Andy → Have you ever had an injury? → I was playing rugby. → I twisted my ankle.
>
> Beth → Have you ever been in a dangerous situation? → I was driving in Spain. → I almost drove into the back of a car.
>
> Cindy → Have you ever been really frightened? → I was crossing a field → I ran away from a horse.

 1. 12 (I = Interviewer; A = Andy)

Andy

I: *Have you ever had an injury?*

A: *Yes, I have. I was playing rugby for the local team, and it was just after kick-off. I was jumping up to catch the ball, when a player from the other team knocked me over, and I fell heavily on my left leg.*

I: *Oh dear. Were you badly hurt?*

A: *Yes, I twisted my ankle and couldn't play rugby for more than three months.*

 1. 13 (I = Interviewer; B = Beth)

Beth

I: *Have you ever been in a dangerous situation?*

B: *Yes I have. I was walking my dog one day with my sister, and we were crossing this field. There was a horse in it, and it suddenly started running towards us, looking really mad.*

I: *What did you do?*

B: *Well, I know you aren't supposed to run away from animals, because they can sense your fear. But we ran away as fast as we could.*

🔊 1. 14 (I = Interviewer; C = Cindy)

Cindy

I: *Have you ever been really frightened?*

C: *Yes, I have. Last summer I was driving on the motorway in Spain. We were getting close to Barcelona, so I started to slow down, ready to turn off the motorway. Suddenly, this black sports car appeared out of nowhere, pulled in front of me and stopped! I almost drove into the back of it, but I just managed to turn off the motorway in time. I've never been so frightened in my life.*

2

• Do the first part of this exercise with the whole class. If necessary, allow them to look at the tapescript on page 151 to see which tenses are used.

• Put the students in pairs and ask them to ask and answer the questions in Exercise 1, giving as many details as possible.

> a) Present perfect simple
> b) Past continuous
> c) Past simple

Grammar (SB page 15)

past simple and continuous

1

• Focus the students' attention on the sentences in the margin. Get them to identify that *was playing* is the past continuous tense and that *fell* and *twisted* are both in the past simple. Remind them that they saw the past continuous used for giving background information and past simple used for main events in the listening text in the previous section.

• Ask them to read the rule and complete the gaps with *simple* or *continuous*.

> 1 continuous   2 simple   3 continuous
> 4 simple

Language notes

Grammar: past continuous + *when* + past simple

• The past continuous is used to talk about the circumstances surrounding an event in the past. It's often used with *when* in sentences where the event (in the past simple) interrupts the circumstances (in the past continuous):
It was raining when I arrived at work.
In these sentences, *when* is always followed by, and refers to, the event (in the past simple).

• It's possible to change the order of the clauses, putting *when* at the beginning of the sentence, without changing the meaning. Where this happens, the two clauses are separated by a comma:
When I arrived at work, it was raining.

Grammar: past simple + *while* + past continuous

• In these sentences, *while* is always followed by, and refers to, the circumstances (in the past continuous):
I dropped my wallet while I was waiting for the bus.

• It's possible to change the order of the clauses, putting *while* at the beginning of the sentence, without changing the meaning. Where this happens, the two clauses are separated by a comma:
While I was waiting for the bus, I dropped my wallet.

2

• Look at the example with the class and then ask them to complete the remaining gaps.

• As the students work, go round giving extra help to anyone who is struggling with the difference between the past simple and past continuous.

> a) moved, was
> b) met, were travelling
> c) had, was learning
> d) woke up, was shining
> e) was walking, bumped into
> f) broke, was playing

3 Grammar *Extra* 2, Part 1

Ask the students to turn to *Grammar Extra* 2, Part 1 on page 128 of the Student's Book. Here they'll find an explanation of the grammar they've been studying and further exercises to practise it.

> **1**
> a) haven't been   e) 've already booked
> b) 've never broken   f) hated
> c) called   g) did
> d) haven't seen   h) haven't finished
>
> **2**
> a) Have you been to the gym recently?
> b) Have you ever broken a bone?
> c) Did your mum call you a few minutes ago?
> d) Have you seen your friends much lately?
> e) Have you booked next year's holiday yet?
> f) Did you hate PE when you were a kid?
> g) Did your great-grandfather do military service?
> h) Have you finished this exercise yet?
>
> **3**
> 1 –   2 –   3 –   4 came   5 –   6 agreed
> 7 –   8 seemed   9 stopped   10 –   11 –
> 12 did

Speaking: anecdote (SB page 15)

For more information about how to set up, monitor and repeat Anecdotes, see page xx in the Introduction.

1 🔊 1.15

- Focus the students' attention on the photo of Jake. Explain that they're going to hear him talking about a time when he was in a dangerous situation. Go through the questions and answers with the class. Explain any unknown vocabulary.
- Play the recording and ask the students to listen and tick the answers that are correct.
- Play the recording again and ask the students to change the answers that are incorrect.

> a) ✔
> b) A few <u>years</u> ago.
> c) ✔
> d) <u>Some friends</u>.
> e) Playing <u>football</u>.
> f) Someone kicked the ball <u>over the fence</u>.
> g) ✔
> h) <u>I've never been so frightened in my life</u>.
> i) ✔
> j) ✔

> 🔊 1.15 (J = Jake; M = Mary)
>
> J: *Have I ever told you about the time a dog nearly attacked me?*
>
> M: *No – what happened?*
>
> J: *Oh well, it was a few years ago. I was still at school, actually, so I guess I was sixteen or seventeen. It was the weekend and it was summer – the sun was shining, and I was with some friends in the garden. We were playing football. Well, we weren't exactly playing football, because there were only three of us, but we were playing with a ball. In fact, we were using my older brother's football. Anyway, we were having a laugh and enjoying the game, when suddenly one of my friends kicked the ball really hard, and it went up in the air, over the fence and into my neighbour's garden. I couldn't believe it. My brother really loved that football and he never let me use it.*
>
> M: *Oh no. What did you do?*
>
> J: *Well, I went and knocked on the neighbour's door, but there was no answer. So I had to climb over the fence. It was really high, and my friends had to push me over. Anyway, as soon as I dropped down on the other side, I realised I wasn't alone.*
>
> M: *The dog?*
>
> J: *Yes, an enormous dog was running towards me, barking like mad. I've never been so frightened in my life.*
>
> M: *What did you do?*
>
> J: *I was absolutely terrified. I couldn't move. But then I noticed a chair near the fence, so I jumped up on it and managed to climb back over the fence.*
>
> M: *What about the ball?*

> J: *I didn't get the ball, but fortunately, the neighbours came back before my brother did. So in the end, he never knew about it. Which is good because my brother is almost as frightening as the neighbour's dog!*

2

Go through the instructions, then ask the students to match the headings to the five stages of Jake's story.

> 1 Introduction
> 2 The background
> 3 The problem
> 4 How you felt
> 5 The resolution

3

- Give the students a minute or two to decide on the situation they're going to talk about. Then ask them to look at the questions in Exercise 1 again and decide how they'd answer them about their story. Allow them to make notes of what they're going to say and how they're going to say it, but discourage them from writing a paragraph that they can simply read out.
- Pairwork. Put the students in pairs and ask them to take turns to tell their partner about a time when they were in a dangerous or exciting situation. Encourage them to ask each other follow-up questions to get further information. Then ask some pairs to report back to the class about what they found out.

Vocabulary & Speaking (SB page 16)

1

Go through the criteria (a–f) with the class. Then ask the students to match the sports in the box to these criteria. Remind them that one sport might go in more than one category. Point out before they start that their answer to e) will depend on what country they come from, and that there aren't necessarily any 'correct' answers. Allow them to justify their choices. For example, some students may include skiing in *Indoor sports* because of places like snow domes. Encourage them to add any more sports that they know of to each group.

> *Suggested answers:*
> a) Water sports: fishing, kite surfing, sailing, scuba diving, surfing, swimming, windsurfing
> b) Team sports: baseball, basketball, football, ice hockey, rugby, volleyball
> c) Indoor sports: badminton, basketball, boxing, ice hockey, judo, karate, skating, swimming, table tennis, volleyball
> d) Sports that collocate with *play*: badminton, baseball, basketball, football, golf, ice hockey, rugby, table tennis, tennis, volleyball
> e) (Depends on country)
> f) Sports that need special footwear: all except bungee jumping, fishing, judo, karate, skydiving, surfing, swimming

Language note

Vocabulary: sports with *go/play/do*

Most sports or activities collocate with *play*, *go* or *do*:

go: *sailing, swimming, riding, running, walking, surfing, snowboarding,* etc.

play: *tennis, golf, table tennis, badminton, football, baseball, basketball,* etc.

do: *gym, aerobics, karate, judo,* etc.

2

Pairwork. Ask the students to take turns talking about each of the things listed. As they work, go round monitoring and take note of anything interesting which can be shared with the class.

Listening & Vocabulary (SB page 16)

1 🔊 1.16–1.17

- Focus the students' attention on the photos of Toby and Kate and ask them to guess what sports they might be interested in.

- Play the recording and ask them to guess what sports the two are talking about. Ask stronger students to tell you what clues they noticed to help them decide.

> Toby: kite surfing
> Kate: rock climbing

> 🔊 1.16 (I = Interviewer; T = Toby)
>
> I: *Toby, where did you learn?*
> T: *I did a beginner's course in Spain. It's the most exciting thing I've ever done.*
> I: *Is it hard?*
> T: *Yes, you have to be strong and fit and also the kind of person who likes showing off!*
> I: *What equipment do you need?*
> T: *A wetsuit, a board, a kite and a harness.*
> I: *Is it similar to wind surfing?*
> T: *I think it's a bit more difficult than wind surfing. But it's similar, because you do it in the sea and you need the right amount of wind.*
> I: *What's so good about it?*
> T: *Everything! But hangtime is by far the best thing about it. That's when you jump, and try to stay suspended in the air for as long as possible. It's awesome.*
>
> 🔊 1.17 (I = Interviewer; K = Kate)
>
> I: *Kate, where do you do it?*
> K: *Wherever there are good cliffs. One of the best places I've ever been is New Zealand. But I usually go to Wales. The cliffs are not as high as in New Zealand, but they're much closer to where I live.*
> I: *Do many women do it?*
> K: *No, there aren't as many women as there are men, but there are female-only courses to get women into the sport.*

> I: *Is it very dangerous?*
> K: *Yes, it is, so you must take the right equipment: waterproof clothes, climbing shoes and ropes.*
> I: *Is it an expensive sport?*
> K: *Not really. In fact, it's slightly less expensive than many other sports, because the mountains are free.*
> I: *Why do you do it?*
> K: *When you get to the top, it's the best feeling in the world.*

2

- Ask the students to work individually to complete the table. Go round giving extra help where needed and making sure the students are putting their words in the correct columns of the table.

- Play the recording again for them to check their answers.

	Sport	Place	Equipment
Toby	Kite surfing	the sea	a board, a harness, a kite, a wetsuit
Kate	rock climbing	cliffs, mountains	waterproof clothes, climbing shoes, ropes

3

- Pairwork. Ask the students to work together to choose five more sports and complete the table with words for the place where they're done and the equipment needed. Remind them that a number of sports are listed in Exercise 1 of the previous section if they need ideas. They may need to use their dictionaries to find the words for the equipment needed for their sports.

- Get the pairs to report back to the class on what they put in their tables.

Grammar (SB page 17)

Comparative and superlative structures

1

- Focus the students' attention on the adjectives in the box and go through the example with them. Point out that *cold*, *high* and *quiet* form the comparative by adding *-er* and the superlative by adding *-est*.

- Ask the students to form three more groups from the adjectives in the box. There should be three adjectives in each group and they should all form the comparative and superlative in the same way. Then check answers.

- Go through the rules with the class and complete the gaps together.
- Finally, remind them that there are some irregular comparative and superlative forms. Ask them to say what the comparative and superlative forms of *bad*, *far* and *good* are.

> Group 1: cold – colder – coldest; high – higher – highest; quiet – quieter – quietest
> Group 2: fat – fatter – fattest; hot – hotter – hottest; sad – sadder – saddest
> Group 3: happy – happier – happiest; lucky – luckier – luckiest; pretty – prettier – prettiest
> Group 4: interesting – more interesting – most interesting; popular – more popular – most popular; relaxed – more relaxed – most relaxed
>
> 1 er/est   2 er/est   3 ier/iest
> 4 more/the most
>
> bad – worse – worst; far – further – furthest; good – better – best

Language notes

Grammar: comparative and superlative structures

- The comparative form can be divided into five categories:
  (1) short adjectives (*old*) take -r/-er (*older*).
  (2) adjectives that end in consonant-vowel-consonant (*th-i-n*), double the final consonant + -er (*thinner*).
  (3) adjectives that end in -y (*happy*), drop the -y and take -ier (*happier*).
  (4) longer adjectives (*interesting*) don't change, but are preceded by *more* (*more interesting*).
  (5) Some adjectives (*good/bad*) are irregular (*better/worse*).
- The superlative form can be divided into five categories:
  (1) short adjectives (*old*) take -est (*the oldest*).
  (2) adjectives that end in consonant-vowel-consonant (*th-i-n*), double the final consonant + -est (*the thinnest*).
  (3) adjectives that end in -y (*happy*), drop the -y and take -iest (*the happiest*).
  (4) longer adjectives (*interesting*) don't change, but are preceded by *the most* (*the most interesting*).
  (5) Some adjectives (*good/bad*) are irregular (*the best/the worst*).

2

- Focus the students' attention on the sentences in the box in the margin. Explain that the words in bold before the adjectives are adverbs and adverbial phrases, which modify the adjectives and allow a more precise comparison. Explain the meaning of *slightly, much more, just as ... as* and *by far the ...* . Also teach *much less, a lot more/less* and *a bit more/less*.

- Focus the students' attention on the table. Go through the sports in the left-hand column and make sure everyone knows what they are. Then go through the example sentence with the class, asking them to find football and rugby in the table and look at the number of participants for each. Point out that 242 million is a much larger figure than 2.4 million, so you can say not only that football is *more popular* than rugby, but that it's *much more popular* than rugby.
- Ask the students to complete the remaining sentences with appropriate sports. When checking answers, accept any that make sense according to the statistics in the table.

> *Possible answers:*
> a) Football is much more popular than rugby.
> b) Judo is slightly more popular than rugby.
> c) Tennis is just as popular as dragon boat racing.
> d) Rugby is a bit less popular than judo.
> e) Tennis is a lot less popular than volleyball.
> f) Volleyball is by far the most popular sport in the world.

Cultural note

Dragon boat racing
Dragon boat racing originated in China in pre-Christian times. It became an international sport in 1976. A dragon boat is a very long and narrow boat with a crew of 20 paddlers sitting in pairs.

3

- Ask the students to work individually to complete the sentences with their own opinions.
- Allow the students to compare their sentences in small groups before checking answers with the class.

4 Grammar *Extra* 2 Part 2

Ask the students to turn to *Grammar Extra* 2, Part 2 on page 128 of the Student's Book. Here they'll find an explanation of the grammar they've been studying and further exercises to practise it.

> 1
> badly dressed – worse-dressed – the worst-dressed
> big – bigger – the biggest
> extreme – more extreme – the most extreme
> fit – fitter – the fittest
> gentle – gentler – the gentlest
> good-looking – better-looking – the best-looking
> healthy – healthier – the healthiest
> intelligent – more intelligent – the most intelligent
> popular – more popular – the most popular
> well-paid – better-paid – the best-paid

2

a) Skydiving is much more extreme than table tennis.
b) Football players are far better paid than squash players.
c) A basketball is a bit bigger than a volleyball.
d) Judo is slightly more popular than rugby.
e) Cyclists are much fitter than golfers.
f) Surfers are a lot better-looking than boxers.

a) Table tennis isn't nearly as extreme as sky-diving.
b) Squash players aren't nearly as well-paid as football players.
c) A volleyball isn't quite as big as a basketball.
d) Rugby isn't quite as popular as judo.
e) Golfers aren't nearly as fit as cyclists.
f) Boxers aren't nearly as good-looking as surfers.

Speaking (SB page 17)

1

Go through the questions with the class and make sure that everyone understands them. Then put the students into pairs and ask them to discuss their answers to the questions. Suggest that they come to an agreement for each one and make a note of their answers.

2

When all the pairs have noted down their answers, ask them to join other pairs to make small groups. They should then compare their answers and discuss how well they know the place where they're studying.

Useful phrases (SB page 18)

1

- Focus the students' attention on the pictures and give them time to take in the situation. Point out that all the people have some kind of injury or complaint.

- Ask them to read each conversation, ignoring the gaps for the moment, and to underline each injury or complaint. Point out that the first one (black eye) has been done for them.

a) black eye	d) blisters
b) twisted ankle	e) sunburn
c) cramp	f) broken thumb

2 🌐 1.18

- Focus the students' attention on the gaps in the conversations and ask them what sort of things they think the people will say in these gaps.

- Go through the useful phrases with the class and point out that they all show ways of giving advice. Ask the students to read the conversations again and match the advice to the appropriate conversations.

- Play the recording for them to check their answers.

---

1 a   2 c   3 f   4 e   5 b   6 d

🌐 1.18

a)
A: *How did you get that black eye?*
B: *I was playing cricket yesterday, and the ball hit me in the face.*
A: *You'd better put a bag of ice on it. It looks terrible.*

b)
C: *Why are you limping?*
D: *I've got a twisted ankle.*
C: *Oh dear. It looks really painful. You really should lie down and keep your leg up.*

c)
E: *Did you have a good swim?*
F: *It was OK at first, but then I got cramp and I had to stop.*
E: *Oh, that's horrible. You're probably dehydrated. You need to drink more water.*

d)
G: *My feet are killing me. I've got terrible blisters.*
H: *You need to put some plasters on them. And then you should wear sandals for a while.*
G: *But it's winter.*

e)
I: *How was the sailing?*
J: *Great, but I think I've got sunburn. My nose is really red.*
I: *You need to put some cream on it immediately.*

f)
K: *Are you OK?*
L: *No, I think I've got a broken thumb.*
K: *Oh dear. You probably need an x-ray. You'd better go to the hospital.*

Language note

Grammar: *should/had better/need to*
When using these phrases for giving advice in the third person, *should* and *had better* remain unchanged (*He'd better go to the doctor's; She should ask for help*), while *need to* takes the third person *s* (*He needs to talk to his teacher*).

3 🌐 1.19

Ask the students to listen and repeat the useful phrases from exercise 2.

4

- Pairwork. Go through the situations with the class and make sure everyone understands them. Then put the students into pairs to discuss the advice they would give.

- Ask the students to choose one of the injuries/ complaints from the list and to write a short conversations. Remind them that they can use the ones in Exercise 1 as a model and to use the useful phrases. Go round, monitoring and giving help where necessary. When they've finished, tell them to practise their conversations out loud. Ask a few confident pairs to perform their conversations for the class.

Vocabulary *Extra* (SB page 19)

Adjectives: exploring synonyms

1

Focus the students' attention on the table. Ask them to look at the list of words under each heading and to cross out the words that aren't synonyms of *important* and *nice*. Allow the students to work in pairs, then ask them to check their ideas with the two dictionary extracts.

important – ~~big~~   nice – ~~sympathetic~~

2

- Focus the students' attention on the diagram. Go through the example for Heading 1 *People* and explain that you can use these synonyms for *nice* with the word *people*. Ask the students to look at the dictionary extract for *nice* in the margin and add the appropriate headings to the diagram.

- Then ask the students to make a similar diagram for the word *important*. Go round giving help where necessary.

1 people
2 weather
3 clothes
4 behaviour
5 food/flowers/gifts/places
6 something that happens or something that you do

3

Go through the example sentence with the class. Then allow the students to work in pairs and ask them to cross out the adjective which is not possible in the remaining sentences.

a) landmark   b) senior   c) top   d) main
e) groundbreaking   f) major

4

Tell students to look at the dictionary extracts to help them complete the sentences with the appropriate synonyms of *important* and *nice*. Allow them to check with a partner before checking as a class.

Sample answers:
a) influential, top / easy-going, friendly, kind, lovely, sweet, thoughtful
b) good, lovely, pleasant
c) beautiful, stylish, smart
d) good, great, lovely, marvellous, wonderful
e) fantastic, great
f) critical, essential, vital

5

- Ask the students to compare the information from the dictionary extracts with that in their own dictionaries. Discuss any similarities and differences as a class.

- Tell the students that not all dictionaries are the same and that they need to become familiar with the way their own particular dictionaries organise and display words.

Further practice material

Need more writing practice?
→ Workbook page 15
- Writing a story.

Need more classroom practice activities?
→ Photocopiable resource materials pages 154 to 156
  Grammar: *Moments in American history*
  Vocabulary: *Guess the sport*
  Communication: *Truth or dare?*
→ Top 10 activities pages xv to xx

Need DVD material?
→ DVD – Programme 2: *Jane Couch*

Need progress tests?
→ Test CD – *Test Unit 2*

Need more on important teaching concepts?
→ Key concepts in *New Inside Out* pages xxii to xxxv

Need student self-study practice?
→ CD-ROM – Unit 2: *Adrenalin*

Need student CEF self-evaluation?
→ CEF Checklists pages xxxvii to xliv

Need more information and more ideas?
→ www.insideout.net

3 Relationships *Overview*

Section & Aims	What the students are doing
Reading SB page 20 Reading for gist and for specific information	Reading a text about the photos people carry around with them. Matching sentences to people.
Grammar SB page 21 Dynamic and stative meanings	Studying verbs with dynamic and stative meanings. Completing descriptions. Underlining the correct verb forms.
Vocabulary SB page 21 Family words	Combining words to describe family relationships. Drawing family diagrams. Talking about family relationships.
Speaking SB page 22 Fluency practice	Talking about 'firsts'.
Reading & Listening SB page 22 Reading for detail Listening for gist	Reading about first dates and giving opinions on relationship success. Completing sentences with information from the text. Listening to find out which relationship failed and why. Talking about the secrets of a successful relationship.
Vocabulary SB page 23 Relationship words	Completing sentences with relationship words. Discussing statements about relationships.
Grammar SB page 23 Present perfect simple and continuous	Identifying the uses of the present perfect simple and continuous. Underlining correct verb forms in sentences. Writing questions using the present perfect simple or continuous.
Vocabulary SB page 24 Qualities	Listening to people talking about the qualities they look for in a partner. Completing a table with qualities. Talking about the qualities of an ideal partner.
Pronunciation SB page 24 Word stress	Listening and repeating words and identifying stressed syllables.
Reading & Speaking SB page 25 Reading for detail and fluency practice	Answering a questionnaire and discussing the results.
Useful phrases SB page 26 'Less direct' language	Listening and answering statements true or false. Matching phrases from a conversation with their more direct meanings. Listening and repeating phrases for talking about things indirectly. Matching comments with less direct versions.
Vocabulary *Extra* SB page 27 Sounds and spelling	Studying the phonemic script. Completing a table with words according to the pronunciation of the letters *ea*. Connecting words according to vowel sounds. Identifying stressed syllables in words. Spelling words written in the phonemic script.
Writing WB page 21	Writing an informal letter.

3 Relationships *Teacher's notes*

Warm up

Ask the students what they think is the best way to meet your life partner (or the best way to meet new friends). List their ideas on the board and perhaps have a class vote on which is the best way.

Reading (SB page 20)

1

- Focus the students' attention on the photos. Ask them what they notice about the photos (all the people are holding photographs of other people). Ask them to discuss in pairs what they think the relationship is between each person and the people in the photos they're holding.

- Ask the students to read the article and check their ideas.

> 1 Alison: mother and twin sons.
> 2 Bruce: husband and wife.
> 3 Chris: boyfriend and girlfriend.
> 4 Debra: woman and the girl who she's sponsoring.

Cultural notes

Action Aid
Action Aid is a charity that encourages people to give aid to the developing world by sponsoring a child. The money the sponsor gives each month, is used to pay for improvements to schools, living conditions, health care, etc. in the community where the child lives. Although the money doesn't go directly to child or its family, the sponsor receives photos, letters and news from the child.

2

- Go through the statements with the class, then ask the students to read the article again and match the people with the statements. Allow them to compare their answers in pairs before checking answers with the class.

- Ask the students to work in pairs and talk about the photos they carry around with them and why. If they have the photos with them, they can talk about them to their partners. If the students don't carry photos around with them, they could talk about a favourite photo they have of someone they know.

> a) Bruce   b) Chris   c) Alison   d) Debra

Grammar (SB page 21)

Dynamic and stative meanings

1

- Ask the students to read the sentence and the two possible meanings of *look*. Ask them to match each example of *look* with the correct meaning. Check answers before moving on to the next part of the exercise.

- Answer the questions with the whole class. Then focus the students' attention on the information in the margin. Explain that some verbs only have dynamic meanings and some only stative meanings, but that there are also some which can have both. Make sure they understand that verbs with dynamic meaning can use either simple or continuous forms, those with stative meanings can only use simple forms, and that those which can have both meanings can use either form, but that the form has to be simple when the meaning is stative.

> 1 to direct your eyes towards something;
> 2 to have a particular appearance
> a) 1   b) 2   c) No.

Language notes

Grammar: dynamic and stative verbs

- Stative verbs describe states or conditions which continue over a period of time. *Like*, *love*, *hate*, *want*, *need*, *hear* and *see* are examples of stative verbs. These verbs aren't normally used in the continuous form*.
  I want to be an engineer one day, not ~~I'm wanting to be an engineer one day~~.

- Dynamic verbs describe things which happen within a limited time. *Come*, *bring*, *buy*, *get* and *learn* are examples of dynamic verbs.
  I'm learning English at the moment, not ~~I learn English at the moment~~.

- Some verbs, such as *have*, *look* and *think* can have both stative and dynamic meanings.

Compare:
  (1) *I have an old car* (state) with *I'm having a great time!* (something happening within a limited time).

(2) *He looks tired* (condition) with *That woman is looking at me in a strange way.* (something happening within a limited time).

(3) *Do you think Brazil will win the World Cup?* (state) with *I'm thinking of going into the city centre today.* (something happening within a limited time).

* In recent times there's been a fashion to make the verbs *like* and *love* take a dynamic form but retain a stative meaning. Thus *I'm really liking that song!* is a modern colloquial way of saying *I really like that song!*

2

- Do the first one as an example with the class, then ask the students to work individually to complete the remaining sentences. Go round while they're working, giving extra help where needed.

- When checking answers, ask the students to identify each time whether the verb is dynamic or stative.

- Then ask the students to match the descriptions to the photos on page 20.

> a) looks, isn't, comes   c) 's smiling, showing
> b) 's posing, seem   d) 's holding, reminds
>
> a) 4   b) 3   c) 1   d) 2

3

- Do the first one with the class, then ask them to work individually to identify whether the verbs describe actions or states and to choose the correct forms. Go round giving extra help where needed. Allow the students to compare in pairs answers with the class. Then check before asking the students to say whether any of the sentences are true for them.

> All the verbs have stative meanings (and so the continuous form is not possible).
> a) think, are   d) hate
> b) have   e) think, look
> c) remind   f) think, take

Vocabulary (SB page 21)

1

Go through the examples with the class, pointing out that in each case, the word is made up of combinations of words or part-words. Ask the students to form at least ten more family words from the elements in the box.

> *Possible answers:*
> ex-: ex-boyfriend (girlfriend, husband, wife)
> grand: grandparent (mother, father, child, daughter, son)

great-: great-aunt, (uncle, nephew, niece, grandparent, grandmother, grandfather, grandchild, granddaughter, grandson)
half-: half-brother (sister)
-in-law: brother-in-law (sister, daughter, son, mother, father)
only: only child
second: second cousin, (husband, wife)
single: single parent (father, mother)
step: stepchild, (brother, sister, father, mother, son, daughter)

Language notes
Vocabulary: *in-laws*
The expression *in-law* can be added to parents, mother, father, daughter and son, sister and brother, to refer to people related by marriage.

sister-in-law
Your sister-in-law could be any of the following: the wife of your brother; the sister of your husband; the sister of your wife.

stepsister
When one of your parents marries again, the children of the person they marry become your stepbrothers and/or stepsisters.

half-sister
Your half-sister shares either the same mother or the same father as you, but not both.

2

Focus the students' attention on the diagram. Ask them to make similar diagrams to describe their own family relationships. You could draw a diagram for yourself on the board. This will be useful for demonstrating the next two exercises. Go round giving help where needed.

3

If you've drawn your own diagram on the board, demonstrate the exercise by underlining, crossing out, etc. according to the instructions. Then ask the students to do the same on their own diagrams.

4

Pairwork. Demonstrate by talking about your own diagram if you've drawn one on the board. Encourage the students to ask you questions about the people. Then put them into pairs and ask them to show each other their diagrams and talk about some of the people in them.

Speaking (SB page 22)

1

Go through the 'firsts' in the box and make sure everyone understands them Ask the students to decide which of their 'firsts' they remember best and to tell the class. Start them off by telling them about your own most memorable 'first'.

2

- Read the example with the class. Then ask the students to choose three of the 'firsts' from the box (or their own ideas if they wish) to tell a partner about. Allow them to make notes if they wish. Again, start them off by talking about one of your own 'firsts'.

- Encourage the students to report back to the class on what they learnt about their partner.

Cultural notes

Rugby

Rugby has its origins in football and dates back to the 19th century. It was named after the school in England where the sport was developed. Points called 'tries' are scored by putting the ball behind the goal line. Goals are scored by kicking the ball over a high bar.

Jonny Wilkinson

Jonny Wilkinson is an English rugby union player. He was as a key member of the national squad during the World Cup final in (and against) Australia in 2003, which England won.

Reading & Listening (SB page 22)

1

- Focus the students' attention on the photos and explain that the text is about the beginning of two very different relationships. Play the recording and ask them to read the text.

- Put the students into pairs and ask them to discuss which relationship they think has the best chance of success. Then find out what the majority view is, encouraging the students to give their reasons.

Students will probably say Clare and Stan have the best chance of success because:
– they have a lot in common
– they have a similar sense of humour
– Clare finds Stan interesting and funny
– they find each other easy to talk to

Language note

Vocabulary: *eligible bachelor*

An *eligible bachelor* is a man who is considered to be a good choice as a marriage partner because he is rich and/or handsome.

2

Ask the students to complete the sentences with the correct names. They may need to look back at the text to find some of the information.

a) Ruth and Bill	d) Clare and Stan
b) Ruth and Bill	e) Clare and Stan
c) Ruth and Bill	f) Clare and Stan

3 🌐 1.20–1.21

Explain that the students are going to hear Ruth and Clare talking about the relationships one year after the text was written. One of the relationships didn't work out. They should listen to find out which one and why. Allow them to take notes if they wish.

Clare's relationship didn't work out because after they met, they realised that they weren't attracted to each other.

🌐 1.20

Ruth

Nobody thought we'd stay together, but we've just had our first wedding anniversary and we're very happily married. My mother-in-law hasn't spoken to us since the day we got married … that's the good news! No, actually we're so upset about it that we've decided to move away from our home town. It's not just because of Bill's mother, but the whole town knows about the competition. We've been trying to live a normal life but we can't walk down the street without people staring at us. Some people have even shouted horrible things, and the tabloid press have made our lives hell. They've been waiting for us to split up so that they can get a story, but it isn't going to happen. We've been together for a year now and we've been planning a big party to celebrate. Only this time, we're not inviting the press. Just our closest friends – the ones who have been there for us from the start.

🌐 1.21

Clare

So it was about a year ago that I went to meet Stan at the airport. I felt really nervous but I couldn't wait to meet him. I spotted him immediately – he looked just like his photo. Over the next week or so, we got on really well and enjoyed one another's company, but unfortunately the relationship didn't work out. There was no real spark. In the end, we knew we weren't attracted to each other and we both agreed that we should just be friends. We stayed in touch for a while, when he went back to Canada, but then he met someone, and I haven't heard from him, since they got married. I'm still looking for Mr Right.

4

Pairwork. Ask the students to discuss the secrets of a successful relationship in pairs. Alternatively, you could ask them to discuss the secrets of a successful friendship instead. Encourage them to report back to the class on their discussion.

Vocabulary (SB page 23)

1

- Most of the answers can be found by looking back at the text on page 22, but encourage the students to try the exercise first without looking back. Allow them to work in pairs if they prefer.
- Check answers with the class to make sure that everyone has filled in the statements correctly.

> a) love, sight   b) dating   c) propose
> d) relationships   e) dreams   f) split up

2

Ask the students discuss the statements in pairs. Go round giving help where needed and encouraging them to give reasons for their opinions.

Grammar (SB page 23)

Present perfect simple & continuous

1

- Do this exercise with the class. Go through the sentences in the margin, pointing out that the first and third sentences are examples of the present perfect simple and that the second is an example of the present perfect continuous.
- Focus the students' attention on the table and read the example sentences aloud. Ask the students to put in them in the correct places in the table.

> 1 b)   2 a)   3 c)

Language notes

Grammar: present perfect simple and continuous

- The present perfect can be used to talk about past experience (completed actions in the past). *I've been to France, but I haven't been to Paris.* Note that no precise time is given for the action in the past and only the present perfect simple form is used when speaking about past experience.

- The present perfect can also be used to speak about actions which started in the past and are still happening now. In these cases it's possible to mention time, using *for* and *since*: Use *for* when you give the length of time – duration – (*for a few days, for years*). Use *since* when you give the beginning of the time – starting point – (*since Tuesday, since 1967*). You usually use the continuous form for verbs with dynamic meanings (*I've been going to the same dentist for years*). However, you can't use the continuous form for verbs with stative meanings (*I've known him since he was born*, not *I've been knowing him since he was born*). See page 130 in the Student's Book for a list of verbs with stative meanings.

- Occasionally, you can use the simple form with verbs with dynamic meanings to indicate unchanging, 'permanent' situations. Compare: *I've been working here since the beginning of summer* with *I've worked here all my life.*

2

- Focus the students' attention on the example. Ask them if the speaker is still learning English (*yes*). Refer them back to the table in Exercise 1 and get them to identify that this sentence matches 1 in the table, and that the correct form is the present perfect continuous. Ask a few students around the class how long they've been learning English.

- Ask the students to choose the correct verb forms in the remaining sentences. Allow them to work in pairs if they wish and to discuss their answers. Go round giving extra help where needed. Check answers with the class before asking the students to say whether any of the sentences are true for them.

> a) 've been learning – An *action* that started in the past and is still happening now.
> b) 've had – A *state* that started in the past and continues now.
> c) has been going out – An *action* that started in the past and is still happening now.
> d) 've been – A *finished action* that happened some time in the past. (We don't know *when*.)
> e) 've known – A *state* that started in the past and continues now.
> f) 've stopped – A *finished action* that happened some time in the past. (We don't know *when*.)

3

- Focus the students' attention on the example. Remind them that the key to deciding which form to use is to think about what the verb is describing: a state or an action, and one that's still happening now or one that has finished.

- Ask the students to make questions for the remaining prompts. Allow them to work in pairs if they wish and to discuss their answers. Check answers with the class and make sure that all the questions are correct before they ask and answer them in pairs.

> a) Have you ever cried at the cinema?
> b) How many times have you travelled by air?
> c) Have you ever read the same book twice?
> d) How long have you had your watch?
> e) How many times have you been to the USA?
> f) How long have you been going to the same dentist?
> g) Have you ever owned a pet?

4 Pairwork

- The pairwork exercise for this unit is on pages 116 and 121 of the Student's Book. Put the students in pairs and tell them who will be Student A, and who will be Student B.
- While they're doing the exercise, go round monitoring and giving help. Take note of any errors which may need particular attention later, and also any examples of good language use, which you can praise in a feedback session.

5 Grammar *Extra* 3

Ask the students to turn to *Grammar Extra* 3 on page 130 of the Student's Book. Here they'll find an explanation of the grammar they've been studying and further exercises to practise it.

1

for:	since:
three years, ages, a while, nearly six months, several hours	I was ten, 2002, I was born, Monday, three o'clock, my birthday, last week, March

2

a) 've been going
b) 've been going
c) 've had
d) 've been studying
e) 've been doing
f) 've known
g) 've been using
h) 've been sitting

a) How long have you been going to the same hairdresser's?
b) How long have you been going to the same dentist?
c) How long have you had your TV?
d) How long have you been studying English?
e) How long have you been doing the same job?
f) How long have you known your oldest friend?
g) How long have you been using the same English dictionary?
h) How long have you been sitting in that chair?

3

a) been   b) been   c) gone   d) gone
e) gone   f) been   g) been   h) gone
Sentences b, f, g

4

a) How many times have you been to the UK?
b) How long have you lived / have you been living at the same address?
c) Which primary school did you go to?
d) When did you learn to ride a bike?
e) How many Harry Potter books have you read?
f) How long have you been going to the same doctor?
g) What time did you get up?
h) Where did you have lunch?

5

1 a) for a long time   b) very well
2 a) for years   b) this evening
3 a) since I was a child   b) at the moment

Vocabulary (SB page 24)

1 🔘 1.22

- Focus the students' attention on the photos and ask them what they think the people are like.
- Ask the students to read and listen to what the people say about the qualities they look for in an ideal partner. Ask them to decide which person is most like them. If the students are reluctant to talk about partners, ask them about qualities they look for in an ideal friend.

🔘 1.22

a) 'I like a man who can look after me. My ideal man has to be athletic, hardworking, down-to-earth, reliable and romantic.'

b) 'Well, I'm quite shy and sensitive. So I'm usually attracted to women who are outgoing and self-assured.'

c) 'I think the most important thing is a good sense of humour and a kind heart. My ideal partner is witty, generous and thoughtful.'

d) 'I couldn't live with a miserable, narrow-minded person. The person I share my life with has to be cheerful, broad-minded and optimistic.'

e) 'I'm looking for a good-looking, kind, faithful partner who can cook really well.'

f) 'My ex-partner was big-headed, demanding and self-centred, So next time I'd like someone modest, easygoing and considerate.'

2

- Focus the students' attention on the table and point out that there are three columns. One has words from the interviews, the next words which have a similar meaning to the words in column 1, and finally words which have opposite meanings to the words in column 1.
- Ask the students to look back through the interviews and find the words to go in column 1. Allow them to use dictionaries if necessary, and go round giving help where needed.

---

a) faithful   b) thoughtful   c) big-headed
d) down-to-earth   e) self-assured
f) outgoing   g) cheerful   h) self-centred
i) reliable   j) witty   k) broad-minded
l) easygoing

Language note

Vocabulary: *considerate* vs *considerable*
The two adjectives are easily confused but the meanings are very different: *considerate = thoughtful*; *considerable = large*.

3

- If your students are uncomfortable about discussing partners, let them talk about ideal friends and the qualities that they think are most important.
- Encourage the students to mingle and compare their lists with other members of the class.

Pronunciation (SB page 24)

1 🌐 1.23

- Play the recording for the students just to listen and repeat the words.
- Play the recording again and ask the students to underline the stressed syllables. Check answers and then ask the students to repeat the words again. When they've done this chorally, ask several students to repeat the words individually. Check that they're stressing the words correctly.

> a) lo<u>y</u>al   <u>cheer</u>ful   <u>faith</u>ful   im<u>prac</u>tical
> b) <u>in</u>teresting   <u>so</u>ciable   <u>mis</u>erable   con<u>sid</u>erate
> c) am<u>bi</u>tious   de<u>man</u>ding   cre<u>a</u>tive   in<u>tell</u>igent

Language note
Pronunciation: word stress
You can check the stress of any word by looking in your dictionary. Dictionaries usually mark the stress of a word as well as giving the phonetic script, i.e. *ambitious* /æmˈbɪʃəs/. In *New Inside Out* the stressed <u>syll</u>able is <u>al</u>ways under<u>lined</u>.

2 🌐 1.24

- Ask the students to say the words aloud as they decide which ones have more syllables. Then play the recording for them to listen and check their answers.

> a) impractical   b) considerate   c) intelligent

Reading & Speaking (SB page 25)

1

Focus the students' attention on the questionnaire and explain that they should cover the panel at the side, which tells them what their score means, and answer the questions, choosing only one answer for each. As they work, answer any questions on vocabulary.

2

- Ask the students to use the panel at the side of the questionnaire to analyse their scores. They should then discuss the results with a partner and decide if they agree with the assessment.
- This questionnaire can also be used for classes which prefer to talk about ideal friends rather than partners.

Useful phrases (SB page 26)

1 🌐 1.25

- Focus the students' attention on the picture and ask them to describe the situation (two friends are talking in a bar). Tell them that they're going to listen to a conversation between the women in the bar.
- Go through the statements with the class before you play the recording so that they know what information to listen out for.

> a) False.   b) True.   c) False.

2

- Ask two students to play the parts of Milly and Rita and to read the conversation to the class. Tell them to ignore the numbers.
- Point out the phrases underneath the conversation and explain that these are more direct ways of saying the phrases that are numbered in the conversation. Ask the students to look at the example and say why someone might want to say *it wasn't particularly interesting* rather than *it was boring* (the less direct expressions soften criticism or personal comments and make them more friendly).
- Ask the students to match the phrases with the numbered ones in the conversation. You could then read out the conversation using the direct phrases to show how much more harsh it sounds with these.

> a) 4   b) 5   c) 7   d) 1   e) 9   f) 2
> g) 8   h) 3   i) 6

3 🌐 1.26

Play the recording and ask the students to listen and repeat the useful phrases. Then ask several students to repeat the phrases individually. Check that the students can pronounce all the words correctly.

> 🌐 1.26
> 1 *He wasn't very talkative.*
> 2 *He's a bit shy.*
> 3 *Liz tends to dominate the conversation.*
> 4 *It wasn't particularly interesting.*
> 5 *You can be so mean.*
> 6 *He's not bad-looking.*
> 7 *Liz isn't exactly old.*
> 8 *She can be rather difficult.*
> 9 *She can be a bit bossy.*

4

Look at the example with the class and then ask the students to match the remaining comments with their less direct versions. When checking the answers, point out that *particularly* and *exactly* both have a similar meaning to *very* in these indirect phrases.

a) 4 b) 5 c) 8 d) 1 e) 10 f) 3 g) 2 h) 6 i) 7 j) 9

Vocabulary *Extra* (SB page 27)

Sounds and spelling

1

- Focus the students' attention on the phonemic chart and point out that the sections are divided up into single vowel sounds, diphthongs and consonant sounds. Go through the sounds with the class before they attempt the exercise.

- Do an example with the class. Ask them to find the symbol in the chart for the vowels in red in the word *beige*. Then tell the students to say each of the words aloud as they do the exercise.

beige /eɪ/   check /e/   jump /ʌ/ mother /ə/   mouth /aʊ/   ring /ɪ/ shop /ɒ/   year /ɪə/ 1 ring   2 year   3 beige   4 check 5 mother   6 jump   7 shop   8 mouth

2

- Focus the students' attention on the words in the margin beginning with the letters *hea*. Tell them to say these words aloud and tell you what they notice about the pronunciation.

- Ask the students to say each of the words in the box aloud as they complete the table. Tell them to check their answers in their dictionaries.

There are five different pronunciations of *ea*.

/iː/	/e/	/ɜː/	/ɪə/	/eɪ/	/eə/
dream	breath	learn	dear	break	bear
meat	health	search	idea	great	wear

3

- Focus the students' attention on the list of words in the margin. Ask them to tell you what vowel sound these words have in common and what they notice about the spelling of these words.

- Go through the example with the class and then ask the students to connect the remaining words according to their vowel sounds. Then tell the students to check their answers in their dictionary.

All the words contain /ɔː/. All the spellings are different. a) /ə/ – arrive – colour – husband – police b) /iː/ – bean – key – niece – people c) /uː/ – blew – fruit – shoe – through d) /ɜː/ – burn – dirty – term – work e) /ɪ/ – busy – pretty – spinach – women

4

- Focus the students' attention on the phonemic transcription of the list of words in the margin. Ask them to tell you how the main stress is indicated.

- Ask the students to underline the stressed syllable in the noun phrases and practise saying the phrases.

The main stress is shown with a stress mark (') before the stressed vowel. a) an eco<u>no</u>mical e<u>con</u>omist b) a philo<u>soph</u>ical phi<u>los</u>opher c) a po<u>lit</u>ical poli<u>ti</u>cian

5

Tell the students to say the words aloud and use the phonemic chart to help them complete the spellings, then check the answers in their dictionaries.

a) although   b) daughter   c) neighbour d) enough   e) laugh   f) thoughtless

6

- Ask the students to find six more words from Units 1–3 that are difficult to spell or pronounce. Then in pairs, compare them and practise saying them.

Further practice material

Need more writing practice?

→ Workbook page 21
- Writing an informal letter.

Need more classroom practice activities?

→ Photocopiable resource materials pages 157 to 159
  Grammar: *Find the correct sentence*
  Vocabulary: *Love is …?*
  Communication: *Parents' day*
→ Top 10 activities pages xv to xx

Need DVD material?

→ DVD – Programme 3: *21ˢᵗ Century dating*

Need progress tests?

→ Test CD – *Test Unit 3*

Need more on important teaching concepts?

→ Key concepts in *New Inside Out* pages xxii to xxxv

Need student self-study practice?

→ CD-ROM – Unit 3: *Relationships*

Need student CEF self-evaluation?

→ CEF Checklists pages xxxvii to xliv

Need more information and more ideas?

→ www.insideout.net

Review A *Teacher's notes*

These exercises act as a check of the grammar and vocabulary that the students have learnt in the first three units. Use them to find any problems that students are having, or anything that they haven't understood and which will need further work.

Grammar (SB page 28)

Remind the students of the grammar explanations they read and the exercises they did in the *Grammar Extra* on pages 126 to 131.

1

This exercise reviews the use of prepositions in questions from Unit 1. Check answers before putting the students in pairs to ask and answer the questions.

a) at   b) on   c) with   d) in   e) about

2

This exercise reviews subject and object questions from Unit 1.

a) loves cooking
b) (film) did you see
c) did you speak to yesterday
d) gave her that watch
e) car did she choose
f) arrived this morning

Cultural note

George Clooney /dʒɔːdʒ ˈkluːni/ (born 1961)
George Clooney is an American actor, director, producer and screenwriter. He also has a keen interest in politics and environmental issues. Clooney uses the money he earns in blockbuster films like *Ocean's Eleven* (2001) and its sequels (in 2004 and 2007) to finance projects that protect the environment.

3

This exercise reviews adverbs of frequency from Unit 1. Check answers before asking the students to tick the sentences which are true for them.

a) I usually work at home.
b) I travel abroad from time to time.
c) I hardly ever come to my English class.
d) I like wearing a hat all the time.
e) I don't often come to school by car.
f) I always walk very fast.

4

This exercise reviews the past simple, present perfect and present perfect continuous for talking about past experience.

1 been
2 've been
3 haven't ridden
4 went
5 did
6 was
7 slept
8 've never seen
9 've been doing
10 taught

5

This exercise reviews the contrast between the past simple and past continuous from Unit 2.

1 invited
2 were
3 had to
4 were having
5 decided
6 was going
7 started
8 was shining
9 was talking and laughing
10 shouted
11 was going
12 tried
13 fell
14 came
15 hit
16 spent

6

This exercise reviews comparative adjectives and adverbs from Unit 2.

a) much taller
b) the biggest
c) not as good
d) by far the most exciting
e) slightly easier
f) most popular

7

This exercise reviews structures used in Units 1, 2 and 3.

1 b) ~~Have you been shopping yesterday?~~
2 a) ~~Who does like chocolate?~~
3 a) ~~They met while they taught together in Spain.~~
4 b) ~~He is by far the more intelligent boy in the class.~~
5 a) ~~Why are you hating football so much?~~
6 b) ~~I've been knowing Olivia for two years.~~

Vocabulary (SB page 29)

1

This exercise reviews friendship expressions from Unit 1.

> a) got on well with   d) drifted apart
> b) have fallen out   e) clicked straightaway
> c) have a lot in common

2

This exercise reviews gradable and non-gradable adjectives from Unit 2.

> a) 4   b) 2   c) 5   d) 6   e) 1   f) 3

3

This exercise also reviews gradable and non-gradable adjectives from Unit 2, putting them in a context.

> a) hilarious   b) frightened   c) good   d) filthy
> e) tired   f) boiling

4

This exercise reviews words for sports from Unit 2.

> a) swimming   b) kite surfing   c) badminton
> d) volleyball   e) sailing   f) football
> g) table tennis   h) skydiving   i) fishing
> j) skiing   k) tennis   l) snowboarding
> m) basketball   n) ice hockey

5

This exercise reviews sports words, asking the students to put them into categories.

> a) badminton, table tennis, tennis
> b) swimming, kite surfing, sailing, fishing
> c) volleyball, football, basketball, ice hockey
> d) kite surfing, skydiving
> e) skiing, snowboarding, ice hockey
>
> Note: *kite surfing* and *ice hockey* appear in two different groups.

6

This exercise reviews relationship expressions from Unit 3.

> 1 split up   5 the woman of his dreams
> 2 relationship   6 love at first sight
> 3 meet   7 proposed
> 4 online dating

7

This exercise reviews words for personal qualities from Unit 3.

> a) considerate   b) cheerful   c) unreliable
> d) dull   e) selfish   f) modest

Pronunciation (SB page 29)

1

Explain to the students that the boxes show the syllables of a word and the large boxes indicate the stressed syllables. Here they're being asked to classify words according to how many syllables they have and where the main stress falls. Encourage them to say each word aloud to get a feeling for what sounds right.

2 🔊 1.27

Point out the main stresses in the example words which are underlined. Ask the students to do the same for the other words in the table. Then play the recording for them to check their answers. Play it a second time for them to listen and repeat.

1 and 2		
A: ☐☐	**B:** ☐☐☐	**C:** ☐☐☐
answer	appointment	normally
friendship	athletics	personal
mobile	extremely	similar
often	remember	somebody
really	together	theatre

Reading & Listening (SB page 30)

1

Tell the students that the people in the photos all share a house with each other. Ask them to read the text quickly and identify each person's favourite housemate.

> Pete's favourite is Ned. Alicia's favourite is Leo.
> Ned's favourite is Alicia. Grace's favourite is Pete.
> Leo's favourite is Alicia.

2

Go through the sentences with the students before they read the text again and underline the correct words.

> a) similar   b) confident; arrogant   c) Alicia
> d) the least   e) amusing   f) Pete   g) Alicia

3 🔊 1.28

Tell the students they're going to hear a conversation between Ned and Alicia. All they have to do is find out what Ned's news is. Play the recording and ask the students what the news is.

> Ned's news is that Pete and Grace have got together as a couple.

1.28 (N= Ned; A =Alicia)

N: Alicia! You're not going to believe what I've just seen.

A: What?

N: I was in the High Street and I saw Pete and Grace in the Grand Café. They were holding hands!

A: Oh, I thought you were going to tell me something I didn't know.

N: You knew?

A: Come on, Ned. You knew they liked each other, didn't you?

N: I knew Pete liked Grace, but I had no idea she liked him.

A: You have to read the signs, Ned. They've liked each other for a long time.

N: But I thought Grace was going out with Dan.

A: Dan? That finished ages ago. They split up about six months ago.

N: Really? I knew they had their ups and downs, but I thought they were still together.

A: OK, well they aren't. Anyway, why are you so excited? Are you interested in Grace?

N: Am I …? Of course not! I'm just surprised to see them together. That's all. Anyway, Pete told me he was seeing his parents this afternoon. I can't understand why he would say that.

A: Maybe he didn't want you to know about Grace. I think you need to find a nice girlfriend, Ned. You and Pete spend too much time together.

N: Mm. Maybe you're right. What are you doing this evening?

A: Washing my hair.

N: Aha! For anyone special?

A: Oh, please!

4

Go through the statements with the students before playing the recording again. Ask them to mark as many statements true or false as they can before they hear the conversation again. Play the recording for them to check their answers and mark any remaining statements.

a) True. b) True. c) False. d) False.
e) False. f) False.

Writing & Speaking (SB page 31)

1

Ask the students to read the email and match the descriptions and the paragraphs.

a) 2   b) 5   c) 3   d) 1   e) 6   f) 4

2

Ask the students to read the text again and decide where the words and phrases could go. Point out that these are alternatives to the expressions already used in the email: students aren't supposed to find a way to introduce the new expressions alongside the old ones.

1 Dear Leo, Hello!
2 How are things?   I hope everything's going well. Thanks for your email.
4 I can't wait to see you.
   I'm really looking forward to hearing from you. Speak to you soon.
5 Best wishes, Love, Regards,
6 I'm sending you the latest photos.

3

Tell the students that they're going to write an email as if they are Leo replying to the email from Ned. Ask them where they are at the moment (in Switzerland). If they are slow to pick up on this, refer them to Ned's first question in his email to Leo. Remind them that they can use Ned's email as a model. Give the students a minute or two to think of ideas, then ask them to write their emails. Go round offering help where needed and making sure that the students are using phrases from Exercises 1 and 2 and including advice about Alicia.

4

Put the students in pairs or small groups to discuss the questions. Go round, monitoring and giving help with vocabulary.

5

Remind the students that they can use the text in Exercise 1 as a model. Tell them to choose one of the emails to write and to make sure they include all the points that are asked for.

Further practice material

Need more classroom practice activities?
→ Photocopiable resource materials page 160
   1.29 **Song:** *You've Got a Friend*
→ TOP 10 activities pages xv to xx

Need progress tests?
→ Test CD – *Test Review A*

Need more on important teaching concepts?
→ Key concepts in *New Inside Out* pages xxii to xxxv

Need student self-study practice?
→ CD-ROM – *Review A*

Need more information and more ideas?
→ www.insideout.net

4 Party *Overview*

Section & Aims	What the students are doing
Reading SB page 32 Reading for detail	Talking about festivals. Reading an article about a Spanish festival and answering questions.
Vocabulary SB page 33 Festivals	Completing a description of a festival. Writing a short summary of a festival.
Vocabulary & Grammar SB page 33 Phrasal verbs	Matching phrasal verbs to their meanings. Studying rules for separable and non-separable phrasal verbs. Making phrasal verb sentences with pronouns.
Listening SB page 34 Listening for detail	Talking about New Year's Eve. Marking statements true or false. Then listening to an interview about Chinese New Year and correcting false statements. Rewriting the statements about New Year's Eve celebrations in their own country.
Vocabulary SB page 34 Collocations with *do* and *make*	Completing sentences with *do* and *make*. Finding collocations and using them to write sentences.
Grammar SB page 35 Future forms	Listening to a conversation and identifying future forms. Choosing appropriate future forms in a conversation. Completing a conversation with future forms.
Speaking & Reading SB page 36 Reading for detail	Discussing different types of parties and what makes a good party. Reading a text and discussing the ideas in it.
Vocabulary SB page 36 Parties	Completing sentences about parties with words from the text. Talking about a party they have had.
Grammar SB page 37 *anybody, somebody*, etc.	Completing a table with *anybody, somebody*, etc. Underlining the correct pronouns in a conversation.
Pronunciation SB page 37 Lyrics from pop songs	Listening and repeating lyrics. Rewriting the lyrics in full sentences.
Speaking: anecdote SB page 37 Fluency practice	Talking about a party they have been to.
Useful phrases SB page 38 Useful phrases for inviting and making excuses	Listening to conversations and identifying which friend a girl doesn't know well. Identifying, listening and repeating useful phrases. Practising conversations. Writing new conversations.
Vocabulary *Extra* SB page 39 Phrasal verbs	Identifying which particles do not go with *take* to form a phrasal verb. Identifying types of phrasal verbs and completing a table. Underlining the idiomatic meanings of phrasal verbs. Completing sentences with phrasal verbs.
Writing WB page 27	Writing letters of thanks and apology.

Warm up

- Write the word *party* in a small circle in the centre of the board. Tell the students to call out words they know that are associated with the word. As the words are called out, draw lines from the circle and add the words in suitable places, gradually building up a spidergram. For example, if a student calls out *decorations*, put this word in and ask the students to give examples of decorations – *balloons*, *streamers*, etc.

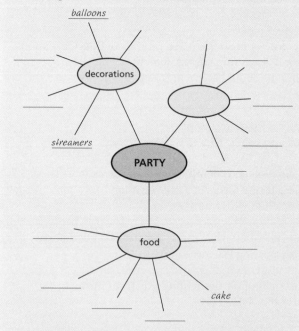

- Show the students how the words have been grouped, and after a few words have been added, invite them to say where in the diagram their new words should go.

- Encourage the students to use spidergrams in their vocabulary notebooks when they note down new words.

Reading (SB page 32)

- Focus the students' attention on the photo behind the text and ask them if the festival it shows looks exciting. Go through the questions with the class, then ask them to think of a festival and make brief notes on their answers to these questions.

- Invite several students to tell the class what they know about the festival they've chosen.

- Ask the students to read the text and find the answers for the questions. Allow them to discuss their answers with a partner before checking with the class.

> a) Las Fallas.
> b) In March. It ends on 19th March.
> c) A week.
> d) It began in the eighteenth century when craftsmen burnt their wooden candelabra on bonfires to celebrate the end of winter. They then started to dress the candelabras up as well-known but unpopular local characters.
> e) They watch fireworks. They go out in the streets. They watch processions. They burn the statues. They set off firecrackers. They eat and drink in the bars.
> f) All the statues are burnt down.

Vocabulary (SB page 33)

1

Encourage the students to try to complete the summary without looking back at the article on page 32. When checking answers, deal with any lingering vocabulary questions. Ask the students which of the words in the box feature in festivals in their countries.

> 1 festival   2 statues   3 bonfires
> 4 firecrackers   5 fireworks   6 procession
> 7 traditional dress   8 parade

2

- Ask the students to write a short summary of a festival they know about. Remind them that they can use the summary in Exercise 1 as a model.

- Ask the students to take turns to read their summaries to each other. Encourage the listening student to ask questions at the end to find out further details.

Cultural note

Chinese New Year

The Chinese New Year falls according to the lunar calendar. It's usually in either January or February. Each year in a twelve-year cycle is represented by an animal. Starting in 2009, the next twelve-year cycle is in this order: the ox, the tiger, the rabbit, the dragon, the snake, the horse, the sheep, the monkey, the rooster, the dog, the pig and the rat.

Vocabulary & Grammar (SB page 33)

Phrasal verbs

1

- Focus the students' attention on the information in the margin. Explain that phrasal verbs are made up of two or more words. Point out the two types, *intransitive* verbs, which don't take an object and *transitive* verbs, which do. Point out that *sth* is an abbreviation for *something*.

- Ask the students to look at the table. Give them time to take in the contents and notice the position of *something* in the separable and inseparable transitive verbs.

- Ask the students to match the verbs in the table with their meanings in the box. Stronger students may be able to do this without looking back at the text on page 32, but encourage them to look at the text so that they see them in context.

- Ask the students to make a list of all the phrasal verbs they know which have the particle *off*. They can then check their list against the examples in a dictionary.

---

go off = explode
join in = participate
burn down = destroy with fire
put something on = organise
dress something up = put special clothes on
keep something up = continue at the same speed
get down to something = start
look forward to something = anticipate excitedly
get over something = recover

Language notes

Grammar: phrasal verbs

- There are many phrasal verbs in English. When your students encounter a phrasal verb in a text, encourage them to try to guess the meaning from the context. This will help if they then look it up in a dictionary, as there can sometimes be several meanings of the same phrasal verb.
  A good dictionary will tell you if the verb needs an object (transitive) or doesn't (intransitive). These are often marked [I] and [T].

- There are two types of transitive phrasal verbs, separable and non-separable.
  In separable phrasal verbs the object can separate the phrasal verb or come after it – *Throw the banana skin **away**. / **Throw away** the banana skin.*
  But if the object is a pronoun, it must separate the phrasal verb – *Throw it **away**.*
  In non-separable phrasal verbs the object always comes after it – *Could you **deal with** the problem? / Could you **deal with** it?*
  If a phrasal verb has two particles (*get on with*), the object always comes after it – *My husband **gets on with** my parents. / He **gets on with** them.*

2

Focus the student's attention on the four sentences. Point out or get them to identify that the differences between them lie in whether the object of the verb is a noun (*the word*) or a pronoun (*it*), and in the position in the sentence of the object. Explain that in these sentences *look up* is a separable transitive phrasal verb. Ask them to say which sentence they think is incorrect. Then ask the students to complete the rule.

---

d) ~~You can look up it in a dictionary.~~
When the object of separable phrasal verb is a pronoun, it always comes between the verb and the particle.

3

- Go through the example with the class, pointing out that it conforms to the rule they've just learnt. You can say *clearing up the mess*, and *clearing it up*, but not ~~clearing up it~~.

- Ask the students to complete the exercise. Tell them that they'll find a mixture of separable and inseparable verbs and to use a dictionary if necessary. Go round giving help where needed and checking that they put the pronouns in the correct place.

- Point out that *look after*, *come up with* and *look forward to* are inseparable verbs. Also point out that *come up with* and *look forward to* each have two particles.

---

a) I hate clearing it up.
b) I look after them.
c) I try them on.
d) I want to turn it down.
e) It's difficult to come up with them.
f) I'm looking forward to it.

Language notes

Vocabulary: phrasal verbs

- Like other words, each phrasal verb can have several different meanings. For example: *go off* = decompose; *go off* = explode, etc.

- Sometimes the meaning is literal and you can guess it from the verb and the particle. For example: *go off* = leave; *take off* = remove, etc.

- Mostly, the meaning is idiomatic and you can only guess it from the context. For example, *go off* = take place/happen; *take off* = start flying, etc.

4 Pairwork

- The pairwork exercise for this unit is on pages 117 and 122 of the Student's Book. Put the students in pairs and tell them who will be Student A, and who will be Student B.

- While they're doing the exercise, go round monitoring and giving help. Take note of any errors which may need particular attention later, and also any examples of good language use, which you can praise in a feedback session.

> **Student A:**
> 1 set off 2 take up 3 go for 4 break up
> 5 finding out 6 comes out
>
> **Student B:**
> 1 get on 2 turn up 3 give in 4 set up
> 5 comes out 6 broken down

Cultural note

Coldplay

Coldplay is a British rock band formed in 1997. The band's hits include *Yellow, Fix You* and *Clocks*. The lead vocalist Chris Martin is married to the actor Gwyneth Paltrow. They have two children.

Listening (SB page 34)

1

- Explain *New Year's Eve* (December 31st). Answer the questions for yourself, telling the students about your own last New Year's Eve.

- Put the students into pairs to talk about their answers to the questions.

2 🌐 1.30

- If you have Chinese students in your class, ask them not to give the answers away at this stage. Ask the students to decide whether they think the statements about Chinese New Year are true or false.

- Play the recording for them to check their answers. Then ask individual students to correct the false statements.

> a) False. It usually takes place in early February.
> b) True.
> c) True.
> d) False. They usually spend New Year's Eve with their families.
> e) False. It's jiaozi – dumplings cooked in boiling water.
> f) True.
> g) True.

> 🌐 1.30 (I = Interviewer; H = Hua)
>
> I: *We're in Beijing, and it's mid-January. Hua, we've already celebrated New Year in England, but you don't celebrate New Year on 1st January, do you?*
>
> H: *No, we don't. Our New Year usually takes place in early February but not always. It depends on the Chinese calendar.*

> I: *I see. So how are you going to celebrate this year?*
>
> H: *Well, everybody spends the month before New Year preparing for it. First of all, I'm going to help my mother to do the housework. We're going to sweep away all the bad luck and make room for good luck to come in.*
>
> I: *Does everybody do that?*
>
> H: *Yes, and some people paint their doors and windows, usually red.*
>
> I: *Is red a lucky colour?*
>
> H: *Yes, traditionally, red is the colour that frightens away bad luck. For New Year, we put red paper decorations on the walls.*
>
> I: *And have you got plans for New Years Eve?*
>
> H: *Yes, we're having a big family dinner.*
>
> I: *Is there a traditional New Year's Eve dinner?*
>
> H: *Yes, we always eat jiaozi, which is dumplings cooked in boiling water.*
>
> I: *Oh, I'm sure it's very nice. Are you going to a New Year's Eve party after dinner?*
>
> H: *No, we always spend the New Year with our family. After dinner everybody watches television or plays cards or other board games, and at midnight, lots of fireworks and firecrackers go off. It's really exciting.*
>
> I: *How long do the celebrations go on?*
>
> H: *For about three days.*
>
> I: *Do you make New Year's Resolutions.*
>
> H: *Not exactly – we make wishes on New Year's Day.*
>
> I : *What are you going to wish for?*
>
> H: *I can't tell you, because it might not come true.*
>
> I: *Well, I hope all your wishes come true. Happy New Year. How do you say that in Chinese?*
>
> H: *Guo Nian Hao.*
>
> I: *Guo Nian Hao!*

3

If you have multinational classes, try to pair up students who come from the same country. Otherwise pairs should work together to produce sentences describing each of their countries. Then ask the pairs to report back to the class.

Vocabulary (SB page 34)

1

- Focus the students' attention on the sentences. Ask them if they can remember what the speaker said.

- Point out that some words collocate with *make* and some with *do*. When checking answers, tell the students that *do* is used with many household tasks.

> 1 do 2 make

Language notes

Vocabulary: *do* and *make*

- *Do* and *make* are combined with nouns to talk about actions you perform.

- *Do* is often used when the action is a noun ending in *ing*. For example, *do the shopping, do the cooking, do some sightseeing*, etc. It's also used to talk about daily activities or jobs. For example, *do (your) homework / the housework / the ironing*, etc.

- *Make* is often used to talk about an activity that creates something. For example, *make food / a cup of tea / a mess*, etc.

- There are a number of fixed expressions using *do* and *make* that don't fit into these categories. For example, *do business / make your bed*. Encourage the students to learn these as complete phrases.

2

- Ask the students to complete the questions.

- Check answers with the class to make sure that everyone has the correct questions before putting the students into pairs to take turns asking and answering them.

a) make	d) doing
b) does	e) made
c) made	f) do, make

3

- Go through the list of words in the box with the class. Then put the students into pairs and ask them to decide which words collocate with *make* and which with *do*.

- Go round giving help where needed and allow the students to use dictionaries if necessary.

- Check answers with the class to make sure everyone has the correct collocations before asking them to write their six sentences. Then ask several students to read their sentences to the class.

> *make*: a comment, a decision, a mistake, a noise, a profit, a suggestion, an excuse, arrangements, money, progress, something clear, sure
>
> *do*: a degree, a job, some decorating, some exercise, some research, some skiing, the ironing, your homework

Grammar (SB page 35)

Future forms

1 🌐 1.31

Focus the students' attention on the photo. Point out that one of the women is crying. Tell the students that the women are flatmates, Sandy and Zoë, and to listen to the recording to find out why Sandy is unhappy.

Because David hasn't rung.

Language notes

Grammar: *will*

- There's no future tense in English, but there are various ways of talking about the future including *will, be going to* and the present continuous.

- *Will* is a modal verb and is used to express a number of functions such as offers (*I'll help her*), promises (*She'll be there at 10 am*), requests (*Will you get me a newspaper?*), orders (*I'll have the steak*) and predictions (*It'll rain tomorrow – it always rains at the weekend*). *Will* is also used to make general statements (of fact) about the future (*The college will be closed*). In this unit *will* is used to express a spontaneous decision.

- The negative of *will* is *will not*. The contraction of *will* is *'ll* and the contraction of *will not* is *won't*. The contractions *'ll* and *won't* are more commonly used than the full form in statements, while in questions and short answers the full form is always used.
  Statement: *I'll* give you a lift, if you want.
  Question: *Will* you help me, please?
  Short answer: Yes, he *will*. (not ~~Yes, he'll.~~)

- *Will* is always followed by the infinitive.

Grammar: *be going to*

- *be going to* is the most common way to talk about future intentions. It's usually used when you've already decided about a future action – you know what you're going to do.

- When *be going to* is used with *go*, it's often shortened. For example: *I'm going to go shopping* becomes *I'm going shopping*.

Grammar: present continuous

- Using the present continuous is the most common way to talk about future arrangements. It's usually used when you've already made plans (with someone else) to do something in the future. Compare:
  I'm going to learn Chinese one day. (*going to* for intention)
  I'm seeing an old friend on Friday. (present continuous for arrangement)

- The present continuous is often used with a time expression to make the future meaning clearer. *I'm having dinner with a friend **this evening**.*

2

- Ask the students to look at the numbered parts of the conversation in Exercise 1. Explain that each is a different way of talking about the future. Explain or get the students to identify the form in each case (1 present continuous, 2 *going to*, 3 *will*).

- Go through the choices and ask the students to match each of them to one of the numbered forms.
- Focus the students' attention on the information on future forms in the margin and go through this with the class.

> a) *will* – (3) I'll phone James
> b) *(be) going to* – (2) We're going to plan
> c) present continuous – (1) Steve's coming round

3 🔘 1.32

- Ask the students to read through the conversation and decide what the situation is for each form choice, i.e. is it a spontaneous decision, an intention or an arrangement? As they work, go round giving extra help where needed.
- Play the recording for the students to check their answers. Then ask a pair of students to perform the completed conversation for the class.

> 1 are you doing   5 I'm going
> 2 I'm meeting   6 I'm going to tell
> 3 I'm meeting   7 I'll believe
> 4 I'll see

> 🔘 1.32 (J = James; S = Sandy; Z = Zoë)
>
> J: Hello.
> S: Hi, James, it's Sandy. What are you doing tonight?
> J: Nothing! Well actually, I'm meeting Alex and Suzy in town, but …
> S: Do you fancy coming to a party? Alex and Suzy can come too.
> J: Yes, that sounds great. I'm meeting them at the Star Bar at 8.30.
> S: OK, I'll see you there. Bye. … (Puts the phone down.) I'm going to the party with James.
> Z: Good idea.
> S: And next time I see David I'm going to tell him the relationship is definitely over.
> Z: Hmm. I'll believe that when I see it.

4 🔘 1.33

- Ask the students to read the conversation and put the verbs in the most appropriate future form.
- As they work, go round giving extra help where needed and making sure that everyone has understood the difference between the forms.
- Play the recording for the students to check their answers. Then ask a pair of students to perform the completed conversation for the class.

> 1 'll get   2 'm having   3 'm going
> 4 'll call   5 's having

5 🔘 1.34

Tell the students they're going to listen to another conversation. Ask them first if they think there's any future in the relationship between Sandy and David. Then play the recording and ask them what has happened and what their answer is now.

> No.

> 🔘 1.34 (S = Sandy; A = Alex; J = James)
>
> S: Hi, James. Hi, Alex. Hey, Alex. Where's Suzy?
> A: Oh, she changed her mind at the last minute. David phoned her and asked her to go for a meal at that new Japanese restaurant.
> S: What? Now I'm definitely going to tell him it's over.
> J: Who's David?

5 Grammar *Extra* 4

Ask the students to turn to *Grammar Extra* 4 on page 132 of the Student's Book. Here they'll find an explanation of the grammar they've been studying and further exercises to practise it.

> **1**
> a) 3   b) 3   c) 3   d) 2   e) 1   f) 3   g) 2   h) 1
>
> **2**
> a) 'Shall I give you a hand?'
> b) 'Shall I dry them?'
> c) 'Shall I open the window?'
> d) 'Shall I help you?'
> e) 'Shall I answer it?'
> f) 'Shall I get it?'
>
> **3**
> 1 's arriving   7 'll buy
> 2 going to tidy   8 'll do
> 3 'll do   9 are you doing
> 4 'll get it   10 'm having
> 5 'll take   11 'll probably play
> 6 going to phone   12 'm doing
>
> 1 b   2 c   3 a   4 d
>
> **4**
> a) 'm going to travel   d) 'll just stay in
> b) 'm playing   e) 'm going to do
> c) is getting married;   f) 'm not going to pass /
>   'll probably be   won't pass

Speaking & Reading (SB page 36)

1

- Focus the students' attention on the list of types of party. Go through it with the class and ask them to discuss in pairs when and why people have these parties.
- Ask them to list any other types of parties they can think of. Encourage them to report back to the class.

> *a housewarming party*: Anytime. When people have just moved in to a new home. To celebrate and meet the neighbours.
>
> *a farewell/leaving party*: When someone is leaving a job or moving abroad.
>
> *an 18th birthday party*: When somebody turns eighteen – a coming-of-age party.
>
> *a surprise party*: Anytime. Usually for somebody's significant birthday (for example, forty or fifty). The person knows nothing about the party and arrives to a complete surprise.
>
> *an office party*: Usually before Christmas. Companies throw parties for their staff.
>
> *a fancy dress party*: Anytime. Often around Christmas. No particular reason.

2

- Ask the students to work in pairs or small groups to discuss what they think are the most important ingredients of a good party. Ask them to share their ideas with the class.
- Focus the students' attention on the text and ask them to read it quickly to find out if any of their ideas are mentioned. Then ask them to read it again more carefully and to discuss whether they agree or not with the other ideas.

Vocabulary (SB page 36)

1

Ask the students to work individually or in pairs to find the words in the article to complete the sentences.

a) fancy	e) mingle
b) guest	f) greet
c) invitation	g) host
d) atmosphere	h) dustpan

2

Students discuss parties they've had in pairs. Ask them to report back to the class on what they learnt.

Grammar (SB page 37)

anybody, somebody, etc.

1

- Focus the students' attention on the information in the margin. Read out the example sentences and point out that *somebody, anything, everywhere* and *no one* are pronouns which refer to people, things and places. Give a few more examples: *I've put my glasses down somewhere. I haven't seen anybody today. I can't find my glasses anywhere. Everybody enjoyed the party.*, etc. Point out that *no one* is the same as *nobody*.
- Focus the students' attention on the table and ask them to complete it.

1 somebody	2 someone	3 somewhere
4 anybody	5 anyone	6 anything
7 nobody	8 nothing	9 nowhere

Language notes

Vocabulary: *anybody, somebody,* etc.

- *everybody, everyone, everything* and *everywhere* refer, in this order, to all people, things and places.
- *somebody, someone, something* and *somewhere* refer to unspecified people, things and places.
- *anybody, anyone, anything* and *anywhere* refer to unlimited people, things and places. You use pronouns beginning with *any* in sentences with negative verbs.
- *nobody, no one, nothing* and *nowhere* refer to no people, things or places. Pronouns beginning with *no* are used in sentences with negative meaning (but positive verbs). For example: *Nobody came to my party. There's nothing here that I like. There is nowhere to hold the party.*
- All these pronouns are used with singular verb forms.

2 🌐 1.35

- Ask the students to read the conversation and decide which pronouns fit best and underline them.
- Play the recording for them to check their answers. Then ask two students to act out the conversation. Find out if they know anybody like Dylan and if their mothers were like this when they were teenagers.

1 Nowhere	2 No one	3 Somewhere
4 Nothing	5 Anything	6 everyone

> 🌐 1.35 (M = Mum; D = Dylan)
>
> M: *Is that you, Dylan? You're late. Where have you been?*
> D: *Nowhere.*
> M: *But you're an hour late!*
> D: *OK, I went to the park.*

M: Who with?
D: No one. I went on my own.
M: Where's Sophie?
D: I don't know. Somewhere in town.
M: What's happened?
D: Nothing! Stop asking questions.
M: What do you want for dinner tonight?
D: Anything. I don't care.
M: We could try that new Chinese restaurant
* – everyone says it's great.*
D: OK.
M: Good. Now, what did you do at school today?

Pronunciation (SB page 37)

1 **1.36**

Focus the students' attention on the sentences and ask them if they notice anything unusual about them. (The sentences are song lyrics and use the short forms *gonna* (*going to*), *wanna* (*want to*), *gotta* (*got to*) and *aint* (*isn't*, though here used instead of *I'm not*). Play the recording and ask the students to listen and repeat.

> **1.36**
>
> *a) We're gonna have a party.*
> *b) Do you wanna dance?*
> *c) I wanna be your man.*
> *d) Just do what you gotta do.*
> *e) Gotta get over you.*
> *f) Ain't never gonna fall in love again.*

Language note

Pronunciation: *gonna, gotta, wanna*
* *going to* is often written in an abbreviated form as *gonna* in pop songs.
* *have got to* (= have to) is often written in an abbreviated form as *gotta* in pop songs.
* *want to* is often written in an abbreviated form as *wanna* in pop songs. Encourage students to use the full form of each when doing their own writing. (Unless they're writing pop songs!)

2

Point out that song lyrics often use non-standard English. Ask the students to rewrite the lyrics using full forms and standard English grammar. When checking answers, point out that in f) it is not good English to use *never* with a negative verb as the word *never* is, itself, a negative form.

> a) We're going to have a party.
> b) Do you want to dance?
> c) I want to be your man.
> d) Just do what you've got to do.
> e) I've got to get over you.
> f) I'm never going to fall in love again.

Speaking: anecdote (SB page 37)

For more information about how to set up, monitor and repeat Anecdotes, see page xx in the Introduction.

1 **1.37**

* Focus the students' attention on the photos of Paul before and after the party. Explain that they're going to hear him talking about a fancy dress party he went to. Ask them if they can guess from the bottom photo who he went dressed as.

* Go through the questions and the answers with the class. Explain any unknown vocabulary. Then play the recording and ask the students to listen and find which question Paul doesn't answer.

* Ask the students to match the questions and answers. Then play the recording again for them to check their answers.

> He doesn't answer question *k*.
> a) 6   b) 8   c) 1   d) 4   e) 3   f) 2   g) 7
> h) 9   i) 5   j) 10   k) –

> **1.37**
>
> *I went to a great party last summer. My friend, Maggie, was leaving our town and moving abroad to live. So she had a leaving party, but she also came up with a really good theme – it was fancy dress, and everybody had to dress up as something beginning with the letter M. She chose the letter M, because it's the first letter of her name. I thought it was a great idea, and people came dressed as all sorts of things – Mickey Mouse, Madonna, Medusa – I went as Marilyn Monroe. It was fun, but I didn't particularly enjoy wearing lipstick or high heels. I don't know how women do it all the time. The party was at Maggie's house, but it was summer, so we were in the garden a lot of the time. The garden looked really beautiful. They had fairy lights in the trees and lots of mirrors, so that the lights were reflected, and it made the garden look much bigger.*
>
> *There must have been at least seventy people there. I think she invited everyone she knew. I didn't know everybody, but it didn't matter. The fancy dress was a perfect ice-breaker and everybody mixed really well. The food was great too – Maggie was moving to Thailand, so the food was Thai. She got the local Thai restaurant to do it, and it was delicious. We even had Thai beer to go with it. Maggie's brother is a DJ, so the music was fantastic, and I danced a lot – without my heels on.*

Cultural notes

Madonna /məˈdɒnə/ (born 1958)
Madonna is one of the most successful recording artists of all time, with songs such as *Material Girl* and *Into the Groove*. She's also appeared in the films *Desperately Seeking Susan* and *Evita*. She continues to produce best-selling albums.

Medusa /məˈduːsə/
In Greek mythology Medusa was a beautiful woman, who was transformed by a jealous goddess Athena into a hideous monster. She changed her lustrous hair into hissing serpents, and Medusa became so grotesque that no living creature could look at her without being turned to stone.

Marilyn Monroe /ˈmærəlɪn mənˈrəʊ/ (1926–1962)
Marilyn Monroe was a Hollywood actress and an icon of 1950s America. She starred in such films as *Gentlemen Prefer Blondes* (1953) and *Some Like It Hot* (1959). She was married three times and her love affairs were as famous as her film roles. She was romantically linked with young politicians John and Robert Kennedy.

2

- Give the students a minute or two to decide what they're going to talk about. Then ask them to look at the questions in Exercise 1 again. Allow them to make notes of what they're going to say about the party and how they're going to say it, but discourage them from writing a paragraph that they can simply read out. If the students can't think of a party that they've been to, adapt the questions to suit talking about a festival or a family occasion such as a wedding.

- Pairwork. Put the students in pairs and ask them to take turns to tell their partner about their party. Encourage them to ask each other follow-up questions to get further information.

- Ask some pairs to report back to the class about what they found out.

Useful phrases (SB page 38)

1 1.38

Focus the students' attention on the illustrations, which show Rose making a series of phone calls. Ask them to read and listen to the four conversations and decide which friend she doesn't know very well.

> She doesn't know Alan very well.

🌐 1.38

a) (R = Rose; I = Ian)
R: *Do you fancy coming to the cinema tonight?*
I: *Yes, good idea. What are you going to see?*
R: *The new James Bond film.*
I: *Oh no, I've seen it.*
R: *Oh what a shame. Is it any good?*
I: *No, it's terrible.*

b) (R = Rose; L = Lucy)
R: *Would you like to come to the cinema tonight?*
L: *I'd love to but I'm working tonight.*
R: *Oh, what a shame.*
L: *I know. What are you going to see?*
R: *The new Bond film.*
L: *Oh, I've heard it's really good – the best one so far.*

---

c) (R = Rose; M = Maggie)
R: *Are you doing anything tonight?*
M: *No, why?*
R: *I'm going to see the new Bond film. Do you fancy coming?*
M: *No, I'm afraid I can't. I have to get up really early tomorrow. Why don't you ask Alan?*
R: *Alan? No, I can't. I don't know him well enough.*
M: *Don't be silly. He'd be really pleased.*

d) (R = Rose; A = Alan)
R: *Oh, hi Alan. It's Rose.*
A: *Hi Rose. How are you?*
R: *Very well, thanks. Um, I was wondering if you'd like to go to the cinema tonight.*
A: *Yes, that sounds great. What's on?*
R: *Well, I was thinking of seeing the new James Bond film.*
A: *Great. What time do you want to meet?*

Cultural note

James Bond /dʒeɪmz bɒnd/
James Bond is a fictional British spy, code named 007. The first Bond novel *Casino Royale* was written by Ian Fleming in 1953. The first Bond film *Dr No* was shown in 1962. Bond has been played by six actors including Sean Connery, Roger Moore, Pierce Brosnan and Daniel Craig.

---

2 🌐 1.39

- Go through the things the students have to find with the class. Then ask them to find them in the conversations. You could do this as a race between teams, if you wish, or set a time limit.

- Check answers, then play the recording for the students to listen and repeat the useful phrases.

> See answers in the audioscript below.

🌐 1.39

a) *Do you fancy coming to the cinema tonight?*
    Would you like to come to the cinema tonight?
    I was wondering if you'd like to go to the cinema tonight.
b) *Yes, good idea.*
    Yes, that sounds great.
c) *I'd love to but I'm working tonight.*
    No, I'm afraid I can't.
d) *Are you doing anything tonight?*
e) *Oh, what a shame.*

3

Ask the students to work in pairs and practise the conversations. Go round and identify some particularly good pairs who could perform for the class.

4

- Put the students into pairs and ask them to write a new conversation, based on the situation described.
- Ask the students to practise their conversations, taking turns to be Student A and Student B. Go round while they're practising and identify some particularly good pairs who could perform for the class.

Vocabulary *Extra* (SB page 39)

Phrasal verbs

1

- Pairwork. Ask the students to cross out the particle in each list which doesn't go with the word *take* to form a phrasal verb. Then tell them to check their answers with the dictionary extract.
- Ask the students to look at the dictionary extract for *take* in the margin and tick the phrasal verbs they know. Then discuss as a class.

> a) about   b) at   c) without

2

Focus the students' attention on the table and go through the example with them. Tell them to look back at the work they did on phrasal verbs in this unit. (See Language note on page 35 for additional information.) Ask them to complete the table with the dictionary example for each phrasal verb in the box.

Intransitive:	Transitive (separable):	Transitive (not separable):
take off	take sth back take sb on take sth up	take after sb take to sb/sth

a) The object (sb/sth) goes between the verb and the particle (e.g. *back/on/up*).
b) The object (sb/sth) goes after the verb and the particle.

3

Ask the students to underline the correct idiomatic meaning of each of the phrasal verbs.

> a) admit that you said sth wrong
> b) write sth
> c) understand and remember sth
> d) aircraft: start flying
> e) get sth official from a bank, etc.
> f) start doing sth new

4

- Tell the students to use the phrasal verbs from Exercise 3 to complete the sentences.
- Then ask them to discuss with a partner whether the sentences are true for them.

> a) taking off   b) take out   c) take up
> d) take it back   e) take in   f) take down

5

- Ask the students to cross out the alternative which isn't possible in each of the sentences. Do not confirm answers at this stage.
- Ask the students to check their answers in their dictionaries.

> a) dog   b) car   c) rent   d) having a baby
> e) sleeping

6

- Ask the students to look in their dictionaries and find examples their dictionary gives for these phrasal verbs with *take* and report back to the class.

Further practice material

Need more writing practice?
→ Workbook page 27
- Writing letters of thanks and apology.

Need more classroom practice activities?
→ Photocopiable resource materials pages 161 to 163
  Grammar: *The bluffing game*
  Vocabulary: *Make & do*
  Communication: *Party animal or party pooper?*
→ Top 10 activities pages xv to xx

Need DVD material?
→ DVD – Programme 4: *Festival*

Need progress tests?
→ Test CD – *Test Unit 4*

Need more on important teaching concepts?
→ Key concepts in *New Inside Out* pages xxii to xxxv

Need student self-study practice?
→ CD-ROM – Unit 4: *Party*

Need student CEF self-evaluation?
→ CEF Checklists pages xxxvii to xliv

Need more information and more ideas?
→ www.insideout.net

5 Edible *Overview*

Section & Aims	What the students are doing
Reading & Speaking SB page 40 Reading for detail Fluency work	Reading questions and statements about chocolate. Deciding whether statements are true or false and listening to check. Making new statements with other food items. Discussing whether they agree or disagree with statements about food.
Grammar SB page 41 Nouns and quantity expressions	Completing statements about countable and uncountable nouns. Studying nouns which can be both countable and uncountable. Completing questions with *many* and *much*.
Vocabulary SB page 41 Partitives	Matching words to make common collocations. Talking about personal consumption of items.
Speaking SB page 42 Fluency work	Completing sentences about food and drink with names of classmates. Asking questions to check ideas.
Vocabulary & Pronunciation **SB page 42** Food; syllable stress	Identifying food items in a photo. Categorising food into types. Practising pronunciation of food items. Completing questions with contrasting words.
Listening SB page 43 Listening for detail	Talking about the taste of unusual food items. Matching dishes with descriptive adjectives.
Vocabulary & Speaking SB page 43 Ways of cooking; taste and texture; fluency work	Categorising words. Describing the taste and texture of food. Describing best and worst meals.
Reading SB page 44 Reading for gist	Reading a text to find someone's food preferences. Identifying whether statements are true or false. Rewriting sentences to make them true.
Grammar SB page 45 *used to/would*	Studying the use of *used to* for repeated actions or states and *would* for repeated actions. Changing sentences to include *used to* or *would*, then rewriting sentences so they are true for them.
Speaking: anecdote SB page 45 Fluency practice	Talking about their childhoods.
Useful phrases SB page 46 Useful conversational phrases at a restaurant	Listening to a conversation and matching it to the correct picture. Identifying the differences between two versions of a conversation. Listening and repeating useful phrases. Completing and practising conversations.
Vocabulary *Extra* SB page 47 Nouns and articles	Completing a table with correct noun types. Classifying nouns. Completing a poem with *a* or *the*. Crossing out the incorrect use of *the*.
Writing WB page 33	Writing a letter of complaint.

Warm up

Ask the students to think about their favourite dish and explain what the ingredients are and, if possible, how to make it to the class. Extend the discussion to typical dishes from their country or countries.

Reading & Speaking (SB page 40)

1

- Go through the questions with the class and explain any unknown vocabulary. You may like to point out that *chocoholic* is a made-up word for someone who is addicted to chocolate. The form of the term *alcoholic*, someone who is addicted to alcohol, is often used to form similar words for other addictions. Students may also have come across *workaholic* to describe someone who works too hard.

- Put the students into pairs, but ask them to work individually at first to guess how they think their partner would answer the questions. Don't let them compare notes at this stage.

- When the students have decided on their answers for all their questions, let them discuss them with their partners to see if they guessed correctly. In a class feedback session, find out who the chocoholics of the class are.

2 🎧 2.01

- Go through the statements with the class and ask the students to decide whether they think they are true or false. Don't confirm or deny any answers at this stage, but encourage discussion.

- Play the recording for the students to check their answers. Then, in a class feedback session, find out if they were surprised by any of these.

1	True
2	True
3	True
4	True
5	False (A little chocolate can make a dog sick. A lot of chocolate can kill it.)
6	False (The Swiss consume more chocolate.)
7	True
8	False (Chocolate contains very little caffeine.)
9	True
10	True

🎧 2.01

Number 1. A little chocolate each day is good for your health. Chocolate contains antioxidants which help to protect the body against cancer. It also contains several minerals and some protein. In fact, one bar of chocolate contains more protein than a banana, so this statement is true.

Number 2. White chocolate doesn't contain any cocoa, so this statement is true.

Number 3. Chocolate contains chemicals that produce the same reaction in the body as falling in love, so this statement is true.

Number 4. The healthy part of chocolate is the cocoa, and dark chocolate has at least 50–70% cocoa. On the other hand, a lot of commercial milk chocolate bars have hardly any cocoa in them at all, so this statement is true.

Number 5. A little chocolate can make a dog sick. A lot of chocolate can kill it, so this statement is false.

Number 6. Americans consume a lot of chocolate, but per capita, the Swiss consume more. The Swiss consume ten kilograms per person per year, so this statement is false.

Number 7 is true.

Number 8. Chocolate contains much less caffeine than coffee, so this statement is false.

Number 9 is true.

Number 10 is true. In fact, they used a lot of chocolate sauce because the scene took seven days to shoot.

Cultural notes

Psycho /ˈsaɪkəʊ/ (1960)
Psycho is one of film director Alfred Hitchcock's most famous films. It tells the story of a young woman who steals some money, and while escaping, stops at the Bates Motel, where she meets psychotic killer Norman Bates.

3

- Focus the students' attention on the example and explain or get them to identify that *chocolate* takes a singular verb (*is*) whereas *chips* takes a plural verb (*are*), and that *chocolate* is an uncountable noun, whereas *chips* can be counted.

- If the students point out that you can also count *chocolates*, focus their attention on the two photos on this page. One shows *chocolates*, the other *chocolate*. When you talk about individual chocolates, as in the items in a box of chocolates in the top photo, they can be counted. When you're talking about the substance, as in the bottom photo, *chocolate* is uncountable. The example sentence is about chocolate in general, i.e. chocolate the substance, so the noun and verb are singular.

- Point out that all the words in the box, including *chip* are singular. The students must decide whether each item is countable or not. If it is, they must use a plural form and plural verb as in *Chips are good for you*. As the students write their new statements, go round checking the everyone is using singular/plural forms appropriately. Then check their answers.

- Put the students into pairs to discuss the statements and decide which ones they agree with.

> *is:* fish, fruit, milk, salt, sleep, sugar, travel, work
> *are:* chips, crisps, vegetables, vitamins

Grammar (SB page 41)

Nouns and quantity expressions

1

Go through the statements with the class and ask them to complete them. Then ask them to suggest some more examples of countable and uncountable nouns.

> 1 Countable   2 Uncountable

Language notes

Grammar: countable nouns / uncountable nouns
- Countable nouns are the names of individual objects, people or ideas which can be counted. Countable nouns have plurals (*shop*, *shops*).
- Uncountable or mass nouns are the names of materials, liquids, collections without clear boundaries, which aren't seen as separate objects, e.g. *water*, *weather*, *air*. Uncountable nouns don't have plurals (*weathers*).

2

- If the issue of *chocolate* being both countable and uncountable didn't come up in the previous section, explain when it can be countable and when uncountable, using the pictures on this page and on the previous one. Explain that even in a bar, chocolate is still a substance rather than an individual item and that if you wanted to count it, you would have to say *two bars of chocolate* or *two chocolate bars*, rather than *two chocolates*.

- Ask the students to look at the other items in the box and decide which of those can sometimes be countable and sometimes uncountable.

> Uncountable + occasionally countable: beers, cakes, coffees, salads, whiskies, yoghurts

Language note

Grammar: nouns that are both countable and uncountable
Certain food items can be both countable and uncountable with a difference of meaning, e.g. *beer*, *cake*, *cereal*, *cheese*, *chicken*, *chocolate*, *coffee*, *fish*, *meat*, *whisky*, *yoghurt*. In some cases this is because you can divide the item and eat it in pieces. This includes *cake*, *lettuce* and *cucumber*. In other cases it is a shorter way of making a sentence, particularly when referring to liquids. For example *Two whiskies / Two beers / Two coffees* (instead of *Two glasses of whisky, two glasses of beer, two cups of coffee*).

3

- Focus the students' attention on the information in the margin on quantity expressions. Point out that some of the expressions can be used with both countable and uncountable nouns, but that some are specific to one or the other.

- Read the example question with the class and point out, or get the students identify, that you use *How many?* in questions with countable nouns and *How much?* in questions with uncountable nouns.

- Ask the students to work individually to complete the remaining questions. Tell them not to worry about the answers just yet.

- Check that everyone has formed the questions correctly before looking at the example again with the class and pointing out that *a little* cannot be the answer to the first question because *friends* is countable and *a little* can only be used with uncountable nouns. Ask the students to choose the answers which are not possible for the remaining questions.

- After checking their answers, ask the students to underline the answers that are true for them. Then ask them to work in pairs and take turns asking and answering the questions.

> a) many; A little   d) many; Too much
> b) much; A lot of   e) much; Not many
> c) many; So much   f) much; Lots of

Language notes

Grammar: *How much/many ...?*
When enquiring about the quantity of chocolate remaining in the bar on page 41, the question would probably be *How much chocolate is there?* The chocolate in the bar can't be counted. The same question for the individual chocolates from a box would be *How many chocolates are there?* because the chocolates can be counted.

Vocabulary: quantity expressions

- You can use *some* with plural countable nouns: *some restaurants*. Other words commonly used with, or referring to, countable nouns are: *none, (not) any, (a) few, several, many, a lot, lots, plenty.*

- You can use *some* with uncountable nouns: *some water*. Other words commonly used with, or referring to, uncountable nouns are: *none, (not) any, (a) little, a bit, much, a lot, lots, plenty.*

Vocabulary: *little*

Generally speaking, if a student makes a mistake with a quantity expression, they'll still be understood. If, for example, one of your students says *Bill Gates has many money*, although the sentence is grammatically incorrect, the meaning is clear. The word *little* presents a bigger problem: if used with a countable noun, *little* refers to the size of the noun; if used with an uncountable noun, it refers to the quantity. This can produce problems with meaning. It's therefore important that the teacher is aware that sentences like *There were little people at the party* are probably grammatically rather than politically incorrect, the desired sentence being *There were few people at the party*, or, more naturally *There weren't many people at the party*.

Vocabulary: *not enough / too much/many*

- *not enough* suggests you have less than you need of something.
  I don't have enough petrol = I need more petrol.
  It can be used with both countable and uncountable nouns.

- *too much/many* suggests you have more than you need of something.
  I have too much homework = I want less homework.
  I have too many things to do today = I want fewer things to do today.
  When used with uncountable nouns, you use *too much*. With countable nouns you use *too many*.

4 Grammar *Extra* 5

Ask the students to turn to *Grammar Extra* 5 on page 134 of the Student's Book. Here they'll find an explanation of the grammar they've been studying and further exercises to practise it.

1	
a) – advice U	m) an orange C
b) an aubergine C	n) – progress U
c) – baggage U	o) – rice U
d) – furniture U	p) – spaghetti U
e) – hair U	q) a suggestion C
f) – homework U	r) – traffic U
g) – information U	s) – travel U
h) – jeans P	t) – trousers P
i) – justice	u) – underpants P
j) – knowledge U	v) a user C
k) – luck U	w) – veal U
l) – machinery U	x) – weather U

3
a) watch   b) jacket   c) comb   d) fridge
e) idea   f) house   g) book   h) interview

4
beer, coffee, Coke, tea, whisky, yoghurt

5
a) ~~some~~   b) ~~a few~~   c) ~~A little~~   d) ~~much~~
e) ~~so much~~   f) ~~some~~   g) ~~any~~   h) ~~some~~

Vocabulary (SB page 41)

1

- Focus the students' attention back on the chocolate photos. Remind them that individual chocolates are countable but that liquid chocolate, or chocolate in a block, is uncountable. Then point out the example in this exercise and explain that there is a way to count uncountable things and that is to use expressions like *a bar of* or *two bottles of*. Point out that the photo on the right could be described simply as *chocolate* or as *a bar of chocolate*.

- Ask the students to try to match the remaining collocations.

1 and 2
a) 2: a bar of chocolate / soap
b) 6: a bowl of fruit / sugar (+ cereal / grapes / rice / soup / spaghetti)
c) 5: a box of chocolates / matches (+ cereal / tissues / tools)
d) 1: a bunch of bananas / flowers (+ grapes / keys)
e) 4: a jar of honey / instant coffee (+ marmalade / raspberry jam)
f) 3: a packet of cigarettes / crisps (+ biscuits / cereal / rice / seeds / soup / spaghetti / tea / tissues)

Language notes

Vocabulary: containers

- It's sometimes possible to 'package' an uncountable noun and make it countable, e.g. *three bottles of water, two pieces of steak.*

- Note that in different countries, food items can be sold in different packaging. So, for example, biscuits are often sold in boxes in the United States, whereas in the UK packets of biscuits are more common.

- Other common UK household containers are:
  carton (of milk, orange juice)
  can (of cola, beer)
  tube (of toothpaste, cheese spread)
  tin (of tuna, tomatoes)

2

- Pairwork. Ask the students to work together to add the words to the correct lists to make more collocations
- Check answers with the class before asking the students to discuss their own consumption or use of the items.

> See answers in Exercise 1.

Speaking (SB page 42)

1

Go through the sentence endings with the class and make sure everyone understands them. Then ask the students to work individually and in silence to add names to the sentences.

2

- Focus the students' attention on the example question. With weaker classes, ask the students to form all the questions they'll need to ask to check their ideas. If your classroom layout allows, ask the students to mingle and ask questions of the people whose names they put in their sentences to see if they guessed correctly.
- In a class feedback session, find out what information about eating habits and preferences they found out about.

Vocabulary & Pronunciation

(SB page 42)

1

- Focus the students' attention on the photo. Ask them to identify as many items of food in it as they can. As they call out words, write them in a spidergram on the board. Put the word *food* in the centre with lines out to *fruit, vegetables, meat* and *dairy products*. As students identify items in the photo, ask them to say which category they should go in.
- When you've exhausted the possibilities of the photo, allow them to add any other food words they know.

2 🌐 2.02

- Students discuss the various food items listed and decide what the colours represent. Ask them to check any words they don't know in their dictionaries. Point out that peppers, tomatoes, olives and aubergines are technically fruit but are generally thought of as vegetables.
- Play the recording and ask the students to listen and repeat the words. Play it a second time for them to mark the stressed syllables. Then ask them what is different about the last word in each row.

> red = meat
> purple = fish and seafood
> orange = fruit
> green = vegetables

> a) veal   cod   limes   trout   beans   <u>tu</u>na
> b) leeks   plums   hake   figs   prawns
>   <u>pea</u>ches
> c) <u>tur</u>key   <u>o</u>lives   <u>mus</u>sels   <u>me</u>lons
>   <u>mush</u>rooms   sar<u>dines</u>
> d) <u>gar</u>lic   <u>cher</u>ries   <u>lob</u>ster   <u>on</u>ions
>   <u>grape</u>fruits   cour<u>gettes</u>
> e) <u>pep</u>pers   <u>ba</u>con   <u>sal</u>mon   <u>spin</u>ach
>   <u>man</u>gos   <u>cau</u>liflower
> f) <u>sau</u>sages   <u>let</u>tuces   <u>cab</u>bages   <u>or</u>anges
>   <u>ra</u>dishes   po<u>ta</u>toes
> g) <u>au</u>bergines   <u>straw</u>berries   <u>cu</u>cumbers
>   <u>cel</u>ery   <u>rasp</u>berries   to<u>ma</u>toes
>
> The last word has a different stress pattern.

> 🌐 2.02
> a) *veal   cod   limes   trout   beans   tuna*
> b) *leeks   plums   hake figs   prawns   peaches*
> c) *turkey   olives   mussels   melons*
>   *mushrooms   sardines*
> d) *garlic   cherries   lobster   onions*
>   *grapefruits   courgettes*
> e) *peppers   bacon   salmon   spinach*
>   *mangoes   cauliflower*
> f) *sausages   lettuces   cabbages   oranges*
>   *radishes   potatoes*
> g) *aubergines   strawberries   cucumbers*
>   *celery   raspberries   tomatoes*

3

- Go through the items in the box and point out the pronunciation of *draught*. Read the example to the class and explain that all the words in the box are contrasts with the words in the questions.
- Ask the students to complete the questions.
- Check answers before getting the students to take turns asking and answering the questions to find out each other's food preferences. Ask if any pairs had exactly the same preferences.

> a) cooked   b) heavy   c) white   d) frozen
> e) weak   f) mild   g) draught   h) sweet

Listening (SB page 43)

Warm up

Tell the class about the most unusual thing you have ever eaten. Describe the texture and the taste and say whether you enjoyed it and whether you would eat it again. Ask if anyone else has eaten this thing and whether anyone would consider eating it.

1

- Focus the students' attention on the photos and ask if anyone has ever eaten any of these things. If they have, get them to tell the class about it and to describe the taste and the texture.

- Then ask the students to say what they think each thing would taste like. You could draw their attention to the list of words in Exercise 2 if they need help with words to describe taste and texture.

Cultural note

A Mars Bar is a popular chocolate bar in the UK. In some places, particularly in fish and chip shops in Scotland, it's possible to buy them deep-fried, that is dipped in batter (a mixture of milk, flour and eggs) and fried in a pan of oil.

2 🌐 2.03

- Tell the students that they're going to hear someone who's eaten all these things describing the taste. First, draw their attention to the columns, which explain how the items were cooked and that describe the taste and texture of these things. Explain any new words.

- Play the recording for the students to match the dishes with the descriptions. Play it again if necessary. Then check answers with the class.

a) 5　b) 4　c) 2　d) 1　e) 6　f) 3

🌐 2.03 (I = Interviewer; M = Mark)

I:　Mark, you've tasted some of the more unusual dishes from around the world. Can you tell us about them and what they taste like?

M:　Yes, well, I've just come back from China where I ate cobra for the first time.

I:　Cobra? I imagine it tastes fishy.

M:　No, not at all. In fact tastes meaty, like chicken. It was a little tough and chewy, but delicious.

I:　Really? I find that hard to imagine.

M:　And before that I was in Thailand. I ate lots of fried grasshoppers there. They're really crisp and tasty.

I:　Hm. I'm not sure I'd like to eat insects.

M:　Well, that's because you're not used to them. In many parts of the world insects are a good source of protein and minerals. Last time I was in Indonesia, I had a feast of insects. In fact, for one meal, the main course was roasted cockroaches.

I:　What did that taste like?

M:　Well, they're crunchy on the outside, and on the inside there's a rich liquid which tastes quite sweet and fruity.

I:　What other insects have you eaten?

M:　While I was in Africa, I ate caterpillars. They boil them and dry them in the sun, so they taste a bit dry and bland. But they're really good for you.

I:　Oh.

M:　One of my favourite insects to eat is ants. Did you know that in Colombia, some cinemas serve roasted, chocolate-covered ants instead of popcorn?

I:　Really? What are they like?

M:　Sweet and crisp – like popcorn.

I:　Oh.

M:　What about you? Have you ever eaten anything unusual?

I:　Well, I'm not as adventurous as you, and I haven't travelled much. But the strangest, and, I must say, the most revolting thing I've ever eaten was in Scotland recently. It was deep-fried Mars Bar.

M:　What? You mean, like fish and chips – Mars bar and chips.

I:　That's right. Greasy and horribly sweet. Disgusting!

Extra activities

- Put the students into groups. One student thinks of a type of food and the others have to ask yes/no questions to find out what it is. For example, *Is it sweet? Do you fry it?* Students have a maximum of ten questions to find out what the food is. If they succeed, they get a point. If not, the person who chose the food gets a point.

- Ask the students to think of the most disgusting food combinations they possibly can. For example, chocolate-covered oysters in a spicy custard sauce. The class then vote on the most disgusting dish.

3

Put the students into pairs to discuss the questions. Ask them to report back to the class on what they found out.

Vocabulary & Speaking (SB page 43)
1

Remind the students of the words for ways of cooking food that they met in the previous section. Then go through the taste and texture words in the table, making sure that students can tell the difference. Texture has to do with the way something feels or looks, taste is simply how the tongue perceives it. Ask them to complete the table with taste and texture words from the previous section.

Ways of cooking food: boil, grill, bake, fry (deep-fry), roast
Ways of describing taste: bitter, salty, spicy, bland, sweet, fruity, disgusting, tasty, meaty, delicious
Ways of describing texture: creamy, dry, crunchy, greasy, crisp, tough, chewy

2

Pairwork. Go through the example sentences with the class, then ask students in pairs to take turns to describe one of the food items or guess what's being described.

3

Pairwork. Students take turns to describe their best and worst meals. Encourage them to report back to the class on what they found out.

Reading (SB page 44)

1

Ask the students if they know who Emma Bunton is. (See note below.) Ask them to skim the text quickly to find out the answers to the two questions. Then ask them to read the article more carefully. Point out that this is an interview and she uses quite a lot of slang. However, much of this is explained in the glossary.

> Favourite food: the classics – shepherd's pie, roast dinners, spaghetti bolognese
> Food she didn't like: peas

Cultural notes

Emma Bunton /ˈemə ˈbʌntən/ (born 1976)
Emma Bunton is an English pop singer, songwriter and actor. She is also a member of the 1990s girl group the Spice Girls in which, as the youngest, she was known as Baby Spice.

Shepherd's pie /ˈʃepədz paɪ/
A dish of minced lamb covered with mashed potato and topped with melted cheese. The same dish but made with minced beef is called a 'Cottage pie'.

Roast dinners
Roast dinners are the traditional meals that British people eat on Sundays. They consist of roast meat (beef, lamb, chicken or pork), potatoes and vegetables. Yorkshire pudding (which is made from flour, milk and eggs) is also traditionally served with roast beef. The meal is popular throughout Britain and Ireland, and also in Canada and Australia.

Spaghetti bolognese /spəˈgeti bɒləˈneɪz/
Spaghetti bolognese is the name used in Britain to describe a pasta dish which originally came from Bologna in northern Italy. The traditional dish is served with tagliatelle rather than spaghetti, and is served with a meat sauce (ragu alla Bolognese). This sauce is made with beef, pancetta, onions, carrots, celery, tomatoes and white wine. It's cooked very slowly.

2

Students decide which of the statements are true and which false. When checking answers, encourage the students to correct the false statements.

---

a) False. (Her mother would 'try' to cook well. Her father was a great cook.)
b) True.
c) True.
d) True.
e) False. (Restaurants were a treat.)
f) True.
g) True.
h) False. (On Saturdays they ate from trays in front of the TV.)
i) True.
j) True.

3

• Go through the example with the class, then ask them to change the other sentences to the first person.

• Check answers before asking the students to change the information so that it is true for them.

Grammar (SB page 45)

used to / would

1

• Focus the students' attention on the statements on page 44 and go through the table with them. Point out that in the examples, sentence a) matches description 2 (a state in the past), and sentence b) matches description 1 (a repeated action in the past). Ask them to match the remaining sentences with the descriptions.

• Go through the information about *used to* and *would* in the margin. Draw their attention to the correct form of *used to* in a question (*Did he use to?* not *Did he used to?*). Point out that sentence a) could be rewritten with *used to*: *Emma's mother used to be a better cook than her father.* Sentence b) could be rewritten with *used to*: *Her family used to enjoy eating new things,* or with *would*: *Her family would enjoy eating new things* (*enjoy* here is acts as an active verb). Explain that there's nothing wrong with the original sentences, but *used to* and *would* are ways of emphasizing the repeat nature of actions or states in the past. In f) *had* means *ate*, so it acts as an active verb. Also draw the students' attention to descriptions 3 and 4 where *used to* and *would* cannot be used.

> a) 2   b) 1   c) 3   d) 4   e) 1   f) 1   g) 1
> h) 1   i) 1   j) 4

Language notes

Grammar: *used to / would*
• You can use *used to* when you want to talk about past habits or states. It's always followed by the infinitive. It can't be used to talk about (1) something in the past which happened once, or (2) something which is still true. Compare: *We used to live in Singapore (but we don't now).*

(Past state.)

He used to smoke (but he doesn't now). (Past habit.)
We went to France last year. (Single action, so ~~We used to go to France last year.~~ is not possible.)

- The question form is *Did you use to…?* (not ~~Did you used to..?~~)

- You can use *would* to talk about repeated actions in the past. It often suggests a nostalgic reminiscence. *I'd spend hours with my friends by the river.*

- You can't use *would* to talk about past states.

- *would* is often contracted to *'d*.

- This use of *would* is less common in the question form.

2

- Do the first two with the class as examples and then ask the students to decide which sentences can be rewritten with *used to* and which with *would*.

- Check answers before asking the students to rewrite the sentences so that they are true for them.

> 1 = a), b), d), e), f), g), j)
> 2 = a), b), f), j)

3 Pairwork

- The pairwork exercise for this unit is on pages 117 and 122 of the Student's Book. Put the students in pairs and tell them who will be Student A, and who will be Student B.

- While they're doing the exercise, go round monitoring and giving help. Take note of any errors which may need particular attention later, and also any examples of good language use, which you can praise in a feedback session.

Cultural note

Nirvana /nəvɑːnə/
American grunge band active in the late 1980s and early 1990s. In 1994, lead vocalist Kurt Cobain committed suicide, bringing the band to a premature end at the peak of its popularity.

Speaking: anecdote (SB page 45)

For more information about how to set up, monitor and repeat Anecdotes, see page xx in the Introduction.

1 🌐 2.04

- Focus the students' attention on the photos of Julio. Explain that they're going to hear him talking about his life when he was a child between the ages of five and ten. Go through the questions with the class. Explain any unknown vocabulary. Point out again the form of *used to* in questions (*Did you use to …?*).

- Play the recording and ask the students to listen and find which two questions Julio doesn't answer.

- Ask the students to match the questions and answers. Then play the recording again for them to check their answers.

> He does not answer questions e) and f).
> a) 2   b) 4   c) 7   d) 8   e) –   f) –
> g) 1   h) 3   i) 9   j) 5   k) 6

🌐 **2.04**

There were five of us at home when I was growing up – my father, my mother, my brother, my sister and me. My mother did most of the cooking, but we all helped her. Well, sort of helped her. We each had a special job: I used to chop vegetables; my brother helped with the washing up; and my sister set the table. I used to love everything my mother cooked, except for one thing – meat. I didn't like it, and that made life difficult for my mother, because everyone else liked it. So she used to cook meat for everyone else, and a vegetarian meal for me.

Teatime was always really important in my house – I think it's because my mother is half English. We'd have tea and cakes at about four o'clock in the afternoon. My mother would invite the neighbours round, and we'd have a tea party! I used to love those times. My father would come home from work at about seven o'clock in the evening, and then we used to have our dinner in the kitchen. Then we would help to clear the table, and we'd be in bed by 8.30. The weekends were a bit different. Every Saturday, we used to go to the restaurant for dinner, and on Sundays we'd have pasta as a treat. My father is of Italian origin, so pasta was his favourite dish. My favourite dish when I was a child was rice and beans – it's a popular dish in Brazil, but nobody makes it like my mum.

2

- Give the students a minute or two to think back and decide what they're going to talk about. Then ask them to look at the questions in Exercise 1 again. Allow them to make notes of what they're going to say and how they're going to say it, but discourage them from writing a paragraph that they can simply read out. Go round, monitoring and giving help.

- Put the students in pairs and ask them to take turns to tell their partner about their life when they were a child. Encourage them to ask each other follow-up questions to get further information.

- Ask some pairs to report back to the class about what they found out.

Useful phrases (SB page 46)

1 🔘 2.05

Focus the students' attention on the illustrations, which show two different scenarios in a restaurant. Give the students time to take in what the illustrations show and to identify the differences between them. Play the recording and ask the students which picture best illustrates what they heard. Although neither of the speech bubbles shown in the pictures actually appears in the conversation, the students should be able to recognise from the speakers' intonation, if not the actual words, that the couple in the conversation are rude and unpleasant.

> The conversation goes with picture *a*.

🔘 2.05 (Wa = Waiter; M = Man; W = Woman)

Wa: Good afternoon. Do you have a reservation?
M: Yes. The name's Brown.
Wa: Oh, yes. Is this table OK for you?
M: No. We want to sit near the window.
Wa: Yes, of course. Follow me.

Wa: Are you ready to order yet?
W: No. Go away and come back a bit later.
Wa: Of course. Would you like to order some drinks?
W: Yes. Two gin and tonics.

W: Oy! Come here. We want to order now.
Wa: Very good. What can I get you?
W: Give me the lamb.
Wa: OK. And sir?
M: I want the grilled salmon steak.

Wa: Would you like to see the dessert menu?
W: No.
M: Bring me two coffees and the bill.
Wa: Certainly. How was your meal?
W: Good.

Language note

Grammar: *Would you like some ...?*
Note that in some circumstances it's possible to ask questions using *some* (generally when the speaker is confident of an affirmative response). In the restaurant the waiter asks *Would you like to order some drinks?* (rather than *Would you like any drinks?*) as he is confident of an answer in the affirmative.

2 🔘 2.06

- Tell the students that they're now going to hear another version of the conversation. Ask them to make a note of any differences they notice.
- Play the recording and get feedback from the class.

> The second version of the conversation is more polite.

🔘 2.06 (Wa = Waiter; M = Man; W = Woman)

Wa: Good afternoon. Do you have a reservation?
M: Yes, a table for two in the name of Brown.
Wa: Oh yes. Is this table OK for you?
M: Do you have anything near the window?
Wa: Yes, of course, follow me.

Wa: Are you ready to order yet?
W: Not quite. Could you give us a few more minutes?
Wa: Of course. Would you like to order some drinks?
W: Yes, two gin and tonics, please.

W: Excuse me. We're ready to order now.
Wa: Very good. What can I get you?
W: I'll have the lamb, please.
Wa: OK. And sir?
M: I'll have the grilled salmon steak.

Wa: Would you like to see the dessert menu?
W: No, I'm all right, thank you.
M: Can we have two coffees and the bill, please.
Wa: Certainly. How was your meal?
W: It was lovely, thank you.

3 🔘 2.07

Play the recording for the students to listen and repeat the phrases. After they've done this chorally, ask several students to repeat the phrases individually, and check that everyone is pronouncing them correctly.

🔘 2.07

a) *Excuse me. We're ready to order now.*
b) *Can we have two coffees and the bill, please?*
c) *Yes, a table for two in the name of Brown.*
d) *Yes, two gin and tonics, please.*
e) *I'll have the grilled salmon steak.*
f) *Do you have anything near the window?*
g) *No, I'm all right, thank you.*
h) *I'll have the lamb, please.*
i) *It was lovely, thank you.*
j) *Not quite. Could you give us a few more minutes?*

4

- Ask the students to work individually to put the phrases in the correct places in the conversation. Play recording 2.06 for them to check their answers before moving on to the next stage of the exercise.
- Put the students into pairs (or threes) and ask them to practise the conversation, taking turns to be the man, the woman and the waiter.

> 1 c   2 f   3 j   4 d   5 a   6 h (e)
> 7 e (h)   8 g   9 b   10 i

Vocabulary *Extra* (SB page 47)

Nouns and articles

1

- Focus the students' attention on the table and go through the examples with them. Tell the students to complete the 'noun type' column with the correct option from the box.
- Ask the students to copy the table into their notebooks. Then focus their attention on the list of nouns in the margin and the information about these words. Tell the students to complete the table using these nouns.

Noun type	Singular			Plural	
	no article	with *a/an*	with *the*	no article	with *the*
a) Countable nouns	*book* child index sheep	*a book* a child an index a sheep	*the book* the child the index the sheep	*books* children indexes sheep	*the books* the children the indexes the sheep
b) Uncountable nouns	*advice* behaviour knowledge research	*xxx*	*the advice* the behaviour the knowledge the research	*xxx*	*xxx*
c) Plural nouns	*xxx*	*xxx*	*xxx*	*jeans* clothes scissors trousers	*the jeans* the clothes the scissors the trousers

2

- Ask the students to look in their dictionary to see how it shows whether a noun is countable, uncountable or plural.
- Then ask students to use their dictionaries to classify the nouns in the box and to find out what they all have in common.

> They are all uncountable. (In many other languages these are considered countable)

3

Ask the students to read the dictionary entry in the margin. Then focus their attention on the five examples in the entry and ask them to add these examples under the correct heading in the table.

The person or thing has already been mentioned	The person or thing is known about	The person or thing is 'the only one'
She bought me some cake and some coffee, but the cake was stale.	Have you locked the door? I have to look after the children.	The sun was hidden behind a cloud. the best hotel in Paris

4

Ask the students to read through the poem first. Draw their attention to the questions on the right and ask them to complete the poem. Ask a volunteer student to read out the poem aloud to check. Then ask the students what happened to the young lady.

> 1 a   2 a   3 the   4 the   5 the   6 the
> 7 the

5

Ask the students to read the note in the margin. Then ask them to cross out *the* in the sentences if it isn't used to refer to people and things in a general way.

> a) The men are better drivers than the women.
> b) The life gets harder as you get older.
> c) The time is more important than the money.
> d) The women are more careful with money than the men.
> e) The children are getting fatter: they don't do enough exercise.
> f) It's impossible to live without the music.

Further practice material

Need more writing practice?
→ Workbook page 33
- Writing a letter of complaint.

Need more classroom practice activities?
→ Photocopiable resource materials pages 164 to 166
  Grammar: *Just a minute!*
  Vocabulary: *Best of the bunch*
  Communication: *Did you use to …?*
→ Top 10 activities pages xv to xx

Need DVD material?
→ DVD – Programme 5: *First date*

Need progress tests?
→ Test CD – *Test Unit 5*

Need more on important teaching concepts?
→ Key concepts in *New Inside Out* pages xxii to xxxv

Need student self-study practice?
→ CD-ROM – Unit 5: *Edible*

Need student CEF self-evaluation?
→ CEF Checklists pages xxxvii to xliv

Need more information and more ideas?
→ www.insideout.net

6 Time Overview

Section & Aims	What the students are doing
Speaking & Reading SB page 48 Fluency work; reading for detail	Talking about idioms and expressions to do with time. Reading and completing a questionnaire about time-keeping.
Grammar SB page 49 Prepositions of time	Choosing the correct prepositions in sentences about time. Identifying which sentences are true for them and their partner.
Vocabulary SB page 49 Time expressions	Following instructions to circle dates on a calendar. Talking about things they have done recently and things they plan to do in the future.
Pronunciation SB page 49 Ordinal numbers	Listening to and ordering groups of ordinal numbers, then dictating numbers to a partner. Practising saying dates and saying why they are important.
Reading SB page 50 Reading for detail	Talking about how you remember things. Reading a text about lists and matching people with photos.
Vocabulary SB page 50 Phrasal verbs	Replacing verbs in sentences with phrasal verbs and saying whether any of the sentences are true for them.
Grammar SB page 51 Modal verb structures	Completing explanations about the use of *must* and *should*. Writing sentences about priorities. Choosing the correct verb structures in a text about working from home. Completing a table about the uses of *have to, don't have to, must, mustn't* and *can*. Completing sentences with modal verbs.
Listening SB page 52 Listening for detail	Listening and comparing three people's working conditions. Marking sentences true or false. Replacing expressions with modal verb structures.
Vocabulary SB page 52 Work	Matching work expressions to definitions in sentences. Talking about ideal working conditions.
Writing SB page 53 Business letters	Completing sentences with phrases often used in business letters. Matching phrases and functions. Improving a letter of application.
Useful phrases SB page 54 Time idioms and expressions	Matching conversations to pictures. Inserting time expressions and idioms in conversations. Listening and repeating useful phrases. Writing and practising conversations.
Vocabulary *Extra* SB page 55 Words that are sometimes confused	Explaining the difference between *job* and *work*. Completing questions with *job/jobs* or *work*. Completing dictionary extracts with more words that are sometimes confused. Completing questions with appropriate words.
Writing WB page 39	Writing a letter requesting information.

6 Time *Teacher's notes*

Warm up
Ask the students about attitudes to time in their countries. Is it acceptable to be late for a business meeting? What about a dinner party? How late is acceptable? Is it acceptable to arrive early?

Speaking & Reading (SB page 48)

1

- Go through the sayings with the class and ask them what they think they mean.

- Find out if there are sayings about time in the students' language. If so, get them to write them on the board and then help them to translate them into English.

> a) The person who is earliest gets the best opportunities.
> b) It's best to act now (rather then wait).
> c) It's better to do something late than not to do it at all.

2

Focus the students' attention on the questionnaire. Explain that *time-keeping* means being on time, i.e. not late. Give the students time to read the questionnaire and decide on their own answers. Then put them into pairs and ask them to compare their answers. Finally, get them to look at the *What your score means* section and discuss whether they agree with the analysis or not.

3

Pairwork. Explain *waste of time*. Then ask the students to work in pairs and to decide on at least three activities which are a waste of time. Start them off with some ideas of your own. For example, blow-drying your hair when it's raining, asking children to keep their bedrooms tidy. Get them to report back to the class on their ideas.

Grammar (SB page 49)

Prepositions of time

1

- Go through the information in the margin. Point out that names of seasons are not spelt with capital letters, and make sure the students are clear about the difference between *on time* and *in time*. For example: *The train arrived on time. I got to the cinema just in time to see the film.*

- Go through the example with the class and then ask the students to choose the correct prepositions in the remaining sentences. Check answers before asking the students to discuss them in pairs.

> a) at   b) on   c) at   d) in   e) in
> f) in, on   g) during   h) on   i) during
> j) in

Language notes
Vocabulary: *in/at*
Note: you say *in the morning/afternoon/evening*, but *at night*.

2 Grammar *Extra* 6, Part 1

Ask the students to turn to *Grammar Extra* 6, Part 1 on page 136 of the Student's Book. Here they'll find an explanation of the grammar they've been studying and further exercises to practise it.

> **1**
> a) in   b) at   c) on   d) in   e) at   f) on
> g) In   h) on   i) in   j) at
>
> **2**
> a) during   b) during   c) for   d) for
> e) during   f) during   g) for   h) during

Vocabulary (SB page 49)

1

- Focus the students' attention on the planner. Go through the instructions carefully and make sure they understand *leap year* (see note on page 55) and *fortnight* (two weeks). Ask them what is special about February 14th. If students don't know, tell them that it's Valentine's Day.

- Tell the students to follow the instructions carefully, crossing out, underlining, circling and bracketing the days specified.

- Check answers and then check understanding by asking questions using today's date, such as *What day/date is the day after tomorrow/a week yesterday?* Students can then test each other.

Mon	Tue	Wed	Thu	Fri	Sat	Sun
		(1)	2	3	4̲	5̲
(6)	(7)	(8)	(9)	(10)	11	12
13̲	1̶4̶	15	⑯	17̲	⑱	(19)
20	21	㉒	㉓	24	25	26
27̲	28	2̶9̶				

Still free: 2nd , 3rd, 11th, 12th, 20th, 21st, 24th, 25th, 26th, 28th

Cultural notes

Valentine's Day (14th February)
St Valentine is the patron saint of lovers and on St Valentine's Day people send gifts and cards (often anonymously) to the ones they love.

Leap year
A leap year is a year containing an extra day to keep the calendar year synchronized with the astronomical year. Consequently, in the Gregorian calendar, February has 29 days (it usually has 28 days) every four years.

2

Pairwork. Students use the expressions in Exercise 1 to discuss some of the things they've done recently and their plans for the future.

Pronunciation (SB page 49)

1 🔘 2.08

- Focus the students' attention on the lists of ordinal numbers. Explain that ordinal numbers are used in dates and also to talk about the order of things, e.g. *He came fourth in the race*.

- Play the recording and ask the students to number the groups as they hear them. The first one is done for them. Then play the recording again and ask them to repeat the numbers. After they've done this chorally, ask several students to repeat the numbers individually, and check that everyone is pronouncing them correctly.

- Put the students into pairs and ask them to write the numbers in any order and then dictate them to each other. They should then check that their written versions match.

---

a) 4   b) 2   c) 1   d) 3

🔘 2.08

1	*fourth*	*fifth*	*first*	*second*	*third*
2	*first*	*fourth*	*fifth*	*third*	*second*
3	*fifth*	*first*	*fourth*	*third*	*second*
4	*first*	*second*	*third*	*fourth*	*fifth*

Extra activity

Divide the class into two teams. Write various ordinal numbers on the board and ask the teams to compete to be the first to draw a circle around the correct one as you read them out.

2 🔘 2.09

- Focus the students' attention on the first date and ask them how they think it should be said. Then ask them to work in pairs and decide how to say the remaining dates.

- Play the recording for them to check their answers. Then play it again for them to listen and repeat.

- Finally, ask the students to say why each date is important.

---

a) 14/02: the fourteenth of February.
   St Valentine's Day
b) 01/04: the first of April. April Fools' Day
c) 01/05: the first of May. May Day
d) 31/10: the thirty-first of October. Halloween
e) 05/11: the fifth of November.
   Guy Fawkes Night
f) 25/12: the twenty-fifth of December.
   Christmas Day

🔘 2.09

a) *The fourteenth of February*
b) *The first of April*
c) *The first of May*
d) *The thirty-first of October*
e) *The fifth of November*
f) *The twenty-fifth of December*

Cultural notes

April Fools' Day (1st April)
There is a tradition in the UK of playing practical jokes on April Fools' Day. These have to be done before midday. Even national newspapers sometimes get involved and print fake stories.

May Bank Holiday (1st May)
May Bank Holiday or May Day is a national holiday to celebrate workers. In the UK, it's celebrated on the first Monday in May.

Halloween (31st October)
Originally an Irish celebration, when on the evening of 31st October, the day before the Christian feast of All Saints, people would dress up in costumes to frighten evil spirits away. Halloween is now a popular celebration in the United States and in Britain. On the evening of 31st October, children dress up as witches and ghosts and play 'trick or treat'. They knock on their neighbours' doors to ask for treats such as sweets, or play tricks on the neighbours if they receive nothing.

Guy Fawkes /gaɪ fɔːks/ (5th November)
Guy Fawkes Night commemorates the discovery and prevention of a plot to blow up King James I and the Houses of Parliament in 1606. Guy Fawkes was one of the leaders of the gang which placed gunpowder under the Houses of Parliament. The conspiracy was discovered just in time. Bonfires are lit and fireworks set off on this night. Sometimes an effigy of Guy Fawkes is put on top of the bonfire.

Christmas Day (25th December)
Christmas Day is a religious holiday celebrating the birth of Jesus Christ. It's a national holiday in the UK. People normally spend the day with their family and exchange presents. They also eat a big meal, usually turkey, roast potatoes and vegetables, followed by a special Christmas pudding. Lots of people also have a Christmas tree in their house, which they decorate.

Reading (SB page 50)

1

Put the students into pairs to talk about how they remember the things they have to do. You could start them off by talking about your own methods.

2

- Give the students plenty of time to read the article. Answer any questions about difficult vocabulary and then ask them to match the people with the photos. They might find it helpful to underline the names in the text so that they can refer to them quickly.

- Check answers with the class and then get the students' reactions to the text. Ask them to say what their own lists are like.

Julie Rost – b	Des O'Brien – d
Jane Levy – c	Kerry Johns – a

Vocabulary (SB page 50)

1

- Focus the students' attention on the example. Point out that phrasal verbs that they need are all in the article in the previous section and that the line numbers are given so that they can find them easily.

- Ask the students to find the remaining phrasal verbs.

a) calms me down	d) coming up with
b) cross something off	e) put off
c) get by	f) rely on

Language note
Grammar: phrasal verbs
(See notes about phrasal verbs on page 35.)

2

Ask the students to read the sentences and decide whether they are true for them or not. Then ask them to compare with a partner.

Grammar (SB page 51)
Modal verb structures

1

- Focus the students' attention on the information in the margin on *must* and *should*. Read out the example sentences or ask several students to read them aloud. Ask them to look at the table and make sure they understand *urgent*. Point out that something can be important/not important and urgent, or important/not important but not urgent.

- Ask the students to complete the explanations with *must* or *should*. Allow them to compare with a partner before checking with the class.

- Ask the students to copy the table, leaving plenty of room for new sentences to be added in each category. As they write sentences, go round giving extra help where necessary and making sure that everyone has understood the difference between *must* and *should*.

- Put the students into pairs and ask them to tell each other about their priorities using *must* and *should*.

1 must	2 should	3 must	4 should
5 must	6 should		

Language notes
Grammar: modal verbs
- There are nine single-word modal verbs in English: *can, could, may, might, must, shall, should, will* and *would*. They don't take the third person *s*. (*He can ski* not ~~He cans ski~~.) They're followed by the infinitive. (*I must go* not ~~I must to go~~.) To make negatives add *not* or *n't*. (*I shouldn't* not ~~I don't should~~.) To make questions invert the subject with the verb. (*Could you help?* not ~~Do you could help?~~)
- Two-word modal verbs like *have to* and *need to* take the third person *s* and use the auxiliary *do* to form negatives and questions. (*Do you have to go?* not ~~Have you to go?~~ / *She needs to be here before four o'clock* not ~~She need to be here before four o'clock~~).

should/shouldn't
- In this unit, *should* is used to give advice – to say you think it's a good idea to do something. *I don't feel well. You **should** see a doctor / You **shouldn't** smoke.*

must/mustn't
- In this unit, *must* is used to give advice which is stronger and more authoritative than using *should*. *You **must** hand in your homework on time / You **mustn't** watch so much TV. It's bad for you.*

2 🌐 2.10

- Focus the students' attention back on the information in the margin on *has to* and *doesn't have to*. Explain that *have to* is similar to *must* in that it is used for things which are important or necessary. The negative form is used for things which are not necessary. In this, *have to* is different from *must* as the negative form of *must* (*mustn't*) implied prohibition rather than lack of necessity. Also look at the sentences with *can* and *can't* and explain that *can/can't* is used for permission.

- Go through the instructions and the example with the class, then ask them to read the text and choose the correct verb structures. Go round as they do this, offering extra help where needed.

- Play the recording for students to check their answers. Ask them to discuss other advantages and disadvantages of working at home in pairs.

1	don't have to	6	can
2	don't have to	7	must
3	don't have to	8	mustn't
4	can	9	can't
5	don't have to	10	have to

🌐 2.10

I love working from home. I don't have to drive to work, I don't have to sit in traffic, and parking is not my problem any more.

I don't have to get dressed in the morning – I can wear my pyjamas all day. In fact, I don't really have to get up in the morning! If I like, I can work all night. It's up to me.

There's nobody to tell me, 'You must be punctual. You mustn't make personal phone calls. You can't do your shopping online …'

There are only a couple of down-sides. I have to phone somebody if I want a chat or a gossip, and I can't blame anything on anybody else – I'm the only person here!

Language notes

have to/don't have to
- *Have to* is used to talk about necessity (i.e. that you're required to do something).
- *Don't have to* is used to talk about something which isn't necessary.
  *In Illinois motorcyclists **don't have to** wear a crash helmet (It isn't required by law, but motorcyclists can wear a helmet if they want to).*

can/can't
- *can* is used in this unit to talk about permission (i.e. what you are permitted to do). *Can I go home early today?* (i.e. is it permitted for me to go home early?) *No, you **can't**.* (i.e. you are not permitted).

3

Tell the students to refer back to the examples in the margin and the text in Exercise 2 to decide where the headings should go.

A: It's necessary	C: It's permitted
B: It's not necessary	D: It's not permitted

4

While the students are completing the sentences, go round checking that everyone is using the modal verbs correctly. Check answers before asking the students to say whether any of the sentences are true for them.

a)	don't have to	d)	mustn't
b)	have to	e)	can't
c)	had to	f)	could / couldn't

5 Grammar *Extra* 6, Part 2

Ask the students to turn to *Grammar Extra* 6, Part 2 on page 136 of the Student's Book. Here they'll find an explanation of the grammar they've been studying and further exercises to practise it.

1

	can	must	should
Affirmative	He can go.	He must go.	He should go.
Negative	He can't go.	He mustn't go.	He shouldn't go.
Question	Can he go?	Must he go?	Should he go?

	have to	need to
Affirmative	He has to go.	He needs to go.
Negative	He doesn't have to go.	He doesn't need to go.
Question	Does he have to go?	Does he need to go?

2

1	don't have to	6	don't have to
2	should	7	should
3	should	8	mustn't
4	mustn't	9	should
5	mustn't	10	don't have to

3

a) have to	b) must	c) must	d) have to
e) have to	f) must	

Listening (SB page 52)

1 🌐 2.11–2.13

- Focus the students' attention on the photos. Ask them to say what jobs they think the people do and what they think their working conditions are like.

- Play the recording for them to check their answers.

Job 1: lawyer
Job 2: journalist
Job 3: train driver

Job 1

I work in London for a big law firm. It's an American firm, and Head Office is in Washington DC, so I have to go to the States about once a month for meetings. Here in London, we're supposed to start work at nine, but I often start later and work until nine or ten o'clock at night. Unfortunately, we don't get extra money for working overtime. We have to dress smartly, so I always wear a suit and tie to work. Female lawyers aren't allowed to wear trousers or miniskirts. In London, we have to wear cloaks in court. Recently, Head Office brought in a new rule – we're not allowed to have relationships with people in the same company. I think it's ridiculous to ban office romance – where else are you going to meet somebody?

🔘 2.12

Job 2

This is the newsroom, where I work as a journalist. I'm actually responsible for foreign news. As you can see, we work in open-plan offices, so it can get quite noisy. We're allowed to work at home one day a week, so when I want to do some quiet work, I don't come into the office. We work flexible hours because news is coming in all the time. We're supposed to have a break every two hours, but when you're working to a deadline, you can't afford to take time for a break. Sometimes I work right through my lunch hour – it's mad really. In fact, you have to be mad to work here. As far as dress is concerned, we can wear anything we like.

🔘 2.13

Job 3

You have to be at least 21 to be a train driver, but you don't have to have any particular qualifications to get on a training course. I earn a good salary, but my job involves a lot of responsibility, and I work unsociable hours. I often work at night or at weekends and I'm supposed to work four or five shifts a week. You can't work a shift of more than twelve hours and you have to have twelve hours off between shifts. My job affects my social life, because I can't have a few drinks and go to bed late in the evening if I'm driving the next day. We have to wear a uniform and we're supposed to wear our hats all the time, but it gets a bit hot.

2

Read the sentences for each job aloud, one by one. Get the class to put their hands up if they think the sentence is true and keep their hands down if they think its false. Play the recording again for them to check their answers.

Job 1
a) False. (You don't get extra pay for working overtime.)
b) False. (Women aren't allowed to wear trousers.)
c) True.

Job 2
a) False. (They're allowed to work at home one day a week only.)
b) False. (We're supposed to have a break ever two hours.)
c) True.

Job 3
a) True.
b) False. (They have twelve hour shifts and work four to five shifts a week.)
c) True.

3

- Do the first one with the class as an example. Then ask the students to replace the remaining highlighted expressions. Make sure that they understand that their new sentences must have the same meaning as the original ones.

- Check answers with the class. Then ask the students whether they would like to do one of these jobs.

---

1 b) can   c) mustn't
2 b) shouldn't
3 c) should

Vocabulary (SB page 52)

1

Do the first one as an example with the class and point out that the expressions in the box are a much shorter way of saying the underlined phrases. Ask the students to replace the remaining underlined expressions.

---

a) unsociable hours   d) works flexible hours
b) open-plan office   e) qualifications
c) work to a deadline   f) shifts

2

Pairwork. Ask the students to take turns asking and answering the questions in Exercise 1, then discuss their ideal working conditions and report back to the class.

3 Pairwork

- The pairwork exercise for this unit is on pages 117 and 122 of the Student's Book. Put the students in pairs and tell them who will be Student A, and who will be Student B.

- While they're doing the exercise, go round monitoring and giving help. Take note of any errors which may need particular attention later, and also any examples of good language use, which you can praise in a feedback session.

Writing (SB page 53)

1

- Ask the students for examples of occasions when they might write a business letter (to apply for a job, to complain about something, to ask for information, etc.). Ask them to say what is special about the style of business letters (they're written in formal English).
- Ask the students to read the phrases and complete them with the words in the box. Check answers with the class and deal with any questions.

> a) Unfortunately   b) 16th May   c) enclose
> d) grateful   e) pleased   f) complain
> g) hearing   h) confirm   i) response   j) apply

Language note

Vocabulary: *flight attendant*

Flight attendant is a non gender-specific word, whereas the job title *air hostess* is gender-specific (female) and is regarded as quite old-fashioned these days. *Cabin crew* is a collective term for the team that help and serve the passengers on board an aircraft.

Cultural note

The Guardian /ðə ˈɡɑːdɪən/
The Guardian is a British newspaper, founded in Manchester in 1821. Its political position is centre-left and its daily circulation is 351,000.

2

Do the first one as an example, then ask the students to match the remaining phrases with their functions.

> 1 d   2 j   3 b   4 g   5 a   6 e   7 f
> 8 i   9 h   10 c

3

- Read the advertisement aloud to the class or get a student to do this. Then ask the students to read Antonia's letter. Give them plenty of time to do this. Tell them to focus on the style when they decide how suitable it is. Note: Worldwide airlines is a fictitious airline.
- Check answers and ask the students to identify which parts of the letter are too informal.

> Not suitable – too informal.

4

Ask the students to use the phrases in Exercise 1 to improve Antonia's letter. Point out that they'll have to make other changes to. For example, *Dear Mr or Mrs* isn't the correct way to open a letter. Elicit or explain that this should be *Dear Sir or Madam*.

156b East 49th Street
Santa Barbara
California

Worldwide Airlines Inc.
PO Box 2983
Chicago
Illinois

February 5th 2009

Dear **Sir or Madam**,

Application for the post of flight attendant

I **am writing in response to** your advertisement in the Morning Post and I **would like to apply for the position of** flight attendant.

I am 21 years old, and I have just graduated from university. I **enclose my curriculum vitae for your attention** and **I would be pleased to attend an interview at any time convenient to you.**

I would be grateful if you could send me an application form and some additional information about the job.

I look forward to hearing from you.

Yours faithfully,

Antonia Clifford

Antonia Clifford

Useful phrases (SB page 54)

1

Focus the students' attention on the pictures and give them time to take in what they show. Ask the students to read the conversations and match them with the pictures. Note: The Global Earth Party is a fictitious political party

> a) 2   b) 3   c) 1

2 🌐 2.14

- Go through the time expressions with the class and ask them to match the expressions with the underlined phrases in the conversations.
- Play the recording for them to check their answers.

> a) 6   b) 1   c) 3   d) 5   e) 7   f) 2
> g) 8   h) 4

> 🌐 2.14
> a)
> A: *We're making good time.*
> B: *Yes, hopefully we'll be there in time for dinner.*
> A: *Oh yes, I should think so. In fact, we may even have time to spare.*
> B: *Well, that's OK. If we have some time before dinner, we can go to the gym.*
> A: *The gym? I'd rather kill time in the mall!*

b)

The Global Earth party will put the environment at the top of the agenda. We've asked the same question time and time again: when will the government do something about global warming? We're running out of time – we need to act now. Vote for the Global Earth Party today!

(T = Teacher; C = Child)

T: *Come along children. Stop running. OK, one at a time. Ruben, stop pushing. Come on children, let's go back to class.*

C: *But we didn't have time to finish our game, Miss.*

T: *Yes, I know, time flies when you're having fun. But we have work to do.*

3 🔘 2.15

Play the recording for the students to listen and repeat the phrases. After they've done this chorally, ask several students to repeat the phrases individually, and check that everyone is pronouncing them correctly.

🔘 2.15

1 *We're making good time.*
2 *We'll be there in time for dinner.*
3 *We may even have time to spare.*
4 *I'd rather kill time in the mall!*
5 *We've asked the same question time and time again.*
6 *We're running out of time.*
7 *One at a time.*
8 *Time flies when you're having fun.*

4

- Pairwork. Ask the students to work with a partner and choose three expressions from Exercise 2. Tell them to write a short conversation including them.

- Ask the students to practise their conversations. Ask any particularly good pairs to perform theirs for the class.

Vocabulary *Extra* (SB page 55)

Words that are sometimes confused

1

Focus the students' attention on the box in the margin and ask them to read the information about the differences between the words *job* and *work*. Then elicit the key difference between these words.

---

job is countable and *work* is uncountable.

2

Ask the students to complete the questions with *job/jobs* or *work*. Then ask them in which sentences you can use both.

---

a) job   b) job/work   c) work/jobs   d) jobs
e) work   f) job

3

Focus the students' attention on the words in a) to g). Explain that these words are often confused. Ask them to read through the dictionary definition of these words in the margin and then complete the dictionary examples with the correct alternative. Go round monitoring and giving help.

---

a) actually; currently   e) lend; borrow
b) trip; travel   f) argue; discuss
c) career; course   g) missed; lost
d) fun; funny

4

- Ask the students to complete the questions with appropriate words from Exercise 3. Point out that they may need to change the grammar of the word.

- Then ask the students to ask and answer the questions in pairs.

---

a) argued   b) funny   c) trip   d) borrowed
e) travel   f) course   g) missed   h) lent
i) lost j) career

Further practice material

Need more writing practice?

→ Workbook page 39
- Writing a letter requesting information.

Need more classroom practice activities?

→ Photocopiable resource materials pages 167 to 169
   Grammar: *Rules and regulations*
   Vocabulary: *How well organised are you?*
   Communication: *Detectives*
→ Top 10 activities pages xv to xx

Need DVD material?

→ DVD – Programme 6: *The model agency*

Need progress tests?

→ Test CD – *Test Unit 6*

Need more on important teaching concepts?

→ Key concepts in *New Inside Out* pages xxii to xxxv

Need student self-study practice?

→ CD-ROM – Unit 6: *Time*

Need student CEF self-evaluation?

→ CEF Checklists pages xxxvii to xliv

Need more information and more ideas?

→ www.insideout.net

Review B *Teacher's notes*

These exercises act as a check of the grammar and vocabulary that the students have learnt in the Units 4–6. Use them to find any problems that students are having, or anything that they haven't understood and which will need further work.

Grammar (SB page 56)

Remind the students of the grammar explanations they read and the exercises they did in the *Grammar Extra* on pages 132 to 137.

1

This exercise reviews the position of pronouns with phrasal verbs from Unit 4.

> a) ✔
> b) ✗ I've used these boots so much I've worn <u>them</u> out ~~them~~.
> c) ✗ My brother was ill last week, and I had to look ~~him~~ after him.
> d) ✔
> e) ✗ Before you buy that shirt you should try <u>it on</u> ~~it~~.
> f) ✔

2

This exercise reviews future forms from Unit 4.

> a) 'll open
> b) 'm going to train
> c) 's meeting
> d) 'm going to stay in
> e) 'll try
> f) 's arriving

3

This exercise reviews *pronouns* from Unit 4. Check answers and then ask the students to practise the conversation in pairs.

> 1 everywhere   2 someone   3 anyone
> 4 no one   5 anything   6 nothing   7 nowhere

4

This exercise reviews *used to* and *would* from Unit 5. Check answers before asking the students to discuss in pairs which sentences are true for them.

> a) I used to have blond hair.
> b) ✔
> c) I didn't use to believe in ghosts.
> d) I used to love everything my mother cooked.
> e) ✔
> f) ✔

5

This exercise reviews prepositions in time expressions from Unit 6.

> 1 on   2 in   3 in   4 During   5 At   6 at
> 7 During   8 at   9 on   10 At   11 on
> 12 on

6

This exercise reviews modals of obligation and permission from Unit 6.

> a) should
> b) don't have to; can
> c) shouldn't
> d) can't
> e) mustn't
> f) must
> g) have to

7

This exercise reviews structures used in Units 4, 5 and 6.

> 1 a) ~~Have you got your coat? ... Put on it.~~
> 2 a) ~~I'm calling you tomorrow.~~
> 3 b) ~~How many time do we have?~~
> 4 a) ~~He would be very fat.~~
> 5 b) ~~She can to come anytime she likes.~~
> 6 a) ~~Sshh! You don't have to speak in here.~~

Vocabulary (SB page 57)

1

This exercise reviews phrasal verbs from Unit 4.

a) go on	d) got over
b) go off	e) are heading for
c) are putting on	f) join in

2

This exercise reviews collocations with *make* and *do* from Unit 4.

make:	do:
a mistake, a noise, a suggestion, a promise, a wish, money	the shopping, your homework, the ironing, some exercise, some research, the cooking

3

This exercise reviews party vocabulary from Unit 4.

1 invitation	4 mingle
2 fancy dress	5 guests
3 host	6 atmosphere

Cultural note

Frankenstein's Monster, the Bride of Frankenstein and Count Dracula

Frankenstein's monster was a character generally known in a book by Mary Shelley (1818) as the 'creature'. The Bride of the Frankenstein was a film by James Whale and not a character in the original book. Count Dracula is a character in a book by Bram Stoker (1897). They have since become standard horror characters in books and films.

4

This exercise reviews partitives from Unit 5.

a) bunch   b) bar   c) packet   d) box   e) jar
f) bowl

5

This exercise reviews words for ways of cooking, taste and texture from Unit 5.

(1) bake, (2) roast
(3) boil
(4) fry
(5) delicious, (6) tasty
(7) bland, (8) disgusting
(9) crisp, (10) crunchy
(11) creamy, (12) greasy

6

This exercise reviews time expressions from Unit 6.

Answers will vary according to today's date.

7

This exercise reviews work vocabulary from Unit 6.

1 rely   2 open-plan   3 unsociable   4 get
5 calms   6 put   7 make   8 shift

Pronunciation (SB page 57)

1

Remind the students that the boxes show the syllables of a word and the large boxes indicate the stressed syllables. Here they are being asked to classify words according to how many syllables they have and where the main stress falls. Encourage them to say each word aloud to get a feeling for what sounds right.

2 ● 2.16

Point out the main stresses in the example words, which are underlined. Ask the students to do the same for the other words in the table. Then play the recording for them to check their answers. Play it a second time for them to listen and repeat.

1 and 2		
A: ☐☐	**B:** ☐☐☐	**C:** ☐☐☐
cour<u>gettes</u>	ar<u>rang</u>ement	<u>au</u>bergine
de<u>gree</u>	ba<u>nan</u>a	<u>cin</u>ema
re<u>lax</u>	de<u>cis</u>ion	<u>cu</u>cumber
sar<u>dines</u>	per<u>miss</u>ion	<u>Jan</u>uary
week<u>end</u>	sug<u>gest</u>ion	<u>sau</u>sages

Reading & Listening (SB page 58)

1

- Focus the students' attention on the two photos and ask them what they think is happening in each one.
- Go through the questions with the class and ask them to read the descriptions quickly just to find the information to answer these questions.

a) Midsummer in Sweden is the older festival.
b) *Midsummer:* fish (herring or salmon), potatoes, strawberries and cream with cold beer or schnapps
Oyster Festival: seafood, pasta, salad, oysters with champagne or Guinness

Cultural notes

Galway, Ireland /ˈɡɔːlweɪ/
Galway is a city on the west coast of the Republic of Ireland with a population of 74,000. Galway has a great music culture and every July hosts an arts festival.

Guinness /ˈɡɪnɪs/
Guinness is a dry stout beer from the brewery of Arthur Guinness in Dublin, Republic of Ireland, first brewed in 1759. Its characteristics in the glass are a deep black body with a creamy white head of froth.

2

- Ask the students to read the descriptions more carefully and to decide whether the statements are true or false.
- When checking answers, encourage the students to correct the false statements.

> a) True.
> b) False. (It celebrates the middle of summer. Many people start their summer holidays on that day.)
> c) True.
> d) False. (Everyone goes to bed late on Midsummer Day as there is dancing all night long.)
> e) True.
> f) True.
> g) False. (People go to the festival from all over the world.)

3 🌐 2.17

Tell the students they are going to hear Carol talking to her friend Rob about what her family do at Christmas. Point out that they have to note down the food and drink for four different meals over the Christmas period. You may need to explain that Boxing Day is what people in the UK call the day after Christmas Day.

> *Christmas Eve:*
> fish (sometimes salmon), fruit dessert
> *Christmas Day (breakfast):*
> smoked salmon and champagne
> *Christmas Day (lunch):*
> turkey and Christmas pudding
> *Boxing Day (lunch):*
> cold meat and salad with fresh fruit

🌐 2.17 (C = Carol; R = Rob)

C: *What are you doing for Christmas this year? Are you staying here in London?*

R: *Oh, I don't know, actually.*

C: *Do you want to come and spend it in Somerset with my family?*

R: *Maybe. What are you planning?*

C: *Well, I'm going to take the day off and drive down on Christmas Eve, because Mum's having a little party. She always does. Everyone will be there – my brother, Ken, and his wife, Michelle, with their kids. And my sister, Di. My Grannie – she's 92 now! And my mum's sister, Betty, with all my cousins.*

R: *Oh, right.*

C: *Then, we'll have dinner together. Dad always used to make it, but since they split up, Mum does it. We always have fish, usually salmon or something, with a light fruit dessert. Then, before bed, we're allowed to open one present each, from under the Christmas tree.*

R: *We always used to do that too, when we were kids! Do you go to church on Christmas Day?*

C: *Yes, we get up early and go to church. Then we'll have a smoked salmon and champagne breakfast before we spend the morning opening presents. After that we have lunch. I think Ken is going to cook it again this year. He's a brilliant cook. We usually have turkey, followed by Christmas pudding – you know, the traditional stuff.*

R: *What about the afternoon?*

C: *Dad's coming over in the afternoon, with his new wife. I'm a bit worried about it actually. I don't know what Mum's going to say. She isn't too happy about it. But she had to invite him, and Christmas just wouldn't be the same without Dad.*

R: *Oh.*

C: *Anyway, in the afternoon we'll all stay at home and play games, or watch a film on TV and eat chocolates.*

R: *And are you coming home the next day?*

C: *You mean Boxing Day? No, I'm staying for that. We always have a big lunch with friends. We eat cold meat and salad for lunch, with fresh fruit. Then we go for a walk, if it's not too cold or wet. I'll come back the next day.*

R: *That sounds lovely, Carol. But I think I'll stay at home on my own.*

Cultural notes

Christmas Eve (24th December)
Christmas Eve is the day before Christmas Day and signals the beginning of the Christmas holiday.

Christmas Day (25th December)
(See notes about Christmas Day on page 56.)

Christmas pudding
A cake made with dried fruit, nuts and alcohol, usually steamed in a bag and eaten on Christmas Day. It's a popular Christmas Day dessert in the UK.

Boxing Day (26th December)
Boxing Day is the day after Christmas Day and is also a national holiday in the UK, Canada, New Zealand and Australia. Traditionally, less fortunate members of society were given boxes of charitable gifts on this day, hence the name.

4

Go through the statements with the students before playing the recording again. Ask them to underline as much correct information as they can before they hear the conversation again. Then play the recording for them to check their answers and underline the correct information in the remaining statements.

> a) mum
> b) dad
> c) go to church
> d) has remarried
> e) stay at home
> f) the day after Boxing Day

Writing & Speaking (SB page 59)

1

Pairwork. Ask the students to read the notes. Then work with a partner and match the notes with the questions.

> a) 4   b) 2   c) 5   d) 6   e) 1   f) 3

2

Ask the students to read the text and match the different sections of the text with the questions in Exercise 1.

> a) Mardi Gras takes place …
> b) It's a big carnival, …
> c) Mardi Gras officially starts …
> d) Mardi Gras has been celebrated …
> e) In the two weeks just before 'Fat Tuesday' …
> f) People eat all kinds of rich food …

3

• Tell the students that they're going to write an account of a festival their partner has been to. Ask them to decide on a festival they have been to which they will describe to their partner.

• Then put the students in pairs to talk about their festivals. Encourage them to ask each other questions to find out as much detail as they can, and to write the answers about their partner's festival in note form.

4

Remind the students that they can use the text in Exercise 2 as a model and point out how the notes in Exercise 1 have been expanded to make a coherent text. As they write their paragraphs, go round giving extra help where needed.

> **Further practice material**
>
> **Need more classroom practice activities?**
> → Photocopiable resource materials page 170
>   🌐 2.18 **Song:** *It's My Party*
> → TOP 10 activities pages xv to xx
>
> **Need progress tests?**
> → Test CD – *Test Review B*
>
> **Need more on important teaching concepts?**
> → Key concepts in *New Inside Out* pages xxii to xxxv
>
> **Need student self-study practice?**
> → CD-ROM – *Review B*
>
> **Need more information and more ideas?**
> → www.insideout.net

7 News *Overview*

Section & Aims	What the students are doing
🔘 **Listening SB page 60** Listening for specific information	Discussing celebrities in the news. Listening to an interview with a paparazzo and choosing sentences which match his views. Discussing the issue of photographing celebrities.
Grammar SB page 61 Verb patterns	Completing sentences with verbs. Completing a table of verb patterns. Choosing the correct verb patterns in sentences.
Vocabulary SB page 61 Adjectives	Completing sentences with adjectives.
Reading & Vocabulary SB page 62 Reading for gist; crime vocabulary	Matching news stories with headlines. Completing sentences with words from news stories. Completing three more news stories.
🔘 **Pronunciation SB page 63** Past participle endings	Listening and repeating past participle endings. Putting past participles in a table according to their pronunciation.
Grammar SB page 63 Passives	Rewriting sentences in the passive. Examining the structure of the passive. Rewriting newspaper extracts in the passive.
Reading & Listening SB page 64 Reading for detail; listening for gist	Matching photos to headlines and predicting the content of news items. Matching words with meanings. Listening and matching radio news items to headlines. Writing a radio news story.
Reading & Writing SB page 65 Reading for specific information; writing an email	Completing an email. Answering questions on the content of the email. Writing a reply to the email.
🔘 **Useful phrases SB page 66** Useful conversational phrases for personal news	Matching conversations with pictures. Choosing appropriate responses to personal news. Classifying phrases as positive or negative responses. Listening to pieces of good and bad news and responding appropriately.
Vocabulary *Extra* SB page 67 Verb patterns	Completing common verb patterns. Choosing the correct verbs in sentences. Completing a joke with *say* or *tell*. Completing questions with the appropriate verb.
Writing WB page 45	Writing an essay.

Warm up

Ask the students if they've ever seen anyone famous. If so, who did they see? Where were they? What were they doing? Did they take photos?

Listening (SB page 60)

1

- Focus the students' attention on the photo. Ask them what they can see and who they think the celebrity is.

- Go through the questions with the class. Explain the term *paparazzi* if students are unfamiliar with it. (See note below.) Either ask the students to discuss the questions in pairs or have a class discussion.

Cultural note

Paparazzi

The paparazzi are photographers who take photos of celebrities, often in private or compromising situations. The (plural) name *paparazzi* is taken from Paparazzo, a character (news photographer) in the Italian film *La Dolce Vita* (Federico Fellini, 1960), who rode around on a scooter in Rome, taking photos of the rich and famous.

2 🌐 **2.19**

- Tell the students they're going to listen to an interview with Jack, a paparazzo, and that first they should predict what his views are. Go through the statements and ask them to underline *OK* or *not OK* according to what they think Jack will say.

- Play the recording for them to check their ideas. Then ask them to discuss in pairs whether or not they agree with Jack.

> a) OK   b) OK   c) OK   d) not OK
> e) OK   f) not OK   g) not OK

> 🌐 **2.19** (I = Interviewer; J = Jack)
>
> I: *People are increasingly obsessed with reading stories and looking at photographs of celebrities. Today there are more paparazzi on the street than ever, all of them trying to get the definitive celebrity photo. We talk to Jack, a paparazzo with fifteen years' experience, about his job. Jack, thank you for joining us.*

> J: *You're welcome.*
>
> I: *Jack, why are people so interested in reading about the private lives of celebrities?*
>
> J: *Because they're young, beautiful, rich and photogenic and they lead glamorous lifestyles.*
>
> I: *But the photos that appear in the tabloid press are not always glamorous. They're often unflattering photos of celebrities just trying to lead their lives. For example, I remember seeing a photo of Matt Damon getting a parking ticket. What's so interesting about that?*
>
> J: *Well, people also want to think that these celebrities are just normal people, so they enjoy seeing photos of them doing ordinary things like shopping. I also think it's fine to take unflattering photos of them because it gives us hope when we realise that they're just like us really!*
>
> I: *I understand that, but where do you draw the line?*
>
> J: *Well, we're not completely insensitive. We try not to involve children. For example, Kate Moss asked us not to take photographs of her daughter, and we haven't. Do you remember seeing photos of her daughter in the press?*
>
> I: *No, but I did read an interview with Kate Moss, where she said that she can't walk anywhere because the paparazzi follow her everywhere. That must be awful. In the same interview, she said that a female photographer was chasing her in New York and fell over a water hydrant. She cut her lip and was bleeding, so Kate stopped to ask her if she was OK. The woman just continued taking photographs! That's a bit desperate, isn't it?*
>
> J: *The woman was just doing her job. Listen, so many of these celebrities refuse to cooperate with the paparazzi. We try reasoning with them. We explain that we don't want to upset them, but they shout and swear at us. So we follow them everywhere. It's a game. Have you ever seen a bad photo of Nicole Kidman in the press?*
>
> I: *Er, no.*
>
> J: *That's because she plays the game. She always agrees to smile for the camera, and we get our shot. Then we leave her alone. If you ask me, I think these celebrities are hypocritical. On the one hand they need to have their photos in the press, and on the other hand they tell us that we're invading their privacy. If they don't like the attention, I suggest that they change jobs.*

Grammar (SB page 61)

Verb patterns

1

Ask the students to complete the sentences using the verbs in the box.

> a) enjoy   b) asked   c) explained   d) agrees
> e) tell

Cultural notes

Kate Moss /keɪt mɒs/ (born 1974)
Kate Moss is an English model. Her 'waifish' looks and her height were unusual for a supermodel when she first came on the scene. Since then she has attracted publicity for her high profile relationships and lifestyle.

Nicole Kidman /nɪkɒl ˈkɪdmən/ (born 1967)
The Australian actress Nicole Kidman has made countless films, such as *The Others* and *Moulin Rouge*, and won an Oscar for the film *The Hours* in 2002. She was married to the film star Tom Cruise for eleven years. In 2006 she married country singer Keith Urban. They have a daughter, Sunday Rose Kidman Urban.

2

Focus the students' attention on the table. Point out that certain verbs follow certain patterns. Go through the headings of the table and point out the example sentences in the margin. Explain that *sth* is short for *something* and *sb* is short for *somebody*. Ask the students to complete the table with the verbs in the box in Exercise 1. Then ask them to make some example sentences of their own with each verb pattern. Go round, monitoring and giving help.

> 1 enjoy   2 agree   3 explain   4 ask   5 tell

Language notes

Grammar: verb patterns
Different verbs can be followed by different structures. In unit 7, five different patterns follow a selection of verbs. The same verbs can occur in different patterns. This usually, but not always, changes the meaning of the sentences.

- verb + *ing* form
  Many of the verbs connected with enjoyment (*enjoy, like, don't like, love, hate, can't stand, detest, mind, don't mind*, etc.) take this form, e.g. *I love playing tennis, but I don't really like watching it.* Other common verbs that take this form include: *avoid, deny, fancy, involve, miss, understand.*

- verb + *to*-infinitive
  In this unit we see the verbs *need, promise, try, want* and *agree*. Other common verbs include: *arrange, decide, forget, learn, manage, prepare* and *start*, e.g. *Oh, no! I forgot to lock my car.*

- verb + *that*
  In this unit we see the verbs *realise, say, suggest, think* and *explain*. Other common verbs used with this pattern are *believe, feel, know, see* and *show*, e.g. *I know that he's an honest person and I feel that he's telling the truth.*

- verb + *somebody* + (*not*) *to*-infinitive
  In this unit we see the verbs *ask, tell* and *warn*. Other common verbs used with this pattern are *allow, force, invite, persuade* and *remind*, e.g. *I finally persuaded Tim not to go to Australia.*

- verb + *somebody* + *that*
  In this unit we see the verbs *warn* and *tell*. Other common verbs used with this pattern are *advise, promise, remind* and *show*, e.g. *Kate reminded me that I owe her £50.*

3

- Go through the example with the class and make sure everyone is clear that in each sentence two of the verbs are correct and one is not.
- Check answers with the class before asking the students to discuss in pairs who they think made each statement.

> a) said   b) enjoy   c) tell   d) suggested
> e) tell   f) don't mind; explain
>
> A paparazzo said statements c), e) and f).
> A celebrity said statements a), b) and d).

Vocabulary (SB page 61)

1

Explain to the class that the words in the box are adjectives which are often used when talking about celebrities and photography. Ask them to use the adjectives to complete the sentences.

> a) obsessed   b) unflattering   c) insensitive
> d) hypocritical   e) photogenic   f) desperate

2

Ask the students to discuss in pairs whether any of the sentences in Exercise 1 are true for them.

Reading & Vocabulary (SB page 62)

1

- Focus the students' attention on the news stories and the accompanying photos. Ask them to match the stories with the headlines.
- Check answers and point out that newspaper headlines are rarely full sentences. They seek to encapsulate in a few words the main features of the story. Ask the students to say which stories they like best and encourage them to give reasons for their answer.

1 b – POLICE THEFT	4 f – KIND JUDGE
2 a – DON'T ASK	5 c – KIDNAPPED
3 d – SLOW LANE	6 e – UNFIT TO GUARD

Cultural notes

Liverpool
A city in northwest England with a population of 440,000. Liverpool is best known as the home of The Beatles and Liverpool F.C. People from Liverpool are called Liverpudlians or, more informally, Scousers. In 2008 it held the title of European Capital of Culture along with Stavanger, Norway.

FBI
Based in Washington DC, the FBI (Federal Bureau of Investigation), formed in 1908, is a US Government agency responsible for investigating crime and gathering intelligence for the US Department of Justice.

M4 motorway
The M4 motorway links London, England with Wales. The 305 km motorway crosses the River Severn via a toll bridge.

Texas
Texas is the second largest US state in both area and population. It has a population of 24 million and the state capital is Austin. Texas joined the United States as the 28th state in 1845. Until then it had been part of Spain's colony of Mexico. The discovery of oil in the early 20th century led to an economic boom in the state.

2

Ask the students to use the highlighted words in Exercise 1 to complete the sentences.

a) police officer	d) judge
b) traffic police	e) convicted thief
c) 'wanted' list	f) fugitive

3

Students complete the stories with the words in the box. Check answers by asking several students to read out their completed stories. Answer any questions on difficult vocabulary.

1 thief	2 arrested	3 chase	4 traffic police
5 escorted	6 court	7 stolen	8 burglar

Pronunciation (SB page 63)

1 🌐 2.20

- Focus the students' attention on the table. Explain that the words are all past participles, formed by adding *ed* to the stem of the verb, and that there are three different ways of pronouncing the endings.
- Play the recording and ask the students to listen and repeat the verbs. After they've done this chorally, ask several students to repeat the words individually, and check that everyone is producing the sounds correctly.
- Ask the students if the statement under the table is true.

It is true.

🌐 2.20

/t/:   asked   based
/d/:   believed   called
/ɪd/:   arrested   decided

Language notes

Pronunciation: *ed* endings
- The *ed* ending on regular past simple verbs ending in /t/ or /d/ is pronounced with an extra syllable (/ɪd/). For example: *started, waited, ended*.
- For all other regular past simple verbs there's no extra syllable. After unvoiced sounds: /k/, /p/, /f/, /s/, /ʃ/ and /tʃ/, *ed* is pronounced /t/. For example, *stopped, walked, watched*. After voiced sounds, *ed* is pronounced /d/. For example, *arrived, changed, used*.

2 🌐 2.21

- Focus the students' attention on the verbs in the box. Read each one aloud, asking the students to give the past participle form. They should then add them to the correct column of the table in Exercise 1.
- Play the recording for the students to check their answers and then ask them to listen and repeat.

ed = /t/:	ed = /d/:	ed = /ɪd/:
asked	believed	arrested
based	called	decided
checked	described	expected
escaped	involved	needed
forced	named	reported
stopped	used	treated

🌐 2.21

/t/: checked   escaped   forced   stopped
/d/: described   involved   named   used
/ɪd/: expected   needed   reported   treated

Grammar (SB page 63)

Passives

1

- Focus the students' attention on the example sentences in the margin and explain that the passive is formed with the verb *be* + a past participle. Remind them that they looked at various past participles in the previous section. Tell them that the passive is often used in newspaper articles.

- Ask the students to work individually to rewrite the sentences in the passive. Discourage them from looking back at the news stories on page 62 until they've had a go at rewriting all the sentences. When they've finished, allow them to compare with a partner.

- Check answers and review the way the passive is formed. Point out that all passive sentences in this exercise demonstrate different tenses. If the students find it helpful, get them to identify what the tenses are (a) past simple passive b) past continuous passive, c) present perfect passive d) past perfect passive. Then ask them to find and underline other examples of passive structures in the news stories on page 62. See if they can identify the tenses.

> a) A television set was stolen.
> b) He was being treated for asthma.
> c) We have been kidnapped.
> d) It had been put there by four unhappy children.
>
> It is formed by combining *be* + past participle.
>
> *Other examples from exercise 1:*
> was arrested; was stopped; was escorted;
> was being pushed; was sentenced; were involved;
> was spotted; have been embarrassed;
> *Other examples from exercise 3:*
> was arrested; were involved in

Language note

Grammar: passives
You use the passive when the person, people or thing that does an action isn't important.

Compare: *This bridge was built in 1750* with *Someone built this bridge in 1750.*

It's natural to want to make the bridge the subject of the sentence (as in the first example) and by using the passive this is achieved. It's formed with the verb *be* in the correct form (*will be, is/are going to be* to talk about the future; *is/are (being)* or *has been* to talk about the present; *was/were* or *had been* to talk about the past) + the past participle.

2

Ask the students to look at the sentences they wrote in Exercise 1. Read the explanations aloud and ask the students to put their hands up if they think they're correct. When they all reach agreement, they can tick them.

> a) ✔   b) ✔   c) ✔

3

- Read the example with the class. Explain or get the students to identify that the passive sounds more natural in this sentence because the 'doer' of the action (the Oscar committee) is obvious and doesn't need to be mentioned.

- Ask the students to rewrite the remaining sentences. As they work, go round giving extra help where needed.

- Check answers by getting several students to read out their sentences. Ask them which of the stories sounds most interesting to them. Lead a class discussion on the kinds of news stories that people find interesting.

> b) The troubled film star is being treated for 'exhaustion' at Meadows Rehabilitation Centre in Arizona.
> c) The singer's long-awaited album has been released to rave reviews.
> d) The hostages were released last night and they are on their way home to their relieved families.
> e) Interest rates will be reduced by 1% before the end of the year according to most financial observers.
> f) The fashion industry has been accused of encouraging young girls to go on starvation diets.

Cultural note

The Academy Awards
The Academy Awards (more commonly known as The Oscars) were designed to recognise excellence in the film industry. First held in Hollywood in 1929, the Academy Awards ceremony is watched around the world every February/March.

4 Pairwork

- The pairwork exercise for this unit is on pages 118 and 123 of the Student's Book. Put the students in pairs and tell them who will be Student A, and who will be Student B.

- While they're doing the exercise, go round monitoring and giving help. Take note of any errors which may need particular attention later, and also any examples of good language use, which you can praise in a feedback session.

Questions:

Student A:

a) Have you ever been burgled?

b) Have you ever been stopped and searched by customs?

c) Have you ever been let down by a friend?

d) Have you ever been mistaken for somebody else?

e) Have you ever been asked to make a speech?

f) Have you ever been told that you look like somebody on TV?

Student B:

a) Have you ever been injured playing a sport?

b) Have you ever been bitten by a snake?

c) Have you ever been given a present you didn't like?

d) Have you ever been invited to a fancy dress party?

e) Have you ever been interviewed on radio or TV?

f) Have you ever been given too much change in a shop?

5 Grammar *Extra* 7

Ask the students to turn to *Grammar Extra* 7 on page 138 of the Student's Book. Here they'll find an explanation of the grammar they've been studying and further exercises to practise it.

1

a) arrested, invented, jailed, murdered – Rule: add *ed*

b) accused, created, produced, prosecuted – Rule: add *d*

c) classified, identified, tried, copied – Rule: replace *y* with *ied*

d) acquitted, banned, kidnapped, mugged – Rule: double the consonant and add *ed*

e) built, grown, made, stolen – Rule: irregular

Verbs used to describe crime: arrested, jailed, murdered, accused, prosecuted, identified, tried, acquitted, banned, kidnapped, mugged, stolen
Verbs used to describe processes: invented, created, produced, classified, copied, built, grown, made

2

a) was written, directed and produced – Past simple (In a newspaper report / on a poster)

b) are requested; engines have been switched off – Present simple; present perfect (On a plane)

c) is now being served – Present continuous (In a canteen / in a diner / on a ship / in a school)

d) is strictly prohibited – Present simple (In a zoo)

e) must be submitted – *must* modal (On an application form / on a web page)

f) cannot be held – *can't* modal (In a public building / offices / a cinema / a theatre)

g) to be taken – Infinitive structure (On a prescription label)

3

a) My mother was born / wasn't born …

b) She was brought up / wasn't brought up …

c) She was educated / wasn't educated …

d) She was taught / wasn't taught …

e) She was awarded / wasn't awarded …

f) She was married / wasn't married …

g) She has been employed / hasn't been employed …

4

a) by Indians

b) by anybody

c) by the brain

d) by French people

e) by people

f) by people

g) by anybody

h) by King Camp Gillette

5

a) I was given money …

b) I'm being shown around …

c) I'm not paid …

d) I've been sent …

e) I was taught …

f) I'm told …

Cultural notes

Stephen Spielberg /ˈstiːvən ˈspɪəlbɜːg/ (born 1946) Award-winning American film director and producer, Spielberg is one of the most influential people in the film industry. Spielberg directed his first hit film (*Jaws*) in 1975. Throughout the 1980s he had continued success with *E.T.* (1982) and the *Indiana Jones* films, and into the 1990s with *Schindler's List* (1993), *Jurassic Park* (1993) and *Saving Private Ryan* (1998).

The Statue of Liberty, New York
The statue was a gift to the people of America from France to commemorate the centennial of the United States. It was completed in Paris in 1884 and stands on Liberty Island, at the mouth of the Hudson River in New York Harbour.

Reading & Listening (SB page 64)

1

• Tell the students they're going to listen to some more news stories. First they have to match the headlines to the photos.

• Go through the headlines with the class and point out the abbreviated form of the headlines, e.g. short punchy words, the lack of articles, the use of the present simple instead of the past or present perfect, and the use of the *to* infinitive instead of the *going to* future. Explain that this is typical newspaper style and is done for impact and space reasons.

• When you've checked the answers, ask the students to predict what each story is about. You could ask them to suggest some vocabulary they'd expect to see in each item. Also ask them to say which one they'd read first.

a) 2   b) 4   c) 6   d) 5   e) 3   f) 1

Extra activity

Ask the students to rewrite the headlines in
Exercise 1 as full sentences. Accept any which are
grammatically correct and make sense.

2

- Explain that newspaper headlines tend to use short,
  dramatic words to catch people's attention. Ask
  the students to match the underlined words in the
  headlines with the phrases.

- Check answers. Then ask students if there are any
  similar stories in today's news. If there are, encourage
  them to tell the stories, giving as many details as
  possible.

a) hits	b) to wed	c) quits	d) row
e) soar	f) cash	g) bars	h) jobless
i) probe	j) talks		

3 🌐 2.22

Tell the students they're going to hear a radio broadcast
which covers the same stories as the newspaper
headlines in Exercise 1. Ask them to listen and match
the news items to the headlines. Ask them to say if their
predictions about the stories were correct.

a) 2	b) 5	c) 1	d) 3	e) 4	f) 6

🌐 2.22

And here are the news headlines.

a)
Robert Holmes, Minister for the Environment,
has resigned. The Prime Minister has ordered an
investigation into the mysterious disappearance of a large
sum of money. A spokesman for the Minister told us that
he was out of the country and not available for comment.

b)
The total number of unemployed people in Britain has
increased significantly. The opposition has called for the
government to provide more jobs for school-leavers.

c)
Peace negotiations have ended after an argument broke
out between delegates. According to our reporter at the
conference, delegates were unable to agree on the order
of matters to be discussed.

d)
A freak hailstorm has severely damaged fruit harvests
in eastern regions of Spain. Meteorological experts have
reported hailstones the size of footballs.

e)
Schoolgirl, Pauline Gates, has not been allowed back
into school after the summer holidays because she has
had her nose pierced. According to headmistress, Jean
Bradley, Paula knew that piercing was against the
school rules. The girl will be allowed back into school
when she removes the offending nosering.

f)
And finally, to end on a happier note, wedding bells are
ringing for 81-year-old Max Williams, who won
£16 million in the lottery last month. He is going to
marry 22-year-old dancer, Sally Lister. The happy
couple posed for photographers outside the millionaire's
luxury home in Essex, and Sally held out her hand to
show off her £10,000 engagement ring for the cameras.

4

- Pairwork. Ask the students in their pairs to choose
  one of the headlines and to brainstorm ideas for
  what the story might be. Go round giving help where
  needed and encourage the students to be creative
  with the details they make up.

- Then ask them to write their stories as radio news
  reports. They may want to present them with a
  newsreader, who introduces the story initially, and an
  on-the-spot reporter, who supplies extra details and
  the latest updates on the story. Go round helping with
  structure and style. Make a note of any particularly
  good stories. Then ask the pairs to deliver their news
  broadcasts to the class.

Reading & Writing (SB page 65)

1

Encourage the students to read through the whole email
first, ignoring the gaps. Then ask them to complete the
email with the words in the box.

1 great	2 sorry	3 pleased	4 Well
5 Actually	6 news	7 heard	8 apparently
9 let	10 Apart	11 forward	12 Anyway
13 touch	14 getting		

2

Ask the students to read the email again and answer the
questions.

a) Pia	b) Ian	c) Ian	d) Pia
e) Anna and Giorgio		f) Giorgio	

3

- Pairwork. Go through the skeleton email with the
  class and ask the students to suggest ideas for what
  Ian might say in reply to Pia.

- They then work with their partner to write Ian's
  reply. As they work, go round giving extra help
  where needed. Encourage them to be creative in their
  explanations of what happened to Giorgio.

Useful phrases (SB page 66)

1

Focus the students' attention on the pictures. Ask the students to read the eight conversations and decide which two match the pictures. Tell them to ignore the alternative expressions for now. Ask them to give reasons for their answers.

> Picture a: conversation 6
> Picture b: conversation 3

2 2.23

- Explain that each conversation shows people responding to either good or bad news. Ask the students to read them again and underline the appropriate responses.

- Play the recording for them to check their answers.

> a) Oh, I'm sorry to hear that.
> b) Well done!
> c) You lucky thing!
> d) Oh no, that's terrible!
> e) Oh, congratulations!
> f) How annoying!
> g) Oh, that sounds interesting.
> h) How exciting!

> 2.23
>
> a)
> A: *How's Shirley?*
> B: *Actually, we've split up.*
> A: *Oh, I'm sorry to hear that.*
> B: *It's OK. Um, this is Sandra.*
>
> b)
> C: *Hello. You're looking very pleased with yourself.*
> D: *I am! I've just passed my driving test!*
> C: *Well done! Was it your first time?*
> D: *No, my sixth.*
>
> c)
> E: *Guess what! I've won a holiday to Florida.*
> F: *You lucky thing! Is it a holiday for two?*
> E: *Yes, I'm taking my mum.*
> F: *Oh.*
>
> d)
> G: *You don't look very happy.*
> H: *No, I've just got my exam results. I've failed them all.*
> G: *Oh no, that's terrible! What happened?*
> H: *I didn't do any work.*
>
> e)
> I: *Have a glass of champagne!*
> J: *Thank you. What are you celebrating?*
> I: *My wife's just had a baby.*
> J: *Oh, congratulations!*

> f)
> K: *You don't usually take the bus!*
> L: *No – my car's broken down again.*
> K: *How annoying!*
> L: *I know. But it is twenty-five years old.*
>
> g)
> M: *What did you do last night?*
> N: *I watched a documentary about snow leopards.*
> M: *Oh, that sounds interesting.*
> N: *Yes, unfortunately I fell asleep halfway through.*
>
> h)
> O: *What are you up to today?*
> P: *I'm having my first sailing lesson.*
> O: *How exciting! Are you nervous?*
> P: *I am actually. I can't swim.*

3 2.24

- Ask the students to put the useful phrases into the table, according to whether they are positive or negative responses.

- Play the recording for them to check their answers. Then play it again for them to listen and repeat. Encourage them to match the speaker's intonation for each phrase.

Positive responses	Negative responses
Well done!	Oh, I'm sorry to hear that.
You lucky thing!	Oh no, that's terrible!
Oh, congratulations!	How annoying!
Oh, that sounds interesting!	
How exciting!	

> 2.24
>
> **Positive responses**
> *Well done!*
> *You lucky thing!*
> *Oh, congratulations!*
> *Oh, that sounds interesting!*
> *How exciting!*
>
> **Negative responses**
> *Oh, I'm sorry to hear that.*
> *Oh no, that's terrible!*
> *How annoying!*

4 2.25

- Tell the students that they're going to hear several pieces of news. They should listen to each, decide if it's good news or bad news and respond appropriately.

- Play the recording, pausing after each piece of news to allow the students to respond. You could either ask all the students to respond to each piece of news (although their responses may vary) or select a different student each time.

Suggested answers
a) Congratulations!
b) How annoying!
c) How exciting! or You lucky thing!
d) You lucky thing!
e) Oh, that sounds interesting.
f) Oh no, that's terrible!
g) You lucky thing!
h) Oh, I'm sorry to hear that / Oh no, that's terrible!
i) Well done! or Congratulations!

🌐 2.25

a) *We got engaged last week.*
b) *My internet's down again.*
c) *I'm going snowboarding for the first time at the weekend.*
d) *I've just won £1,000 on the lottery.*
e) *I'm reading Nelson Mandela's autobiography.*
f) *My wallet's been stolen.*
g) *My mum's going to give me her car.*
h) *I think my boyfriend might lose his job.*
i) *I passed all my English exams.*

Vocabulary *Extra* (SB page 67)

Verb patterns

1

- Ask the students to complete the verb patterns with *ask*, *explain*, *say* or *tell*. Allow them to work with a partner if you wish. Then tell the students that they can check their answers by looking at the dictionary extracts in the margin.
- When they've finished, ask them which two verbs nearly always have a person as a direct object.

a) explain   b) ask   c) explain   d) say
e) tell   f) ask   g) tell   h) ask   i) ask
j) ask

ask, tell

2

Ask the students to underline the correct option in the sentences. Then tell them to check their answers by looking at the dictionary extracts in the margin.

a) said   b) tell   c) say   d) tell, said
e) Tell, said   f) told

3

Ask the students to read through the joke first before they complete it with *say* or *tell*. Remind them that *tell* is nearly always followed by a person as the direct object.

1 said   2 tell   3 said   4 tell   5 tells
6 tells   7 tells   8 tell

4

- Remind the students to look at the dictionary extracts for *ask*, *explain*, *say* and *tell* to help them to complete the questions.
- Ask the students to ask and answer the questions in pairs.

a) told   b) said   c) told   d) explained
e) asked   f) said   g) asked   h) explained
i) said   j) told

5

Ask the students to look at the extracts for *ask*, *explain*, *say* and *tell* in their own dictionaries. Then ask them what example sentences they have in their dictionaries for these words.

Further practice material

Need more writing practice?

→ Workbook page 45
- Writing an essay.

Need more classroom practice activities?

→ Photocopiable resource materials pages 171 to 173
   Grammar: *It's happened to me!*
   Vocabulary: *A true crime story*
   Communication: *Making news*
→ Top 10 activities pages xv to xx

Need DVD material?

→ DVD – Programme 7: *Paparazzi*

Need progress tests?

→ Test CD – *Test Unit 7*

Need more on important teaching concepts?

→ Key concepts in *New Inside Out* pages xxii to xxxv

Need student self-study practice?

→ CD-ROM – Unit 7: *News*

Need student CEF self-evaluation?

→ CEF Checklists pages xxxvii to xliv

Need more information and more ideas?

→ www.insideout.net

8 Journey *Overview*

Section & Aims	What the students are doing
Reading SB page 68 Reading for specific information	Discussing reasons for going travelling. Reading an extract from a novel and marking statements true or false.
Speaking SB page 68 Fluency practice	Making a list of places they have travelled to. Describing the locations of places and discussing when and why they travelled there.
Reading & Vocabulary SB page 69 Reading for specific information; location	Matching an extract from *The Beach* to a photo and marking statements true or false. Completing descriptions of places. Talking about places in their country.
Listening SB page 70 Listening for gist	Identifying locations in photos, then listening to people discussing photos and numbering them in order. Identifying features in photos.
Grammar SB page 71 Modals of deduction	Completing explanations of the use of modals of deduction. Matching countries with statistics and writing sentences saying how they deduced which was which.
Pronunciation SB page 71 Geographical features	Listening to and repeating the names of mountains, rivers, continents and oceans, and marking the stress. Putting geographical features in a table according to their size.
Reading & Listening SB page 72 Reading for detail; listening for gist	Reading about a motorbike trip across the US and answering questions. Listening to the end of the story and commenting on what happened.
Vocabulary SB page 72 Fixed expressions	Studying fixed expressions which use pairs of words. Completing fixed expressions in sentences.
Grammar SB page 73 Past perfect	Studying the form and use of the past perfect. Completing sentences with the past perfect to make a story.
Speaking: anecdote SB page 73 Fluency practice	Talking about a journey they have been on.
Useful phrases SB page 74 Useful conversational phrases for asking for directions	Reading and listening to a conversation and answering questions. Completing useful phrases, then listening and repeating them. Rewriting questions using less direct language, then asking questions and giving directions from where they are now to various places.
Vocabulary *Extra* SB page 75 Dictionary labels	Matching dictionary labels with their definitions. Giving appropriate dictionary labels as headings. Identifying public notices and where you might see them. Rewriting sentences from American English into British English and saying if they are true for them.
Writing WB page 51	Writing a description.

8 Journey *Teacher's notes*

Warm up

Write on the board: *It is better to travel than to arrive.* Ask the students what they think this means and if they agree that the journey someone makes can be more enjoyable than arriving at their destination.

Reading (SB page 68)

1

- Go through the list of reasons for going travelling and ask the students to discuss in pairs whether they've ever travelled for one of these reasons. Point out that *to go travelling* is different from *to travel* and implies a longer journey, perhaps to more than one country, undertaken for a reason that goes beyond simply wanting to reach a given destination.

- Ask the students to make a list of other reasons they can think of to go travelling. Then have a class feedback session on what they pairs came up with.

2

- Ask the students if they have read *The Beach* by Alex Garland or have seen the film. (See note below.)

- Ask the students to skim-read the extract and say why the author went travelling. Point out the footnotes with the difficult vocabulary under the text.

> He was running away because he was depressed about splitting up with his girlfriend.

Cultural note

The Beach
The Beach (1996) is Alex Garland's first novel. It tells the story of Richard, a young man travelling in Thailand who is given a map, which leads him to a secret and secluded beach on a forbidden island. Here he finds a community of fellow travellers living a seemingly utopian existence in harmony with nature. Life there seems ideal until tragedy strikes and the dream turns into a nightmare.

3

- Ask the students to read the extract again more carefully and to decide whether the statements are true or false. When checking answers, encourage them to correct the false statements.

- Have a class discussion on whether travel can help you escape from your problems.

a) False. (It was in Greece.)
b) True.
c) True.
d) False. (He left England by plane.)
e) False. (England became meaningless the moment he got on the plane.)

Language note

Vocabulary: *lend* and *borrow*
You *lend* someone something and you *borrow* something from someone. In the extract on page 68, he *borrows* some money from his father (= his father *lends* him some money).

Speaking (SB page 68)

1

Pairwork. Ask the students to make a list of places they have travelled to in pairs. These could be either in their own country or abroad.

2

- Focus the students' attention on the ways of describing where a place is in the box. Ask for a few examples of where places are using these expressions and write the students' suggestions on the board. Then ask them to choose five places from their list and think about how to describe where they are, using the expressions in the box. Allow them to make brief notes if they wish.

- Ask the students to tell each other about where they've travelled to, saying when they went there and why. Go round giving help and encouragement. Encourage the pairs to report back to the class.

Extra activity

You could get the students to list all the places they have been alphabetically and see how many have been to the same place. Try to find one place for each student where nobody else has been. For example:

ABC	Country/Region/ City	Student Name
A	Austria	Maria
B	Brussels	David, Eva, Toni
C	Catalonia	Eva, Maria

Reading & Vocabulary (SB page 69)

1

- Ask the students to look at the three photos of beaches and to say whether they've ever been to any beaches like these. Ask which one they'd most like to visit and encourage them to give reasons.

- Tell the students that they're going to read another extract from the novel *The Beach*. Ask them to read it quickly and decide which of the photos it describes.

> Photo b)

2

Go through the statements with the class, then ask the students to read the extract again more carefully and decide whether they are true or false. When checking answers, encourage the students to correct the false statements.

> a) False. (The lagoon is hidden from the sea by a wall of rock.)
> b) True.
> c) True. (The travellers fish but they don't use dynamite, so the beach is unspoilt.)
> d) True.
> e) False. (The island has jungle all around it rather than forests.)
> f) False. (The visitors are a select community of travellers. *Select* suggests a small number.)

3

Pairwork. Tell the students to work together to complete the two descriptions using the words and expressions in the box. When they've finished, check answers and ask them which description matches which photo in Exercise 1.

> 1 white sands   6 overlooking
> 2 beach community   7 sandy
> 3 popular with tourists 8 hidden
> 4 southern   9 surrounded by
> 5 spectacular views 10 sun loungers
>
> Bondi Beach: photo b)
> Portinatx Beach: photo a)

4

- Go through the list with the class and make sure that they understand all the items.

- Pairwork. Ask the students to discuss places in their city or country that match the descriptions in the list in pairs. Go round giving help and encouragement. Ask some students to give their descriptions to the class.

Listening (SB page 70)

1 🌐 2.26

- Focus the students' attention on the photos and ask them to discuss in pairs where they think they are. Then ask the students to report back to the class, giving reasons for their decisions. Do not confirm or deny anything at this stage.

- Play the recording for the students to check their ideas. Find out if anyone got any of the places correct. Then play the recording again and ask the students to number the photos in the order they are mentioned.

> *Probable answers:*
> a) Argentina   b) Singapore
> c) Vietnam   d) Thailand
> 1 c   2 b   3 d   4 a

> 🌐 **2.26** (A = Amy; J = Joe)
>
> A: *Have you heard from Conrad lately? Is he still going round the world?*
>
> J: *Yes, lucky thing. He's in South America now – I had a message from him yesterday.*
>
> A: *How's he getting on?*
>
> J: *He's having a great time – here, come and have a look at the photos on his web page.*
>
> A: *Oh, great.*
>
> J: *Right – here we are.*
>
> A: *Oh wow! Look at those waterfalls. Where is that?*
>
> J: *Well, he hasn't put the name of the place, but I suppose it could be Vietnam.*
>
> A: *Or it could be India.*
>
> J: *No, it can't be India, because he hasn't been there. I'm pretty sure it's Vietnam. I know he went trekking in the hills there.*
>
> A: *Oh, I'd love to go to Vietnam.*
>
> J: *Mm, me too. Now this one must be Singapore. Look at that skyline – it's so built-up.*
>
> A: *Or it could be Hong Kong.*
>
> J: *No, he didn't go to Hong Kong, but I know he stopped off in Singapore.*
>
> A: *Ah. Wow, look at these statues. They look really old. Is it a Buddhist temple?*
>
> J: *Yes, I think so. That's probably Thailand. He was there for the New Year.*
>
> A: *Lucky man. Now this is different – I didn't know Conrad could ride a horse.*
>
> J: *He can't – I don't think that's him.*
>
> A: *So where is this then?*
>
> J: *I'm not sure, but it's probably southern Argentina.*
>
> A: *Oh look here's a good one. What is he doing?!*

2

- Go through the items in the box and make sure everyone understands them. Then ask them to match them with the photos in Exercise 1.
- Check answers with the class before asking the students to work in pairs and discuss whether they can see any of these things in their own countries.

> a) grasslands, snow-capped mountains
> b) built-up skyline, high-rise buildings
> c) forests, waterfalls
> d) ancient ruins, Buddhist temples

Grammar (SB page 71)

Modals of deduction

1

- Focus the students' attention on the explanations and remind them that they heard two people in the last section discussing where photos might have been taken. Explain that you use *must*, *may/might/could* and *can't* to indicate how certain you are that things are true or not true.
- Focus the students' attention on the examples in the margin. Point out that the second sentence uses *can't* to express certainty that something is not true. You cannot use *mustn't* in this situation.
- Ask the students to complete the explanations with *must* or *can't*.

> a) must   c) can't

Language note

Grammar: modals of deduction

- When you are not 100% sure of something, the best you can do is make deductions based on the information you have. The language necessary to make these deductions is a group of modal verbs: *must*, *can't*, *might*, *may* and *could*. As with all modal verbs, there is no *-s* in the third person singular and each modal verb is followed by the main verb in the infinitive, without *to*.
- To express the greatest degree of certainty use *must* with a positive sentence (i.e. *I'm sure it is*) and *can't* with a negative sentence (i.e. *I'm sure it isn't*). For example: *Jane looks very tired today: She must be ill / She can't be well.*
- To express possibility use *may/might/could*. For example: *Jane might have a cold.*
- The choice of language indicates the level of certainty the speaker feels given the information available.

2

- Focus the students' attention on the table and point out that these are descriptions of countries, but that the names of the countries are missing. They have to look at the information and decide in each case which country they think it refers to. The countries are all in the box, but there are four names they won't need. Ask them to work individually to make their decisions.
- When they have completed their tables, ask them to discuss their ideas in pairs. Then ask them to write sentences to show how they decided. Go through the example with the class and point out that the writer has used *must* because he or she is certain that Brazil is the correct answer. Encourage them to use all the verbs in their sentences, not just *must*. Go round giving extra help where needed.
- Finish by asking the students to discuss in pairs whether or not they have been to any of the countries listed.

> a) Spain   b) Portugal   c) Brazil
> d) Mexico   e) Argentina   f) Angola

Cultural notes

Angola /æŋˈɡəʊlə/
Angola is a republic in south-west Africa with a population of 16 million. It borders Namibia to the south, the Republic of the Congo to the north, Zambia to the east and the Atlantic Ocean to the west. Portuguese is the official language.

Mozambique /məʊzæmˈbiːk/
Mozambique is a republic bordering on the Indian Ocean in south-eastern Africa, It lies north of South Africa and south of Tanzania, with Zambia and Zimbabwe to the west. Portuguese is the official language.

3 Grammar *Extra* 8, Part 1

Ask the students to turn to *Grammar Extra* 8, Part 1 on page 140 of the Student's Book. Here they'll find an explanation of the grammar they've been studying and further exercises to practise it.

> **1**
> a) 3   b) 6   c) 5   d) 2   e) 1   f) 4
>
> **2**
> a) You must be really cold.
> b) You must be joking.
> c) Your keys can't be far away.
> d) You might not enjoy the film.
> e) You must know who she is.
> f) It can't be far from here.
> g) You might meet the love of your life.
> h) She can't be that old.

Pronunciation (SB page 71)

1 🌐 2.27

- Ask the students to look at the words in the box and say what they are (names of rivers, mountain ranges, continents and oceans. Play the recording and ask the students to listen and repeat the names. After they've done this chorally, ask several students to repeat the names individually, and check that everyone is pronouncing them correctly.

- Then ask the students to underline the stressed syllables. Remind them that they can check the stress on any word by looking in their dictionary.

> the <u>A</u>mazon   the <u>An</u>des   An<u>tar</u>ctica
> <u>A</u>sia   At<u>lan</u>tic   the <u>Dan</u>ube   <u>Eu</u>rope
> the Hima<u>lay</u>as   <u>In</u>dian   the <u>Nile</u>   Pa<u>ci</u>fic
> the Pyre<u>nees</u>

Cultural notes

The Amazon /ði: ˈæməzən/
The Amazon River is the largest river (by volume) in the world and could be up to 7,000 km long. It flows through Bolivia, Brazil, Colombia, Peru and Venezuela.

The Andes /ði: ænˈdiːz/
The Andes is the longest mountain range in the world, running along the length of the western side of South America for 7,000 km. The average height of the range is 4,000 m and it runs through Argentina, Bolivia, Chile, Colombia, Ecuador, Peru and Venezuela.

Antarctica /æntˈɑːktikə/
Antarctica is the Earth's southernmost continent and is 98% covered in ice. It is home to penguins, seals and many varieties of Antarctic gull.

The Danube /ði: ˈdænuːb/
The Danube is the second longest river in Europe after the Volga. It flows through ten countries (Austria, Bulgaria, Croatia, Germany, Hungary, Moldova, Romania, Serbia, Slovakia and Ukraine) for 2,850 km.

The Himalayas /ði: hɪməˈleɪjəs/
The Himalaya Range sits between Bhutan, India, Nepal and the Tibetan region of China. Its highest point is Mount Everest (8,874 m), the highest point on Earth.

The Nile /ði: ˈnaɪəl/
The Nile is the longest river in Africa and possibly the longest river in the world (6,650 km). It flows south to north through ten African countries (Burundi, Congo, Egypt, Eritrea, Ethiopia, Kenya, Rwanda, Sudan, Tanzania and Uganda).

The Pyrenees /ði: pɪrəˈniːz/
The Pyrenees are a range of mountains that form a natural border between France and Spain. At their highest point they are 3,400 m high. They are 430 km long and run between the Bay of Biscay and the Mediterranean Sea.

2 🌐 2.28

- Focus the students' attention on the table and point out that in each category, the example which is the biggest, longest, etc. should be at the top of the column and the example which is the smallest, shortest, etc. should be at the bottom. Ask the student to decide where each of the things in the box in Exercise 1 should go in the table.

- Play the recording for the students to listen, check their answers and repeat the words.

	Continents	Mountain ranges	Oceans	Rivers
+	Asia	the Himalayas	Pacific	the Nile
↓	Antarctica	the Andes	Atlantic	the Amazon
−	Europe	the Pyrenees	Indian	the Danube

Reading & Listening (SB page 72)

1

Ask the students to read the article quickly to find out what problems Nick Campbell had.

> His motorbike broke down three times.

Cultural notes

Harley-Davidson /ˈhɑːli ˈdeɪvɪdsən/
Harley-Davidson Motor Company is a motorcycle manufacturer based in Milwaukee, Wisconsin, USA. It was founded in 1903 by William S Harley and Arthur Davidson (and Arthur's brothers Walter and Will). Harley-Davidsons are used by many US police forces. It was once the world's largest motorcycle manufacturer. The average age of a Harley rider these days is 47 years old.

Miami /maɪˈæmi/
Miami is a port city in Florida, USA, with a population of just over five million. In 2008 the city was ranked as the cleanest city in the United States.

Atlanta /ætˈlæntə/
Atlanta is the capital of Georgia (the US state that lies to the north of Florida) and has a metropolitan population of over five million.

Kansas /ˈkænsəs/
Kansas is a state in the centre of the United States with a population of 2.7 million. Named after the Kansa tribe of native Americans, Kansas entered the Union in 1861. The main industry in Kansas is agriculture.

Denver /ˈdenvə/
Denver City is the capital of the US state of Colorado and has a metropolitan population of 2.5 million. Denver is surrounded by mountains with the Rocky Mountains to the west and the High Plains to the east.

San Francisco /sæn frənˈsɪskəʊ/
A west coast US city founded in 1776 by Spanish settlers and named after Saint Francis of Assisi, San Francisco experienced rapid growth during the California Gold Rush in 1848. In 1906 an earthquake devastated the city, but it was quickly rebuilt, and has become a popular tourist destination as well as being home to 750,000 residents.

2 🌐 **2.29**

- Pairwork. Ask the students to read the text again more carefully and discuss the questions. The first three questions only require them to scan the text for the answers. The fourth question requires more thought and discussion. Encourage them to think of several reasons why the mechanic said what he did. Get them to report back to the class on their ideas and write all the suggestions on the board.
- Play the recording and ask the students to listen to the full story. Then have a class discussion on whether the mechanic was fair and how they think Nick felt.

> a) $600
> b) $2,000
> c) $3,000
> d) The bike had belonged to Elvis Presley. There was an engraving on the underside of the seat saying 'To Elvis. Love James Dean'.

🌐 **2.29**

Coast to coast

Nick Campbell sat at the side of the road and wondered what to do next. He looked at the second-hand Harley Davidson he'd bought from a back-street garage in Miami at the beginning of his trip six weeks before.

For years he had dreamt of crossing the United States from east to west by motorbike and he'd finally decided that it was now or never. He'd given up his job, sold his car and set off for the journey of his dreams. He'd been lucky, or so he thought, to find this old Harley Davidson and had bought it for a very reasonable price – it had cost him just $600. But five kilometres from Atlanta, he had run out of luck. The motorbike had broken down.

He pushed the bike into town and found a garage. The young mechanic told him to leave the bike overnight and come back the next day. The following morning, to his surprise, the man asked if the bike was for sale. 'Certainly not,' he replied, paid his bill and hit the road.

When he got to Kansas the old machine had run out of steam again. This time Nick thought about selling it and buying something more reliable, but decided to carry on. When the bike was going well, he loved it.

However, in Denver, Colorado the bike broke down yet again, so he decided to take it to a garage and offer it for sale. The mechanic told him to come back in the morning.

The next day, to his amazement, the man offered him $2,000. Realising the man must be soft in the head, but clearly not short of money, Nick asked for $3,000. The man agreed, and they signed the papers. Then the mechanic started laughing. In fact it was several minutes before he could speak, and when he could he said, 'That's the worst deal you'll ever make, boy.'

The mechanic removed the seat. Engraved on the underside was the inscription, 'To Elvis. Love James Dean.'

Cultural notes

Elvis Presley /ˈelvɪs ˈprezliː/ (1935–1977)
An American singer, musician and actor, Elvis Presley is known as 'The King' (of Rock and Roll). The teenage Presley got his break in 1953. Over the next two decades he became an international star with recordings like *Jailhouse Rock* (1957), *It's Now or Never* (1960) and *Suspicious Minds* (1969). From 1973, Presley's health declined. He put on weight and became increasingly dependent on prescription drugs. In 1977, he died of a heart attack at the age of forty-two.

James Dean /dʒeɪmz diːn/ (1935–1955)
James Dean was an American film actor and cultural icon of the 1950s. He played the roles of a troubled teenager. His most famous films were *East of Eden* (1955), *Rebel Without a Cause* (1955), and *Giant* (1956). His death at an early age in a road accident guaranteed him legendary status. He received two posthumous Oscar acting awards.

Vocabulary (SB page 72)

1

Focus the students' attention on the extract from the article and ask them to decide what the underlined expression means. Explain that there are several fixed expressions in English that involve pairs of words.

> b)

2

- Put the students into pairs and ask them to complete the sentences and try to complete them with the words in the box.

- When checking answers, make sure everyone understands the expressions. Use dictionaries to check, if necessary. Then ask them to say whether or not the sentences are true for them.

> a) take   b) peace   c) clean   d) give
> e) Sooner   f) all   g) come

Grammar (SB page 73)

Past perfect

1

Ask the students to look at the diagram of Nick Campbell's route and answer the questions.

> a) (five kilometres from) Atlanta
> b) Miami
> c) Denver, Colorado

2

- Focus the students' attention on the extracts and ask them to write the names of the cities where the events happened.

- Point out the use of the past perfect in extracts b), c) and d) and its form, *had* + past participle. Ask the students why they think this tense is used, or explain to them that this tense used to look back at a past event from another, more recent, point in the past.

- Focus the students' attention on the sentences in the margin. Point out that in the first one, the first part is in the past simple and that the second part is in the past perfect and describes something even further back in the past.

> a) Atlanta   b) Miami   c) Miami   d) Miami
> e) Kansas   f) Denver
>
> Because the events that happened in Miami happened before all the other events described.

Language note

Grammar: past perfect
You use the past perfect when you're talking about the past and want to talk about something that happened before the time you're speaking about. It's formed with *had* + past participle.

3

- Pairwork. Ask the students to work in pairs to complete the sentences with the past perfect and make a story.

- While they're doing this, go round monitoring and giving help. Make sure everyone is forming the past perfect correctly and using it appropriately. Then ask several pairs to read their stories to the class.

> *Possible answers:*
> a) … he'd never been there before / he'd always wanted to see the Kremlin / he'd enjoyed his last trip so much.
> b) … his alarm clock hadn't gone off / he'd had to get his children ready for school / he'd woken up late.
> c) … there had been an accident / the traffic lights had stopped working / it had rained and the roads were wet.
> d) … all the other seats had been taken / he hadn't managed to pre-book.
> e) … the plane hadn't arrived / the plane had developed a fault / the pilot had fallen ill.
> f) … he hadn't said goodbye to his wife / he hadn't locked his car / he hadn't packed any underwear.

4 Pairwork

- The pairwork exercise for this unit is on pages 118 and 123 of the Student's Book. Put the students in pairs and tell them who will be Student A, and who will be Student B.

- While they're doing the exercise, go round monitoring and giving help. Take note of any errors which may need particular attention later, and also any examples of good language use, which you can praise in a feedback session.

> **Student A:**
> a) were flying   i)   had been
> c) was having   k)   had put
> e) was leaving   m)   located
> g) realised   o)   had broken
>
> **Student B:**
> b) came out   j)   was
> d) asked   l)   'd stored
> f) closed   n)   managed
> h) 'd locked   p)   was cruising

Cultural note

Nairobi /naɪˈrəʊbi/
With a population of around 4 million, Nairobi, the capital of Kenya is around eight and a half hours flying time from London.

5 Grammar *Extra* 8, Part 2

Ask the students to turn to *Grammar Extra* 8, Part 2 on page 140 of the Student's Book. Here they'll find an explanation of the grammar they've been studying and further exercises to practise it.

1

1 *All forms the same:* bet – bet – bet; burst – burst
   – burst; cost – cost – cost; hurt – hurt – hurt; let
   – let – let; shut – shut – shut; split – split – split;
   spread – spread – spread

2 *Two forms the same:* dig – dug – dug; feed – fed
   – fed; fight – fought – fought; mean – meant
   – meant; shine – shone – shone; slide – slid
   – slid; stick – stuck – stuck; win – won – won

3 *All forms different:* drink – drank – drunk; fly
   – flew – flown; ring – rang – rung; rise – rose
   – risen; shrink – shrank – shrunk; sing – sang
   – sung; sink – sank – sunk; swim – swam
   – swum

2

a) I'd had breakfast …
b) I'd read …
c) I'd travelled …
d) I'd done the shopping …
e) I'd passed my driving test …
f) This lesson had started …

Using the past perfect changes the order in which
the actions occur. The action in the past perfect
happened before the action in the past simple.

3

Students' own answers.

Speaking: anecdote (SB page 73)

For more information about how to set up, monitor and
repeat Anecdotes, see page xx in the Introduction.

1 2.30

- Focus the students' attention on the photo. Explain
  that they're going to hear Suzi talking about her visit
  to this place. Go through the questions and answers
  with the class. Explain any unknown vocabulary.

- Play the recording and ask the students to listen and
  cross out the wrong information in the answers.

- Ask the students to correct the information, then play
  the recording again for the students to check their
  answers.

> a) ~~Dead~~ (It should be the Red Sea.)
> b) ~~Christopher's~~ (It should be Catherine's.)
> c) ~~diving~~ (It should be windsurfing.)
> d) ~~big van~~ (It was a mini-van.)
> e) ~~and windy~~ (There was no wind.)
> f) ~~seven~~ (There were eight tourists.)
> g) ~~three~~ (It took two hours.)
> h) ~~sea~~ (She looked at the scenery.)
> i) ~~food~~ (She bought a necklace.)
> j) ~~own car~~ (She would do it in a hired car in her
>   own time.)

 2.30

*I once went on a trip through the Sinai desert in
Egypt, from the Red Sea to a historical place called
St Catherine's Monastery. I was actually on a
windsurfing holiday with some friends in a small
resort called Dahab. It's a perfect place for water
sports, but one day, the weather was useless for
windsurfing – basically, there was no wind at all.
My friends decided to go diving, but I don't like
being under the water, and
I hate sunbathing. So I signed up for a trip to
St Catherine's Monastery.*

*We left the hotel at about 10 a.m., and the weather
was just beginning to get hot. There were ten of us
in a minivan including eight tourists, one guide
and one driver. Fortunately, the minivan was
air-conditioned. The guide spoke five languages,
so during the trip, he told us the history of the
monastery in English, Spanish, French and German.*

*The journey took about two hours, and as we drove
through one of the driest deserts in the world, I just
stared out of the window at the wonderful scenery.
The sandy colour of the mountains looked fantastic
against the blue sky. We stopped once on the way at
a place where the view is spectacular and everybody
got out and took photographs. There were Bedouins
selling souvenirs, and I bought a lovely necklace.*

*By the time we arrived at the monastery, it was
really hot and there were loads of other tourists there,
but I was glad I'd come. It's a very special place, and
I'd love to do the trip again, but next time I'd hire a
car and do it in my own time.*

Cultural notes

Sinai Peninsula /saɪnaɪ/
The Sinai Peninsula is an Egyptian-controlled
triangular stretch of land, which sits between
mainland Africa and the Suez Canal to the west,
Israel and Arabia to the east, the Mediterranean Sea
to the north and the Red Sea to the south.

The Red Sea
The Red Sea is an inlet of the Indian Ocean dividing
the northern part of Africa from Asia. In the north
are the Suez Canal and the Gulf of Aqaba with
the Sinai Peninsula between them. The Red Sea is
around 2250 km long and 355 km wide.

St Catherine's Monastery
St Catherine's Monastery, a Coptic monastery
situated on the Sinai Peninsula, is the oldest
monastery in the world. It's the most popular
tourist attraction on the peninsula.

Dahab /dæhæb/
Dahab is a town in Egypt, situated on the Gulf of
Aqaba, near the southern tip of Sinai. Until the
1960s, it was a sleepy Bedouin fishing village, but
increased tourism has turned it into a busy resort,
popular with scuba divers.

The Bedouin /ˈbeduɪn/
The Bedouin are a nomadic people found mainly across the Sahara Desert, Sinai Desert and Arabian Desert. Traditionally, Bedouins ride camels and live in tents in the desert.

2

- Give the students a minute or two to decide on the journey they're going to talk about. Then ask them to look at the questions in Exercise 1 again and decide how they'd answer them about their journey. Allow them to make notes of what they're going to say and how they're going to say it, but discourage them from writing a paragraph that they can simply read out.

- Put the students in pairs and ask them to take turns to tell their partner about their journey. Encourage them to ask each other follow-up questions to get further information. Then ask some pairs to report back to the class about what they found out.

Useful phrases (SB page 74)

1 🌐 2.31

Focus the students' attention on the picture. Explain that the people in the car are Angie and Rick and that Rick is driving. Go through the questions. Then play the recording and ask the students to listen and read the conversation to find the answers.

> a) Andover.
> b) The A34.
> c) They pass it three times.

2 🌐 2.32

- Ask the students to read the conversation again and complete the useful phrases. Tell them to look back at the conversation in Exercise 1 if they need help.

- Play the recording for the students to listen and check their answers. Then play it again for them to repeat the useful phrases. When they've done this chorally, ask several students to repeat the useful phrases individually, and check that everyone is pronouncing them correctly.

> a) to get to
> b) for the road to
> c) we can get onto
> d) way we need to go
> e) the A34 is
> f) round, the first turning on
> g) come to a roundabout

> h) exit
> i) you come to a petrol station
> j) the signs

🌐 2.32

Saying what you're looking for
a) *Excuse me, I'm trying to get to Andover.*
b) *Excuse me, we're looking for the road to Andover.*

Asking for directions
c) *Do you know how we can get onto the A34?*
d) *Could you tell me which way we need to go?*
e) *Do you have any idea where the A34 is?*

Giving directions
f) *You need to turn round and then take the first turning on the left.*
g) *Go to the end of the road and you'll come to a roundabout.*
h) *Take the third exit.*
i) *Go straight down here until you come to a petrol station.*
j) *Turn left and follow the signs.*

3

- Remind the students that you often use less direct language when asking questions to strangers, as it sounds more polite. Go through the instructions and the example with the class, pointing out that *Excuse me* is a polite way of attracting someone's attention. Then put the students into pairs and ask them to rewrite the questions in less direct language.

- Check answers with the class before asking the students to take turns asking the questions and giving appropriate directions from where they are now.

> a) Excuse me. Do you know / Could you tell me / Do you have any idea where the nearest bank is?
> b) Do you know / Could you tell me / Do you have any idea how I can get to the airport from here?
> c) Excuse me. Do you know / Could you tell me / Do you have any idea which way I need to go?
> d) Do you know / Could you tell me / Do you have any idea how to get to the centre of town from here?
> e) Do you know / Could you tell me / Do you have any idea where I can get a taxi?
> f) Do you know / Could you tell me / Do you have any idea how I can get to the cinema from here?

Vocabulary *Extra* (SB page 75)

Dictionary labels

1

Ask the students to match the dictionary labels (a–d) with their definitions.

> a) 4　 b) 2　 c) 1　 d) 3

2

Ask the students to use the labels from Exercise 1 to complete the headings for the word lists (1–3). Then tell them they can check their answers by looking at the dictionary extracts in the margin.

> 1 American　 2 spoken　 3 formal

3

- Pairwork. Focus the students' attention on the public notices. Tell them to discuss with their partner what each of the notices mean and where they'd expect to see them. Remind them to look at the dictionary extract in the margin to help.

- Ask the students to write a less formal version of each notice. Then compare as a class.

> a) Please don't smoke around here. (In any public space.)
> b) Please get off the ferry using the steps at the front. (On a ferry.)
> c) Get off your bike. (At the entrance to a pedestrian-only zone.)
> d) You can't use your calculator. (In an exam.)
> e) Don't get off the train when it's still moving. (On a train.)
> f) People under 18 can't buy alcohol. (In a shop, supermarket or bar.)

4

Ask the students to rewrite the sentences in British English. Check with the class before they ask and answer the questions with their partner.

> a) Last year, I went on holiday in the autumn.
> b) We keep our dustbin in the garden.
> c) I never eat sweets or biscuits between meals.
> d) I get angry with lorry drivers who go too fast on the motorway.
> e) When I go to the city centre, I walk or use the underground.
> f) There's a postbox on the pavement in front of my house.

5

Ask the students to look at their own dictionaries to find out what kinds of labels are used. Ask them to write these labels down and an example from their dictionaries for each one.

Further practice material

Need more writing practice?

→ Workbook page 51
- Writing a description.

Need more classroom practice activities?

→ Photocopiable resource materials pages 174 to 176
 Grammar: *Past perfect dominoes*
 Vocabulary: *Holiday emails*
 Communication: *Globetrotters*
→ Top 10 activities pages xv to xx

Need DVD material?

→ DVD – Programme 8: *Journey*

Need progress tests?

→ Test CD – *Test Unit 8*

Need more on important teaching concepts?

→ Key concepts in *New Inside Out* pages xxii to xxxv

Need student self-study practice?

→ CD-ROM – Unit 8: *Journey*

Need student CEF self-evaluation?

→ CEF Checklists pages xxxvii to xliv

Need more information and more ideas?

→ www.insideout.net

9 Opinions *Overview*

Section & Aims	What the students are doing
Speaking & Reading SB page 76 Fluency practice; reading for detail	Categorising statements into those said by men or women. Answering a questionnaire and comparing with a partner.
Reading SB page 77 Reading for detail	Reading and completing a survey on men's and women's opinions. Talking about what the results of the survey might be in their country.
Grammar SB page 77 Reported statements	Studying the use of reporting verbs. Studying how to form reported speech. Completing sentences in direct speech.
Speaking SB page 78 Fluency practice	Finding out about classmates' leisure pursuits.
Listening & Vocabulary SB page 78 Listening for gist; books, films, music	Listening to conversations and identifying the topics. Completing a table with book, film and music vocabulary. Matching extracts from film soundtracks to their genres.
Reading & Grammar SB page 79 Reported questions	Reading a web report of an interview with actor Tom Hanks. Rewriting reported questions in direct speech. Studying the form of reported questions.
Speaking: anecdote SB page 79 Fluency practice	Talking about a film they have enjoyed.
Vocabulary & Speaking SB page 80 *-ed* and *-ing* adjectives; fluency practice	Choosing the correct adjectives to complete a text and talking about how they choose books. Categorising *-ed* and *-ing* adjectives. Talking about feelings.
Pronunciation SB page 80 Syllable stress in adjectives	Categorising adjectives according to syllables and stress pattern.
Reading & Vocabulary SB page 81 Reading for gist; describing a book	Reading the synopsis of a novel and saying if they'd like to read it. Matching book reviews with scores. Matching words and expressions and talking about a book or a film.
Writing SB page 81 Book review	Writing a book review.
Useful phrases SB page 82 Useful phrases for giving your opinion	Discussing the advantages and disadvantages of owning a car. Completing a conversation. Categorising useful phrases. Writing a new conversation using the useful phrases for giving opinions.
Vocabulary *Extra* SB page 83 Collocations	Combining verbs with the appropriate noun. Discussing statements about collocations. Choosing the correct collocation in dictionary examples. Completing questions with appropriate collocations.
Writing WB page 57	Writing a film review.

9 Opinions *Teacher's notes*

Warm up

• Write *Men are from Mars, women are from Venus* on the board and ask your class if they think men and women come from different planets and what the main differences between men and women are.

Speaking & Reading (SB page 76)

1

• Pairwork. Put the students into pairs (mixed sex if possible). Tell them that they're going to discuss a number of comments and they should discuss these and put them into the table according to whether they think they're things women never say or things men never say. Go round giving help where needed.

• Ask the pairs to add one other comment to each column. In a class feedback session, find out how much consensus there is. Ask a number of pairs to read out their new comments and see if other students agree with their place in the table.

Probable answers:	
Things women never say:	**Things men never say:**
b), c), e), h)	a), d), f), g)

2

• Ask the students to work individually to read and complete the questionnaire.

• Ask the students to compare their answers with a partner. In a class feedback session try to find out if male students and female students tended to give different answers to the questions.

Reading (SB page 77)

1

Point out that the text they are about to read reports the findings of the survey, which used the questionnaire they've just completed. Ask them to read it carefully and decide if each gap should be filled with *men* or *women*. Allow them to compare answers in pairs but do not confirm or deny anything at this stage.

1 men	2 women	3 women	4 men
5 women	6 men	7 men	8 women
9 women	10 men	11 women	12 men

2 🌐 2.33

Play the recording for the students to check their answers. Then have a class discussion on whether the results would be different in their country or countries.

🌐 2.33

Survey results: Men and Women

On attraction

Three out of four women said that they had bought new clothes to attract somebody, compared with only one in five men. Similarly, while just under half of the women told us that they had dieted so that they would be more attractive, only one in ten men admitted that they had done the same. However, a significant number of both men and women admitted that they had lied about their age, with the important difference that men tended to say they were older, while women were more likely to knock a few years off their age.

On dating

The majority of people said that they expected to be called within three days after a first date. However, 35% of women insisted that they expected to be phoned the next day, while only 19% of men gave this answer. On average, men are prepared to wait on a first date if the woman doesn't arrive on time. 18% of women said that they would only wait for five minutes, whereas 67% of men claimed that they would wait half an hour or more.

On birthdays

The results of the survey suggest that women attach greater importance to birthdays than men. 49% of women admitted they got angry or upset if their partner forgot their birthday, while more than three-quarters of the men interviewed claimed that they didn't care.

On marriage

The results of the survey show that men are more in favour of marriage than women. 41% of women said that they considered marriage to be unnecessary, and 20% told us that they didn't mind whether they got married or not. When we asked men about marriage, four out of five told us that they definitely intended to get married one day.

On childcare

65% of women are in favour of fathers staying at home to look after the children. However, when we asked men for their opinion, the majority replied that it was not appropriate.

Grammar (SB page 77)

1

- Focus the students' attention on the reporting verbs in the box and ask them which they think they can use to complete the statement. When you've established that the only verb which can be used in this sentence is *told*, ask them to look at the examples of direct and reported statements in the margin and to say which word they'd have to delete from the original statement if they wanted to use any of the other reporting verbs in the box. Point out the different structures *He told us …* and *She said …* (See notes below.)

- Tell the students that *told*, *said* and *replied* mean much the same thing, but that the other verbs you can use to report statements have slightly different meanings or implications. For example, *admitted* is used for something you've done and which you regret or are embarrassed about. Ask them to check the other meanings in a dictionary.

> *told* is the only one.
> Delete *us*.

Language note

Reporting verbs
- *Say, tell, ask* are the most common reporting verbs, but there are many others you can use.

- *Tell* and *ask* are always followed by an object pronoun (*me, him/her*, etc.), e.g. *He told me he wanted to go home. Warn* also follows this pattern.

- *Say* is followed by an optional *that*, e.g. *She said (that) she was on a diet.*
  Other common reporting verbs that follow this pattern are: *admit, claim, explain, insist, reply, suggest* and *promise.*

2

- Look again at the reported statement in Exercise 1 and point out the past perfect verb form *had dieted*. Ask the students to decide which of the sentences the women actually said.

- Go through the explanation about tense changes in reported statements with the class and make sure that everyone understands that the explanation is true.

> c) 'Yes, I've dieted.'
> True.

Language notes

Grammar: reported statements
- There are two principal ways which you can report speech. The first way is to repeat the exact words that someone used as direct speech.
  He said 'I don't want to go'.

- The second way is to incorporate the words that someone said as part of your sentence, using the conjunction *that* and 'backshifting' the tense of the verb. This is called indirect speech. Unit 9 concentrates on indirect speech.
  He said that he didn't want to go.

- The present simple in direct speech is usually backshifted to past simple: Compare '*I go to the gym every week*' (direct speech) with *He said **he went** to the gym every week* (reported speech).

- Present continuous backshifts to past continuous: Compare '*He's living in a shared house*' with *She said that **he was living** in a shared house.*

- Past simple backshifts to past perfect: Compare '*We went to Spain in August*' with *He said that **they had gone** to Spain in August.*

- Present perfect backshifts to past perfect: Compare '*They've been to Paris*' with *She said that **they had been** to Paris.*

- *will* backshifts to *would*: Compare '*I'll wait until 2.30*' with *He said that **he would** wait until 2.30.*

3

- Go through the example sentence with the class and then ask them to work individually to complete the remaining sentences. Remind them to look back at the survey to see how the sentences were reported to help them. Go round checking that everyone has understood the concept of reported statements and is manipulating the verb tenses correctly.

- Check answers with the class and then ask them to say whether they think that the statements were made by a man, a woman or both.

> | a) 've bought | d) get angry; forgets |
> |---|---|
> | b) 've lied | e) don't mind; get |
> | c) 'll wait | f) isn't |

4 Grammar *Extra* 9

Ask the students to turn to *Grammar Extra* 9 on page 142 of the Student's Book. Here they'll find an explanation of the grammar they've been studying and further exercises to practise it.

> **1**
> a) 3: 'Albert Einstein shows no promise.'
> b) 5: 'Everything that can be invented has been invented.'
> c) 6: 'The aeroplane will never fly.'
> d) 2: 'Who the hell wants to hear actors talk?'
> e) 4: 'There's a world market for maybe five computers.'
> f) 1: 'Sean Connery can't play the sophisticated James Bond because he looks like a bricklayer.'

2

1 it had just missed her head and had hit her arm
2 she had felt a nasty pain on her arm, which had started bleeding heavily
3 she was glad it hadn't hit her on the head
4 there was a good chance (that) it was a meteorite
5 the chances of being hit by one were incredibly small
6 most meteorites disintegrated as they entered the atmosphere

3

a) said   b) told   c) asked   d) said   e) said
f) told   g) asked   h) told

4 *Possible answers:*

a) He said that he hated spending money on new clothes.
b) She told him that she wasn't wearing that outfit again.
c) She asked him if he thought she looked fat in those trousers.
d) She said that she had to go on a diet.
e) He told her that he'd checked the oil and had put some air in the tyres.
f) She asked him not to forget that it was their anniversary the following day.
g) He said he didn't want to get married until he was forty.
h) He asked her what time her salsa class finished.

Cultural notes

Sean Connery /ʃɔːn ˈkɒnəri/ (born 1930)
Scottish actor Sean Connery is probably best known for his role as James Bond, which he played between 1962 and 1971.

Warner Brothers (founded 1918)
Warner Brothers is one of the biggest producers of film and television entertainment in the world. Warner Brothers produced *The Jazz Singer* (1927), the first full-length feature film with sound.

Albert Einstein /ælbət aɪnstaɪn/ (1879–1955)
Einstein was a German-born scientist. He is most famous for his *Theory of Relativity*. In 1921, he won the Nobel Prize in Physics.

Speaking (SB page 78)

Go through the questions the students will need to ask to find out the information. Then, if possible, ask them to mingle and ask questions to find out how many people in the class match each of the things in the list.

Listening & Vocabulary (SB page 78)

1 🌐 2.34

- Ask the students to write the numbers 1 to 7 on a piece of paper. Tell them to write *B*, *F* or *M* next to each number as they listen to the conversations. Play the recording, pausing it after each conversation if necessary.

- When checking answers with the class, ask the students to say what clues helped them decide what the people were talking about.

1 M	2 F	3 B	4 F	5 B	6 F	7 M

🌐 **2.34**

1
A: Which is your favourite track on the album?
B: The last one – it's amazing. I can't wait to see them performing live.

2
C: What did you think of it?
D: I thought the acting was brilliant and the photography's superb. Apart from that, it was dead boring.

3
E: Have you finished it yet?
F: Nearly.
E: What's it like?
F: Really good. I reckon it's going to be a best-seller.

4
G: I enjoyed that. What did you think of it?
H: I thought it was rubbish – a sentimental tearjerker – and the ending was predictable.
G: Well, it made you cry anyway.
H: No, it didn't – I've got a cold.

5
I: Are you enjoying it?
J: Yes. I found it a bit difficult to get into, but now that I'm past the first few chapters, I can't put it down.

6
K: What did you think of the special effects?
L: What special effects?
K: It was all done with computers.
L: Oh no – I thought it was real. You've spoilt it now.

7
M: Did you have a good time?
N: Not really – I can't stand all that techno stuff. I like it when you can actually hear the lyrics.
M: Old hippy.
N: What did you say?
M: Nothing.

2

- Focus the students' attention on the table and point out that there are three columns of words, which come from the conversations they've just heard. Ask them to write the correct heading above each column.

- Check answers before asking the students to add more words to each column. Point out that some may fit in more than one column. Encourage them to add any more words that they know.

a) Films   b) Music   c) Books

a) *Films:* acting, photography, special effects, tearjerker; director, fantasy, a hit, horror, musical, plot, premier, science fiction, soundtrack, storyline, subtitles

b) *Music:* album, lyrics, performing live, techno, track; band, blues, classical, dance, gig, hip-hop, a hit, musical, orchestra, reggae, soundtrack, stereo system

c) *Books:* bestseller, can't put it down, chapters, difficult to get into; fantasy, a hit, horror, novel, paperback, plot, science fiction, short story, storyline

3 🌐 2.35

- Tell the students that they're going to listen to six extracts from film soundtracks. Go through the possible genres in the box and make sure that everyone understands them. Then play the recording, pausing after each extract to give the students a chance to decide what kind of film they think it is.

- Put the students into groups and ask them to think of some films they know in the different genres. Ask them to have a discussion about films and to find out which types of films the students in their group like best. Encourage them to report back to the class.

a) westerns
b) horror films / thrillers
c) love stories
d) comedies
e) action films / science fiction films
f) spy films / thrillers / action films

Language note

Vocabulary: classifying films
There are many ways to classify films according to their genre. Here are a handful of common colloquial classifications:

a *romcom* is a romantic comedy

a *sci fi movie* is a science fiction film

a *road movie* is a film in which the main character(s) change, grow and improve over the course of a road trip, after encountering a series of challenges

a *chick flick* is a film designed to appeal mainly to a female audience

Reading & Grammar (SB page 79)

Reported questions

1

- Focus the students' attention on the text and the photo. Ask them if they know who Tom Hanks is and if they can name any of the films he's been in.

- Explain that *Mr Nice Guy* is a description given to people who are always friendly and considerate. Ask the students to read the report of the interview and find out why Tom Hanks is known as *Mr Nice Guy*.

> He has always cooperated with the press. He usually plays the part of the 'nice guy' in films. He doesn't want to be away from his children.

Language note

Grammar: reporting questions
- In direct questions the auxiliary verb *do* usually comes before the subject. Verbs like *can, have, be* come before the subject.

- In reported questions the subject usually comes before the verb. *Yes/No* questions are reported using *if* or *whether*.

- There are no question marks in reported questions.

- Questions are usually reported using the verb *ask*.

Direct question: *Where's Sara?*
Reported question: *He asked where Sara was.*

Direct question: *Do you like tea?*
Reported question: *She asked whether I liked tea.*

Direct question: *Can you swim?*
Reported question: *He asked if I could swim.*

Cultural note

Tom Hanks /tɒm hæŋks/ (born 1956)
Tom Hanks is an actor, director and writer from California. Some notable film roles include *Forrest Gump* (1994) and *The Green Mile* (1999).

2

- Ask the students to find and underline the five reported questions in the report.

- Focus the students' attention on the example questions in the margin. Point out that as with reported statements there is a shift backwards in the tenses. Point out the difference between an information question like *How do you feel?* and a *yes/no* question like *Have you ever had problems?* When reporting *yes/no* questions, you need to use *if* or *whether*.

- Ask the students to look back at the first of the underlined questions in the text, *We asked him how he felt about his 'nice guy' persona.* Explain that the actual question was *How do you feel about ...?* Ask the students to write the actual questions used for each of the other underlined reported questions.

We asked him how he felt about his 'nice guy' persona. – 'How do you feel about your "nice guy" persona?'
We asked him where this reputation had come from. – 'Where has this reputation come from?'
We asked him whether he had ever had problems … – 'Have you ever had problems …?'
We asked the *Forrest Gump* star why he always played … – 'Why do you always play …?'
We asked him what his current plans were. – 'What are your current plans?'

3

Go through the instructions with the class and ask them to mark the statements true or false.

> a) True.   b) True.   c) True.

4 Pairwork

- The pairwork exercise for this unit is on pages 119 and 124 of the Student's Book. Put the students in pairs and tell them who will be Student A, and who will be Student B.

- While they're doing the exercise, go round monitoring and giving help. Take note of any errors which may need particular attention later, and also any examples of good language use, which you can praise in a feedback session.

Speaking: anecdote (SB page 79)

For more information about how to set up, monitor and repeat Anecdotes, see page xx in the Introduction.

1 🎧 2.36

- Focus the students' attention on the photo of Tom Hanks. Explain that they're going to hear a woman called Alice talking about a film she enjoyed from which this photo is taken. Go through the questions and answers with the class. Play the recording and ask the students to listen and tick the answers that are correct.

- Play the recording again and ask the students to change the answers that are incorrect.

> a) ✔
> b) The other night ~~at the cinema~~. (on television)
> c) ✔
> d) ✔
> e) A ~~true story~~. (novel)
> f) ~~A thriller~~. (drama)
> g) ✔
> h) ✔
> i) ✔
> j) ~~A happy ending~~. (A tear-jerker)
> k) ~~No I wouldn't~~. (Yes, it's the best film of all time.)

🎧 2.36

One of my favourite films is Forrest Gump. *I know it's quite an old film but I've never seen anything better. Actually, I've seen it three times. The last time I saw it was the other night on television, and it made me laugh and cry all over again. I love Tom Hanks and I think he's brilliant in this film. Robin Wright played the part of his girlfriend, and Sally Field was his mum. I can't remember who else was in it, or who directed it. But I do know that it won six Oscars including best film, best director and Tom Hanks got best leading actor. Apparently, it's based on a novel, but I've no idea who wrote it.*

There are so many things I love about this film. I suppose it's a drama, but it's historical and it's funny and it's really sad too. The character of Forrest Gump is brilliant – he's not very clever, and at the beginning of the film he can't walk properly, but he manages to succeed in life without meaning to, and without realising it. I particularly like the bits where he meets famous people like President Kennedy or Elvis Presley. It's so clever the way they mix old black and white footage from the 60s. It's hilarious when Forrest meets Elvis. Forrest has a strange way of walking, and when Elvis imitates him, it looks like the dance that he was famous for. The soundtrack is great too – there are all these classic pop songs including some by Elvis.

But the ending is a bit of a tearjerker – I cry my eyes out every time. I won't spoil it for you in case you haven't' seen it – but you should see it because it's the best film of all time.

Cultural notes

Robin Wright Penn /ˈrɒbɪn reɪt pen/ (born 1966)
Robin Wright Penn is an American actress. She starred in *The Princess Bride* (1987), *Forrest Gump* (1994) and *Beowulf* (2007). She has been married to actor Sean Penn since 1996.

Sally Field /ˈsæliː fiːld/ (born 1946)
Sally Field is an American actress. She starred in *Norma Rae* (1979), *Forrest Gump* (1994) and *Lincoln* (2009). Since 2006, she has starred in the TV series *Brothers and Sisters*.

John F. Kennedy (1917–1963)
John F. Kennedy was the 35th President of the United States (1961–1963). He was assassinated on November 22nd, 1963, in Dallas, Texas, at the age of 46. His brother Robert (Bobby) Kennedy was assassinated five years later, in 1968.

Elvis Presley /ˈelvɪs prezliː/ (1935–1977)
(See notes about Elvis Presley in Unit 8, page 79.)

2

- Give the students a minute or two to decide on the film they're going to talk about. Then ask them to look at the questions in Exercise 1 again and decide how they'd answer them about their film. Allow them to make notes of what they're going to say and how they're going to say it, but discourage them from writing a paragraph that they can simply read out.

- Ask the students to take turns to tell their partner about a film they enjoyed. Encourage them to ask each other follow-up questions to get further information. Then ask some pairs to report back to the class about what they found out.

Vocabulary & Speaking (SB page 80)

1 🌐 2.37

- Focus the students' attention on the introductory text. Make sure they understand that the five people were asked the same question: *How do you choose a book to read?*

- Ask the students to look at the alternatives in the text and say what they notice about them (they are all adjectives, but the first in each pair ends in *-ing* and the second in *-ed*). Ask them to read the text, decide which adjective is correct and underline it. Play the recording for them to check their answers and then ask them to say how they choose a book.

> 1 interesting   2 disappointed   3 interesting
> 4 excited   5 disappointed   6 boring
> 7 fascinated   8 inspiring   9 interesting

> 🌐 2.37
>
> *We asked several people the question, 'How do you choose a book to read?' Here are their replies.*
>
> *'I judge the book by its cover. If the cover looks interesting, I buy the book. Sometimes I'm lucky, and the book is good. And sometimes I'm disappointed.'*
>
> *'I always read book reviews in newspapers and magazines, and when I read about a book that sounds interesting, I write it down in my diary.'*
>
> *'I don't take any risks – I always read books by authors I know. I get really excited when one of my favourite authors brings out a new book, and I buy it immediately. This way I'm never disappointed.'*
>
> *'I read the first page, and if it's boring, I don't buy the book – if I want to turn over the page and carry on reading, I buy the book.'*
>
> *'It's easy – I never read fiction but I'm fascinated by biographies of famous people. I find strong women in history particularly inspiring.'*
>
> *'I tend to choose books written by women. They have a better feeling for characters and the relationships between them, and that's what I find interesting in a book. Having said that, I've just finished* The Beach *by Alex Garland, and it was brilliant!'*

2

- Focus the students' attention on the table and point out that some adjectives can describe either how people feel or the thing or person that causes the feeling. Point out that the adjectives in the two columns have the same basic stem, but those which describe how people feel end in *-ed* and those which describe the cause end in *-ing*.

- Ask the students to add the adjectives from the text in Exercise 1 to the correct columns of the table. Check answers. Then choose several of the adjectives and ask the students to make example sentences.

> *To describe how people feel:* annoyed, challenged, confused, exhausted, relaxed, tired, worried; interested, disappointed, excited, bored, fascinated, inspired
> *To describe the thing (or person) that causes the feeling:* annoying, challenging, confusing, exhausting, relaxing, tiring, worrying; interesting, disappointing, exciting, boring, fascinating, inspiring

3

- Put the students into pairs and ask them to tell each other how they're feeling today and why. Ask several pairs to report back to the class.

- Then ask them to choose three more adjectives and say what makes them feel like this.

Pronunciation (SB page 80)

1

Remind the students that the boxes show the syllables of a word and the large boxes indicate the stressed syllables. Here they are being asked to classify adjectives according to how many syllables they have and where the main stress falls. Encourage them to say each word aloud to get a feeling for what sounds right. Remind them to check the stress of any word in their dictionaries.

1 & 2		
A: ▢▢▢	**B:** ▢▢▢	**C:** ▢▢▢▢
<u>cha</u>llenging, <u>in</u>teresting, <u>wo</u>rrying	an<u>noy</u>ing, ex<u>ci</u>ting, ex<u>haus</u>ting	disap<u>poin</u>ting, enter<u>tai</u>ning, over<u>whel</u>ming

2 🌐 2.38

Point out the main stress in the example words which is underlined. Ask the students to do the same for the other words in the table. Then play the recording for them to check their answers. Play it a second time for them to repeat the adjectives.

> 🌐 2.38
>
> A: *challenging   interesting   worrying*
> B: *annoying   exciting   exhausting*
> C: *disappointing   entertaining   overwhelming*

Reading & Vocabulary (SB page 81)

1

- Focus the students' attention on the web page and find out if anyone has read *Pride and Prejudice* or seen the film. If so, encourage them to tell the class about it.
- Ask the students to read the synopsis of the book and say what kind of book it is and whether or not they would be interested in reading it.

> A classic romantic novel.

Cultural note

Jane Austen /dʒeɪn ˈɒstɪn/ (1775–1817)
Jane Austen is one of the most widely-read and best loved novelists in British literature. She wrote six complete novels, including *Pride and Prejudice* (1813), *Sense and Sensibility* (1811) and *Emma* (1815). Her books are both witty and a commentary on that era, highlighting the dependence of women on marriage for their social standing and economic security.

2

Tell the students to read the reviews and decide what score the reviewer would give the book out of ten. When checking answers, ask them which words gave the review a particularly positive or negative tone.

> *Suggested answers:*
> a) 9/10   b) 6/10   c) 7/10   d) 8/10   e) 1/10

3

- Ask the students to match the italicised words with those in the box which have a similar meaning. Point out that it's important, particularly in writing, to use a variety of vocabulary. Encourage the students to group together words with similar meanings when they record them in their vocabulary notebooks. If they do this, they'll have a bank of different words to use when they need them.
- Check answers. Then put the students into pairs and ask them to tell each other about a book or film that fits each of the descriptions. Encourage them to report back to the class on what they found out.

> a) is set   b) central   c) engaging   d) storyline
> e) gripping   f) thought-provoking

Writing (SB page 81)

- Go through the points that have to be included in the review with the class. Remind the students of the work they've just done on alternative words for describing the same thing.
- The reviews could be written in class or set for homework. Allow time in class for the students to read each other's reviews. You could, perhaps, display them in the classroom for everyone to enjoy.

Useful phrases (SB page 82)

1

Put the students into groups of three and ask them to brainstorm the advantages and disadvantages of owning a car. Then write their suggestions on the board.

2 🌐 2.39

Tell the students they're going to hear three people having a discussion about owning a car. Ask them to listen and find out how many of their ideas they mention.

> 🌐 **2.39** (J = Jess; R = Ryan; K = Kim)
>
> K: *Hi, Ryan. Come in.*
> J: *Hi, Ryan. What happened to you? You're late!*
> R: *Yes, I'm really sorry – I had to wait ages for a bus.*
> J: *What's wrong with your car?*
> R: *I've sold it! I think there are too many cars in this town.*
> J: *Well, that's true, but a car is useful.*
> R: *I'm not so sure about that. The traffic's awful, and I can never find a parking space.*
> K: *But how are you going to get to work?*
> R: *By bicycle.*
> K: *Don't you think bicycles are dangerous?*
> R: *Not really. They're certainly less dangerous for the environment.*
> J: *Well, as far as I'm concerned, a car is essential – I have to drive my kids to school.*
> R: *Your kids should walk to school? If you ask me, children don't get enough exercise.*
> J: *That's rubbish! My kids do football, swimming and tennis – and I need a car to get them there on time.*
> K: *I agree with Jess – I couldn't live without my car. I sometimes work in the evening, and I don't feel safe getting a bus late at night.*
> R: *OK, I take your point, but aren't you worried about pollution?*
> J: *Do you know what I think? It's not my problem. I can't save the planet.*
> R: *But that's nonsense! Everybody can do something!*
> K: *OK, OK, you're right! Now, let's change the subject. What do you think of my new television?*
> J: *It's great – but I hope it's solar-powered!*

3

- Pairwork. Ask the students to complete the conversation in pairs.
- Play the recording again for them to check their answers.

> 1 think   2 but   3 sure   4 Don't   5 as
> 6 me   7 That   8 agree   9 but   10 know
> 11 that   12 right   13 what

4 🌐 2.40

- Point out the highlighted phrases in the conversation and ask the students to put them in the table in the correct columns, according to their function.

- Check answers. Then play the recording for them to repeat the phrases. Tell them to copy the stress and intonation exactly. Ask for individual repetition. Make sure they are getting the stress and intonation correct.

Ask for an opinion	Give an opinion
Don't you think …? What do you think of …?	I think there … … as far as I'm concerned, … If you ask me, … Do you know what I think?
Agree with an opinion	**Disagree with an opinion**
Well, that's true, … I agree with … OK, I take your point, … OK, you're right.	I'm not so sure about that. That's rubbish! That's nonsense!

5
- Groupwork. Put the students into groups of three. Give them a minute or two to decide on their topic and then ask them to note down the advantages and disadvantages. Ask the students to use their notes to write a short conversation. Remind them to use the one in Exercise 3 as a model and that they should include some of the useful phrases from Exercise 4.
- Get the students to practise their conversations. Choose any particularly good ones to be performed for the class.

Vocabulary *Extra* (SB page 83)

Collocations

1
- Pairwork. Focus the students' attention on the table and go through the examples with them. Ask them to work in pairs and decide on which nouns make collocations with the verbs.
- Tell the students that they can check their answers by looking at the dictionary extracts in the margin. Point out the collocations in bold in the example sentences.

	action	advice	a comment	a decision	a mistake	an opinion
give	✗	✓	✗	✗	✗	✓
make	✗	✗	✓	✓	✓	✗
take	✓	✓	✗	✓	✗	✗

2

Pairwork. Ask the students to decide with a partner whether they agree with the statements or not.

> a), b) and c) are all correct.

3
- Ask the students to underline the correct collocation in the dictionary examples.
- Tell the students that they can check their answers by looking at the dictionary extracts for the words *highly* and *opinion* in the margin.

> a) gave   b) high   c) differences   d) of
> e) highly   f) highly

4
- Ask the students to complete the questions. Then tell them to look at the information in the boxes for words often used with *advice* and *mistake*.
- Students then ask and answer the questions in pairs.

> a) ask, for   b) offered   c) accept
> d) ignored   e) expensive

5

Ask the students to look at their own dictionaries to find out how it shows information about collocation. Ask them for a few example sentences from their dictionaries for the words in the dictionary extracts on page 83.

Further practice material
Need more writing practice?
→ Workbook page 57
- Writing a film review.

Need more classroom practice activities?
→ Photocopiable resource materials pages 177 to 179
   Grammar: *Interpreter*
   Vocabulary: *Blockbuster*
   Communication: *Film, books and music*
→ Top 10 activities pages xv to xx

Need DVD material?
→ DVD – Programme 9: *Romance*

Need progress tests?
→ Test CD – *Test Unit 9*

Need more on important teaching concepts?
→ Key concepts in *New Inside Out* pages xxii to xxxv

Need student self-study practice?
→ CD-ROM – Unit 9: *Opinions*

Need student CEF self-evaluation?
→ CEF Checklists pages xxxvii to xliv

Need more information and more ideas?
→ www.insideout.net

Review C *Teacher's notes*

These exercises act as a check of the grammar and vocabulary that the students have learnt in Units 7–9. Use them to find any problems that students are having, or anything that they haven't understood and which will need further work.

Grammar (SB page 84)

Remind the students of the grammar explanations they read and the exercises they did in the *Grammar Extra* on pages 138 to 143.

1

This exercise reviews verb patterns from Unit 7. Check answers before putting the students in pairs to ask and answer the questions.

a) told you that	d) spending
b) having	e) not to do
c) promised to do	

2

This exercise reviews passive structures from Unit 7. (Note: Lewisham is a district of south-east London.)

1 were arrested	5 was found
2 was robbed	6 were taken
3 is believed	7 hasn't been found
4 had been reported	8 is asked

3

This exercise reviews the past simple and past perfect from Unit 8. Remind the students that when you talk about past events, events even further back in the past are expressed in the past perfect.

1 went	7 decided
2 realised	8 saw
3 had left	9 had lost
4 wasn't	10 opened
5 had gone	11 had got
6 had already closed	12 had been

4

This exercise reviews modals of deductions from Unit 8.

a) may	b) could	c) must	d) can't

5

This exercise reviews reported statements from Unit 9.

a) was	d) hadn't been
b) wasn't	e) had never seen
c) had been	f) hadn't robbed

6

This exercise reviews structures used in Units 7, 8 and 9.

1 a) ~~These computers are using all over the world.~~
2 b) ~~I told him to not talk to anybody.~~
3 b) ~~You've worked really hard. You can't be exhausted!~~
4 a) ~~When I got to the airport, the plane was already left.~~
5 a) ~~They said me they weren't hungry.~~
6 b) ~~She asked me did I need help?~~

Vocabulary (SB page 85)

1

This exercise reviews words from Unit 7.

a) hypocritical	b) obsessed	c) photogenic
d) insensitive	e) unflattering	f) desperate

2

This exercise reviews crime words from Unit 7.

a) thief	b) escorted	c) stolen
d) arrested, chase	e) court	f) sentenced

3

This exercise reviews the words to describe places from Unit 8.

> 1 southern   2 white sands   3 surrounded
> 4 spectacular   5 popular   6 unspoilt

Cultural note

Jamaica /dʒəˈmeɪkə/
Jamaica is an island in the Caribbean Sea about 150 km south of Cuba. It has a population of around 2.6 million and is home to the Rastafari movement, popularized by its most famous son, singer/songwriter Bob Marley.

4

This exercise reviews useful adjectives for describing the features of a landscape.

> a) ancient ruins   d) built-up skyline
> b) Buddhist temple   e) snow-capped mountain
> c) high-rise building   f) waterfall

5

This exercise reviews fixed expressions from Unit 8. Check answers before asking the students to tick the sentences which are true for them, then put the students in pairs to discuss them.

> a) nothing   b) Sooner   c) peace   d) go
> e) take   f) tidy

6

This exercise reviews book, film and music words from Unit 9.

> a) *music:* band, gig, lyrics, musical, orchestra, techno
> b) *films:* comedy, horror, musical, plot,
>   science fiction, storyline, tearjerker, western
> c) *books:* chapter, horror, plot, science fiction,
>   storyline, tearjerker, western

7

This exercise reviews *-ed* and *-ing* adjectives from Unit 9.

> a) fascinated   b) boring   c) interested
> d) confusing   e) worrying   f) disappointed

Pronunciation (SB page 85)

1

Remind the students that the boxes show the syllables of a word and the large boxes indicate the stressed syllables. Here they're being asked to classify words according to how many syllables they have and where the main stress falls. Encourage them to say each word aloud to get a feeling for what sounds right.

2 🌐 2.41

Point out the main stresses in the example words, which are underlined. Ask the students to do the same for the other words in the table. Then play the recording for them to check their answers. Play it a second time for them to listen and repeat.

> **1 and 2**
>
> | A: ☐▢☐ | B: ▢☐☐ | C: ☐▢☐☐ |
> |---|---|---|
> | an<u>noy</u>ing | <u>clas</u>sical | ce<u>leb</u>rity |
> | di<u>rec</u>tor | <u>fan</u>tasy | em<u>bar</u>rassing |
> | dra<u>mat</u>ic | <u>inter</u>viewed | ex<u>per</u>ience |
> | sug<u>gest</u>ed | <u>priv</u>acy | pho<u>tog</u>raphy |

> 🌐 2.41
>
> **A:** *annoying   director   dramatic   suggested*
> **B:** *classical   fantasy   interviewed   privacy*
> **C:** *celebrity   embarrassing   experience   photography*

Reading & Listening (SB page 86)

1

Ask the students to read the article quickly just to find out the answer.

> Sentence b)

2

Ask the students to read the article more carefully and decide if the statements are true or false.

> a) True.
> b) True.
> c) False. (She tore it up / shredded it.)
> d) True.
> e) False. (They made mocking comments and tried to interrupt her.)
> f) False. (She said that she wasn't going to do the story.)
> g) True.

3 🌐 2.42

Tell the students they're going to hear three callers to an American radio phone-on show giving their reactions to what Mika Brzesninski did. Play the recording and ask the students to say whether most of the callers have a positive or negative reaction.

> A positive reaction.

> 🌐 2.42 (DR = Dan Rivero; L = Luke; M = Maria; J = Jason; C = Cathy)
>
> DR: *You're listening to WAZR on 98.6 FM, and I'm Dan Rivero. We're talking about Mika Brzezinski's refusal to cover the Paris Hilton story. What do you think? Give me a call and let me know. … We have our first caller. Is it Luke?*
>
> L: *That's right.*
>
> DR: *Go ahead, Luke.*
>
> L: *Hi, Dan. I just want to congratulate Mika Brzezinski on taking a stand and for saying what most of America is thinking: we've had enough of hearing about these celebrities! That's not news! And what's the problem with Mika's co-hosts? They gave her no support at all when she really needed it.*
>
> DR: *Thanks, Luke. Next up we have Maria.*
>
> M: *You rock, Mika! It takes courage to do what you did. I wish there were more presenters like you. You're an inspiration. I'm going to tell my boss today what I think of him! Yeah! You know, Mika, you're a lot bigger and a lot better than those guys you have to work with.*
>
> DR: *Thanks, Maria. We have Jason on the line. Jason?*
>
> J: *Thanks, Dan. I have to say I was disappointed by Mika Brzezinski's refusal to cover the lead story. It's not up to her to decide which stories she does and doesn't cover. Her job is to read out what she's given. I think her co-presenters were right to tell her that her behaviour was unacceptable.*
>
> DR: *OK, Jason. Thanks for your call. Time for one more. Let's hear from Cathy.*
>
> C: *Hi, Dan. I don't know what your last caller was talking about. I agree with your other callers that Mika was right and the other guys on the show were trying to make her look stupid. And just because the paparazzi are running around taking pictures of Paris Hilton, it doesn't mean we're actually interested in her!*
>
> DR: *OK, let's take a break. We'll be right back after the news with more reactions …*

4

Go through the questions with the students before playing the recording again so that they know what information to listen out for.

> a) most   b) criticises   c) inspired   d) wrong
> e) agrees   f) doesn't feel   g) doesn't think

5

Go through the questions with the students before putting them into pairs and asking them to give and discuss their own opinions. Encourage them to report back to the class.

Writing & Speaking (SB page 87)

1

• Ask the students to work in pairs to compare the notes and the finished article.

• Then ask the students to complete the article with the words in the box.

> 1 was   2 had   3 a   4 a   5 the   6 it
> 7 had   8 been   9 the

2

Ask the students to choose the best headline and justify their choice, saying why the other headlines are unsuitable.

> The best headline is *c*.
>
> The bank cashier wasn't arrested, so *a* is not possible. The man didn't rob the bank. He just made the cashier think he was going to rob the bank, so *b* isn't possible.

3

Give the students a minute or two to look at the notes, the article and the headlines again. Then ask them to underline the correct words in the statements.

> a) leave out
> b) direct, reported
> c) leave out

4

• Put the students in pairs and tell them that they're going to work together to write a newspaper article from a set of notes. Ask them to read the notes and answer questions about any difficult vocabulary.

• As the students write their stories, go round giving help and encouragement. Remind them to think of a suitable headline for their story. Get several pairs to read out their articles to the class.

Possible answer:

Supermarket thief caught

£5,000 was stolen from a supermarket in
Liverpool on 25 May. A local newspaper ran the
story and claimed the thief had taken £7,000.
The thief called the newspaper to complain
and suggested that the supermarket manager
had taken the extra £2,000. The staff at the
newspaper kept him busy on the phone while
the police traced the call. The thief was arrested
ten minutes later, while he was still on the
phone talking to the newspaper staff!

5

Put the students into small groups to discuss the
questions. Encourage them to report back to the class on
what they found out.

Further practice material

Need more classroom practice activities?

→ Photocopiable resource materials page 180
  🌐 2.43 **Song:** *Somewhere Only We Know*
→ TOP 10 activities pages xv to xx

Need progress tests?

→ Test CD – *Test Review C*

Need more on important teaching concepts?

→ Key concepts in *New Inside Out* pages xxii to
  xxxv

Need student self-study practice?

→ CD-ROM – *Review C*

Need more information and more ideas?

→ www.insideout.net

10 Childhood *Overview*

Section & Aims	What the students are doing
Reading & Vocabulary SB page 88 Reading for gist Phrasal verbs	Talking about children they know. Reading definitions of a mother and choosing the one they like best. Underling the correct particle in sentences with phrasal verbs. Answering questions about childcare.
Listening SB page 89 Listening for detail	Listening to children defining things and identifying what they are. Writing explanations of things for a child.
Grammar SB page 89 Defining relative clauses	Studying the structure and use of defining relative clauses. Identifying parts of relative clauses in definitions. Reordering questions about memories of childhood. Asking and answering questions about childhood memories.
Reading SB page 90 Reading for gist	Talking about white lies which people tell children. Reading an article about telling lies to children and discussing the benefits.
Pronunciation SB page 91 Silent letters	Identifying the silent letters in words. Listening and repeating words with silent letters.
Grammar SB page 91 Real conditionals	Studying the form and use of real conditionals. Identifying the rules for making real conditional sentences. Choosing the correct alternatives in sentences.
Vocabulary & Speaking SB page 91 Proverbs	Matching statements to proverbs. Discussing the meaning of proverbs.
Listening & Grammar SB page 92 Listening for gist Indirect questions	Listening to a TV programme and choosing a correct definition. Choosing the correct alternatives in sentences. Matching opinions to speakers. Completing indirect questions. Studying the structure of indirect questions.
Vocabulary SB page 93 *make* and *let*	Rewriting sentences with *make* and *let*. Completing sentences.
Speaking: anecdote SB page 93 Fluency practice	Talking about an activity they did when they were children.
Useful phrases SB page 94 Useful conversational phrases: describing objects.	Matching conversations to pictures. Completing a table with useful phrases for describing objects. Describing the purpose, appearance and material of objects. Writing conversations and descriptions of gadgets.
Vocabulary *Extra* SB page 95 Word families	Discovering how prefixes change meanings of the base word, and matching prefixes to meaning. Matching parts of speech with suffixes. Completing sentences with appropriate words.
Writing WB page 63	Writing a letter of advice.

10 Childhood *Teacher's notes*

Warm up

Tell the students about your earliest memory. Encourage them to ask you questions about how old you were at the time and about the details of your memory. Ask the students what their earliest memories are. Find out who can remember the furthest back and encourage them to give as many details as they can.

Reading & Vocabulary (SB page 88)

1

- Tell the students the names of some children that you know. Get them to ask you questions about the children – whose children they are, how you know them, how old they are, etc.

- Students write the names of three children they know. They then show their names to a partner and take turns to ask questions about them. Encourage them to ask as many questions as they can about these children.

2

- Write the following on the board:

  You have to love your own because everyone else thinks it's a nuisance.

  It's someone who tells you it won't hurt when he's hurting you.

  Tell the students that these are definitions of things written by children. Get them to guess what they are (a baby and a doctor).

- Get individual students to read out the children's definitions of a mother to the class. Explain any unknown vocabulary (*tucks you in* = puts you to bed and tucks the sheets and blankets tightly under the mattress so you feel safe and secure), and ask them to say which one they like best.

- Put the students in pairs and ask them to write similar definitions of a father. Give them plenty of time to do this and go round offering help where needed. They could either write their definitions as a child might or as their grown-up selves.

3

- Point out that the highlighted verbs in these sentences are all phrasal verbs which can be used to talk about childhood. Ask the students to read the sentences and choose the correct particles. Allow them to use a dictionary if necessary.

- Point out that some of the incorrect particles do form phrasal verbs with the main verbs, but don't have the right meaning for the sentence. So, for example, in sentence 1 there is a phrasal verb *to bring someone down*, but it doesn't have the meaning required for this sentence. When checking answers, make sure the students are clear about the meaning of all these phrasal verbs.

- Ask the students to work individually to answer the questions with reference to their own childhoods. They should then compare with a partner.

a) up	b) off	c) about	d) for	e) in
f) at	g) after	h) up		

Language notes

Grammar: phrasal verbs

There are many phrasal verbs in English. When your students encounter a phrasal verb in a text, encourage them to try to guess the meaning from the context. This will help if they then look it up in a dictionary, as there can sometimes be several meanings of the same phrasal verb.

See Language note about phrasal verbs on page 35 for more information.

Listening (SB page 89)

1 🌐 3.01

- Focus the students' attention on the photos. Tell them that they're going to hear the children in the photos defining some of the things from the list. Explain that all three children will give a definition for each item. Go through the list with the class, making sure they understand all the items.

- Play the recording and ask the students to listen and number the five items defined by the children in the correct order. Allow them to compare their answers in pairs before playing the recording again and checking answers with the class.

a) 2	b) 1	c) 3	d) –	e) 5	f) 4
g) –	h) –	i) –			

1
It's something that lived a very long time ago. It looks very scary.
A thing that lived long time ago.
Um ... It's a big monster.

2
It's a man and he lives in ... , he lives up in space.
He's someone who lives ... who's died and he looks down on people.
A person that helps people, in heaven.

3
It's something that's very cold and it's ... it's a ... it's a stone.
It's a sort of big piece of ice that cracks off a bigger piece.
It's a big ice cube.

4
A place where animals have been put up to show.
Somewhere where they show you things that are very old.
It's somewhere where people will show things like dinosaurs and olden days things.

5
It's a person who takes toys away.
It's someone that in the middle of the night ... and it's got a ... something around his face with round holes and he's got a T-shirt that's got black and white and he robs things.
It's someone who steals things when you're asleep.

Language note

Vocabulary: *robber*
Strictly speaking, a *robber* is someone who takes money/property by force or by the threat of force. Someone who steals money/property is a *thief*, and a *thief* who breaks into a house to steal from you is a *burglar*. A *thief* who steals from you on the street, without your knowledge, is a *pickpocket*.

2

- Pairwork. The students choose other things from the list and try to describe them in terms that a four-year-old child would understand. First give them some examples. Write on the board the words *sandwich* and *magazine* and get the students to say something like *It's a sort of food, It's like a book.*

- Students then write their own explanations. Go round the class. Take note of any particularly good explanations. Invite several pairs to read out one of their explanations without saying what it is they are talking about. Get the rest of the class to guess. Then put the students in pairs to read out their explanations and identify what is being described.

Grammar (SB page 89)

Defining relative clauses

1

- Focus the students' attention on the examples in the margin. Point out that the highlighted expressions are defining relative clauses; they give a definition of the preceding word or phrase.

- Ask the students to look at the two examples of children's definitions in the exercise. Ask them to work in pairs and to answer the questions below.

- Check answers with the class and make sure that everyone has understood the concept of defining relative clauses. Make sure that they understand that relative pronouns cannot be left out when they're the subject of the verb. (See notes below.)

> 1 In sentence b.
> 2 In sentence a.
> 3 No. Because the relative pronoun is the subject of the verb.

Language notes

Grammar: defining relative clauses

- A defining relative clause gives essential information about the noun or noun phrase it describes. The defining relative clause joins two ideas together with a relative pronoun (e.g. *who, which, that*). For example:
I've got a friend. He lives in the United States.

  This becomes one sentence when the relative pronoun *who* replaces the pronoun *he*:

  *I've got a friend **who** lives in the Unites States.*

- The relative pronoun *who* is used when talking about people (it replaces the pronoun *he* or *she*).

  The relative pronoun *which* is used when talking about things (and replaces the pronoun *it*).

  The relative pronoun *that* can be used to talk about people or things in a defining relative clause, although it's mainly used in spoken English rather than written.

- The relative pronoun can be omitted in a sentence only if it's the object of the verb. Compare these sentences:

  *Is she the woman **that** everyone's talking about?*
  Is she the woman everyone's talking about?

  The relative pronoun *that* is the object of the verb *talking*, so it can be omitted.

  When the relative pronoun is the subject of the verb it can't be omitted.

  *Isn't he the man **that** won the prize?*

  The relative pronoun *that* is the subject of the verb *won* so it has to stay in.

2

Working in the same pairs, the students read some more definitions and identify the relative clauses, the subjects and verbs and the relative pronouns that can be omitted.

1

a) <u>who stays away from school</u>
b) <u>that protects babies' clothes</u>
c) <u>which you put in a baby's mouth</u>
d) <u>who you employ</u>

2

a) subject = *who*; verb = *stays*
b) subject = *that*; verb = *protects*
c) subject = *you*; verb = *put*
d) subject = *you*; verb = *employ*

3

You must keep the relative pronouns in definitions *a* and *b* because *who* and *that* are the subject of the relative clause in these sentences.
You can leave out the relative pronouns in *c* and *d* because *which* and *who* are not the subject of the relative clause in these sentences – *you* is.

---

3 Pairwork

- The pairwork exercise for this unit is on pages 119 and 124 of the Student's Book. Put the students in pairs and tell them who will be Student A, and who will be Student B.

- They take it in turns to read out a word with three definitions for their partner to guess which is the correct one. While they're doing the exercise, go round monitoring and giving help. Take note of any errors which may need particular attention later, and also any examples of good language use, which you can praise in a feedback session.

4

- Go through the example with the class. Ask the students to work individually to write the remaining questions.

- Check answers with the class before asking them to answer the two questions underneath. If anyone raises the issue of whether the preposition can go anywhere other than the end, point out that these are informal questions. In very formal questions, people might ask *What can you remember about the school to which you went/the toys with which you played, etc.?*

- Pairwork. Finally, put the students into pairs to ask and answer the questions for themselves. For question f), you might like to point out the difference between *dream of* (which usually refers to aspirations, e.g. *He dreamt of becoming a firefighter*) and *dream about* (which usually refers to the contents of dreams at night, e.g. fairytales, castles, monsters, etc.).

---

a) the school that you went to?
b) the toys that you played with?

---

c) the parties that you were invited to?
e) the books which you were interested in?
f) the things that you were worried about?
g) the things that you used to dream of?

1 A preposition.
2 Yes. Because it is not the subject of the verb in the relative clause.

---

5 Grammar *Extra* 10, Part 1

Ask the students to turn to *Grammar Extra* 10, Part 1 on page 144 of the Student's Book. Here they'll find an explanation of the grammar they've been studying and further exercises to practise it.

1

a) A babushka is a headscarf which/that women tie under their chin.
b) A pestle is a tool which/that you use to crush nuts and seeds.
c) A woodlouse is a small insect which/that eats dead wood.
d) A farrier is a person who/that makes and fits horseshoes.
e) A fandango is a dance which/that originated in Spain.
f) A burglar is a person who/that breaks into your house and steals things.
g) A rolling pin is a kitchen utensil which/that you use to make pastry.

The relative pronoun can be removed from sentences a), b), and g).

2

a) OK.
b) My mother is the only person who/that really understands me.
c) The issue which/that worries me most is global warming.
d) OK.
e) I've got a lot of friends who/that live in the United States.
f) OK.
g) The people who/that live next door to me are really friendly.

Reading (SB page 90)

1

- Explain that a 'white lie' is a trivial lie told for diplomatic or well-intentioned reasons. For example, if a friend asks if you like her sweater, you might tell her that you do, even if you hate it, because giving your true opinion would be hurtful.

- Point out that white lies are often told to children when a more truthful explanation would be too complicated or when parents need to persuade them to do something. Go through the list, reading each one aloud or asking a student to do this.

- Put the students into pairs and ask them to discuss which of the white lies they heard when they were children. In a class feedback session, encourage them to contribute any other white lies that they were told.

Language notes
- **pillow**
  A soft object on which you rest your head in bed.
- **crusts**
  The hard brown edges of a piece of bread.
- **curl** (verb)
  To make something form a curved or round shape.

Cultural notes
Father Christmas
Also known as Santa Claus, Father Christmas brings presents at Christmas to children around the world.

The tooth fairy
The (mythical) tooth fairy gives children money in exchange for a tooth left under a child's pillow when they are asleep.

2
- Focus the student's attention on the statements and read them aloud, or get a student to read them. Ask the students to think about the statements and decide which ones they agree with.
- Tell the students that they're going to read an article about lying to children and they should find out which statement psychologists agree with.

> The psychologists agree with statement b.

3
- Focus the student's attention on the example and point out that it uses *avoid* from box A and *awkward truths* from box B. Ask the students to refer back to the article and make similar pairings in order to write sentences giving the potential benefits of telling white lies.
- Check answers with the class before putting them into pairs to discuss the questions. Encourage them to report back to the class on their discussions.

> White lies can …
> help avoid awkward truths.
> develop children's language skills.
> help children to eat up their vegetables.
> protect children's innocence.
> stimulate children's imagination.

Pronunciation (SB page 91)

1 🌐 3.02
- Explain that some English words have silent letters, letters which aren't pronounced. Read out the example, pointing out that the words *know*, *knee* and *knife* are all spelt with a *k* but that the *k* isn't pronounced; it is silent.
- Play the recording and ask the students to listen to each group of words and decide which letter is silent.

> a) k   b) h   c) b   d) t   e) w   f) p

2
Play the recording again for the students to listen and repeat.

Grammar (SB page 91)
Real conditionals

1
- Focus the students' attention on the extract from the article. Ask them to say how they could complete the second sentence so that it has the same meaning.
- Focus attention on the sentences in the margin and point out that *unless* has the meaning *if … not*. This is why a negative verb is needed in the gap in the second sentence to give it the same meaning.
- Point out the heading of the information in the margin and explain that the conditionals they're going to be studying are all *real*: they deal with things which are true or possible.

> doesn't eat

Language notes
Grammar: real conditionals
- Real conditionals present possible scenarios in sentences with two clauses: the *if* clause (the condition) and the main clause (which contains the outcome resulting from the condition). They usually follow this pattern:

if clause:	main clause:
if + present	*will / might / may / can* + infinitive
If we have a picnic,	*I might / may / 'll invite Joe.*
	imperative:
	bring something to drink.

- The two clauses can change position. When they do, the comma separating the clauses goes. You don't use *will*, etc. in the *if* clause.
- Real conditionals are used to talk about possible situations which include:
  threats: *If you touch that chocolate, I'll hit you.*
  warnings: *If you don't do your homework, your teacher might punish you.*
  promises: *If you help me, I'll give you £20.*

> • Unless = if ... not and won't = will not.
>   Unless you work harder, you won't pass your exams
>   = If you don't work harder, you won't pass your
>   exams.

2

- Go through the rules with the class and ask them to say whether they are true or false.
- Get the students to link the rules with the examples in the margin, identifying the *if*-clauses and the main clauses; establishing that they all deal with things that are true or possible.

> a) True. b) True. c) True. d) True.
> e) True.

3

- Go through the example with the class, pointing out that *you're* is correct here because it's in the *if*-clause and *if*-clauses use the present tense.
- Get the students to work in pairs to discuss the meaning of the sentences and to choose the correct alternatives. Check answers with the class and then ask them to say how old they think the child would be in each case.

> a) you're
> b) you fall off
> c) you're phoning
> d) Unless
> e) you haven't finished
> f) you've finished
> g) If
> h) you're going to play

4 Grammar *Extra* 10, Part 2

Ask the students to turn to *Grammar Extra* 10, Part 2 on page 144 of the Student's Book. Here they'll find an explanation of the grammar they've been studying and further exercises to practise it.

> **1**
> a) 2 b) 5 c) 8 d) 1 e) 4 f) 3 g) 6
> h) 7
>
> **2**
> a) If / unless b) unless c) If d) Unless
> e) unless f) If g) If
>
> **3**
> a) is; 'll go
> b) rains; won't go
> c) will go; is
> d) earn; 'll visit
> e) 'll go; is
> f) 'll see; have to

Vocabulary & Speaking (SB page 91)

1

- Focus the students' attention on the example and point out that there's a mistake in each of these sentences. In the example, the verb has to be *is* rather than *will be* as *if*-clauses use the present tense. Ask the students to work individually to correct the remaining statements.
- Check answers before asking the students to match the statements to the proverbs. Point out that a proverb is a short saying which is supposed to express a basic truth. Ask them if they have the same proverbs in their own language.

> a) If the boss ~~will be~~ is away, nobody will do any work. (6)
> b) If you ~~will~~ get something easily, you won't be sorry to lose it. (4)
> c) Unless you ~~will~~ consider something carefully, you might fail. (5)
> d) Unless you ~~will~~ concentrate, you won't succeed. (1)
> e) If you ~~will~~ fail the first time, you might not want to try again. (3)
> f) Unless you ~~will~~ make an effort, you won't succeed. (2)

2

Pairwork. If possible, pair up students from the same country or who speak the same language. Ask them to think about proverbs in their own language and to translate them into English using *If ...* or *Unless ...* . As they do this, go round making sure they are forming sentences with *If ...* and *Unless ...* correctly. Encourage several pairs to read out their translated proverbs to the class.

Listening & Grammar (SB page 92)

1 🌐 3.03

- Focus the students' attention on the photos in the margin. Explain that the man and woman are the parents of the little girl. Ask the students what they might be arguing about.
- Tell the students that they're going to listen to a television programme about bringing up children. This programme uses the expression *pushy parents*. Read the definitions with the class, then play the recording and ask the students to say which definition they think is best.

> Definition b)

3.03 (D = Dale; R = Rachel; G = George)

D: *Welcome to* Dale's Dilemmas. *I'm Dale Rogers, and the subject of today's dilemma is pushy parents. Are today's parents too ambitious for their children? Should they let children be children and stop organising their lives? Should we congratulate them for developing their children's potential, or should we say 'back off and leave the kids alone'?*

In the studio we have George and Rachel from Chicago. They disagree about how to bring up their daughter, and we're going to hear what they have to say. … George and Rachel, welcome to the show.

G and R: *Thanks.*

D: *Rachel, if we could start with you. Can you tell us a little about your daughter?*

R: *Yes, my daughter Hayley is five years old, and I think she has what it takes to be a film star. So I'm doing everything I can to get her into films.*

D: *And what exactly does that involve?*

R: *Hayley goes to acting classes twice a week. She has a singing teacher who comes to the house once a week, and we watch a lot of movies together at home. Then at the weekends we go to auditions. Sometimes we have to travel to New York or Los Angeles, but I'm willing to do whatever it takes.*

D: *That's a lot of travelling. What do you think about it, George?*

G: *I think my wife is obsessed. I don't think she should make Hayley do this. It isn't Hayley's choice. Rachel wanted to be a child star, and that's why she's making Hayley go though this.*

R: *I'm not making her do anything against her will. Hayley loves it and she wants to be a star.*

D: *But at five years old, does she understand what it means?*

G: *No, of course not. I want to let Hayley grow up like a normal child. There's too much pressure in the film world. She's a kid – let her play, let her have friends.*

D: *It's true that being a child star can be a very isolating experience.*

R: *I know that, but if you don't try, you don't succeed. When Hayley is famous and she's doing movies, you're going to look back and thank me.*

D: *Thank you Rachel and George. In just a moment, we'll be meeting Mark and Charlene who want their two-year-old son to be the next Tiger Woods. But first, it's over to the studio audience. Who has a question for Rachel and George?*

Cultural note

Tiger Woods (born 1975)
Tiger Woods is considered to be one of the greatest golfers ever. Woods, who is of mixed race, is credited with prompting a surge of interest in golf among minorities and young people in the United States.

2

Go through the sentences and the alternatives with the class, then play the recording again and ask the students to underline the correct ones. Ask them for their reactions to what they've heard and for their opinions about the way George and Rachel are bringing up Hayley?

a) disagree	b) five	c) film	d) week
e) auditions	f) obsessed	g) Rachel	

3 🌐 3.04

- Read out the questions and answers to the class. After each one, ask the students to write G and R next to the answers they think each parent gave.
- Play the recording for them to check their answers.

a) R: 'She enjoys life.'
   G: 'She's too young to know.'
b) R: 'Continue doing auditions. We've invested a lot of time and money.'
   G: 'Stop doing auditions. Our child isn't a business.'
c) G: 'Yes.'
   R: 'No.'
d) G: 'Our son misses his mom.'
   R: Our son is proud of his little sister.'
e) G: Very stressful.'
   R: 'We can cope.'

🌐 3.04 (D = Dale ; W1 and W2 = woman 1, woman 2; R = Rachel; G = George; M1, M2 = man 1, man 2)

D: *Who has a question for Rachel and George? Yes, the woman in the red dress please …*

W1: *Do you know how Hayley feels?*

R: *She enjoys her life and she wants to be a film star.*

G: *I think she's too young to know how she feels. She says she's happy because she wants to please her mom.*

D: *Thank you. Another question now please. … Yes, the woman with the blue shirt.*

W2: *Can you tell me what you're going to do when Hayley starts school?*

G: *I'd like her to stop doing auditions and focus on being a normal school kid.*

R: Well, I think it would be wrong to stop now after all the time and money we've invested. After all, you don't invest in a business and then give up after six months if you're not making a profit.

G: But Hayley is not a business – she's a child. Our daughter.

D: OK, … let's have one from the man in the green jacket.

M1: Do you think you're depriving Hayley of a normal childhood?

G: Yeah. I worry about that.

R: Well, I don't. She's special and I want to help her to fulfil her potential.

D: Yes, the young man with the baseball cap.

M2: Could you tell me whether you have any other children and how they are affected?

G: We have a seven-year old son, and he misses his mom.

R: He's very proud of his little sister.

D: The woman in the red dress again.

W1: Do you have any idea how stressful it is to be a film star?

G: Very stressful. I don't think my wife has thought about the negatives at all.

R: We can cope. I just hope that I can come back here in ten years' time and we can do a follow-up story when Hayley's a star.

D: Well, I'm afraid that's all we've got time for now. Thank you to …

4 🌐 3.05

- Focus the students' attention on the information in the margin. Point out that in each pair of sentences, the first one is a direct question, the second is indirect, beginning with *Do you know …* and *Can you tell me …* Explain that the effect of this is to make a question sound gentler, more polite and less confrontational.

- Look at the example with the class. Point out that question a) in Exercise 3 is direct. What the audience actually asked on the recording was an indirect question: *Do you know how Hayley feels?* Ask them to complete the remaining indirect questions using the beginnings given.

> a) … how Hayley feels?
> b) … what you're going to do when Hayley starts school?
> c) … you're depriving Hayley of a normal childhood?
> d) … whether/if you have any other children and how they are affected?
> e) … how stressful it is to be a film star?

🌐 3.05 (W1 and 2 = 2 women in the audience; M1 and 2 = 2 men in the audience;)
a) W1: Do you know how Hayley feels?
b) W2: Can you tell me what you're going to do when Hayley starts school?
c) M1: Do you think you're depriving Hayley of a normal childhood?
d) M2: Could you tell me whether you have any other children and how they are affected?
e) W1: Do you have any idea how stressful it is to be a film star?

Language notes

Grammar: indirect questions

- Indirect questions are often used as a way of putting a little (polite) distance between the person who is asking the questions and the person they're asking.

- In indirect questions you don't put the auxiliary before the subject. The word order (subject + verb) is the same as affirmative sentences.

  Direct question: *When did they meet?*
  Indirect question: *Do you know when they met?*

- In direct questions the auxiliary verb *do* usually comes before the subject. Verbs like *can, have, be* come before the subject.

  Direct question: *What is your favourite colour?*

  Indirect question: *Could you tell me what your favourite colour is?*

- Yes/No questions use *if* or *whether* in indirect questions.

  Direct question: *Are they happy?*
  Indirect question: *Can you tell me if they are happy?*

5

Pairwork. Ask the students to look at the indirect questions they've just written and answer the questions about their construction.

> a) No.   b) Yes.   c) Yes.

6

Go through the example with the class, then ask them to put the remaining questions in the right order. Check answers before putting the students into pairs to take turns asking and answering the questions.

> a) your parents were 'pushy parents'?
> b) if your parents were born in the same city?
> c) how your parents met?
> d) children have enough freedom these days?
> e) what your ambitions for your children are?

Vocabulary (SB page 93)

1

- Make sure the students know the difference in meaning between *make someone do something* (force them to do it) and *let someone do something* (allow them to do it). Ask them to rewrite the sentences. When checking answers, write the correct sentences on the board. Then ask which comment was made by Rachel and which by George.

- Focus the students' attention on the sentences on the board and ask the students to say which pattern they demonstrate.

> a) 'I'm not making her do anything against her will.' (Rachel)
> b) 'She's a kid – let her play, let her have friends.' (George)
> 2 *make/let* + somebody + infinitive without *to*

2

- Students complete the sentences. Explain that *make* and *let* both fit grammatically, but the context will determine whether *make* or *let* is a better choice. Point out that in the example sentence it's more likely that parents would allow a child to wear jewellery to school than that they'd insist on her wearing it.

- When you've checked the answers, ask the students to decide how many of the sentences are true for them. Give them a few minutes to change the statements into questions, then ask them to take turns to ask and answer in pairs. Point out the follow-up question *Did yours?* in the example. With weaker students, check that they've formed the questions correctly before putting them into pairs.

> a) let me
> b) made me/us
> c) let us
> d) let me
> e) made me
> f) let me
> g) let me
> h) made us
>
> a) Did your parents let you wear jewellery to school?
> b) Did your parents make you do the washing up after dinner?
> c) Did your school teachers let you use their first names?
> d) Did your sister ever let you borrow her clothes?
> e) Did your parents make you keep your room tidy?
> f) Did your brother sometimes let you borrow his MP3 player?
> g) Did your parents let you dye your hair?
> h) Did you sports teacher make you play outside in bad weather?

Speaking: anecdote (SB page 93)

For more information about how to set up, monitor and repeat Anecdotes, see page xx in the Introduction.

1 **3.06**

- Focus the students' attention on the photo of Ryan. Explain that they're going to hear Ryan talking about an activity he used to do when he was a child. Go through the questions and the answers with the class.

- Play the recording and ask the students to underline the correct information.

- Ask the students to match the questions and answers. Then play the recording again for them to check their answers.

> a) Martial arts.
> b) I liked kung fu movies.
> c) My idea.
> d) Yes, I was obsessed with it.
> e) Two or three times a week.
> f) At a gym in the city centre.
> g) My parents drove me there.
> h) Yes I do.
> i) Yes, definitely.

> **3.06**
> *My mother plays the piano really well, so she was very keen for me to learn the piano too. I had lessons for a while, but I was useless, and eventually my piano teacher begged my parents to stop sending me. So that was the end of my music career! But what I really wanted to do was martial arts, and my parents let me join a club when I was about nine. I used to love those kung fu movies – Bruce Lee was my hero, and I had posters of him all over my room, and that was how I got the idea. I was a bit disappointed at first, because our classes weren't like the films, but then I got quite obsessed with it and I was doing martial arts two or three times a week. We did it at a gym in the city centre, so my parents drove me there because it was quite far away from my house. But when I was about fourteen I decided that I didn't want my friends to see my parents dropping me off, so I took the bus instead. I'm still doing martial arts now after ten years, and I've started getting more and more interested in kick-boxing. I'd definitely encourage my own children to do martial arts. It's not just about fighting – of course, you learn self-defence – but you also learn other skills such as mental discipline and self-confidence.*

Cultural notes

Martial Arts
Martial Arts were devised and developed in Asian countries. Karate, Judo and jujitsu are Japanese combat styles; Kung Fu and Wing Chun are Chinese; Taekwondo is a Korean kicking martial art.

Kickboxing
Kickboxing is a Japanese sport which takes elements of karate, boxing and Thai boxing. Although similar to Thai Boxing, kicks below the belt aren't allowed.

Bruce Lee /brus liː/ (1940–1973)
Bruce Lee was an American-born martial artist and actor. He popularized the martial arts genre with such films as *Way of the Dragon* (1972) and *Enter the Dragon* (1973).

2

- Give the students a minute or two to decide what they're going to talk about. Then ask them to look at the questions in Exercise 1 again. Allow them to make notes of what they're going to say and how they're going to say it, but discourage them from writing a paragraph that they can simply read out.

- Pairwork. Put the students in pairs and ask them to take turns to tell their partner about their childhood activity. Encourage them to ask each other follow-up questions to get further information.

- Ask some pairs to report back to the class about what they found out about their partner.

Useful phrases (SB page 94)

1 3.07

- Focus the students' attention on the illustrations. Ask them if they know what any of the things are.

- Explain *gadget* and tell the students that they're going to listen to four people describing their favourite gadgets. Ask them to listen and read the conversations and then match them to four of the pictures.

> a) 6   b) 1   c) 5   d) 4

2 3.08

- Focus the students' attention on the table and point out the three columns for three different ways of describing an object. Ask them to complete the table with the highlighted phrases from the conversations in Exercise 1.

- Play the recording for the students to listen and repeat. When they've done this chorally, ask for individual repetition of the useful phrases.

> a) It's one of those things you use to massage your head.
> b) It's for cooling yourself down.
> c) You use it to peel a pineapple.
> d) It looks like a big spider.
> e) It's round with a long handle.
> f) It's made of metal.

3.08

> a) It's one of those things you use to massage your head.
> b) It's for cooling yourself down.
> c) You use it to peel a pineapple.
> d) It looks like a big spider.
> e) It's round with a long handle.
> f) It's made of metal.

3

Ask the students to look at the words and phrases in the box and decide which ones can be used to complete which of the useful phrases b, c, e and f in Exercise 2.

> b) It's for removing stains / storing things / straightening your hair.
> c) You use it to light the gas / recharge your mobile phone / unblock toilets.
> e) It's long and thin / rectangular / small and square.
> f) It's made of cardboard / plastic / stainless steel.

4

- Pairwork. Put the students into pairs and ask them to write conversations describing the purpose, appearance and material of the two other objects in Exercise 1 which were not described. If they don't know what these are, encourage them to be creative in writing convincing dialogues about what they think the objects might be. (The objects are a jewellery organiser and a hair straightener. You can decide whether or not to tell the students.)

- Tell the students to practise their dialogues. Go round and note any particularly good pairs. You can then ask to perform their conversations for the class.

5

Ask the students to describe their own favourite gadgets to their partners, using the useful phrases.

Vocabulary Extra (SB page 95)

Word families

1

- Pairwork. Ask the students to discuss the words in lists a) to c) and to decide which word in each list does not exist. Encourage them to do this without looking up the answers in the dictionary extracts. They could use various techniques, for example, explaining to each other the meaning of any words they already know, reading the word aloud to see which ones they recognise, etc.

- Then focus the students' attention on the dictionary extracts and ask them to check their answers and tick the words they know.

- In a class feedback session, get the students to explain the words they've ticked to each other.

> a) undernational b) misqualify
> c) overnationalistic

2

- Ask the students to look at the dictionary extracts and the prefixes in the box. Ask them to think about how each prefix alters the meaning of the base word. It might help to begin by first picking out which ones have a predominantly negative or positive meaning.

- Ask the students to match the prefixes to their approximate meanings.

> a) un/in b) over c) mis d) dis
> e) re f) under

3

Remind the students to look at the base words and the prefixes. If they know the base word and the rough meaning of the prefix, they can make a good guess at the overall meaning of the word. Get them to check their answers in their dictionaries.

> a) continue no longer (stop doing)
> b) print wrongly
> c) sleep too much (more than you should have slept)
> d) do again
> e) not aware
> f) not pay enough

4

- Remind the students of the abbreviations used in dictionaries to show parts of speech. Point out that suffixes are often used to change a base word from one part of speech to another. Ask them to copy and complete the table.

- Ask the students to refer to the words in the table as they match the parts of speech to the typical suffixes.

Verb	Adjective	Noun	Noun (person)
advise	(in)advisable, advisory	advice	adviser
cook	cooked, overcooked, under-cooked	cooker, cookery, cooking	cook
employ	(un)employed (un)employable	(un)employment	employer, employee
nationalize	national, multinational, international, nationalized, nationalistic	nation, nationalism, nationality, multinational	
qualify, disqualify	qualified, disqualified, unqualified	qualification, qualifier	
use, misuse, reuse	used, useful, useless, reusable, disused	usage, misuse, use	user

> a) verb – 4 b) adjective – 1 c) noun – 2
> d) noun (person) – 3

5

- Ask the students to work individually to complete the sentences. Then allow them to compare with a partner before checking answers with the class.

- Make sure the students are clear about the difference between a *cooker* (a kitchen appliance) and a *cook* (a person who does the cooking).

- Finally, ask the students to say if any of the sentences are true for them.

> a) cook b) nationalistic c) adviser (also advisor) d) qualifications e) reuse
> f) unemployed

6

Give the students time to look at their own dictionaries and see how the word families are presented there. They could then report back to the class.

Further practice material

Need more writing practice?
→ Workbook page 63
- Writing a letter of advice.

Need more classroom practice activities?
→ Photocopiable resource materials pages 181 to 183
  Grammar: *When I was at school …*
  Vocabulary: Make *and* let
  Communication: *Definition auction*
→ Top 10 activities pages xv to xx

Need DVD material?
→ DVD – Programme 10: *Childhood*

Need progress tests?
→ Test CD – *Test Unit 10*

Need more on important teaching concepts?
→ Key concepts in *New Inside Out* pages xxii to xxxv

Need student self-study practice?
→ CD-ROM – Unit 10: *Childhood*

Need student CEF self-evaluation?
→ CEF Checklists pages xxxvii to xliv

Need more information and more ideas?
→ www.insideout.net

11 Age *Overview*

Section & Aims	What the students are doing
🔘 **Listening & Vocabulary** **SB page 96** Listening for gist Attitude adverbs	Talking about rock and pop music. Reading and listening to an interview about a Rolling Stones gig. Completing the interview with attitude adverbs. Talking about going to live concerts.
🔘 **Pronunciation SB page 97** Syllable stress in attitude adverbs	Categorising attitude adverbs according to number of syllables and stress.
Vocabulary SB page 97 Adverbs	Identifying the correct position for adverbs. Reordering sentences and discussing which ones are true for them.
Grammar SB page 97 Unreal conditionals (1)	Studying the structure and use of unreal conditionals. Writing sentences with *If …* and discussing which ones are true for them.
Reading SB page 98 Reading for detail	Inventing an identity for a man in a photo. Reading a poem to see if it fits the character they have invented.
Grammar SB page 99 Wishes and regrets	Completing sentences with wishes and regrets. Matching facts to wishes and regrets. Writing more wishes and regrets.
Speaking SB page 99 Fluency practice	Writing wish or regret sentences based on pictures. Talking about bad decisions.
🔘 **Reading & Speaking SB page 100** Reading for specific information Fluency practice	Talking about upper or lower age limits for activities. Reading an article and deciding if statements are true. Writing a conversation based on the article. Discussing questions to do with age.
Grammar SB page 101 Unreal conditionals (2)	Studying the form and use of unreal conditionals. Underlining the correct alternatives. Writing and discussing unreal conditional sentences.
🔘 **Reading & Speaking** **SB page 101** Reading for specific information Fluency practice	Predicting the content of stories. Completing stories and discussing what they would have done in the same circumstances.
🔘 **Useful phrases SB page 102** Useful conversational phrases: on the telephone	Reading useful telephone phrases and deleting incorrect ones. Completing telephone conversations with the appropriate useful phrases. Listening and repeating useful phrases for talking on the telephone. Writing and practising telephone conversations.
Vocabulary *Extra* SB page 103 Idiomatic expressions	Replacing phrases with suitable binomials. Correcting idiomatic phrases. Completing idiomatic phrases.
Writing WB page 67	Writing a story.

Age *Teacher's notes*

Warm up

Ask the students to say at what age they think the following stages of life begin and end:

- childhood
- middle age
- adulthood
- old age

Listening & Vocabulary (SB page 96)

1

- Pairwork. Ask the students to make notes on their answers to the questions.
- In a class feedback session, compare the opinions of the different pairs.

2 🌐 3.09

- Find out if the students are familiar with the Rolling Stones and if they've been to one of their concerts. Ask them to listen and read the interview to find out what Matt and Ella think about Mick Jagger and Keith Richards.
- Allow them to compare their answers in pairs before checking with the class.

> a) Matt thinks Mick Jagger looked pretty good. Ella has a problem with Mick Jagger's dancing.
> b) Matt doesn't think Keith Richards looks good, but he plays the guitar beautifully. Ella thinks it's a miracle that Keith Richards is still alive.

Cultural note

The Rolling Stones
The Rolling Stones is an English rock band formed in 1962 by Brian Jones, Mick Jagger and Keith Richards. They've released 29 albums, and had 37 top ten singles, including *Satisfaction*, *Honky Tonk Woman* and *Brown Sugar*.

3

- Ask the students to look at the adverbs in the lists. Make sure that they understand the implications of each of the adverbs. Ask them to use them to complete the interview.
- Play the recording for them to check their answers. Then ask them to discuss the final question in pairs.

> 1 obviously   2 unfortunately   3 Basically
> 4 definitely   5 Personally   6 Actually

Pronunciation (SB page 97)

1

Remind the students that the boxes show the syllables of a word and the large boxes indicate the stressed syllables. Here they are being asked to classify words according to how many syllables they have and where the main stress falls. Encourage them to say each word aloud to get a feeling for what sounds right. Point out the main stress in the example word, which is underlined. Ask the students to do the same for the other words in the table.

A: ☐☐☐	B: ☐☐☐☐	C: ☐☐☐☐
<u>ac</u>tually	<u>de</u>finitely	a<u>pp</u>arently
<u>na</u>turally	<u>for</u>tunately	in<u>cre</u>dibly
<u>ob</u>viously	<u>po</u>sitively	pre<u>dic</u>tably
<u>prac</u>tically	<u>re</u>gularly	sur<u>pri</u>singly

2 🌐 3.10

Play the recording for the students to check their answers. Play it a second time for them to listen and repeat.

Vocabulary (SB page 97)

1

Focus the students' attention on the sentence and ask them to identify in which position it's possible to use *beautifully*. When checking answers, read out the complete sentence so that the students get to hear the whole thing and can develop a sense for what sounds right.

> Position 4.

Language note

Vocabulary: adverbs of manner
It's important to note that although this Vocabulary section deals with adverbs, they're adverbs of manner, not attitude (which are dealt with in the preceding two exercises). Adverbs of manner usually come at the end of the sentence, as practised here, whereas adverbs of attitude can occur at the beginning, middle or end of a sentence.

2

- Do the first one with the class as an example and then ask the students to reorder the remaining sentences.
- Check answers before asking the students to think about whether the sentences are true for them. Tell them to rewrite any that aren't to make them true, then to compare their sentences with a partner.

> a) I don't know the Rolling Stones' music very well.
> b) I like English bands a lot.
> c) I like playing my music very loud.
> d) I can't play any musical instruments very well.
> e) I don't enjoy karaoke very much.
> f) I don't remember the last concert I went to very well.

Grammar (SB page 97)

Unreal conditionals (1)

1

- Remind the students that they studied real conditionals in Unit 10 and that they were used to talk about things which are true or possible. Tell them that now they're going to look at unreal conditionals that are used to talk about things which are unreal or imaginary.
- Read out the unreal conditional sentence from the article. Ask the students to look at situations *a*, *b* and *c* and to decide which one the conditional sentence is based on. Draw the students' attention to the fact that the example sentence could equally well begin with the *if*-clause, i.e. that the two clauses are interchangeable.
- Tell the students to look at the sentences below and ask them to choose the correct alternative in each one.
- Go through the information and examples in the margin and make sure that everyone understands.

> Sentence *a*: They are popular. They are talented.
> 2 Use the past simple / *would* + infinitive in the main clause.

Language notes

Grammar: unreal conditionals

- The examples in this unit relate to a hypothetical or imaginary situation in the present, and not the past. *If* is followed by the simple past form to 'remove it one step from reality', not because the situation relates to the past.
- The type of conditional in this unit is also known as the 'second conditional'. There are two clauses in this type of sentence: the *if* clause (*if* followed by the verb in the past simple form) and the main clause (*would*/*wouldn't* followed by the infinitive without *to*). For example: *If I **was** an animal,* (*if* + past simple form) *I'd be cat.* (*would* + infinitive).

- The clauses can be reversed without changing the meaning, but the punctuation changes: When the *if* clause comes after the main clause, they aren't separated by a comma. When the *if* clause comes before the main clause, they are separated by a comma.

2

- Go through the example with the class, then ask the students to write unreal conditional sentences based on the other situations.
- Check answers with the class before asking the students to discuss with a partner whether the sentences are true for them.

> a) If I had a car, I'd be able to drive to work.
> b) If I could cook, I'd invite my friends round for dinner.
> c) If I lived abroad, I wouldn't see my family very regularly.
> d) If I didn't go out every night, I wouldn't always be tired.
> e) If I had time, I'd do my English homework.
> f) If I didn't have to learn English, I could learn / 'd be able to learn another language.

3 Pairwork

- The pairwork exercise for this unit is on pages 120 and 125 of the Student's Book. Put the students in pairs and tell them who will be Student A, and who will be Student B.
- While they're doing the exercise, go round monitoring and giving help. Take note of any errors which may need particular attention later, and also any examples of good language use, which you can praise in a feedback session.

Reading (SB page 98)

1

- Groupwork. Ask the students to look at the photograph of the man. Discourage them from reading the text at this stage. Ask them to work together to decide on an identity for the man, using the questions for guidance. Encourage them to use their imaginations and to invent as many details as possible.
- Ask the groups to compare their ideas with other groups. This could be done by getting a representative of each group to stand up and introduce the man as if he were a speaker at some kind of event.

2 🌐 3.11

- Ask the students (still in their groups) to read and listen to the poem and decide whether it fits the character they've invented. Point out that some of the difficult vocabulary is glossed.

- In a class feedback session ask the students for suggestions as to how the man in the poem feels about his life.

> *Possible answer:*
> He feels disappointed, sad and regretful that his life has been too safe and he has been too sensible. He wishes he could live his life again as he would make sure he had more fun.

Grammar (SB page 99)

Wishes and regrets

1

- Ask the students to look back at the poem on page 98 and use it to help them complete the sentences.

- Check answers with the class and then focus on the structure of the sentences. Explain that the man is talking about his regrets about the past and this is expressed using *If only I ...* or *I wish ...* + the past perfect.

> a) anxious b) adventurous c) risks
> d) fun   e) sensible   f) seriously   g) enjoy
> h) over

2

- Ask the students to look at the information about expressing wishes or regrets in the margin. Point out the differences in tenses between facts (present simple or past simple) and wishes/regrets (past or past perfect). Explain that we use the past for wishes/regrets about the present and the past perfect for wishes/regrets about the past.

- Get the students to identify that the sentences in Exercise 1 are all regrets about the past apart from the last one, which is a regret about the present. Go through the example with them and ask them to write the corresponding fact for each of the other regrets.

- Finally, ask them to underline the correct alternatives in the sentences describing the ways to express past and present wishes/regrets.

> a) I was anxious.
> b) I wasn't adventurous.
> c) I didn't take many risks.
> d) I didn't have much fun.
> e) I was sensible.
> f) I took life seriously.
> g) I didn't do many of the things I enjoy.
> h) I don't have my life to live over.
>
> a) past   b) past perfect

Language notes

Grammar: wishes or regrets

- The concept of 'backshifting' to remove the situation one step from reality continues here. We last saw this in the second conditional:
  *If I **was** a millionaire ...* is an unreal situation.
  *I'm **not** a millionaire* is a real situation.
  I wish/If only + one step back. For example:
  I'm not rich but I would like to be. = *I wish/If only I **was** rich.*
  Even though the past form is used, it refers to a regret about the present.
  *I **didn't study** Spanish at school* = *I wish/If only I **had studied** Spanish at school.*
  In this case the regret is about the past, so the sentence backshifts to the past perfect.

- A regret about the present simple usually backshifts to past simple.

  A regret about the present continuous backshifts to past continuous.

  A regret about the past simple backshifts to past perfect.

  A regret about the present perfect backshifts to past perfect.

  am going to backshifts to *was going to*.
  will backshifts to *would* and *can* to *could*.

3

- Pairwork. Ask the students to work together to write wishes or regrets for each of the facts. Go through the example with the class first, establishing that it's a regret about the past so it requires the past perfect. With weaker classes, go through all the facts before the students start writing their sentences, identifying whether each one is referring to the past or the present. As the students work, go round giving extra help to anyone who is struggling.

- Check answers with the class before asking the students to discuss in pairs whether or not any of the sentences are true for them.

> a) I wish/If only I'd been able to go to the last U2 gig.
> b) I wish/If only I'd done English at school.
> c) I wish/If only I was married.
> d) I wish/If only I knew how to play chess.
> e) I wish/If only I could play the guitar.
> f) I wish/If only I wasn't going on a training course next week.
> g) I wish/If only I wasn't studying for exams at the moment.
> h) I wish/If only I could/I'd been able to swim when I was a child.

Cultural note

U2

Formed in 1976, U2 are a rock band from Dublin, Ireland. The members of the band are: Bono (lead singer), The Edge (lead guitar), Adam Clayton (bass) and Larry Mullen (drums).

4 Grammar *Extra* 11, Part 1

Ask the students to turn to *Grammar Extra* 11, Part 1 on page 146 of the Student's Book. Here they'll find an explanation of the grammar they've been studying and further exercises to practise it.

1
a) I wish/If only I could play the piano.
b) I wish/If only I lived near a beach.
c) I wish/If only I liked my job.
d) I wish/If only I wasn't/weren't getting old.
e) I wish/If only I had more free time.
f) I wish/If only I was/were better at English.
g) I wish/If only I didn't have a stressful life.
h) I wish/If only I earned more money.

2
a) I wish I had been born in another country.
b) If only I had studied English more at school.
c) I wish I had gone to a better school.
d) If only I had travelled more when I had the chance.
e) I wish I hadn't got married so young.
f) If only I had worked harder at university.

Speaking (SB page 99)

1

- Pairwork. Ask the students to look at the pictures and decide what has happened. They should then think about what the people in the pictures might regret and write sentences beginning *I wish ...* or *If only ...* As the students work, go round giving extra help to any pairs that need it.

- Check answers by getting several pairs to read out their sentences for each picture.

Possible answers:
a) I wish I hadn't got involved in a fight.
b) If only I hadn't had children.
c) I wish I hadn't had my hair cut so short.
d) If only I hadn't stolen that car.
e) I wish I hadn't bet on that horse.
f) If only I hadn't got these tattoos.
g) I wish I hadn't got dressed up.
h) If only I hadn't become a teacher.

2

- Pairwork. Ask the students to talk to their partners about any bad decisions which they've made which they regret. Tell them to give as much detail as they can, and to use the *I wish ...* and *If only ...* structures as much as possible.

- Encourage the students to report back to the class on what they found out about their partners.

Reading & Speaking (SB page 100)

1

- Read the list of activities to the class. Ask the students to say whether they think there should be an upper or lower age limit for each of them. If they think there should be, try to get a consensus on what the limits should be. Write these on the board next to the name of the activity.

- Put the students in pairs and ask them to discuss their views and to say whether they agree with the limits set by the class. Ask them to discuss whether they think there are any other activities which should have age limits.

2

- Focus the students' attention on the photo and ask them how old they think the woman is. Discourage them from trying to find the answer in the text. Ask them what clues in the picture helped them decide and how easy they think it is to tell the age of a person just by looking at them.

- Tell the students that they're going to read an article written by the woman in the photo which is to do with her age. Go through the statements with the class, then ask them to read the article and decide which of them are true for the writer.

- When you've checked the answers, ask the class for their reactions to the story.

---

b), c) and e) are true

---

3 🌐 3.12

- Pairwork. Ask the students to decide how the man will react when the woman tells him the truth about her age. Tell them to write the conversation using the beginning given. Go round giving help and encouragement where necessary.

- Ask the students to practise their conversations in pairs. Get any particularly good pairs to perform their conversation for the class. Try to choose some pairs who portrayed a positive reaction from the man and some who portrayed a negative reaction.

- Play the recording and ask the students to compare the conversation with the ones they've written. Ask them which they prefer. They should then discuss what they'd do now if they were in the writer's position.

🔘 3.12

M: *You look worried. What's on your mind?*

W: *Actually, there is something I've been meaning to tell you …*

M: *Look, if it's about last night, it really doesn't matter. I shouldn't have said anything.*

W: *No, no, it's nothing to do with that. Or rather I suppose it is, in a way.*

M: *I knew it – if only I'd kept my mouth shut.*

W: *Look, I agree with you – Bryan Adams is old-fashioned, and I wish I'd never put that CD on.*

M: *It's not a bad CD. It's my fault – I shouldn't have called him a boring old dinosaur.*

W: *No, it's my fault – I shouldn't have reacted like I did. It's just that that CD brings back special memories for me.*

M: *Look, I understand.* My *parents used to play Bryan Adams too.*

W: *No, you don't understand – I was in my teens when that record first came out.*

M: *Ah, right. I see what you mean. Well, you look very good for your age.*

W: *Oh, shut up.*

M: *No, what I mean is that I don't care how old you are – and anyway, I've got something to tell you. I'm not 31. I'm 26.*

W: *What?!*

Cultural note

Bryan Adams /ˈbraɪən ˈædəms/ **(born 1959)**
Bryan Adams is a Canadian rock singer / songwriter whose best-known hits (like *Cuts Like a Knife* (1983) and *Everything I Do* (1991)) were released during the 1980s and 1990s.

4

Groupwork. Ask the students to discuss the questions, giving as much detail as possible about any situations they're familiar with or experiences they've had.

Grammar (SB page 101)

Unreal conditionals (2)

1

* Remind the students of the work they did on unreal conditionals on page 97. Point out that there they were looking at unreal or imaginary situations in the present. Here they'll look at unreal or imaginary situations in the past.

* Focus the students' attention on the example sentence from the article on page 100. Read it aloud to the class or get a student to read it. Ask the students to identify which of the situations (*a*, *b* or *c*) the sentence is based on.

* Ask the students to read the sentences describing the structure of unreal conditionals in the past and to underline the correct alternatives.

* Check answers with the class, then go through the information and example sentences in the margin.

Sentence *b*: I didn't tell him. It became a big issue
2 Use the past perfect / *would + have* + past participle in the main clause.

Language notes
Grammar: unreal conditionals

* The type of conditional in this unit is also known as the 'third conditional'. There are two clauses in this type of sentence: the *if* clause (*if* followed by the verb in the past perfect form) and the main clause (*would/wouldn't* + *have* + *past participle*). For example:
  If you **had knocked** on the door, (*if* + past perfect) I **would have heard** you. (*would* + *have* + past participle).

* The clauses can be reversed without changing the meaning, but the punctuation changes:
  When the *if* clause comes after the main clause, they aren't separated by a comma.
  When the *if* clause comes before the main clause, they are separated by a comma.

* The examples in this unit relate to hypothetical or imaginary situations in the past.

2

* Go through the example with the class, pointing out how it matches the rules outlined in Exercise 1. Then ask the students to write unreal conditional sentences based on the remaining situations.

* Check answers with the class before putting the students into pairs to discuss whether any of the sentences are true for them.

a) If I'd seen you yesterday, I'd have said hello.
b) If I hadn't stayed up late last night, I wouldn't have overslept this morning.
c) If I'd been able to find a parking space, I wouldn't have arrived late for the class.
d) If my sister hadn't travelled round the world, she wouldn't have met her future husband.
e) If I'd learnt to drive when I was 18, I'd have had a car at university.
f) If it hadn't rained yesterday, I'd have gone for a walk.

3 Grammar *Extra* 11, Part 2

Ask the students to turn to *Grammar Extra* 11, Part 2 on page 146 of the Student's Book. Here they'll find an explanation of the grammar they've been studying and further exercises to practise it.

1

a) What would you do if you found £100 in the street?

b) If you were able to change your nationality, what would you be?

c) If you could have dinner with a famous person, who would you choose?

d) If you had to change one part of your body, what would it be?

e) What would you do if you saw someone stealing something in a shop?

f) If you could meet one person from history, who would you choose?

Sample answers:

a) If I found £100 in the street, I'd keep it.

b) If I was/were able to change my nationality, I'd be Italian.

c) If I could have dinner with a famous person, I'd choose David Bowie.

d) If I had to change one part of my body, it would be my nose.

e) If I saw someone stealing in a shop, I wouldn't do anything.

f) If I could meet one person from history, I'd choose William Shakespeare.

2

a) If I'd been paying attention, I wouldn't have walked into a lamppost.

b) If I hadn't studied hard, I wouldn't have passed my exams.

c) If I'd studied hard, I wouldn't have failed my exams.

d) If I hadn't forgotten to set my alarm clock, I wouldn't have overslept.

e) If I hadn't missed the bus, I wouldn't have been late for work.

f) If I hadn't bought a lottery ticket, I wouldn't have won any money.

g) If I'd had a map, I wouldn't have got lost.

h) If the weather had been good, we'd have gone camping.

Reading & Speaking (SB page 101)

1

Pairwork. Focus the students' attention on the pictures and the list of words for each story. Explain any difficult vocabulary and then ask them to work in pairs and to speculate on what they think each story is about.

2 🌐 3.13

• Ask the students to work individually to read the stories and complete them with the words from Exercise 1.

• Check answers and then put the students into pairs and ask them to discuss what they'd have done in each situation. Remind them that they'll need to use unreal conditional sentences to describe what they'd have done. As they work, go round giving extra help where needed.

• Encourage the pairs to report back to the class on what they decided. Then play the recording for them to listen and find out what the people actually did. Have a class discussion on whether they think the people did the right thing.

> a) 2   b) 3   c) 1
> (for each text, the words are in order)

> 🌐 3.13
>
> a)
> *Of course I didn't say anything – I mean, the cashier should have asked to look in her bag, shouldn't she? If it had been a small shop, I probably would have said something, but a big supermarket like that can afford it.*
>
> b)
> *Well, I picked it up, brushed the cat hairs off and served it. What you don't see you don't worry about, do you?*
>
> c)
> *I don't know if he saw me, but I didn't want to embarrass him, so I just carried on walking. I often think about him and wonder how he ended up on the streets.*

Useful phrases (SB page 102)

1

Focus the students' attention on the lists of phrases. Ask them to identify in each one a phrase that is unusual or incorrect. Encourage them to read the phrases aloud in order to get a feel for what sounds right.

> 1 ~~Speak me.~~   5 ~~I am me.~~
> 2 ~~Is there (*name*)?~~   6 ~~What do you do later?~~
> 3 ~~Are you (*name*)?~~   7 ~~To tomorrow.~~
> 4 ~~One instant.~~

2 🌐 3.14–3.15

• Ask the students to read the phone conversations and complete the gaps with the most appropriate phrase from Exercise 1. Draw their attention to the fact that the first call is to a friend and the second to a bank manager. Ask what difference this will make to what Phil says and help them to identify that the register is likely to be informal with the friend and informal with the bank manager. With weaker classes, go through the lists of phrases in Exercise 1 with the class and identify which of the phrases in Exercise 1 are formal and which informal.

• Play the recording for them to check their answers.

Conversation A

1 Hello.
2 Is Maddy there?
3 Is that Phil?
4 Hang on, I'll go and get her.
5 It's me.
6 What are you up to later?
7 See you tomorrow then.

Conversation B

1 Good morning.
2 I'd like to speak to Mr Moore, please.
3 Who's calling, please?
4 Hold on, please. I'll try to put you through.
5 This is Philip Jones here.
6 Are you available later on today?
7 I'll look forward to seeing you tomorrow.

🌐 **3.14**

Conversation A (J = Janet; P = Phil; M = Maddy)

J: Hello.
P: Oh, hi. Is Maddy there?
J: Is that Phil?
P: Yes, hello Janet. How are you?
J: Fine, thanks. Hang on, I'll go and get her.
M: Hello.
P: Hi! It's me.
M: Hello you. What have you been up to?
P: Oh, just working. Listen, I can't chat now. What are you up to later?
M: I've got to work this evening but I thought we could go to the cinema tomorrow.
P: OK, I'll come round at about seven.
M: See you tomorrow then.
P: Bye.

🌐 **3.15**

Conversation B (R = Receptionist; P = Phil; Mr M = Mr Moore)

R: Good morning. Northminster. Can I help you?
P: Yes, I'd like to speak to Mr Moore, please.
R: Who's calling, please?
P: My name's Philip Jones.
R: OK, Hold on, please. I'll try to put you through. … Oh, Mr Jones, I'm afraid, he's on the other line. Would you like to hold?
P: Yes, thank you. …
Mr M: Anthony Moore.
P: Oh, hello. This is Philip Jones here.
Mr M: Oh, yes. Mr Jones. Thank you for getting back to me so promptly. There seems to be a problem with your account.
P: Oh, dear. What sort of problem?
Mr M: Well, you've exceeded your limit by more than £500. You really need to come to the bank to discuss it. Are you available later on today?

P: I'm afraid I'm rather tied up today. Would tomorrow be convenient for you?
Mr M: Yes, that's fine. Ten thirty?
P: Yes, ten thirty's fine for me.
Mr M: Well, thank you for ringing. I'll look forward to seeing you tomorrow.
P: Goodbye.

---

3 🌐 3.16

Ask the students to listen and repeat the useful phrases. Pause the recording between those for Conversation A and those for Conversation B.

🌐 **3.16**

Conversation A

1 Hello.
2 Is Maddy there?
3 Is that Phil?
4 Hang on. I'll go and get her.
5 It's me.
6 What are you up to later?
7 See you tomorrow then.

Conversation B

1 Good morning.
2 I'd like to speak to Mr Moore, please.
3 Who's calling, please?
4 Hold on, please. I'll try to put you through.
5 This is Philip Jones here.
6 Are you available later on today?
7 I'll look forward to seeing you tomorrow.

4

- Pairwork. Go through the situations with the class and make sure everyone understands them. Then put the students into pairs to write telephone conversations for one of the situations. Try to make sure that several pairs choose each option. Go round helping with vocabulary where needed and making sure that the students get the register right for the conversation they've chosen.

- Ask the students to practise their conversations out loud. Ask a few confident pairs to perform theirs for the class.

Vocabulary *Extra* (SB page 103)

Idiomatic expressions

1

- Go through the instructions with the class. Point out that the prefix *bi-* usually has the meaning *two*. Focus attention on the binomials in the dictionary extracts. The students should be able to recognise that each consists of two main words, generally separated by *and*.

- Ask the students to read sentences *a–e* and decide which of the binomials in the dictionary extracts could be used in place of the underlined phrases.
- When you've checked their answers, get them to look in their dictionaries and see which word they need to look for first.

---

a) in leaps and bounds   d) here and there
b) pick and choose   e) now and then
c) in black and white

In the *Macmillan Essential Dictionary* the idiomatic expression always appears under the first word (*black, here, leaps, now, pick*).

2

- Ask the students to look at the sentences and the dictionary extracts and try to identify the mistakes. Remind them that these are 'fixed' expressions and cannot usually be altered even a tiny bit without the meaning disappearing or the speaker sounding very odd.
- When you've checked their answers, ask the students to discuss in pairs whether any of the descriptions match anyone they know.

---

a) has ~~the~~ her hands full
b) ~~over~~ up to her neck in debt
c) her heart is in ~~its~~ the right place
d) ~~one~~ an eye for fashion
e) keeps his head above ~~the~~ water.
f) landed on his ~~foot~~ feet

3

Encourage the students to try to complete the expressions first without looking at the dictionary extracts. They can then use the extracts to check their answers.

---

a) stitches   d) arms
b) minds   e) weather
c) moon   f) dumps

4

- Remind the students that not all dictionaries are the same and that they need to become familiar with the way their own particular dictionaries organise and display words.
- Ask them to look up their six chosen expressions and answer the questions for each one.
- In a class feedback session find out what information the students discovered from their dictionaries.

Further practice material
Need more writing practice?
→ Workbook page 67
- Writing a story.

Need more classroom practice activities?
→ Photocopiable resource materials pages 184 to 186
  Grammar: *If …*
  Vocabulary: *Then and now*
  Communication: *Unreal!*
→ Top 10 activities pages xv to xx

Need DVD material?
→ Test CD – Programme 11: *If …*

Need progress tests?
→ Test CD – *Test Unit 11*

Need more on important teaching concepts?
→ Key concepts in *New Inside Out* pages xxii to xxxv

Need student self-study practice?
→ CD-ROM – Unit 11: *Age*

Need student CEF self-evaluation?
→ CEF Checklists pages xxxvii to xliv

Need more information and more ideas?
→ www.insideout.net

12 Style *Overview*

Section & Aims	What the students are doing
Reading SB page 104 Reading for gist / specific information Describing a person with style	Discussing clothes and style. Reading two article and matching opinions to the writers. Underlining correct information.
Vocabulary & Listening **SB page 105** Clothes; listening for detail	Completing descriptions of clothes. Listening to people talking about clothes. Matching them with pictures.
Grammar SB page 105 Adjective order	Categorising adjectives. Putting adjectives in the correct order to describe clothes. Talking about the most interesting item in their wardrobe.
Reading & Writing SB page 106 Reading for specific information Writing a physical description	Reading an article and identifying true and false statements. Completing a description of themselves. Discussing first impressions.
Pronunciation SB page 106 Vowel combinations	Linking words with the same vowel sounds.
Vocabulary SB page 107 Physical description Completing a physical description	Categorising words for describing people. Matching descriptions to film roles played by Johnny Depp. Writing a description of a film character.
Speaking: anecdote SB page 107 Fluency practice	Talking about someone they met for the first time recently.
Listening SB page 108 Qualities	Guessing the ages of people in photos. Listening to friends discussing a TV make-over programme. Describing what people have done to change their appearance.
Grammar SB page 108 *have something done*	Studying how to talk about having things done. Completing a table with correct verb forms. Completing questions about having things done.
Vocabulary & Speaking SB page 109 Morning routines; fluency practice	Matching verbs and noun phrases to make expressions. Talking about their morning routines.
Reading & Vocabulary **SB page 109** Reading for specific information Morning routines	Underlining correct alternatives in texts about morning routines. Completing questions about getting ready to go out. Describing how they get ready for different occasions.
Useful phrases SB page 110 Small talk	Identifying common conversational topics at weddings. Matching conversations to topics. Completing a table with useful phrases and writing a conversation.
Vocabulary *Extra* SB page 111 Exploring meaning	Discussing meanings of the word *suspect*. Matching homographs to their correct pronunciation. Matching meanings of *soft* to its correct dictionary definition.
Writing WB page 71	Writing a description of a person.

12 Style *Teacher's notes*

Warm up

Ask the students what they think is stylish at the moment. Encourage them to talk about fashions in clothes and image. Ask them to name a celebrity who they think is the most stylish at the moment.

Reading (SB page 104)

1

• Read the statements aloud or ask several students to read them. Explain any difficult vocabulary, then put the students into pairs to discuss which ones are similar to their own views about clothes and style.

• Ask the pairs to report back to the class.

2

• Focus attention on the two photographs and ask the students if they know who Carla Bruni and Vanessa Paradis are. Ask them which one they think is most stylish. Tell the students to read the two articles and match the women with the statements in Exercise 1.

• Allow them to compare their answers in pairs before checking answers with the class.

> a) VP   b) VP   c) VP   d) CB   e) VP
> f) CB

Cultural notes

Carla Bruni /kɑːlə ˈbruːni/ **(born 1967)**
Carla Bruni is the wife of French President Nicolas Sarkozy. Before her marriage she was as a singer/songwriter and model. Although Italian, she's spent most of her life living in France.

Vanessa Paradis /vəˈnesə ˈpærədi/ **(born 1972)**
Vanessa Paradis is a French pop singer and actress. Her most famous hit was *Joe, le Taxi* (1987). In 1991 she helped to promote Coco, a fragrance by Chanel. She modelled for Chanel again in 2006. She's lived with US actor Johnny Depp since 1998. They have two children Lily-Rose (born 1999) and Jack (born 2002).

Coco Chanel /ˈkəʊkəʊ ʃəˈnel/ **(1883–1971)**
Gabrielle 'Coco' Chanel was a French fashion designer who is arguably the most influential figure in haute couture of all time.

3

• Ask the students to read the articles again and underline the correct information.

• Check answers with the class and then ask the students to replace the names with the names of people they know, making true sentences (but discourage them from writing anything unflattering about a fellow member of the class). They can use any of the alternatives in their new sentences.

• Ask several students to read their sentences to the class.

> a) has   b) never   c) has   d) always wears
> e) never

4

• Pairwork. Give the students a minute or two to think of someone they know who has style. Then ask them to take turns to describe this person to their partner.

• Encourage several pairs to report back to the class on what they found out.

Vocabulary & Listening (SB page 105)

1

Ask the students to look at the pictures and complete the descriptions. Allow them to use dictionaries and to work in pairs if they wish.

> a) cowboy boots   b) suit   c) jeans   d) hoody
> e) miniskirt   f) belt   g) boots   h) jeans
> i) shirt   j) top   k) dress   l) jumper

2 🌐 3.17

• Tell the students that they're going to listen to four people talking about clothes and that they should listen and identify each person's favourite from the list in Exercise 1. Before playing the recording, ask the students to look at the photos of the four people and try to predict which item of clothing they'll choose as their favourite.

• Check answers and then ask the students to say which of the items of clothing they like or dislike.

1 Al: fabulous American snakeskin cowboy boots
2 Fran: red low-waisted miniskirt
3 Jay: old black skinny jeans
4 Bea: beautiful long blue silk evening dress

🔊 **3.17**

1
Al: *I'm really proud of my fabulous American snakeskin cowboy boots. Most of my friends hate them and wouldn't be seen dead in boots like these, but I like that fact that they're different. I wear them for work with a smart suit and tie and I think the contrast looks great. I like to stand out from the crowd.*

2
Fran: *I usually wear jeans and a hoody during the day, but for going out, my favourite thing is my red low-waisted miniskirt. I wear it with a wide black leather belt and short boots, and it looks fantastic with my old black leather jacket.*

3
Jay: *I have about twenty-five pairs of jeans, but my favourites are my old black skinny jeans. I play the guitar in a band and I always wear my black skinny jeans and a black polo-neck top when we're playing. It's like a uniform.*

4
Bea: *I'm really into vintage clothes and I've just bought a beautiful long blue silk evening dress. I haven't worn it yet – I'm waiting for the right occasion. It would look great on the red carpet at the Oscars.*

Grammar (SB page 105)

Adjective order

1

- Point out that in the descriptions of clothing in the previous section, most of the items were described with more than one adjective. Tell the students that there's a correct order for adjectives when more than one is used with a noun and that it depends on what aspect of the thing the adjective describes

- Ask them to look at the table and the headings. Point out that the first six columns are for different types of adjectives, the final one for the noun that they're describing. Go through the example, explaining that *fabulous* describes the speaker's opinion of the boots and that this comes first in the description. We don't know anything about their size, age or pattern/colour, but we do know their origin, *American*, which comes next in the description. We also know that they are made of *snakeskin*, which comes next, just before the noun. Explain that this order is the same for all descriptions, regardless of what aspects are or are not present in the description.

- Ask the students to add the descriptions of Fran, Jay and Bea's favourite clothes to the table. Go round making sure they are doing this correctly. Check answers with the class. Point out that for Bea's dress, the material (*silk*) comes before the style (*evening*).

	ADJECTIVE					NOUN
Opinion	Size / Shape	Age	Pattern / Colour	Origin	Material / Style	
1 fabulous				American	snakeskin	cowboy boots
2 (fantastic)			red		low-waisted	miniskirt
3		old	black		skinny	jeans
4 beautiful	long		blue		silk evening	dress

Language note

Grammar: word order
In this exercise, the students are asked to combine adjectives and nouns to describe clothes. When two or more adjectives come before a noun, they usually have to be put in a particular order. You say *brown leather jacket*, not ~~leather brown jacket~~. Although the rules are complex, generally, when there are two adjectives, the order is:

opinion (*beautiful, lovely*)
size/shape (*long, big, small*)
age (*straight, curly, wavy*)
pattern/colour (*red, dark, striped, plain*)
origin (*American, French*)
material/style (*cotton, leather, evening*)

So, for example, you could say:

She's wearing a beautiful long silk dress.
He's in a scruffy old white cotton shirt.

2

- Focus the students' attention on the example and point out that it fits the rule established in the previous exercise. Ask the students to reorder the other descriptions. Go round giving help where needed.

- Check answers before asking the students to write a three-adjective sentence describing the most interesting item in their wardrobes.

a) an elegant dark blue linen jacket
b) a brand-new black V-neck T-shirt
c) an expensive white silk blouse
d) a plain beige woolly jumper
e) an old Russian fur hat
f) scruffy blue suede shoes

3 Pairwork

- The pairwork exercise for this unit is on pages 120 and 125 of the Student's Book. Put the students in pairs and tell them who will be Student A, and who will be Student B.

- While they're doing the exercise, go round monitoring and giving help. Take note of any errors which may need particular attention later, and also any examples of good language use, which you can praise in a feedback session.

> *Differences between Pictures A and B:*
> **The man**
> A: baggy jeans   B: tight jeans
> A: a leather jacket   B: no jacket
> A: a striped T-shirt   B: a plain black T-shirt
> A: black cowboy boots   B: brown cowboy boots
>
> **The woman**
> A: a red mini-skirt   B: a long black skirt
> A: a thick belt   B: a thin belt
> A: a black pullover   B: a red pullover
> A: a check hat   B: a plain green hat
>
> **The little girl**
> A: blue jeans   B: a red skirt
> A: a check scarf   B: a striped scarf
> A: a blue and white   B: a plain green hoody
>   striped hoody

Reading & Writing (SB page 106)

1

- Tell the students that they're going to read an extract from a novel called *Come Together*. It's unusual in that it was written by a couple, Josie Lloyd and Emlyn Rees. They each wrote alternate chapters of the book, which tells the story of the same relationship from the point of view of the man and the woman.

- Go through the statements with the class. Then ask the students to read the extract and say whether they are true or false. Answer any questions they may have about difficult vocabulary. It would be worth explaining *build* at this point as the word will come up again in later exercises. Here it refers to body type, e.g. *average, skinny, plump, fat, thin, muscular, stocky.*

> a) True.   b) False.   c) False.   d) True.

2

- Go through the sentences with the class, then ask them to work individually to complete them with information about themselves.

- Allow the students to compare their sentences with a partner, then ask several of them to read them to the class.

3

Pairwork. Explain that a 'first impression' is the opinion you form the first time you see someone or something. Ask the students to discuss the questions. Encourage them to report back to the class on their ideas.

Pronunciation (SB page 106)

1

- Focus the students' attention on the example and read the words *medium, green* and *jeans* aloud, emphasizing the vowel sound which they all share. Point out the phonemic symbol which represents this sound, and which the students will find in a dictionary which gives a guide to pronunciation as well as meaning. Tell the students that learning the phonemic symbols is very useful as it means they'll always be able to check the correct pronunciation of a word. Point out that in the normal spelling of these words, the vowel sound is represented in different ways: *e, ee* and *ea.*

- Ask the students to link the other words with the same vowel sounds and to match them with the correct phonemic symbol. Encourage them to say all the words aloud as they do this so that they get a sense for what sounds right.

> a) /iː/   medium   green   jeans
> b) /uː/   two   blue   suits
> c) /ɜː/   third   worse   fur
> d) /ɔː/   short   bald   author
> e) /eɪ/   plain   beige   suede
> f) /eə/   wear   their   hair

2 🔘 3.18

Play the recording for the students to check their answers. Play it a second time for them to listen and repeat.

Vocabulary (SB page 107)

1

Explain *build* if you haven't already done so. Ask the students to look back at the text on page 106 and complete the information for the man described there.

> Age: between 25 and 30
> Height: just under six feet tall
> Build: average
> Eyes: brown
> Hair: brown
> Distinguishing features: a scar across left eyebrow

2

The students match the words to the categories. Go round giving help where needed and encouraging them to think of one new word of their own for each category. Explain any words they don't know.

> Age: in her early thirties, in her mid-twenties,
>   in his late teens
> Height: just over 1 metre 80, medium
> Build: medium, overweight, slim, stocky, well-built
> Eyes: deep-set, hazel
> Hair: bald, blond streaks, ginger, messy, receding,
>   sideburns, shoulder-length
> Distinguishing features: freckles, a goatee, a mole,
>   a tattoo

3

- Focus attention on the photo of Johnny Depp in the margin and find out if he is popular with the students and if they've seen any of his films.
- Tell the students to look at the photos of Johnny Depp in three of his film roles. Read out each of the descriptions in turn and ask them to match it to one of the photos. Check answers and explain any difficult vocabulary.

> a) 3 (Captain Jack Sparrow in) *Pirates of the Caribbean 1* – 2003
> b) 1 *Edward Scissorhands* – 1990
> c) 2 *Sweeney Todd* – 2007

Cultural note

Johnny Depp /ˈdʒɒni dep/ (born 1963)
Johnny Depp's film debut was in *Nightmare On Elm Street* (1984). Six years later, he starred in the film *Edward Scissorhands* (1990). His most popular role to date is probably that of pirate Jack Sparrow in the *Pirates of the Caribbean* films. In 2007 Depp played the role of *Sweeney Todd: The Demon Barber of Fleet Street* (the fictional London barber who murdered his customers and turned them into meat pies).

4

Give the students time to write their descriptions, giving help with vocabulary where needed. Then put them in pairs to take turns reading out their descriptions and guessing who their partner has described.

Speaking: anecdote (SB page 107)

For more information about how to set up, monitor and repeat Anecdotes, see page xx in the Introduction.

1 🌐 3.19

- Focus the students' attention on the photo of Martin. Explain that they're going to hear him talking about a person he met for the first time recently. Go through the questions and answers with the class. Explain any unknown vocabulary.
- Play the recording and ask the students to listen and cross out any answers that are wrong.
- Play the recording again and ask the students to change the answers that are incorrect.

> a) At a friend's ~~engagement~~ birthday party.
> b) –
> c) –
> d) I thought she was ~~funny~~ friendly and very confident.
> e) She was ~~tall~~ tiny with long curly black hair.
> f) She was wearing a turquoise ~~ring~~ necklace.
> g) –
> h) –
> i) ~~Yes, I have~~ No, I haven't.

🌐 **3.19**

I was invited to a friend's birthday party recently, and there were quite a few people there who I'd never met before. I'm not very good at introducing myself to strangers, so I just stayed with the people I knew, and that was nice because I hadn't seen them for a while. But then this woman came over and introduced herself, and asked who I was. I thought she seemed really friendly and very confident. She was tiny, with long curly black hair, and I remember she was wearing a beautiful turquoise necklace. I admired the necklace, and she told me that it was from Egypt. We talked about Egypt, and it turned out that we'd both been on holiday to the same Egyptian holiday resort, but not at the same time. Small world. I haven't seen her since then, but she works with my friend, so I think I'll probably bump into her again some time. I hope so.

2

- Give the students a minute or two to decide on the person they're going to talk about. Then ask them to look at the questions in Exercise 1 again and decide how they'd answer them about their person. Allow them to make notes of what they're going to say and how they're going to say it, but discourage them from writing a paragraph that they can simply read out. Go round monitoring and giving help.
- Pairwork. Put the students in pairs and ask them to take turns to tell their partner about somebody they met for the first time recently. Encourage them to ask each other follow-up questions to get further information.
- Ask some pairs to report back to the class about what they found out.

Listening (SB page 108)

1

- Focus the students' attention on the photos of Tony and Angela. Explain that they took part in a television programme called *Ten Years Younger* in which ordinary people, who look older than their age, are helped to make themselves look younger. This is achieved by a combination of surgery, make-up, advice on choosing the right clothes, etc. Point out that the two pairs of photos are before and after photos.
- Ask the students to discuss the questions in pairs. In a class feedback session find out how much agreement there is, but don't confirm or deny suggestions about their age at this point.

2 🌐 3.20

Tell the students that they're going to listen to two friends who watched the programme featuring Tony and Marilyn discussing what they saw. Ask them to listen and see if their ideas in Exercise 1 were right.

3.20 (A = Annie; B = Betty)

A: *Did you see* Ten Years Younger *last night?*

B: *No, I missed it. I had to work. Why, was it good?*

A: *It was brilliant. They had a man and a woman on, and honestly, the transformation was incredible.*

B: *What did they look like?*

A: *Well, the man looked about sixty, even though he was only forty-four.*

B: *Oh no!*

A: *He had this horrible long grey hair, and he dressed a bit like an old rock star.*

B: *Urgh!*

A: *Anyway, he had his hair cut and coloured and he had his teeth whitened.*

B: *Oh yes, that makes such a difference.*

A: *And I think he had his eyelids lifted.*

B: *Oh well, of course if you can afford to have plastic surgery, you're bound to look better.*

A: *Yes, but I think that's all he had done. Oh, and he had his clothes chosen by a stylist.*

B: *What about the woman? Did she have lots of plastic surgery?*

A: *No, she didn't actually. But she looked as if she'd had a major facelift, it was amazing. Before the makeover, everybody thought she was about fifty-five, and in fact the poor woman was only forty.*

B: *Oh dear. What did she have done?*

A: *She had her hair cut and coloured, of course. And she had her make-up done by an expert and her clothes chosen by a stylist.*

B: *Oh, I'd love that. How old did they think she was after the makeover?*

A: *Thirty-eight.*

B: *Oh, she must have been pleased. Hey, do you think I need to have my hair cut?*

3

- Do one sentence with the class as an example. Then ask the students to make more sentences about what Tony and Marilyn had done.

- Play the recording again for the students to check their answers, then check with the class, making sure they've structured the sentences correctly.

- Explain that the expression *you look young for your age* means that you look younger than you are. Ask the students to discuss in pairs anybody they know who looks young for their age.

> Tony had his hair cut and coloured.
> Tony had his teeth whitened.
> (Annie thinks) Tony had his eyelids lifted.
> Tony had his clothes chosen by a stylist.
> Marilyn had her hair cut and coloured.
> Marilyn had her make-up done by an expert.
> Marilyn had her clothes chosen by a stylist.

Grammar (SB page 108)

have something done

1

- Focus the students' attention on the two sentences and ask them to discuss in pairs who cut Tony's hair in each of them.

- Check answers and point out that there were a number of sentences in the previous section using the structure *have something done*. Go through the example sentences in the margin.

> In sentence a) it was Tony who cut his hair.
> In sentence b) it was somebody else – we don't know who – who cut Tony's hair.

Language notes

Grammar: *have something done*

- There are certain jobs that people pay others to do for them, like cutting their hair, for example. Compare the two sentences:

  Phil had his jacket cleaned.
  Phil cleaned his jacket.

  In the first sentence Phil (probably) paid for someone to clean his jacket; in the second sentence he cleaned it himself.

- The word order is always the same:

  have + object + past participle

  Note that the past participle follows the object.

  *When did you have your car **fixed**?*
  *Are you going to have your teeth **whitened**?*
  *I want to have my house **painted**.*

- Instead of using *have*, it's possible to use *get*:

  *I'm going to **get** my hair cut this afternoon.*

  This is more common in spoken English.

2

- Pairwork. Put the students in pairs to complete the table with the correct verb forms.

- Check answers with the class and then ask the students to decide which, if any, of the sentences are unlikely or unusual. They should cross these out and then tick any that are true for them.

> a) I like having my hair washed.
> b) I never have my hair coloured.
> c) ~~I'm testing my eyes next week.~~ I'm having my eyes tested. (This is something you can't really do for yourself.)
> d) ~~I cleaned my teeth last month.~~ (If this refers to brushing your teeth, then you would do it every day and not refer to it a month later; if it refers to a professional clean, then it would normally be done by a dentist.)
> e) ~~I've pierced my ears.~~ I've had my ears pierced. (This is something you can't really do for yourself, though it is possible.)
> f) I want to repaint my bedroom.

3

• Go through the example with the class and then ask the students to complete the remaining questions.

• Check that they've formed all the questions correctly before putting them into pairs to take turns asking and answering them.

> a) … would you have it washed or would you wash it yourself?
> b) … would you have it cleaned or would you clean it yourself?
> c) … would you have it repaired or would you repair it yourself?
> d) … would you have it done or would you do it yourself?
> e) … would you have them sharpened or would you sharpen them yourself?
> f) … would you have them taken up or would you take them up yourself?

4 Grammar *Extra* 12

• Ask the students to turn to *Grammar Extra* 12 on page 148 of the Student's Book. Here they'll find an explanation of the grammar they've been studying and further exercises to practise it.

• Then ask the students to do the Test yourself exercises to revise and check the grammar they've studied from the whole book.

> **1**
> a) having our house decorated
> b) clean my car
> c) have your eyes tested
> d) have the roof fixed
> e) cooking dinner
> f) had her car repaired
>
> **2**
> a) have/get delivered
> b) have/get serviced
> c) have/get cut
> d) have/get checked
> e) have/get done
> f) have/get taken
>
> **3**
> a) Have you ever had your appearance changed?
> b) How often do you get your eyes tested?
> c) Have you ever had anything stolen?
> d) Have you ever had your ears pierced?
> e) Have you ever had your car vandalised?
> f) How often do you have your hair cut?
>
> **Test yourself**
> 1 b 2 a 3 c 4 a 5 a 6 a 7 b 8 b 9 c 10 c
> 11 b 12 c 13 c 14 b 15 a 16 b 17 c 18 a
> 19 b 20 a
> 21 c 22 b 23 c 24 b 25 a 26 a 27 a 28 c
> 29 b 30 a
> 31 a 32 c 33 a 34 a 35 b 36 b 37 c 38 b
> 39 a 40 c

Vocabulary & Speaking (SB page 109)

1

• Ask the students to look at the picture and say what time of day it is (morning). Ask what the person has just done (woken up) and what they think the person will do next.

• Ask them to match the verbs in box A with the nouns in box B to make things that people do in the morning before they leave the house.

• When checking answers, point out that some noun phrases can go with more than one word, but with a different meaning. For example, *make breakfast* means to prepare it, *have breakfast* means to eat it. Explain any items the students don't know. You may need to point out that *make the bed* refers to straightening sheets and blankets or shaking a duvet to make the bed tidy rather than actually constructing a bed.

> *do:* my exercises, my homework, the washing up
> *get:* the children ready, dressed, the mail
> *have:* breakfast, some coffee, a cup of tea, a shower
> *make:* the bed, breakfast, some coffee, a cup of tea
> *put:* the computer on, my make-up on, the radio on, the TV on
> *read:* the mail, the paper

2

• Ask the students to take a moment or two to think about their own morning routines. Encourage them to make notes, putting the activities in order and deciding how long each one takes.

• Put the students into pairs and ask them to compare notes and discuss their morning activities. Encourage them to report back to the class on the differences between them.

Reading & Vocabulary (SB page 109)

1 🌐 3.21–3.22

• Focus the students' attention on the two texts and explain that they describe the morning routines of two very different people. Ask them to read the texts and underline the correct alternatives.

• Check answers with the class. Then ask them whether they think they are descriptions of a man or a woman. Then play the recording for them to listen and find out.

> **Person A** (a woman)
> 1 get dressed   6 goes with
> 2 wear   7 try on
> 3 put on   8 looks
> 4 fit   9 feels
> 5 take them off   10 match
>
> **Person B** (a man)
> 1 put on   4 match
> 2 had on   5 suit
> 3 goes with   6 look like

2

- Ask the students to complete the questions with the words in the box.
- Check answers before putting the students into pairs to take turns asking and answering the questions. You may need to point out the difference between the verb *suit* (to look good on someone) and the noun *suit* (a combination of trousers and jacket or skirt and jacket.) Also point out the difference between *suit* and *fit* (to be the right size).

> a) suit
> b) get dressed
> c) trying on
> d) wear
> e) fit (possibly also *suit* but with different meaning)
> f) match

3

- Go through the list of occasions. Ask the students which of them they'd wear smart clothes for and which casual clothes.
- Put the students into pairs and ask them to choose some of the situations and describe to each other how they'd get ready for them and what they'd wear. Go round offering help and encouragement where necessary.

Useful phrases (SB page 110)

1

- Ask the students when they last went to a wedding and whose wedding it was. Ask them who they talked to at the wedding and what they talked about.
- Read out each of the items in the box to the class and ask them to put up their hands if they think it is something that people are likely to talk about at a wedding. Try to work out a list of the three topics that they think are the most likely.
- Explain *bride* and *groom* (the woman and man getting married) and see if the students know any other terms for people at weddings, such as *best man* (usually the groom's best friend or brother who acts as his assistant and takes charge of the ring) and *bridesmaids* (friends of the bride or little girls from the family who help the bride by carrying her flowers, etc.). They'll need to know these words for Exercise 4.

2 🌐 3.23

- Play the recording and ask the students to read the conversations as they listen.
- Ask the students to match each conversation with one of the topics in Exercise 1.

> 1 c   2 b   3 d   4 h   5 f

3 🌐 3.24

- Focus attention on the table and point out the three headings: *making positive comments*, *giving and receiving compliments* and *thanking and accepting thanks*. Explain that a *compliment* is a nice comment, often made about a person's clothes or appearance (though it could be on any subject so long as it amounts to personal praise of some sort). Ask the students to complete the useful phrases in the table by looking back at the conversations.
- Play the recording for the students to check their answers. Draw their attention to the different ways of responding to a compliment. These range from simple thanks to modest self-deprecating comments like the one here made about the dress, denying that it is anything special, and making out that it is old rather than new. In the UK it's considered polite to respond modestly to compliments rather than agree that the dress, hat or whatever is fantastic.
- Play the recording again for the students to repeat the useful phrases. When they've done this chorally, ask for individual repetition and make sure that they copy the speakers' intonation and sound sincere.

> **Making positive comments**
> a) 'Oh, she looks so beautiful.'
> b) 'What a lovely day!'
> c) 'This dessert is delicious.'
>
> **Giving and receiving compliments**
> d) 'What a lovely dress.' 'Oh this – I've had it for ages.'
> e) 'Blue really suits you.' 'Do you think so?'
> f) 'That's a very nice hat.' 'I'm glad you like it.'
>
> **Thanking and accepting thanks**
> g) 'Thank you so much for a lovely day.' 'You're welcome.'
> h) 'Thank you for inviting us.' 'Don't mention it.'

> 3.24
> *Making positive comments*
> *a) 'Oh, she looks so beautiful.'*
> *b) 'What a lovely day!'*
> *c) 'This dessert is delicious.'*
>
> *Giving and receiving compliments*
> *d) 'What a lovely dress!' 'Oh this, I've had it for ages.'*
> *e) 'Blue really suits you.' 'Do you think so?'*
> *f) 'That's a very nice hat.' 'I'm glad you like it.'*
>
> *Thanking and accepting thanks*
> *g) 'Thank you so much for a lovely day.' 'You're welcome.'*
> *h) 'Thank you for inviting us.' 'Don't mention it.'*

4

Pairwork. Ask the students to choose one of the options and to write a conversation between the two people. Explain *best man* and *bridesmaid* if you have not already done so. As the students work, go round giving help and encouragement. When they've finished, ask them to practise their conversations and then ask several pairs to perform them for the class.

Vocabulary *Extra* (SB page 111)

Exploring meanings

1

- Focus attention on the dictionary extract for *suspect* and allow time for the students to read it thoroughly.
- Ask the students to work in pairs to find the answers to the questions.

> a) Three.
> b) As a verb.
> c) *Suspect* is pronounced *suspect* as a verb and *suspect* as a noun.
> d) Three.
> e) To believe that something is true.

2

Ask the students to read the sentences and match them to the various meanings of *suspect* given in the dictionary extract. Tell them that it will help to decide first what part of speech *suspect* is in each sentence. Point out that they'll need to use the superscript numerals in the dictionary extract to identify the different entries. If necessary, go through the example with the class.

> a) suspect¹ meaning²
> b) suspect² meaning¹
> c) suspect¹ meaning¹
> d) suspect³ meaning²
> e) suspect³ meaning¹

3

- Explain *homograph* before you start and put an example on the board in which the pronunciation is vastly different, e.g. *moped* /məʊˈped/ (a motorised bicycle) and /məʊpt/ *moped* (sulked). Then ask the students to look at the sentences and the pronunciation choices for the words in bold. Ask them to match the words to the correct pronunciation. Encourage them to do this first without looking in the dictionary extracts. They can then use these to check their answers.

- When you've checked answers with the class, ask the students to use their own dictionaries to look up the different meanings and the correct pronunciation of each for six more homographs in the box.

- When checking with the class, make sure that all the words have been covered.

> 1 a) 2   b) 1
> 2 a) 1   b) 2
> 3 a) 2   b) 1

4

- Focus the students' attention on the dictionary entry for *soft*. Point out the number of meanings.
- Ask the students to read the sentences and match them to the seven meanings of *soft*.
- Check answers with the class, then put the students into pairs to discuss which statements they agree with.

> a) 3   b) 6   c) 1   d) 4   e) 7   f) 2   g) 5

5

- Remind the students that not all dictionaries are the same and that they need to become familiar with the way their own particular one displays information.
- Ask them to look at their dictionaries and find out how they show the information for words that belong to more than one word class and/or have more than one meaning.
- In a class feedback session, find out what information the students discovered from their dictionaries

Further practice material

Need more writing practice?

→ Workbook page 71
- Writing a description of a person.

Need more classroom practice activities?

→ Photocopiable resource materials pages 187 to 189
  Grammar: *Ever had it done?*
  Vocabulary: *First impressions*
  Communication: *Phonetics guessing*
→ Top 10 activities pages xv to xx

Need DVD material?

→ Test CD – Programme 12: *Party*

Need progress tests?

→ Test CD – *Test Unit 12*

Need more on important teaching concepts?

→ Key concepts in *New Inside Out* pages xxii to xxxv

Need student self-study practice?

→ CD-ROM – Unit 12: *Style*

Need student CEF self-evaluation?

→ CEF Checklists pages xxxvii to xliv

Need more information and more ideas?

→ www.insideout.net

Review D *Teacher's notes*

These exercises act as a check of the grammar and vocabulary that the students have learnt in Units 10–12. Use them to find any problems that students are having, or anything that they haven't understood and which will need further work.

Grammar (SB page 112)

Remind the students of the grammar explanations they read and the exercises they did in the *Grammar Extra* on pages 144 to 149.

1

This exercise reviews defining relative clauses from Unit 10. Check answers before asking the students to make true sentences and putting them in pairs to compare their sentences.

> a) India is the country ~~which~~ I'd most like to visit.
> b) –
> c) I still have the first CD ~~that~~ I ever bought.
> d) –
> e) The person ~~who~~ I spend most time with is my friend Ben.

2

This exercise reviews real conditionals from Unit 10. Remind the students that when the situation is real or possible, we use the present tense in the *if*-clause and *will, can, might*, etc. or an imperative in the main clause.

> a) Unless you wear a coat, you'll catch a cold.
> b) If they don't arrive in the next five minutes, we'll have to go.
> c) Unless they work, they'll fail the exam.
> d) If you don't ask him, he won't come to the party.
> e) Unless you save your money, you won't be able to buy that car.

3

This exercise reviews indirect questions from Unit 10. Check answers before putting the students into pairs to take turns asking and answering the questions.

> a) Do you know what you're doing next weekend?
> b) Can you tell me where you bought your shoes?
> c) Do you think politics is an interesting topic?
> d) Could you tell me where you were born?

4

This exercise reviews unreal conditionals from Unit 11. Remind the students that when we talk about unreal or imaginary situations in the present, we use the past simple in the *if*-clause and *would* + infinitive in the main clause, and in the past, we use the past perfect in the *if*-clause and *would* + *have* + past participle in the main clause.

> a) were, 'd drive
> b) 'd studied, 'd have passed
> c) 'd learn, could
> d) hadn't fallen, 'd have seen
> e) could, had
> f) wouldn't have bought, 'd known

5

This exercise reviews wishes and regrets from Unit 11. Check answers with the class before asking the students to discuss in pairs which statements are true for them.

> a) could have done   b) was   c) were
> d) hadn't started   e) had   f) had been

6

This exercise reviews *have something done* from Unit 12.

> a) He's cut his hair.
> b) He's had his hair cut.
> c) She's having her car fixed.
> c) She's fixing her car.

7

This exercise reviews structures used in Units 10–12.

> 1 b) ~~A blog is a diary that you write it on the internet.~~
> 2 a) ~~We'll go out on Sunday if it will be fine.~~
> 3 a) ~~If I didn't eat so much I won't be so fat.~~
> 4 b) ~~I wish I didn't buy that shirt – I hate it now.~~
> 5 a) ~~Sean always wears the same leather black old jacket.~~
> 6 b) ~~She has her house decorated at the moment.~~

Vocabulary (SB page 113)

1

This exercise reviews phrasal verbs from Unit 10.

> 1 for me   2 after me   3 me in   4 about me
> 5 me off   6 at me   7 me up

2

This exercise reviews *make* and *let* from Unit 10.

> 1 let   2 let   3 made   4 made   5 let

3

This exercise review attitude adverbs from Unit 8.

> a) Apparently   b) incredibly   c) very well
> d) Hopefully   e) definitely   f) very much
> g) Basically

4

This exercise reviews words to describe clothes from Unit 12.

> a) *material:* cotton, leather, linen, silk, suede
> b) *shape/design/pattern:* baggy, checked, long-sleeved,
>   plain, striped
> c) *clothes:* blouse, boots, suit, sweater, top

5

This exercise reviews words for describing people from Unit 12.

> a) 1 slim 2 mid-forties 3 short 4 deep-set eyes.
> b) 5 shoulder-length 6 skinny 7 freckles
>   8 tattoo
> c) 9 twenties 10 bald 11 sideburns 12 goatee

6

- This exercise reviews verbs for morning routines from Unit 12.
- Check answers before putting the students into pairs to take turns asking and answering the questions.

> a) do b) get c) have d) put e) read

Pronunciation (SB page 113)

1

Remind the students that the boxes show the syllables of a word and the large boxes indicate the stressed syllables. Here they're being asked to classify words according to how many syllables they have and where the main stress falls. Encourage them to say each word aloud to get a feeling for what sounds right.

2 🌐 3.25

Point out the main stresses in the example words which are underlined. Ask the students to do the same for the other words in the table. Then play the recording for them to check their answers. Play it a second time for them to listen and repeat. Be careful with *desert*.

Exercises 1 and 2			
A: ☐☐☐	**B:** ☐☐	**C:** ☐☐☐	**D:** ☐☐☐☐
comfortable	christmas	develop	adventurous
dinosaur	language	expensive	apparently
talented	naughty	museum	psychiatrist
vegetables		pyjamas	ridiculous

Reading & Listening (SB page 114)

1

Ask the students to read the texts quickly just to find the names to complete the sentences.

> a) Brad b) Colin c) Anna

2

Ask the students to read the texts again more carefully and decide if the statements are true or false. Encourage them to correct the false statements.

> a) False. (She had a difficult time when she was a teenager and is glad those years are over.)
> b) True.
> c) True.
> d) False. (She says he can get one when he leaves home.)
> e) False. (He thinks the best years are where you are now and he is happier now than when he was young.)
> f) False. (He wishes he had spent less time worrying about things that don't matter. He thinks only family and health are important enough to worry about.)

3 🌐 3.26

Tell the students they're going to hear Colin talking about his past. Play the recording and ask them to say what he regrets about his past.

Nothing.

🔘 **3.26** (I = Interviewer; C = Colin)

I: *Colin, tell me about your childhood. You never knew your real parents, did you?*

C: *That's right. I was brought up in children's homes – I moved several times when I was very young – and then went to live with my foster parents, Flo and Isaac, when I was ten.*

I: *Was it a difficult childhood?*

C: *Well, some people might see it that way, but I have very good memories. In that part of London at that time, everyone there was poor – we never had any money – but we didn't complain. There was a real neighbourhood spirit. Everyone helped each other.*

I: *Can you tell me what your memories of that time are?*

C: *We used to make our own entertainment – there was no TV, no video games. We played in the fields and down by the canal. All the kids together.*

I: *And you left school quite young, didn't you?*

C: *Yes. I left school at fourteen and went to work in a factory. But I didn't like it. I only stayed there two years. I always wanted to work for myself, so I trained to be a taxi driver. I worked as a driver for ten years until I got married.*

I: *But you didn't stay a taxi driver?*

C: *No. I was ambitious! We already had two children, and another on the way. I wanted a good life for my kids, so I started my own business from nothing, but soon had fifty cars and drivers. I sold the business a few years ago, and made enough money to buy a holiday home in Spain.*

I: *How did you meet your wife?*

C: *We met at a dance. She was wearing a beautiful yellow silk dress. I thought she was the prettiest thing I'd ever seen. We got married six months later.*

I: *Any regrets? Would you change anything about your life?*

C: *Not a thing! I feel like the luckiest man in the world!*

4

Go through the events with the students. Play the recording again and ask them to number them in order.

| 1 e | 2 f | 3 b | 4 c | 5 a | 6 g | 7 d |

Writing & Speaking (SB page 115)

1

Ask the students to read the email, ignoring the gaps. Then ask them to read it again and complete it with the words in the box. Point out that the missing words are linking words which help make a text flow more smoothly.

| 1 but | 2 After | 3 When | 4 While | 5 who |
| 6 unfortunately | 7 although | 8 so | 9 and |

2

Ask the students to match the questions to the paragraphs of the email.

| 1C | 2B | 3E | 4A | 5D |

3

Give the students a minute or two to think about their own answers to the questions and ask them to make notes. Discourage them from writing complete sentences which they may be tempted just to read out in the next exercise.

4

Put the students in pairs and tell them to use their notes to tell each other about their life up to now and their hopes for the future. Encourage them to maintain eye contact with their partner as they speak. The listening partners could ask questions for clarification or to extract more details.

5

Ask the students to write an email to an old childhood friend about their life up to now, what they're doing and what their hopes are for the future. Encourage them to divide the email into three paragraphs, each one dealing with a different part of the task.

Further practice material

Need more classroom practice activities?

→ Photocopiable resource materials page 190
🔘 **3.27 Song:** *Dedicated Follower of Fashion*
→ TOP 10 activities pages xv to xx

Need progress tests?

→ Test CD – *Test Review D*

Need more on important teaching concepts?

→ Key concepts in *New Inside Out* pages xxii to xxxv

Need student self-study practice?

→ CD-ROM – *Review D*

Need more information and more ideas?

→ www.insideout.net

Resource materials

Worksheet	Activity and focus	What the students are doing
Unit 1		
1 Grammar *Reasons to be famous*	Group, pair and individual work: interview Mixed tense questions and modals	Practising interviewing techniques; writing a short biography
1 Vocabulary *You in pictures*	Pair or groupwork: discussion Personal attributes	Using images to describe and interpret personal characteristics
1 Communication *Questions, questions, questions*	Pairwork: question puzzle	Finding out and sharing personal information
Unit 2		
2 Grammar *Moments in American history*	Pairwork: information gap Past simple and past continuous	Interviewing each other using picture and word prompts
2 Vocabulary *Guess the sport*	Groupwork: guessing game Sports	Guessing sports
2 Communication *Truth or dare?*	Team game Mixed tense questions and instructions	Writing questions and playing a board game
Unit 3		
3 Grammar *Find the correct sentence*	Pairwork: sentence quiz Present perfect	Identifying correct uses of present perfect tense forms
3 Vocabulary *Love is ...?*	Pair and groupwork: debate Gradable/non-gradable adjectives	Discussing different romantic situations and giving opinions
3 Communication *Parents' day*	Group or pairwork: roleplays Qualifying adverbs Personality characteristics	Describing people Roleplaying parent interviews
Review A *You've Got a Friend*	Pairwork: song Revision of grammar and vocabulary from Units 1–3	Listening to and reading a song and matching sounds to phonetic symbols
Unit 4		
4 Grammar *The bluffing game*	Groupwork: using diaries Arrangements, invitations and excuses Present continuous	Inviting and refusing invitations Making arrangements and excuses
4 Vocabulary *Make & do*	Individual work: mime game Common expressions with *make* and *do*	Miming common expressions for other students to guess

Worksheet	Activity and focus	What the students are doing
4 Communication *Party animal or party pooper?*	Pairwork: questionnaire Party activities	Interviewing a partner about party habits
Unit 5		
5 Grammar *Just a minute!*	Whole class or groupwork: categories game Countable/uncountable nouns Quantifiers	Completing a list of words to make a correct phrase
5 Vocabulary *Best of the bunch*	Group or pairwork: pelmanism game Noun collocations	Making correct collocations from pairs of cards
5 Communication *Did you use to ...?*	Whole class: mingle activity Used to	Finding out about classmates
Unit 6		
6 Grammar *Rules and regulations*	Groupwork: collaborative writing Rules for public places Modals of obligation, prohibition, permission	Producing a poster with rules about public places for classmates to identify
6 Vocabulary *How well organised are you?*	Individual and pairwork: questionnaire Personal organisation and time management	Reading questions, noting answers and interviewing a partner
6 Communication *Detectives*	Groupwork: murder mystery game	Making deductions and sequencing events to explain a mystery
Review B *It's My Party*	Pairwork: song Revision of grammar and vocabulary from Units 4–6	Listening to and reading a song and answering true/false questions
Unit 7		
7 Grammar *It's happened to me!*	Whole class: mingle activity Passive forms	Asking and finding out about things which have happened to classmates
7 Vocabulary *A true crime story*	Pair and groupwork: story telling Crime	Reading, making notes and re-telling a story to find differences
7 Communication *Making news*	Individual, pair and groupwork: picture card news stories Topical issues	Writing, listening to and reporting a short news story with picture prompts
Unit 8		
8 Grammar *Past perfect dominoes*	Group or pairwork: dominoes game Past perfect	Playing dominoes by matching two halves of a sentence
8 Vocabulary *Holiday emails*	Pairwork: holiday emails Holidays Descriptions	Completing holiday emails about good and bad holiday experiences
8 Communication *Globetrotters*	Pair and groupwork: survey and discussion Travel and transport	Discussing questions and identifying a group member for an award

Worksheet	Activity and focus	What the students are doing
Unit 9		
9 Grammar *Reported interviews*	Groupwork or pairwork: memory game Reporting interviews	Reading and reporting statements from interviews
9 Vocabulary *Blockbuster*	Groupwork: presentation Film outlines Narrative	Planning and writing details for a film and presenting to the rest of the class
9 Communication *Film, books and music*	Group and pairwork: crossword Films, books and music	Writing clues for crosswords, guessing words from partner's clues
Review C *Somewhere Only We Know*	Pairwork: song Revision of grammar and vocabulary from Units 7–9	Listening to and reading a song and discussing places to go
Unit 10		
10 Grammar *When I was at school ...*	Pairwork: game Defining relative clauses Schooldays	Playing a board game and completing sentences
10 Vocabulary Make *and* let	Groupwork: debate Recommendations and opinions *Make* and *let*	Agreeing on good qualities for teachers, parents and employers
10 Communication *Definition auction*	Team game Defining relative clauses	Reading and bidding for correct word definitions in auction-style game
Unit 11		
11 Grammar *If ...*	Whole class: chain game Conditionals	Writing chain sentences using *if* clauses
11 Vocabulary *Then and now*	Pairwork: discussion Past and present tenses	Comparing life changes with a partner
11 Communication *Unreal!*	Team game Unreal conditionals	Using prompts on a board to make conditional sentences
Unit 12		
12 Grammar *Ever had it done?*	Whole class: mingle activity *Have something done*	Making questions from prompts to find classmates who answer *yes*
12 Vocabulary *First impressions*	Individual and groupwork: interviews Interview protocol	Writing and discussing advice for a first job interview
12 Communication *Phonetics guessing*	Groupwork: board game Vocabulary revision Pronunciation	Playing a board game and guessing a word from a definition and phonetic symbol
Review D *Dedicated Follower of Fashion*	Pairwork: song Revision of grammar and vocabulary from Units 10–12	Listening to and reading a song Vocabulary work

Teacher's notes

1 Grammar Reasons to be famous

Page 151

Activity

Groupwork, pairwork and individual work: interviewing.

Focus

Mixed tense question forms including modals.

Preparation

Make one or two copies (depending on class size) of the worksheet and cut them up into cards as indicated.

Procedure

- Divide the class into two groups. Ask one group to brainstorm answers to the question: 'What are people famous for?' Ask the other group to brainstorm answers to the question: 'What information do people like to know about famous people?'

- Ask the two groups to report back on their discussion.

- Divide the students into pairs. Tell them that they have all suddenly become famous and give everyone a 'Reasons to be famous' card. (Use the blank cards if you need them. Students can write in their own 'Reasons to be famous'.) Allow a minute or two for students to check vocabulary – either with you or in dictionaries.

- Explain that they are going to interview each other for a glossy magazine (like *Hello!*). Tell them that the person they are going to interview is incredibly busy and can only spare five minutes for the interview, and they need to find out as much interesting information as possible in the time given. Then allow a few minutes for students to decide what their name is, what they are doing before and after the interview, and how/why the interview is going to end after five minutes.

- Ask the students to begin the interview. After five minutes, tell the students to swap roles.

- Ask the students to work individually and write the opening paragraph for their article. When they've finished, let them read each other's work.

Follow up

Ask students to bring in passport-size photographs of themselves, and the articles and photographs could be displayed on a 'Class Biographies' poster.

Note: This activity works well with classes who do not know each other very well and can be used as an extended icebreaker. It is also a good diagnostic activity at the beginning of a course.

Hello! is a popular British magazine that often has interviews with celebrities and photos of their houses and families.

1 Vocabulary You in pictures

Page 152

Activity

Pair and groupwork discussion.

Focus

Practising language related to personal characteristics.

Preparation

Make one copy of the worksheet for each student in the class. Take a few minutes to look at the pictures yourself. Think about what the pictures signify to you – although these interpretations may be different for everyone.

Procedure

- Give each student a worksheet.

- Ask the students to think about their own character and to choose the *five* images that best represent this. Then, tick or circle them.

- Ask the students to complete the sentences at the bottom of the worksheet.

- In pairs or small groups, the students explain their choices to each other.

Follow up

Hold a brief open class discussion of which images best represent the class as a whole. Encourage discussion of which characteristics each of the images could represent.

Variations

For classes where the students know each other well, variations on the last stage above are:

- Students guess their partner's choices before the discussion.

- With the writing at the bottom folded out of sight, the worksheets are collected and then randomly distributed. The students have to guess whose worksheet they have got before the discussion can take place.

- With the writing at the bottom folded out of sight, the worksheets are collected and then put on the walls of the classroom. The students walk around the room, in pairs or small groups, deciding whose is whose.

1 Communication Questions, questions, questions

Page 153
Activity
Pairwork: reading, writing and speaking.

Focus
Recognising, answering and asking questions.

Preparation
Make one copy of the worksheet for each student in the class.

Procedure
- Give out one worksheet to each student. Tell students to read through the answers and check the meanings of any words they don't understand, either with you or using dictionaries.
- Working in pairs, the students have to find all the questions and write them next to the appropriate answers.
- The students now take turns to ask each other these questions, writing down their partner's answers in the spaces on the worksheet. Encourage the students to ask follow-up questions to find out more information, e.g.

  Which country would you most like to visit?
  China. And you?
  India.
  Why India?
- Ask each student to report back three interesting things they have learnt about their partner.

> Which country would you most like to visit?
> How often do you speak English?
> Who is your favourite singer?
> Are you reading a book at the moment?
> What kind of music do you like?
> How many countries have you been to?
> Have you ever been to the UK?
> Are you any good at cooking?
> How are you feeling right now?
> Who chose your name?
> What were you doing at midnight last night?
> What is your favourite colour?

2 Grammar Moments in American history

Page 154
Activity
Pairwork: listening and speaking.

Focus
Practising the past simple and past continuous.

Preparation
Make enough photocopies of worksheets A and B for each pair in the class.

Procedure
- Tell students that they are going to interview each other about past events in history.
- Ask students to form pairs of Student As and Student Bs and give each student an A or B worksheet.
- Allow a minute for students to look at their sheets. Explain to them that they have information about the Walton family and what different members were doing at different moments in the history of America.
- Do an example with a student in the class so that students know what they have to do, e.g.:

Student:	*What was Mrs Walton doing when Kennedy was assassinated?*
Teacher:	*She was cooking.*
Student:	*What were you doing when the stock market crashed?*
Teacher:	*I was watching the news on TV.*
- Suggest to students that they take it in turns to ask and answer questions. It is best to work across the page so that the students can substitute the names of the people for pronouns. For the *You* sections, ask them to use their imagination – and invent activities.

2 Vocabulary Guess the sport

Page 155
Activity
Groupwork: speaking.

Focus
Practising vocabulary related to sports and sporting events.

Preparation
Make one copy of the worksheet for every four or five students in the class. Cut up the worksheet as indicated.

Procedure

- Tell the students you have a pack of cards for each group. Each card has the name of a sport and some information about that sport on it.
- Explain the rules of the game:
  1 Students work in groups of four or five.
  2 Each student in the group takes one card and reads it – without showing it to the others.
  3 Students take turns to ask one *yes/no* question to any member to the group:
  Is it a ball game?
  Do you play in teams?

  They must nominate the person they want to ask:
  My question is for Javier.
  4 The student answering the question should give short answers, e.g: *Yes, it is / No, you can't / I don't know / Sometimes / It depends …*
  5 Students can use their turn to make a guess (*Is it tennis?*). They may *only* guess during their turn. If the guess is right, the card holder drops out.
  6 When only one student remains, the game is over and that student is the winner.

  Demonstrate the game if necessary.
- Ask the students to form groups. Make sure that the seating arrangement allows them to listen to each other.
- Give each group a set of cards facing down to be placed in the middle of the group. As they play the game, circulate and monitor.
- When the first groups finish playing, get them to repeat the game with the remaining cards.

Variation

As an alternative procedure, try telling the students that everybody has a starting score of 10 points: a wrong guess loses them 3 points and a correct guess earns them 3 points. Groups should keep their own written record of this. In this case, the winner is the student with the most points at the end.

2 **Communication** Truth or dare?

Page 156
Activity

Team game: speaking and writing.

Focus

Asking and answering questions using the present perfect, past simple and past continuous tenses

Preparation

Make one copy of the worksheet for each group of six to eight students (i.e. two teams of three to four players) in the class.

Procedure

- Divide the class into teams of three or four. Make sure there are even numbers of teams as each team has to play against another team. Tell them they are going to play a game called 'Truth or dare?' (explain that a dare is something funny or difficult or embarrassing to do), but first they have to write some questions.
- Write the following suggestions on the board:
  TRUTH
  Have you ever … ?
  Did you … ?
  When did you last … ?
  How many times have you … ?
  When did you first..?
  What were you doing when … ?

  DARE
  Sing a song in English.
  Imitate a famous person.
  Say the alphabet backwards.
  Make three animal sounds.
  Demonstrate disco dancing.
  Show us everything in your pockets.
- When each team has prepared enough questions, ask two teams to sit facing each other and give them one copy of the worksheet. Refer the students to the 'How to play the game' section on the worksheet and ask them to elect someone to read out the rules.
- The teams play until one team has reached the finish. When the first team has reached the finish, ask the students to stop playing.

3 **Grammar** Find the correct sentence

Page 157
Activity

Pairwork: speaking and writing.

Focus

Use of the present perfect tenses.

Preparation

Make one copy of the worksheet for each student in the class.

Procedure

- Explain that students are going to look at nine pairs of sentences which are similar. However, only one sentence is correct in each pair.
- Give one copy of the worksheet to each student in the class and divide the class into pairs. Ask each pair of students to discuss which sentence is correct and which is wrong and why. They can make notes on their worksheets.
- When students have finished discussing the sentences and have made their choices, conduct an open class feedback.

Answers and commentary

1 b) is correct. a) isn't possible because the verb 'know' is not usually used in the continuous form as it refers to a state. The sentence tells us the speaker met Lindy twenty years ago and still knows her today.

2 a) is correct. It tells us about an activity which started in the early afternoon and has continued until now (late afternoon). As 'all afternoon' refers to past time as well as present time, sentence b) isn't possible. The present continuous tense is used more generally to describe time around now, whereas the present perfect continuous allows the speaker to be more specific.

3 b) is correct. The sentence needs to express past time (when he started living in Rome – five years ago) and present time (he is still living in Rome) and so the present perfect is the correct choice. In many languages sentence a) achieves the same function, but in English you don't use the present continuous to describe an action which started in the past and has continued until now.

4 b) is correct. Whenever possible English speakers prefer to use present perfect continuous to describe an activity which started in the past and has continued until now, especially if it's seen as a short-term activity. Usually when you want to emphasise the completion of an action, you use the present perfect simple. For example 'I've done my homework' tells us the speaker has completed the homework and is now reporting the fact. In sentence a) there appears to be a conflict between the first part of the sentence, which suggests completion, and the second part, which suggests that the homework is not yet completed.

5 a) is correct. In this sentence the speaker tells us that five emails have been completed and the sixth is going to be started shortly. Sentence b) is incorrect because 'I've been writing five emails' suggests the action of writing all five emails was simultaneous. It's possible to say 'I've been writing emails this morning' because the emphasis is on the general activity of writing emails, but adding the number of emails makes it too specific.

6 b) is correct. 'Before I came here' refers to past time and so requires a past tense. The present perfect only ever refers the past when there is a relationship with the present.

7 a) is correct. The question is asking about the activity that led to the person looking tired. The question 'What have you done?' usually refers to the outcome of a completed single action (i.e. I've cut my finger' or 'I've broken your plate').

8 b) is correct. It refers to the outcome of a completed action.

9 a) is correct. b) isn't possible because the verb 'want' is not usually used in the continuous form as it refers to a state.

3 Vocabulary Love is ...?

Page 158

Activity

Pairwork and groupwork: speaking.

Focus

Using adverbs and gradable/non-gradable adjectives.

Preparation

Make one copy of the worksheet for each student in the class.

Procedure

- Draw a picture of a romantic situation on the board, e.g. two people having a meal with candles and roses on the table, or bring in a picture from a magazine. If you like, play a cassette of romantic music. Write *Love is …?* on the board. Ask the students to suggest ways of completing the sentence.

- Give one copy of the worksheet to each student and ask them to read through the twelve situations. Ask them to choose the most romantic situation. Circulate, helping with vocabulary.

- After five minutes ask the students to stop reading and form pairs.

- Explain that each pair is going to discuss how romantic the remaining situations are and grade them using hearts (5 hearts is extremely romantic, 1 heart is only slightly romantic). Explain that the students in each pair do not have to give the same grading.

- Circulate, encouraging discussion and/or helping the pairs with vocabulary where necessary.

- When most of the pairs have finished grading, bring the language at the bottom of the worksheet to their attention. Model and drill for pronunciation. Show how the structure changes for 'not really' and 'not at all'. Go through the results with the whole class, encouraging the students to use the adverbs.

- Ask the students to form new groups of four, each pair joining with another pair of similar opinion. Explain to the new groups that they are going to collaborate to produce another romantic situation. This time, they must agree on one new romantic situation.

- When all the groups have completed their situation, discuss each one as a whole class, and ask the other groups to grade them by giving each situation a number of hearts. Again, encourage the students to use the adverbs.

Follow up

Ask the students to conduct a class or school survey on what makes a romantic situation. The results could be presented in the form of a wall-chart or display.

3 Communication Parents' day

Page 159

Activity

Group or pairwork: speaking.

Focus

Describing people using qualifying adverbs.

Preparation

Make one copy of the worksheet for each group or pair.

Procedure

- Introduce the idea of parents' day (i.e. that parents visit the school and ask the different teachers how their children are doing).

- Divide the class into pairs or groups. Hand out one set of pictures to each pair or group and put the following subjects on the board: *art, maths, science, computers, English, sport.* Ask the students to use the 'useful language' (+ any of their own) to describe each pupil from their appearance in the pictures (e.g. *Karen is very good at maths, quite popular, very hard-working, she likes science,* etc.). Note that students may need help with the qualifying adverbs (e.g. 'very nice' is possible, but 'absolutely nice' is not).

- Compare the ideas of each pair/group.

- Introduce the idea of the 'tactful' teacher and the 'tactless' teacher. Elicit how each would describe one of the students. For example:

Tactful:	Tactless:
Matthew **tends to be** late.	Matthew is always late.
Matthew **can be a bit** quiet at times.	Matthew is boring.
Matthew **is not particularly/ exactly** talkative.	Matthew never talks.

- Divide the students into two equal groups: one group of parents (allocate one pupil picture to each parent) and one group of teachers. Move the teachers to different areas of the room. Parents then visit each teacher and get a report on their son or daughter (teachers give information about all subjects – they can say whatever they choose about any students).

- After finishing, ask the parents which teachers were tactful and which were tactless and why.

Review A You've Got a Friend

Page 160

Activity

Pairwork: song.

Focus

Revision of grammar and vocabulary from *New Inside Out* Intermediate Student's Book, Units 1–3.

Preparation

Make one copy of the worksheet for each student in the class. Get the recording ready.

Procedure

- Ask students to read aloud each of the lettered words in Exercise 1, focusing mainly on the underlined part. Make sure they are familiar with the phonetic symbols in the box and then encourage them to match the sounds to the symbols.

- Ask student to cover the song so that they can only see Exercise 1. Allow them time to listen to the song and tick the words in Exercise 1 as they hear them. Play the song again, if necessary. Students report back to the class on which word isn't in the song.

- Exercise 3: Give students plenty of time to discuss and possibly check the words in their dictionaries.

- Exercise 4: Students tell each other about a friend who is always there for them.

Optional extra activity

Ask students (working in pairs) to give their interpretation of the following lines from the song.

a) And soon I will be there, to brighten up even your darkest night.
   (= *I'll be there to lift your spirits and make you happy even in the worst of times.*)

b) If the sky above you grows dark and full of clouds
   (= *If you become very upset / If you are going through very difficult times.*)

c) Keep your head together
   (= *Stay calm. Be sensible. Think clearly.*)

1
a) c<u>a</u>ll /ɔː/   b) c<u>o</u>me /ʌ/   c) d<u>ar</u>kest /ɑː/
d) fri<u>e</u>nd /e/   e) g<u>oo</u>d /ʊ/   f) g<u>o</u>t /ɒ/
g) h<u>ur</u>t /ɜː/   h) n<u>ee</u>d /iː/   i) s<u>oo</u>n /uː/
j) wint<u>er</u> /ə/   k) th<u>a</u>nk /æ/   l) th<u>i</u>nk /ɪ/

2
The word *thank* isn't in the song.

3
a) troubled   b) close   c) brighten
d) fall (American English)   e) cold
f) desert   g) soul

---

4 Grammar The bluffing game

Page 161

Activity

Groupwork: speaking and writing

Focus

Invitations and refusals, using present continuous for future.

Preparation

Make one copy of the worksheet for each student in the class.

Procedure

- Give one copy of the worksheet to each student. Ask them to write ten arrangements anywhere in their diary page but tell them <u>not</u> to let the other students see what they have written.

- Divide the class into groups of four or five and ask each group to appoint a referee. The referee's job is to check the other players' diaries and award points.

- Explain how to play the game:

  1 Player A invites Player B (on his/her left) to go out.

  2 Player B refuses the invitation and a) reads out the arrangement in his/her diary **or**
  b) invents an arrangement if there is a free space in their diary.

  3 Player A guesses if Player B is telling the truth or bluffing. For example,

    A *Do you fancy going to the cinema on Saturday afternoon?*

    B *I'm afraid I can't – I'm playing tennis with my cousin.*

    A *I think you're telling the truth. / I think you're bluffing*

  4 The referee then checks Player B's diary page and gives 1 point to Player A if he/she guessed correctly and 1 point to B if A did not guess correctly.

  5 Player B invites Player C (on his/her left) to go out, and play continues.

- The student with the most points at the end of the game is the winner.

Note

Before students start playing, tell them to write some false arrangements to use in the game.
For example:
I'm having my hair done.
I'm going to the airport to meet my Australian cousin.
I'm helping my nephew with his homework.
I'm making a cake for my grandmother's birthday.
I'm helping my father to paint the bathroom ceiling.

4 Vocabulary Make & do

Page 162

Activity

Mime game/drill.

Focus

Collocations with *make* and *do*.

Preparation

Make one copy of the worksheet and cut it up as indicated.

Procedure

- If possible, ask the students to sit in a circle or horseshoe.

- Give one card to each student.

- Tell the students that they are going to mime the expression on their card. Give a couple of examples, e.g. *do the ironing* or *make a sandwich* and get the students to guess them.

- Give the students a few seconds to think of a way of miming the expression. Help them if necessary.

- The first student mimes their expression. When another student guesses what it is, they shout it out. When the expression is correctly guessed, the next student in the circle starts miming.

- The process continues round the circle, with each student miming *all* the expressions that came before, while the other students simultaneously chorus the expression. So for example, student number ten will have to mime the previous nine as well as their own.

- The activity continues until all the students have mimed the expressions on their cards.

Notes

This activity works with anything up to twenty students. For larger classes, divide the students into two groups and have two independent activities going on.

Before the activity, the cards can be used to check or teach the collocations. (1) Put the students into small groups and give each group a set of cards. Get the students to group the cards according to whether they are *make* or *do* expressions. (2) Give each student a card and get the students to stand in two groups according to whether they have a *make* or *do* expression.

4 Communication Party animal or party pooper?

Page 163

Activity

Pairwork: questionnaire.

Focus

Phrases related to parties.

Preparation

Make one copy of the worksheet for each student in the class.

Procedure

- Give one copy of the worksheet to each student. Explain that they are going to interview each other in pairs and make a note of each other's answers.
- Divide the class into pairs. Give the students plenty of time to interview each other, noting down the answers.
- When all the students have finished interviewing each other, ask them to check their scores (upside down) at the foot of the page. Once they have checked their scores they can then read the 'What it means' section.
- Conduct a feedback session in open class. Ask students if they think the commentary describes them well.

5 Grammar Just a minute!

Page 164

Activity

Whole class or groupwork: filling in a table.

Focus

Countable and uncountable nouns.

Preparation

Make one copy of the worksheet for each student in the class.

Procedure

- Give one copy of the worksheet to each student.
- Ask the students to look carefully at the grid on the worksheet. Point out to them that there are six columns with quantifiers as headings.
- Explain the rules of the game to the students:
  1 Students have to complete the lines with words that fit the categories you are going to read aloud. If necessary, remind the students of the rules for quantifiers and countable/uncountable nouns. (See Student's Book page 134.)

2 Students have a maximum of one minute to come up with a word under each heading and they must write only one word per category.

3 If a student completes their entire line before the time is up, they have to say *Stop!* and the rest of the class must stop writing.

4 Students score one point for every correct word and two points for every 'original' word – a word that only one student has written.

5 The winner of the game is the student with the most points.

- Read out the first category from the list below. If nobody finishes after one minute, call *Stop!*

> **List of categories**
> 1 Something you have in the kitchen.
> 2 Something you can't live without.
> 3 Something you had when you were a child.
> 4 Something you would like to have.
> 5 Something you can put in your pocket.
> 6 Something you are wearing now.
> 7 Something in the classroom.
> 8 Something you can see in the street.
> 9 Something you can buy with your pocket money/salary.
> 10 Something you would like for your next birthday.

- The students say their words. Check that the phrases are grammatically correct and are appropriate for the context.
- Give the students their points and carry on with the second category on the list.

Follow up

Once you have finished your categories, encourage the students to add some more.

If the students have enjoyed the game, you can use the same procedure to practise any other grammar or lexical field (e.g. vocabulary categories: clothes, food, sports, etc.).

5 Vocabulary Best of the bunch

Page 165

Activity

Pair/groupwork: *Pelmanism* game.

Focus

Using partitives *a bunch / packet / bar / box / jar of* with their collocating nouns.

Preparation

Make one copy of the worksheet for every four students in the class and cut up as indicated.

Procedure

- Write *keys, biscuits, soap, tools* and *marmalade* on the board and *a bunch / packet / bar / box / jar.* Ask students to match each item with its container, or way of counting it when there are a lot. Check answers open class.

- Tell your students they are going to play a game in which they have to do the same thing. Divide the class into pairs and ask one pair to play against another pair. Give each group of four a copy of the worksheet, cut into cards as indicated. Ask them to put all the cards face down on the table.

- Each pair takes it in turns to turn two cards over. The object of the game is to turn over two cards which form one correct collocation (e.g. *a bunch of bananas,* not *a box of bananas*). If a player does this, they keep the pair of cards. As the player turns over the card, they must say the word, otherwise they cannot claim the pair.

- If the cards are not a matching pair, they are turned over again and left for the next pair to try.

- The pair with the most pairs of cards at the end of the game are the winners.

Variation

Pairs try to write down as many collocations as they can remember with the cards face down. They get one point for each correct collocation.

5 Communication Did you use to ...?

Page 166

Activity

Class survey: speaking and writing.

Focus

Used to questions.

Preparation

Make one copy of the worksheet for each group of twelve students in the class and cut up as indicated.

Procedure

- If there are more than twelve students in the class, divide them into groups. Give one card to each student in the class and ask them to make a question starting *Did you use to...*.

- Tell the students they are responsible for finding the answer to the questions on their card by speaking to everybody in their group. Make sure the students know that the answer can only be 'yes' if the situation is no longer the same, i.e. *Yes, I used to own a dog* means the speaker no longer owns a dog.

- Ask the students to go round the class (or their group) asking and answering questions. Tell them that they may need to make notes on a separate piece of paper.

- When they have spoken to everyone in the class (or their group), they should take it in turns to report back to the class (or group) on the information they have found out.

6 Grammar Rules and regulations

Page 167

Activity

Collaborative writing.

Focus

Modals of obligation and permission; paraphrasing.

Preparation

Make one copy of the worksheet and cut it up into cards.

Procedure

- Divide the students into small groups.

- Give a card to each group.

- Tell the students that the aim of the task is to produce a poster giving eight rules for the place on the card. They must strictly follow the instructions about forbidden words: see the lists headed 'Don't use these' on the worksheet. It may help to give them an example before they start:

You can borrow cash from this place.
You usually have to show ID.
You can't buy things in this place.

- Write the modals below on the board:

  You have to/must
  You mustn't
  You can
  You cannot
  You don't have to/needn't

- Number the posters and display them around the classroom. Ask the students to read all the posters and guess the place that each applies to.

6 **Vocabulary** How well organised are you?

Page 168

Activity

Individual and pairwork: speaking, listening and note-taking.

Focus

Questionnaire relating to time and personal organisation.

Preparation

Make one copy of the worksheet for each pair of students in the class. Cut copies into A and B.

Procedure

- Tell the students that they are going to interview each other about their personal organisation and time management.
- Divide the students into pairs and assign A and B within each pair.
- Give A and B students their part of the questionnaire.
- Ask the students to read the instructions and answer their questionnaires, noting their own answers on the side.
- Circulate and help with vocabulary problems.
- Tell the students to start interviewing each other and to make a note of their partner's answers.
- Read out the scores or put them on an OHP to show the class.
- Ask the students to calculate their score in their own questionnaire and that of their partner, to see who's better organised.

Follow up

A conversation could be developed about useful tips for time-saving and better self-organisation, either in the pairs or as a whole class.

Notes

Encourage the students to ask follow up questions, to make the interview more natural.

Encourage students to ask the questions, rather than let the partner 'read' them, so that everybody makes an effort to practise oral communication.

Suggest that they take it in turns to ask one question each. This makes it more entertaining, and gives everybody roughly the same opportunity to speak (if time is limited).

Scoring system

Questionnaire A

1	a 3	b 2	c 1
2	a 2	b 1	c 3
3	a 2	b 1	
4	a 1	b 3	c 2
5	a 1	b 2	
6	a 2	b 1	c 3
7	a 2	b 1	

Questionnaire B

1	a 1	b 2	
2	a 1	b 3	c 2
3	a 3	b 2	c 1
4	a 1	b 2	c 3
5	a 1	b 2	
6	a 1	b 2	
7	a 3	b 2	c 1

Total score

Up to 15 points: You are a disaster. You can't get things done on time because of a total lack of organisation. You should make a plan to start organizing your life today!

Between 16–28 points: You are fairly well organised. On the whole you get things done when they need to be done. You must, however, be aware of a certain tendency to improvise, which may cause you some problems.

Between 29–36 points: You are very well organised. You manage your time extremely well and don't like leaving things to chance. However, keep in mind that your liking for organisation could verge on obsession.

6 **Communication** Detectives

Page 169

Activity

Groupwork: deduction and speculation game.

Focus

Using a sequence of events to work out a murder mystery.

Preparation

Make one copy of the worksheet for each group of three or four students in the class and cut it up as indicated.

Procedure

- Introduce the situation and the characters to the class and explain that they will try and find out what happened and why.

Tony, the victim, was found dead today. (Check day and date with the class.) He had been shot with his own gun.

Jeanette was Tony's wife.

Steve was Tony and Jeanette's driver.

Peter was Tony's business partner.

- Divide the class into groups of three or four.
- Hand out the clues from the worksheet – one set to each group. Give each student a different set of clues, so that each has all the information about one of the four characters.
- Tell the students to exchange the clues they have and come up with a theory explaining Tony's murder. Encourage students to put the facts into chronological order, having established today's date, e.g.
  On the 29th June …
  On the 30th June …
- When they have finished, groups report back to the class with their theories on who did what and why.

> You can either choose the explanation which is the most ingenious or entertaining – or decide which group got closer to the version below.
>
> Steve and Peter both needed money. Steve's salary was small. Peter lost a fortune gambling. They stole from the business together for a year. To divert suspicion they pretended to hate each other. But the money still wasn't enough – especially for Peter.
> Peter played tennis with Jeanette and he knew she was in love with him. He persuaded her to leave her husband and run away to Bangkok with him, though he had no intention of actually going. She bought the tickets and cleared out her and Tony's joint private bank account. There was about £2,000,000 in it: the savings from Tony's share of profits of the business. Meanwhile Peter booked a flight to Rio.
> Tony realised money was disappearing from the business and he hired a private detective. The detective told Tony about Jeanette's visit to the bank and when Tony discovered that she had emptied the account, he confronted her. She panicked and shot him.

Follow up

Students write up a report or a newspaper story telling what happened.

Review B It's My Party

Page 170
Activity
Pairwork: song.

Focus
Revision of grammar and vocabulary from *New Inside Out* Intermediate Student's Book, Units 4–6.

Preparation
Make one copy of the worksheet for each student in the class. Get the recording ready.

Procedure
- Ask students to look at the picture and predict what the song is about.
- Play the recording. Students check their guesses and then identify the three characters.
- Ask students to work on their own or in pairs and choose which sentences are true and which are false. Check answers with the class.
- Students discuss their own parties, based on their answers to the four questions (*a–d*).

> **1 and 2**
> The song is about a disastrous birthday party. The song is sung by a teenage girl who is the host of the party. At some point in the party, Judy, a friend of the host, leaves with Johnny, the boyfriend of the host. When they come back to the party, Judy is wearing Johnny's (friendship) ring, and it's clear that he is now Judy's boyfriend. The singer is miserable and says she has every reason to cry because everything has gone wrong. 'I'll cry if I want to' suggests a rather childish response to a friend's attempt to stop her crying.
>
> **3**
> a) True   b) False   c) False   d) True
> e) True
>
> **4**
> Students' own answers.

7 Grammar It's happened to me!

Page 171
Activity
Class mingle: speaking and writing.

Focus
Questions using the passive voice.

Preparation
Make one copy of the worksheet for each student.

Procedure
- Give one copy of the worksheet to each student in the class. Explain that they are going to ask one another some general questions.
- Explain that they should ask each other the questions and only write down the name of the person in the right-hand column who answers 'Yes' to their questions. Elicit the first question 'Have you been shocked by something recently?'. Ask them to ask follow-up questions to find out more information, e.g. *What have you been shocked about? When did it happen?* etc.
- Ask them to stand up and mingle. Monitor carefully and only stop them when the first student has finished. Conduct a feedback session in open class.

7 Vocabulary A true crime story

Page 172
Activity
Pair and groupwork: story telling.

Focus
Crime vocabulary.

Preparation
Make a copy of the story for each group.

Procedure
- Divide the class into two groups. Give one group story A and one group story B.
- Tell the students to read their stories and make notes to remember them. A good way to help the students to remember their stories is to get each student in the group to prepare five comprehension questions about their story and then get them to read the questions to the rest of the group who then answer them. Move around the groups and help with vocabulary. (If you have a lot of students then make two groups of student As and two groups of student Bs.)
- Regroup the students in pairs so that each pair has one student with story A and one student with story B.

- Ask the students to tell their stories to their partners.
- After both of them have told their stories they should make a list of the differences in their two stories.
- Afterwards, get the pairs to explain the differences they found and list them on the board.
- Tell them that one of the stories is true and the other is false. Take a vote – which one do they think is true? (The true story is the one set in Brazil.)

---

1 … went on holiday to (A) Brazil, (B) America
2 … spent over (A) £1,000, (B) £1,200
3 … went to a rather dangerous part of (A) São Paulo, (B) New York
4 (A) … he picked up a telephone and pretended to speak to someone, (B) … he stood in front of a cigarette machine and bought a packet of cigarettes.
5 (A) … across the road. He was now very nervous and …, (B) … across the road and he was nervous but …
6 … while (A) making a phone call, (B) buying a packet of cigarettes
7 (A) He was so nervous that even though the story wasn't true he started to cry. He gave a description of two men he had seen following him. (B) He told them he had lost a video camera, jewellery, money and clothes.
He wasn't nervous at all. He had always liked acting and totally convinced the police.
8 … every item over (A) £50, (B) £100
9 … a telegram from the police in (A) Brazil, (B) New York
10 (A) to tell him that his information and prompt reporting of the crime had led to the arrest and conviction of two criminals who the police had been pursuing for much more serious crimes and that he was entitled to a reward of £2,500. (B) telling him that a bag that fitted his description had been found in the house of a recently convicted criminal and that some of the contents had also been found. Two weeks later he received a video camera, clothes and jewellery from the police in New York. None of it was, of course, his.

---

7 Communication Making news

Page 173

Activity

Individual, pair and groupwork: note writing, news reporting (story telling) and listening.

Focus

Past tense verbs (both regular and irregular).

Preparation

Make one copy of the worksheet for each group of four or six students. Cut the copies up into cards.

Procedure

- Divide the class into groups of four or six. Ask the students in each group to sit in a circle and number themselves 1–4 or 1–6, clockwise.
- Ask the students to imagine that this morning they heard a surprising piece of news on their local radio station and that they are going to tell a friend about it.
- Give one set of pictures from the worksheet to each group. Ask students who are number 1 to shuffle the pictures well and deal out four to six pictures face down to every student in the group.
- Tell the students that they have five to ten minutes to make up a newsworthy story which includes at least three of their pictures. Explain that the story should take one minute to tell. Ask the students to write short notes about the story. Encourage them to be imaginative.
- Circulate, helping with vocabulary and grammar problems.
- When the students are ready, tell them that the activity is in two rounds and that they only need half of the stories for the first round.

First round

- Ask students 1, 3 and 5 to tell their story to the student on their left, beginning with *This morning I heard on the news that …* Tell the students that the telling-listening periods will be exactly one minute and that you will be giving the 'go' and 'stop' commands.
- Ask students 2, 4 and 6 to pass the story they have just heard on to the student on their left, again beginning with *This morning I heard on the news that …*
- Ask the students to make the stories 'travel' clockwise. Repeat this until the stories have been told to the original storyteller.
- The original storytellers explain to the whole group what in the story is correct and what has been omitted or changed by showing the pictures they used.

Second round

- Repeat the first round, with the other half of the stories. Ask students 2, 4 and 6 to start telling their stories.

Follow up

Ask every group to report to the whole class about the most interesting/credible/incredible/imaginative story.

Students can be asked to write a longer version of the story for homework, expanding the initial information.

The conversation can develop into 'stranger-than-fiction stories', real events that the students know about.

Notes

If you don't have even numbers in your class, you can join in, or you can ask your 'odd-number' student to keep the timing for you (after he/she has made up his/her own story!).

An element of competition can be introduced by asking the last 'tellers' to guess what pictures the story is based on. Give one point per correctly guessed picture.

8 Grammar Past perfect dominoes

Page 174

Activity

Group or pairwork: Dominoes game.

Focus

The past perfect tense.

Preparation

Make one copy of the worksheet for each group of three students in the class and cut up as indicated.

Procedure

- Explain to the students that they are going to play a game of dominoes by matching two halves of a sentence containing the past perfect, and that the object of the game is to get rid of all their dominoes.
- Ask the students to work in groups of three and give each group a set of dominoes. Ask them to deal out three dominoes each and to leave the rest in a pile, face down.
- Before they start, explain the instructions: 1) Player A puts down any one of his/her dominoes face up. 2) The player on their left must put down one of their dominoes, making sure that one of their sentence halves matches one on either side of Player A's domino. The sentences must make sense as well as being grammatically correct. 3) If a player can't put down one of their dominoes, they take a domino from the top of the pile and put it down if they can. 4) The winner is the first player to get rid of all their dominoes.
- When they have finished the game, students can shuffle the dominoes and play again if they like.

8 **Vocabulary** Holiday emails

Page 175
Activity
Pairwork: writing.

Focus
Describing places, travel and geographical location.

Preparation
Make one copy of the worksheet for each pair of students.

Procedure
- Divide the students into pairs.
- Hand out the worksheets – one per pair of students – with a good holiday email and a bad holiday email to fill in.
- Ask the students to complete the two emails describing a good holiday and a bad holiday. Tell them that they can use one or more words to fill each space.
- When the students have finished their emails they read each other's to decide who had the best holiday and who had the worst holiday.

Variation
You can put the emails up around the classroom and have a class vote on the best and worst holiday.

Notes
There is enormous variation in how the email can be completed. Students may need help using the adverbs correctly (*absolutely, quite*, etc.) as well as with vocabulary. Note *look forward to -ing.*

8 **Communication** Globetrotters

Page 176
Activity
Groupwork: discussion.

Focus
The present perfect.

Preparation
Make one photocopy of the worksheet for each student in the class.

Procedure
- Divide the class into groups.
- Tell the students that they have to award the 'Globetrotter Extraordinaire' trophy. Give each student a copy of the worksheet.
- Allow a couple of minutes for silent reading. Circulate, checking that students have understood.

- Ask the students to discuss the questions and complete each line with the name of one student in the group.
- After the discussion the students decide who to award the trophy to.
- Let the spokesman/woman for each group announce the winners.

Follow up
Ask the students to write a prize-giving speech for the award ceremony.

9 **Grammar** Reported interviews

Page 177
Activity
Group or pairwork: speaking and writing.

Focus
Making statements using reported speech.

Preparation
Make one copy of the worksheet, cut in half as indicated, for each pair of students in the class.

Procedure
- Explain to your students that they have spent the day as journalists and they have interviewed some people. Tell them they are going to read the interviews (just to check the facts once more).
- Divide the class into Group A and Group B. Explain that you are going to give each group the same half of the worksheet. Give Worksheet A to each student in Group A and Worksheet B to each student in Group B.
- After your students have read the interviews, ask them to work together, in pairs or small groups with the same worksheet (i.e. A+A), to identify whether the statements 1–6 are true or false. They then have to write a sentence using reported speech which supports their answers (see possible answers below). Point out the examples to the students to get them into the habit of 'back-shifting' the tenses when using reported statements.
- After students have finished writing their statements, ask them to find a new partner from the other group (i.e. A+B), and sit down together. Explain that they are going to play a memory game. Ask all Student Bs to put their worksheet face down. Ask all Student As to read out statements 1–6. Student B has to say if the statement is true or false. A correct answer is worth one point. Then Student B has to make a reported statement which supports their answer (see below). A correct statement is worth two points. So, all together, each statement is worth a total of three points and Student B can score a total of 18 points. For example:
  A: Ella isn't rich.
  B: True. (1 point)
  She said she didn't have much money. (2 points)

- When Student A has read out all of their statements, and Student B has answered them, ask students to repeat the process, but this time Student B reads out their sentences while Student A puts the worksheet face down and answers in the same way, scoring a maximum of 18 points.
- When students have finished, find out who scored the most in the class.

> *Possible answers:*
>
> **Student A**
> 1 ✓ She said that she didn't have much money.
> 2 ✗ She told me that she was going to Milan.
> 3 ✗ He told me that he was from Seville.
> 4 ✗ He said that he had been to the USA ten times.
> 5 ✗ They told me that they were from Kyoto.
> 6 ✓ They said that they had just returned from their honeymoon.
>
> **Student B**
> 1 ✓ She said that she was living in London.
> 2 ✗ She told me that she had just finished.
> 3 ✗ He told me that he had two children.
> 4 ✓ He said that one day he would be the head of his company.
> 5 ✓ They told me that they don't have much free time.
> 6 ✗ They said that they would definitely go back again.

9 Vocabulary Blockbuster

Page 178

Activity

Groupwork: writing, speaking.

Focus

Writing the outline of a narrative.

Preparation

Make one copy of the worksheet for each group of three or four students.

Take a short clip from a well-known film. (Optional)

Procedure

- If you have the equipment, play the first three minutes of a well-known film for the students. Otherwise, write the title of a film on the board (e.g. *Star Wars*). Ask them what type of film it is (e.g. *science fiction*).
- Brainstorm different categories/genres of film and write them on the board, e.g. *romance, adventure, drama, comedy, musical, western, thriller, horror, action, science fiction, animation, documentary*. Elicit films the students have seen in each of the categories.
- Divide the students into groups of three or four.

- Tell them they are going to write an outline for a film. The group with the best outline will get (a notional) $100 million to make their movie.
- Give each group a copy of the worksheet. Ask them to choose at least three items from each column.
- The groups build up the details of a plot, using their chosen location, characters, props and events. Set a time limit. Circulate and help them with vocabulary and ideas as necessary. Each group also thinks of three possible titles for their movie and chooses the actors and actresses to appear in their film.
- Each group, in turn, presents its outline to the rest of the class. The class then decides which of the three titles is the best for the movie that has been described.
- After the presentations, the class votes for the best idea (they can't vote for their own) and a winner is declared.

Follow up

Students write a scene from their film with dialogue. They then rehearse and act out the scene (this could be filmed if your school has a video camera).

Notes

As an alternative for larger classes: each group invents one title for their movie and gives it to the teacher, who writes up all the titles on the board. The class listens to the presentations and guesses which title was written for each film outline.

9 Communication Film, books and music

Page 179

Activity

Group or pairwork: communicative crossword.

Focus

Vocabulary associated with films, books and music.

Preparation

Make one copy of the worksheet, cut in half as indicated, for each pair of students in the class.

Procedure

- Write on the board: *It's a type of film that frightens people. It sometimes features evil people or scary creatures.* Ask students to guess the word (*Horror*). Tell students they are going to write some similar sentences as clues for a crossword.
- Divide the class into Team A and Team B. Explain that you are going to give each group the same crossword but that Team A will have the DOWN words already written in and Team B will have the ACROSS words already written in. They have to write the clues for the words written on their crosswords.

- Give a copy of Crossword A to each student in Team A and a copy of Crossword B to each student in Team B. Ask the students to work together with people in their group to write a clue for each word. Make sure that students write clues related to film, books and music (as some words can have other meanings, e.g. *track* can also mean a small path, or a line on which a train runs).

- When they have finished writing their clues, students should work with a partner from the other group. They must not show each other their crossword. Ask them to sit facing each other and take it in turns to ask their partner for clues for the missing words on their crossword. At the end they can look to check their answers. (Instead of pairwork this activity could be done in open class with both teams facing each other.)

Review C Somewhere Only We Know

Page 180

Activity

Pairwork: song.

Focus

Revision of grammar and vocabulary from *New Inside Out* Intermediate Student's Book, Units 7–9.

Preparation

Make one copy of the worksheet for each student in the class. Get the recording ready.

Procedure

- 1: Play the recording and then ask students to look at exercise 1 and discuss in pairs or small groups which they think is the most accurate summary. Make sure they can back up their ideas with references to lines in the song. Students then report back to the class.

- 2: Students find the words and phrases in the song. Your students may need help in finding the exact phrase – for example e) is *dream of*, not just *dream*.

- 3: Give students enough time to think of a response to each of the items and then decide what they are going to say. Once they have had enough time to prepare, they can talk about each item in pairs.

1

The song apparently refers to a small area of woodland (called Manser's Shaw) near where the members of the band grew up. As children they used to play in this place – it was somewhere only they knew. As adults, their life becames more complicated and they think back to simpler (happier?) days. Summary *c* may therefore be the best option.

2
a) to know it like the back of your hand
b) beneath
c) rely on
d) used to love
e) dream of
f) have a minute
g) talk about

3
Students' own answers.

---

10 Grammar When I was at school ...

Page 181

Activity

Pairwork: speaking.

Focus

Defining relative clauses.

Preparation

Make one copy of the worksheet for each pair of students in the class. Each pair will need a coin.

Procedure

- Introduce the topic of schooldays. Talk about your own. Pre-teach/check: *bully, teacher's pet, trouble-maker, subject*.

- Divide the students into pairs.

- Tell the students they will need a coin to play this game.

  1 They toss the coin. If it is heads, they advance one square, if it is tails they advance two.

  2 Student A tosses a coin and completes the statement on that square. Then it's Student B's turn. If they can't complete the sentence, they miss the next turn.

  3 The activity is finished when one student reaches the *Finish* square and completes the last sentence.

Follow up

Run a class debate about school.

Possible topics are:

- What makes a good school?

- What makes a good teacher?

- Schooldays are the best years in everyone's life.

- Friends are more important when you are a child.

Notes

Not all statements include a relative clause.

10 Vocabulary *Make* and *let*

Page 182
Activity
Groupwork: speaking and writing.

Focus
Using the verbs *make* and *let*.

Preparation
Make one copy of the worksheet for each student and an extra set for the final decision (see Procedure).

Procedure
- Give one copy of the worksheet to each student in the class. Divide the class into groups of three or four.
- Ask students to work together and write two pieces of advice/recommendations in each of the six sections. Students must discuss which two they think are best before they write anything, and they all need to write the same thing once they have agreed.
- When all the students have finished writing their advice/recommendations, make new groups by taking one member from each of the other groups and putting them together. Ask the new groups to compare their ideas for each of the six sections and agree on the best two for each section. Give the group one more copy and ask one student to be the secretary. He/She is responsible for writing the two best ideas for each section, once agreed, onto the new worksheet.
- Once finished, ask each group to display their worksheet on the wall and if there is time, ask them to justify their decisions.

10 Communication Definition auction

Page 183
Activity
Team auction game.

Focus
Defining relative clauses.

Preparation
Make one copy of the worksheet for each student.

Procedure
- Give one copy of the worksheet to each student in the class. Divide the class into teams. Explain that they are going to play a game in the style of an auction. Tell them that the definitions on their worksheet are up for sale at a public auction. Some are correct definitions and others are untrue.

- Each team must try and buy the definitions they think are correct by 'bidding' (offering) more money than the other teams. Each team has a total of £10,000 to spend at the auction. The teacher takes the role of the auctioneer, reads out a word and opens the bidding. Check the pronunciation below for each of the words.
- caretaker /ˈkeəteɪkə(r)/; gargoyle /ˈgɑːɡɔɪl/; pew /pjuː/; dumbwaiter /ˈdʌmweɪtə(r)/; glue /gluː/; rib /rɪb/; knuckle /ˈnʌkl/; miser /ˈmaɪzə(r)/; winkle-picker /ˈwɪŋklpɪkə(r)/; quiff /kwɪf/
- The winner of the game is the team that buys the highest number of correct definitions.

Correct definitions
*A **caretaker** is someone whose job is to look after a large building, like a school.*

*A **gargoyle** is a stone statue of an ugly creature used mainly in old churches for directing water away from the roof.*

*A **dumbwaiter** is a small lift used for moving food between floors in a restaurant.*

*A **rib** is a long, curved bone in the chest.*

*A **quiff** is the font part of (usually) a man's hair which is shaped so that it is higher than the rest.*

11 Grammar If ...

Page 184
Activity
Whole class: reading and writing.

Focus
Conditionals.

Preparation
Make one copy of the worksheet and cut it up as indicated.

Procedure
- Ask the students to get out a pen and a piece of paper.
- Give each student one of the photocopied strips. Tell them to complete the sentence with anything they like as long as it makes sense and it is grammatically correct, and to write the whole sentence at the top of their piece of paper. For example, *If I were a bird, I wouldn't go to school.*
- Ask the students to pass the sentences they have written to the next person on the left.
- Explain what the students have to do.
  1 First they should change the *main clause* of the sentence they have received to an *if clause*. For example, *... I wouldn't go to school* changes to *If I didn't go to school.*
  2 Then they should complete the new *if clause* with a new *main clause*. For example, *If I didn't go to school, I'd miss all my friends.*

3 Then they pass the sentences on again and repeat the procedure. For example, *If I missed all my friends, I'd be unhappy.*

- Repeat the procedure until the sentences have gone full circle.
- Ask the students to read out their 'chains'. The class can vote for their favourite.

11 Vocabulary Then and now

Page 185
Activity
Pairwork: writing and speaking.

Focus
Comparing past and present.

Preparation
Make one copy for every two students in the class and cut the copies up as indicated.

Procedure
- Divide the class into Student As and Student Bs and give them the relevant worksheet.
- Allow a few minutes for them to complete the 'You' column.
- Put the students into pairs with one Student A and one Student B in each pair.
- Ask students to compare their answers with their partner and discuss how they have changed. Encourage students to think about the reasons why they have changed so much (or so little).
- Circulate and monitor.
- Ask students to compare their answers with another pair.

Follow up
Hold a discussion about the reasons why people change as they get older. Write a list on the board.

11 Communication Unreal!

Page 186
Activity
Team game: speaking and reading.

Focus
Unreal conditional sentences.

Preparation
Make one copy of the worksheet for each group of students. Each group will need dice and counters.

Procedure
- Divide the class into small groups. Give one copy of the worksheet to each group. Explain that they are going to play a game in which they have to make unreal conditional sentences.
- Each student places their counter on the START square. They then take it in turns to throw the dice. The first student to throw a six starts the game. He/she throws the dice again and moves his/her counter along the board according to the number on the dice.
- Players then play in turns, moving clockwise around the board. If a player lands on a CUE square they have to use the words on it to make a conditional sentence.
- For example:

 or

- If a player lands on a TRUE square, they have to use the words on it as the beginning of a sentence that is true for them. If a player lands on a FREE SQUARE they don't have to do anything. The first student to reach the FINISH square is the winner.

12 Grammar Ever had it done?

Page 187

Activity

Whole class: speaking.

Focus

Have something done.

Preparation

Make one copy of the worksheet for each student in the class.

Procedure

- Give a copy of the worksheet to each student.
- Explain that the students have to walk around the classroom, asking each other questions in order to complete the sentences with the names of their classmates. Encourage students to find a different person for each sentence.
- Before doing the activity, elicit the questions for the first few items, e.g. *Are you going to have your hair cut in the next few days? Have you had your photo taken in the last week?*
- Circulate and monitor, helping as necessary.
- When they have finished, the students report to the class what they found out about each other.

12 Vocabulary First impressions

Page 188

Activity

Individual and groupwork: writing and speaking.

Focus

Clothes and personal appearance, giving advice, negotiating, expressing opinions.

Preparation

Make one copy of the worksheet for each student.

Procedure

- Tell the students that a female friend of theirs has asked for some advice for a first job interview.
- Give each student a copy of the worksheet.
- Ask students to read the instructions and write down their own ideas.
- Circulate, helping with any grammar and vocabulary problems.
- Divide the students into groups of three or four.
- Ask the groups to agree on the top eight dos and don'ts.
- When most of the groups have finished, ask a few of them to report back to the class.

Follow up

As a whole class activity, build a common list on the board with the most popular tips suggested by all the groups.

Groups can also work on tips they would give to a male friend.

12 Communication Phonetics guessing

Page 189

Activity

Groupwork: vocabulary and pronunciation.

Focus

Recognition of sounds and phonetic symbols.

Preparation

Make one copy of the worksheet for each group.

Procedure

- Divide the students into groups of four to six.
- Give one copy of the worksheet to each group. Tell students they will also need dice or a coin. Distribute counters if available.
- Explain that each box has the definition of a word that they must guess. This word contains the sound that appears in brackets.
- The first player flips a coin. If it is heads, the player moves one square, if it is tails, they move two squares.
  If players guess a word correctly, they stay on that square. If they are wrong, they go back to the previous square.
  When a player lands on a square which has previously been guessed, they must think of another word with the same sound.
- Circulate, checking that students have given a correct answer.

1	/iː/	TEAM
2	/æ/	CAPITAL
3	/ɔː/	WALL
4	/iː/	PLEASED
5	/ɑː/	FATHER/AUNT
6	/ɔː/	(SURF)BOARD
7	/e/	MESSAGE
8	/ɑː/	PARTNER
9	/uː/	SCHOOL
10	/ɪ/	BUSY
11	/ʌ/	MONTH
12	/uː/	TRUE
13	/ɪ/	LIFT
14	/ʌ/	COME
15	/uː/	HOOLIGANS
16	/e/	FRIEND

17	/ʌ/	UNCLE
18	/ʊ/	WOULD
19	/e/	HEAVY
20	/ʌ/	JUMP
21	/ʊ/	CHILDHOOD
22	/e/	SWEPT
23	/ɒ/	COFFEE
24	/ɜ:/	WORDS
25	/e/	HEADLINES
26	/ɒ/	JOB
27	/i:/	NIECE
28	/æ/	MARRY
29	/ɔ:/	AUXILIARY
30	/ɜ:/	CHURCH

2
seek – look for
loud – very brightly coloured
square – boring
dedicated – spending a lot of time and effort on something
boutiques – fashion shops
eagerly – enthusiastically
fads – things that are fashionable for a short time
flattery – (insincere) praise
flits – moves quickly from one place to another
fickle – always changing your mind about what you like

Follow up

Students write the words they have guessed and group them according to the vowel sounds they have in common.

Review D Dedicated Follower of Fashion

Page 190

Activity

Pairwork: song.

Focus

Revision of grammar and vocabulary from *New Inside Out* Intermediate Student's Book, Units 10–12.

Preparation

Make one copy of the worksheet for each student in the class. Get the recording ready.

Procedure

- Play the recording while students listen and decide which activity *isn't* referred to in the song.
- Ask students to work in pairs. Allow them time to find the emboldened words in the song and match them to their synonyms/definitions in the box. (Students can use their dictionaries if they need to.) Play the song once again for pleasure, if your students want to hear it.

1
The song doesn't refer to *catching butterflies*.

---

1 Grammar

Reasons to be famous

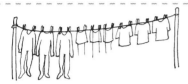

You are the mother/father of 12 children and next month you are expecting triplets.

You have just discovered you can read people's minds.

You are the invisible man/woman.

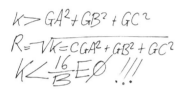

You were born in 2400 and are the inventor of time travel.

You saved the world from a computer-generated disaster.

You have just published your first novel and it is already a best-seller.

You have just flown around the world in a hot-air balloon.

You have just discovered a cure for the common cold.

You are the first person who has been on holiday to the moon.

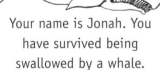

Your name is Jonah. You have survived being swallowed by a whale.

You have just woken up after 20 years in a coma.

You won a record-breaking £25m on the lottery exactly a year ago today and you are giving your first interview to the press.

It is your 150th birthday. You are officially the oldest person on Earth.

You are the first extraterrestrial being to announce your arrival on Earth.

You have just got engaged to

_____

You are _____

_____

_____

_____

You are _____

_____

_____

_____

You are _____

_____

_____

_____

1 Vocabulary

You in pictures

Look at the pictures below. Choose the five that best represent you.

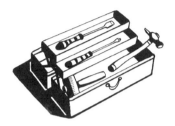   

The pictures that best represent me are ...

... the _____ because _____ .

... the _____ because _____ .

... the _____ because _____ .

... the _____ because _____ .

... the _____ because _____ .

The pictures that best represent the class are _____

because _____ .

 PHOTOCOPIABLE *New Inside Out* Intermediate Teacher's Book © Macmillan Publishers Limited 2009

1 Communication

Questions, questions, questions

Find twelve questions and then write them next to their answers.

wheraedobwhochoseyournamewherdidyeusedopleaswasawhatwereyoudoingatmidnightl
astnightibegetwasiflwhatkindofmusicdoyoulikewerdothowareyoufeelingrightnowhertow
ivuareyouanygoodatcookingdoesahxilwhichcountrywouldyoumostliketovisitdifrilpa
reyoureadingabookatthemomentewhywhereacroapwhoisyourfavouritesingerbitudoyoou
didwathhowmanycountrieshaveyoubeentowhoiservizatdoyuolivatwhatisyourfavourit
ecolourhwomucthdoitsyhaveyoueverbeentotheukenwharhowoftendoyouspeakenglish

Questions	Answers	Your partner's answers
_____ ?	Probably Mongolia.	_____ .
_____ ?	Every day, usually.	_____ .
_____ ?	Frank Sinatra.	_____ .
_____ ?	No, not at the moment.	_____ .
_____ ?	Reggae mainly.	_____ .
_____ ?	Fifteen or so.	_____ .
_____ ?	Yes, once.	_____ .
_____ ?	Well, I can make an omelette.	_____ .
_____ ?	A little tired, actually.	_____ .
_____ ?	My mother, I think.	_____ .
_____ ?	Getting ready for bed.	_____ .
_____ ?	Purple.	_____ .

Moments in American history

A

	October 29, 1929 … the stock market crashed	December 8, 1941 … the USA entered the Second World War	November 22, 1963 … Kennedy was assassinated	July 20, 1969 … the first man landed on the moon
Mr Walton	tour/France		relax	
Mrs Walton		iron		have
Junior Walton	rob		visit	
Grandpa Walton		drink		
You				

✂ -

B

	October 29, 1929 … the stock market crashed	December 8, 1941 … the USA entered the Second World War	November 22, 1963 … Kennedy was assassinated	July 20, 1969 … the first man landed on the moon
Mr Walton		dance/nightclub		lie
Mrs Walton	wash		cook	
Junior Walton		attend		live
Grandpa Walton	drink		drink	
You				

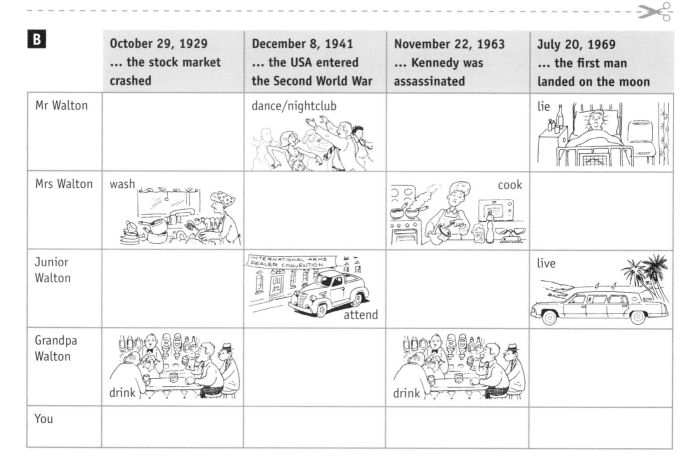

2 Vocabulary

Guess the sport

SQUASH

Individual sport; two players.
Equipment: small rubber ball
and racket.
Place: indoor court.
Objective: to hit the ball so that
the opponent misses it.
Very fast game. Requires a lot of stamina.
You don't usually play for a long time.

SKIING

Individual sport.
Equipment: boots, skis and poles.
Place: outside. Snowy countryside,
hills or mountains.
Objective: to move down hills or
across the countryside in the snow.
In competition, skiers usually race
against the clock. It's a winter sport.

TABLE TENNIS

Individual or doubles sport.
Equipment: bat and small ball.
Place: table with a low net,
usually indoors.
Objective: to hit the ball back
and forth over the net.
Also called ping-pong. The first
player to reach 21 wins.

(FIELD) HOCKEY

Team sport. 11 players in each team.
Equipment: a stick and a ball.
Place: outdoor grass pitch.
Objective: to score goals by hitting
the ball with a stick into a net.
Similar sports are played on ice or
on roller-skates.

WATER POLO

Team sport. Two teams of seven.
Equipment: ball, goalpost.
Place: swimming-pool.
Objective: to score goals by
throwing the ball between goalposts.
You need to be a fast swimmer.
It is played in 15-minute halves.

BOXING

Individual sport. A fight between
two people.
Equipment: big leather gloves.
Place: square ring.
Objective: to knock out or fight better
than the opponent.
A fight is divided into 15 three-
minute rounds.

VOLLEYBALL

Team sport. 6 players in each team.
Equipment: a large leather ball
and a high net.
Place: indoor or outdoor court.
Objective: to hit the ball back and
forth over the net with your hands,
without letting it touch the ground on your
team's side. The first team to reach 15 points wins.

SWIMMING

Individual sport or relay teams of 4.
Equipment: (optional) swimming
cap and goggles.
Place: indoor or open air swimming-
pools, rivers, lakes and the sea.
Objective: to move yourself through
water as quickly as possible.
Strokes: crawl, breaststroke, backstroke and butterfly.

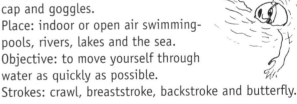

ICE-SKATING

Individual or couples.
Equipment: ice-skates.
Place: ice rink.
Objective: to move across ice on
special boots with thin metal blades.
Speed skating, figure skating and
ice dancing are the main branches
of the sport.

RUGBY

Team sport. 15 players in each team.
Equipment: oval ball.
Place: outdoor grass pitch.
Objective: to kick the ball between
the two upright posts and over the
crossbar or touch the ball down over
the line. Matches are divided into
two 40-minute halves.

2 Communication

Truth or dare?

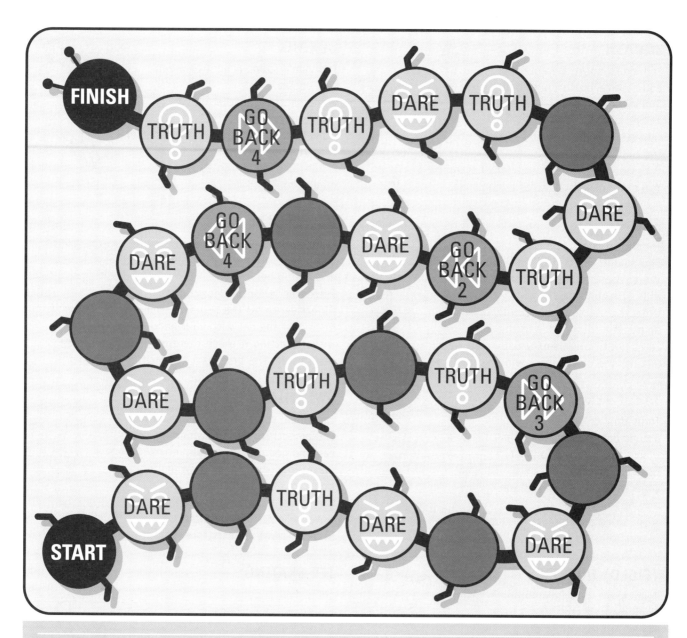

RULES OF THE GAME

How to play

1 Each team throws the dice. The team with the highest score starts.

2 Teams take turns to throw the dice and move their counters round the board according to the number they throw.

3 When a team lands on a TRUTH or a DARE square, they nominate a team member, the 'victim', to answer a question, truthfully, or do a dare from the other team.

4 Teams must nominate a new victim each time until all team members have had a turn.

5 Teams cannot use the same TRUTH or DARE twice, unless they have used all their TRUTHS and DARES.

6 After hearing the TRUTH or the DARE, the victim can say 'change' and take a DARE instead of a TRUTH, or vice versa. After saying 'change', the victim cannot go

back to the original TRUTH or DARE.

7 If the victim will not answer a TRUTH or do a DARE, the team loses its turn and moves its counter back to the square it was on at the beginning of the turn.

8 The winner of the game is the team that reaches the finish first.

3 Grammar

Find the correct sentence

Read the pairs of sentences. In each pair, one sentence is wrong.
Tick (✓) the correct sentence.

1 a) I've been knowing Lindy for twenty years.

    b) I've known Lindy for twenty years.

2 a) He's been trying to mend his car all afternoon.

    b) He's trying to mend his car all afternoon.

3 a) He's living in Rome for the past five years.

    b) He's been living in Rome for the past five years.

4 a) I've done my homework for four hours and I haven't finished yet.

    b) I've been doing my homework for four hours and I haven't finished yet.

5 a) I've written five emails and I'm just about to start the sixth!

    b) I've been writing five emails and I'm just about to start the sixth!

6 a) Before I came here, I've been working in an office.

    b) Before I came here, I worked in an office.

7 a) You look tired – what have you been doing?

    b) You look tired – what have you done?

8 a) I'm afraid there aren't any biscuits left – I've been eating them all!

    b) I'm afraid there aren't any biscuits left – I've eaten them all!

9 a) I've always wanted to visit China.

    b) I've always been wanting to visit China.

3 Vocabulary

Love is ...?

	You	Your partner

1 A candlelit dinner for two at home with romantic music and a log fire.

2 Champagne with strawberries and cream on a summer picnic in the countryside.

3 A kiss and a cuddle in front of the TV on a Friday night.

4 Crying over the same film.

5 A stranger stopping you in the street with a bouquet of flowers.

6 A couple of 86 and 87 celebrating their diamond wedding anniversary.

7 A surprise weekend for two in a 4-star hotel in Paris/Venice/Prague.

8 A card and chocolates on Valentine's Day.

9 A moonlit swim.

10 Saying 'I love you' regularly.

11 Being ill together.

12 Sharing a love of the same things.

I think _____ is	really extremely very quite fairly	romantic
because _____ .		

I don't | really | think _____ is	particularly at all	romantic
because _____ .		

 PHOTOCOPIABLE *New Inside Out* Intermediate Teacher's Book © Macmillan Publishers Limited 2009

3 Communication

Parents' day

Karen	Roger	Jeremy	Dorothy	Glen

Philip	David	Jane	Matthew	Helen

Useful words and phrases:

can be ... tends to be ... isn't exactly ... isn't particularly ...	hard-working confident fit talkative selfish	kind terrible naughty creative late	clever nice lovely overconfident lazy
absolutely really very quite a bit not very not at all	strong average ambitious self-centred	weak aggressive slow big-headed	competitive absent-minded stupid over-sensitive
	interested in _____ ing good/excellent at _____ ing bad/awful at _____ ing		

Review A

You've Got a Friend

Carole King wrote and recorded *You've Got a Friend* in 1971. Since then it's been covered by James Taylor (1971), The Brand New Heavies (1997) and McFly (2005).

1 Match the underlined sound to a phonetic symbol in the box.

/ɑː/	/iː/	/uː/	/ɜː/	/ɔː/	/æ/	/e/	/ɪ/	/ə/	/ʌ/	/ʊ/	/ɒ/

a) c<u>a</u>ll /ɔː/	b) c<u>o</u>me	c) d<u>a</u>rkest	d) fr<u>ie</u>nd	e) g<u>oo</u>d	f) g<u>o</u>t
g) h<u>u</u>rt	h) n<u>ee</u>d	i) s<u>oo</u>n	j) wint<u>er</u>	k) th<u>a</u>nk	l) th<u>i</u>nk

2 🔊 **1.29 Listen to the song and tick the words from Exercise 1 as you hear them. Which word isn't in the song?**

When you're down and troubled
And you need some loving care,
And nothing, nothing is going right.
Close your eyes and think of me,
And soon I will be there,
To brighten up even your darkest night.

You just call out my name,
And you know wherever I am,
I'll come running,
To see you again.
Winter, spring, summer or fall,
All you have to do is call,
And I'll be there.
You've got a friend.

If the sky above you
Grows dark and full of clouds
And that old north wind begins to blow,
Keep your head together
And call my name out loud.
Soon you'll hear me knocking at your door.

You just call out my name, …

Ain't it good to know that you've got a friend,
When people can be so cold?
They'll hurt you and desert you.
And take your soul if you let them.
Oh, but don't you let them.

You just call out my name, …

3 Work with a partner. Find the words in the song with the following meanings.

a) upset *(down and) troubled*	d) autumn	f) abandon
b) shut	e) unfriendly	g) spirit
c) make lighter		

4 Work with your partner. Tell each other about a friend who is always there for you.

	morning	afternoon	evening
MONDAY			
TUESDAY			
WEDNESDAY			
THURSDAY			
FRIDAY			
SATURDAY			
SUNDAY			

4 Vocabulary

Make & do

a decision	a mistake	the bed	a mess
a phone call	dinner	a noise	an effort
friends	an appointment	a coffee	a sandwich
some work	the cleaning	the driving	some damage
nothing	the ironing	the shopping	the cooking
your homework	yoga	the washing	the washing up

 PHOTOCOPIABLE *New Inside Out* Intermediate Teacher's Book © Macmillan Publishers Limited 2009

4 Communication

Party animal or party pooper?

Work with a partner. Take it in turns to interview each other and write down each other's answers.

1 You've been invited to a party but you're working the next morning. Do you
   a) think 'you only live once' and go and have a good time?
   b) go to the party but leave at ten o'clock?
   c) send your apologies and get an early night?

2 It's your birthday. Do you
   a) have a big party and invite everybody you know?
   b) hope that nobody has remembered – you don't want to get older anyway?
   c) have a quiet family get-together, blow your candles out and go to bed early?

3 You've been invited to a party by somebody you don't know very well. Do you
   a) go to the party and hope you'll meet lots of new people?
   b) go to the party but take a friend with you to make sure you'll have someone to talk to?
   c) refuse the invitation – it's too scary?

4 You arrive at a party and realise that the only person you know is the host. Do you
   a) go and introduce yourself to anybody who looks interesting?
   b) end up talking to the most boring person there because nobody else wants to talk to them?
   c) panic and hide in the bathroom?

5 Your favourite song comes on, but nobody else is dancing. Do you
   a) start dancing on your own and enjoy the music?
   b) wait until a few other people are dancing and then join them?
   c) stay where you are – you prefer to dance to your favourite song in the privacy of your own home?

6 Somebody suggests playing party games. Do you
   a) suggest your favourite game and organise it?
   b) feel embarrassed, but join in anyway?
   c) suddenly remember you had to be somewhere else?

SCORE
Give yourself 1 point for every a) answer, 2 points for every b) answer and 3 points for every c) answer.

WHAT IT MEANS

If you scored between 6 and 10:
You are definitely the life and soul of any party.

If you scored between 11 and 14:
You could afford to let your hair down occasionally.

If you scored between 15 and 18: You obviously like the quiet life – but you don't have to take everything so seriously!

5 Grammar

Just a minute!

	only one	a couple of	lots of	several	a little	a few
1						
2						
3						
4						
5						
6						
7						
8						
9						
10						

PHOTOCOPIABLE
New Inside Out Intermediate Teacher's Book © Macmillan Publishers Limited 2009

5 Vocabulary

Best of the bunch

a box of	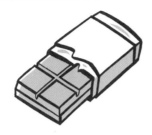	a packet of	a bar of
	a bunch of		a jar of
		a packet of	
a bar of		a box of	a bunch of
	a jar of		
a bunch of			a box of

New Inside Out Intermediate Teacher's Book © Macmillan Publishers Limited 2009   PHOTOCOPIABLE   165

5 Communication

Did you use to ...?

How many people used to smoke?

 Find out

How many people used to have different coloured hair?

 Find out

How many people used to play a musical instrument?

 Find out

How many people used to enjoy school?

 Find out

How many people used to live in a different city?

 Find out

How many people used to do a lot of sports?

 Find out

How many people used to go on holiday with their parents?

 Find out

How many people used to be frightened of the dark?

 Find out

How many people used to own a dog?

 Find out

How many people used to have long hair?

 Find out

How many people used to suck their thumb?

 Find out

How many people used to believe in Santa Claus?

 Find out

PHOTOCOPIABLE
New Inside Out Intermediate Teacher's Book © Macmillan Publishers Limited 2009

6 Grammar

Rules and regulations

Write a set of rules and regulations for one of these places.
There are some *taboo* words that you are <u>not allowed to use</u>.

● LIBRARY

Don't use these
- borrow
- books
- smoke
- eat
- magazines

● ZOO

Don't use these
- animals
- food
- cage
- security area
- grass

● CINEMA

Don't use these
- sit
- popcorn
- film
- refreshments
- talk

● PUB

Don't use these
- drink
- pay
- dance
- consumption
- tables

● AMUSEMENT PARK

Don't use these
- ride
- attraction
- ticket
- queue
- grass

● FOOTBALL STADIUM

Don't use these
- referee
- football players
- pitch
- shout
- cheer

● HOSPITAL

Don't use these
- smoke
- patients
- disturb
- corridor
- quiet

● AIRPORT

Don't use these
- trolley
- baggage
- check-in
- gifts
- boarding pass

---

6 Vocabulary

How well organised are you?

A

Here are some questions about how well you organise your time. Answer them yourself, then ask your partner, making a note of both answers.

	YOU	YOUR PARTNER
1 How do you normally keep your desk? **a)** Perfectly tidy. **b)** Once a week I have to tidy it up before things get too untidy. **c)** It's a mess.	☐	☐
2 How punctual are you for your appointments, classes, work, etc.? **a)** Very early. **b)** Late. **c)** On time.	☐	☐
3 When it comes to organisation, what reputation do you have among your friends and family? They think I'm … **a)** a well-organised person. **b)** a bit of a disaster.	☐	☐
4 Do you have a diary where you write what you have to do during the day/week/month? **a)** No. **b)** Yes, I use it all the time. **c)** Yes, but I hardly use it.	☐	☐
5 Do you find time to relax every day? **a)** Not really, I always seem to have things to do. **b)** Yes, I usually keep some time free during the day to relax.	☐	☐
6 When you have a piece of work to do for your work or studies, how do you organise yourself? **a)** I work to the last minute to finish it. **b)** I start the day before the deadline. **c)** I finish a week in advance.	☐	☐
7 For your friends' and family's birthdays and anniversaries, do you get round to writing or phoning in good time? **a)** Yes, I normally do. **b)** No, I'm usually too late.	☐	☐

- ✂ - - -

B

Here are some questions about how well you organise your time. Answer them yourself, then ask your partner, making a note of both answers.

	YOU	YOUR PARTNER
1 Do you find that you frequently run out of essentials, like sugar or toilet paper? **a)** Yes, I only remember to buy a new supply when I've run out. **b)** No, I usually buy a new supply before I run out.	☐	☐
2 Do you normally write a list of 'things to do'? **a)** No, I hate planning. **b)** Yes, and I try to stick to it. **c)** Yes, but I never manage to do all the things on the list.	☐	☐
3 When you have to do something or go somewhere, do you often … **a)** get up early? **b)** get up on time but end up rushing? **c)** get up late?	☐	☐
4 When you get home from a trip, what do you do with your luggage? **a)** I don't unpack for days. **b)** I start unpacking almost immediately but leave things in the way. **c)** A couple of hours after getting home everything is back in its place.	☐	☐
5 Have you ever missed a train/plane/coach because you didn't give yourself enough time? **a)** Yes. **b)** No, I always allow plenty of time.	☐	☐
6 Do you often leave the dishes unwashed or the bed unmade for more than one day? **a)** Very often. **b)** Almost never.	☐	☐
7 How do you normally keep your wardrobe? **a)** Always perfectly tidy. **b)** Once a week I have to tidy it before clothes start piling up. **c)** It's a mess.	☐	☐

6 Communication

Detectives

Tony was found dead today at home. He had been shot with his own gun. The police have the following information about Tony.

Tony

- [ ] He hired a private detective a month ago.
- [ ] The business he owns with Peter has been in trouble for over a year.
- [ ] His marriage was not a happy one.

Tony was found dead today at home. He had been shot with his own gun. The police have the following information about Steve.

Steve

- [ ] He's always arguing with Peter at work and last week they had a fight.
- [ ] He owes three months' rent on the flat.
- [ ] He has a criminal conviction for theft.

Tony was found dead today at home. He had been shot with his own gun. The police have the following information about Jeanette.

Jeanette

- [ ] She plays tennis regularly with Peter.
- [ ] She has a plane ticket for Bangkok for the day after tomorrow.
- [ ] She wasn't happy in her marriage.
- [ ] She went to her bank the day before yesterday and took out all the money from the joint account she held with Tony: about £2,000,000.

Tony was found dead today at home. He had been shot with his own gun. The police have the following information about Peter.

Peter

- [ ] He has plane tickets for Rio tomorrow and Bangkok the day after – both from London.
- [ ] He is a regular gambler.
- [ ] He's just sold his flat and is staying in a hotel.
- [ ] He's always arguing with Steve at work and last week they had a fight.
- [ ] He plays tennis regularly with Jeanette.
- [ ] Tony and Peter's business has been in trouble for over a year.

Review B

It's My Party

It's My Party was recorded by American singer Lesley Gore in 1963, when she was just sixteen. Although the song had been recorded before by British pop star Helen Shapiro, the Lesley Gore version remains the best-known.

1 Work with a partner. Look at the picture.
What do you think the song is about?

It's my party and I'll cry if I want to,
Cry if I want to, cry if I want to.
You would cry too if it happened to you.

Nobody knows where my Johnny has gone,
But Judy left the same time.
Why was he holding her hand,
When he's supposed to be mine?

It's my party and I'll cry if I want to, …

Play all my records, keep dancing all night,
But leave me alone for a while,
'Til Johnny's dancing with me,
I've got no reason to smile.

It's my party and I'll cry if I want to, …

Judy and Johnny just walked through the door,
Like a queen with her king.
Oh, what a birthday surprise,
Judy's wearing his ring!
It's my party and I'll cry if I want to, …

2 2.18 Listen to the song and check your answer to Exercise 1.
Identify the following three people in the picture:
a) the hostess; b) Johnny; c) Judy.

3 Are the statements true or false?

a) The hostess of the party is upset.
b) The hostess has found out that her boyfriend has had an accident.
c) The hostess just wants to play music and dance all night.
d) Judy and Johnny have become girlfriend and boyfriend.
e) Johnny used to be the hostess's boyfriend.

4 Work with a partner. Take it in turns to describe the last party you organised.
Answer these questions.

a) What type of party was it? (birthday / graduation / etc.)
b) Where was the party? (at your house / at school / etc.)
c) How many people did you invite and who were they?
d) How did the evening end?

7 Grammar

It's happened to me!

Find someone who ...	Name
has been given an award or prize	
was given a really nice present last Christmas	
has been robbed	
has been told off by his/her parents recently	
was woken up by an alarm this morning	
has been introduced to someone famous	
has been questioned by the police	
has been turned down for a job	
was read bedtime stories when he/she was a child	
lives in a house that was built more than 100 years ago	
was chosen to represent his/her school sports team	
has been shocked by something recently	

7 Vocabulary

A true crime story

Story A

In 1990 Mark Brown went on holiday to Brazil for a month where he spent over £1,000 more than he had planned. He had insured himself before going on holiday and so he decided on the last day to go to the police and say he had been robbed, so that he could claim the money back from the insurance company.

He decided to fake the robbery in the street. He left all his bags in the hotel and went to a rather dangerous part of São Paulo. He picked up a telephone and pretended to speak to someone. Suddenly he screamed, 'Help, someone, my bag has been stolen'. To his surprise several people stopped and one man told him to cross the street to where a policeman was standing.

All the people followed him across the road. He was now very nervous and knew he had to continue with his story. He told the policeman that he had left his bag on the ground while making a phone call and that when he looked down it had disappeared. He then began to describe all the things that were in the bag. He had practised this in the afternoon as he knew that the more

things he said, the more money he would get. He was so nervous that even though the story wasn't true he started to cry. He gave a description of two men he had seen following him and was told to go to the police station later that day to collect a report for his insurance company.

When he got back to England he sent the police report to the insurance company who told him that every item over £50 required a receipt. He then sent the receipts off to the company and waited. After about five weeks he was sent another letter from the insurance company telling him that he hadn't taken enough care of his bag and that they would not pay any money. Mark couldn't really complain, after all the story was all a fabrication. However, two days later he received a telegram from the police in Brazil to tell him that his information and the prompt reporting of the crime had led to the arrest and conviction of two criminals who the police had been pursuing for much more serious crimes and that he was also entitled to a reward of £2,500.

Story B

In 1990 Mark Brown went on holiday to America for a month where he spent over £1,200 more than he had planned. He had insured himself before going on holiday and so he decided on the last day to go to the police and say he had been robbed, so that he could claim the money back from the insurance company.

He decided to fake the robbery in the street. He left all his bags in the hotel and went to a rather dangerous part of New York. He stood in front of a cigarette machine and bought a pack of cigarettes. Suddenly he screamed, 'Help, someone, my bag has been stolen'. To his surprise several people stopped and one man told him to cross the street to where a policeman was standing.

All the people followed him across the road and he was now very nervous but he knew he had to continue with his story. He told the policeman that he had left his bag on the ground while buying a packet of cigarettes and that when he looked down it had disappeared. He then began to describe all the things that were in the bag. He had practised this in the afternoon as he knew that the more things he said, the more money he would

get. He told them he had lost a video camera, jewellery, money and clothes. He wasn't nervous at all. He had always liked acting and totally convinced the police. He gave a description of a man he had seen following him and was told to go to the police station later that day to collect a report for his insurance company.

When he got back to England he sent the police report to the insurance company who told him that every item over £100 required a receipt. He sent the receipts off to the company and waited. After about five weeks he was sent another letter from the insurance company telling him that he hadn't taken enough care of his bag and that they would not pay any money. Mark couldn't really complain, after all the story was all a fabrication. However, two days later he received a telegram from the police in New York telling him that a bag that fitted his description had been found in the house of a recently convicted criminal and that some of the contents had also been found. Two weeks later he received a video camera, clothes and jewellery from the police in New York. None of it was, of course, his.

 PHOTOCOPIABLE *New Inside Out* Intermediate Teacher's Book © Macmillan Publishers Limited 2009

7 Communication

Making news

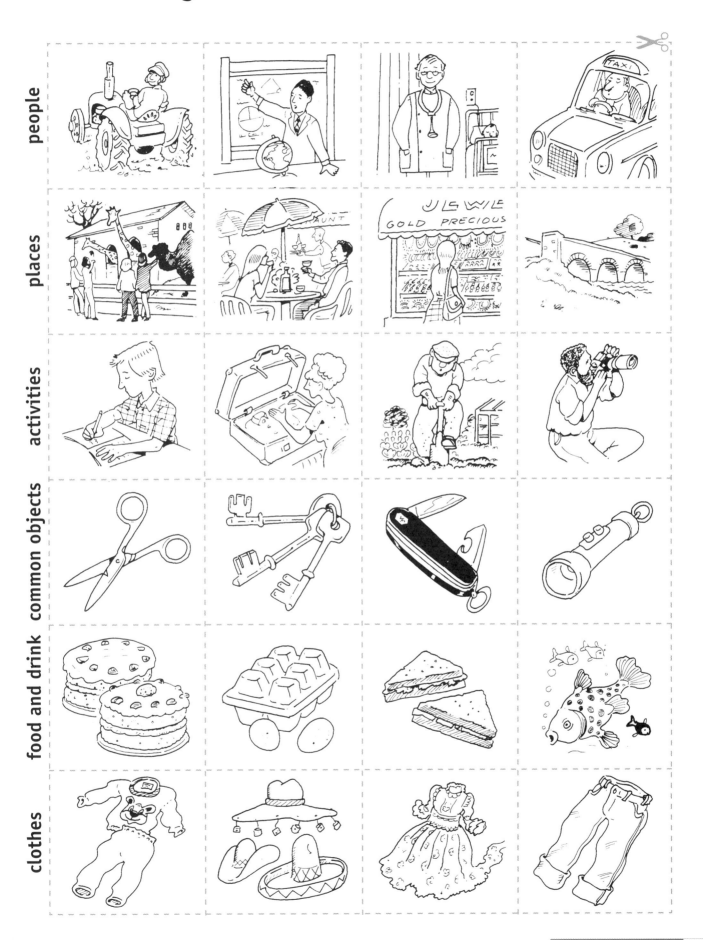

people

places

activities

common objects

food and drink

clothes

8 Grammar

Past perfect dominoes

PHOTOCOPIABLE

she hadn't eaten all day	As soon as the film started,	I realised I'd seen it before.	By the time I got to the station
my train had left.	He had to see the head teacher	because he had hit another student.	The play had already finished
when we arrived at the theatre	I had lost my keys,	so I couldn't get into my house	He loosened his belt
because he had eaten too much	My teacher asked me if	I had done my homework	By the time I got to the shop,
they'd sold out of milk	I had smoked for twenty-five years	by the time I gave up	Halfway up the hill I wished
I had taken a smaller backpack	I hadn't been to Paris	before I flew there last summer	He had already gone to bed
by the time she got home	She had studied Spanish for six months	before she went to Mexico	He had finished dessert
before I even started my main course	My older sister finished university	by the time I started secondary school	We missed the early train
because we had overslept	It was good to see Anna again because	we hadn't spoken to each other for years	She was really hungry because

 PHOTOCOPIABLE *New Inside Out* Intermediate Teacher's Book © Macmillan Publishers Limited 2009

8 Vocabulary

Holiday emails

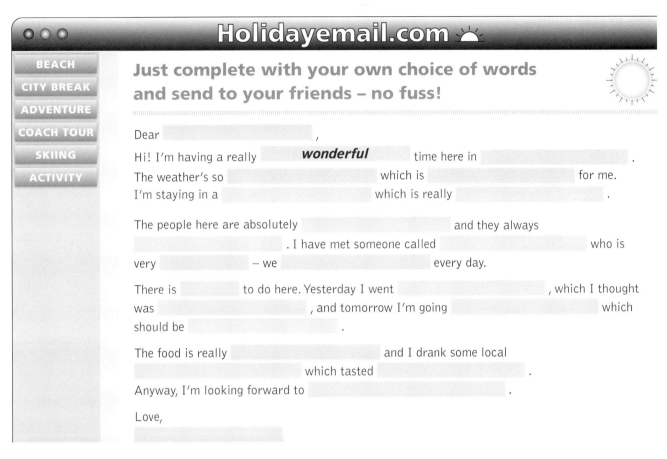

Holidayemail.com

BEACH
CITY BREAK
ADVENTURE
COACH TOUR
SKIING
ACTIVITY

Just complete with your own choice of words and send to your friends – no fuss!

Dear   ,

Hi! I'm having a really   *wonderful*   time here in   .
The weather's so   which is   for me.
I'm staying in a   which is really   .

The people here are absolutely   and they always
                    . I have met someone called   who is
very   – we   every day.

There is   to do here. Yesterday I went   , which I thought
was   , and tomorrow I'm going   which
should be   .

The food is really   and I drank some local
                    which tasted   .

Anyway, I'm looking forward to   .

Love,

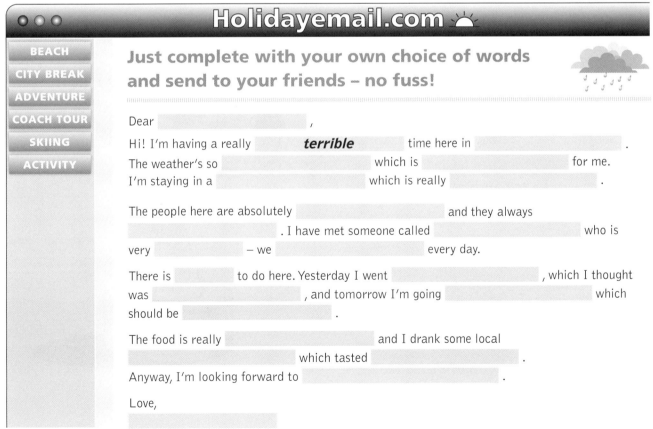

Holidayemail.com

BEACH
CITY BREAK
ADVENTURE
COACH TOUR
SKIING
ACTIVITY

Just complete with your own choice of words and send to your friends – no fuss!

Dear   ,

Hi! I'm having a really   *terrible*   time here in   .
The weather's so   which is   for me.
I'm staying in a   which is really   .

The people here are absolutely   and they always
                    . I have met someone called   who is
very   – we   every day.

There is   to do here. Yesterday I went   , which I thought
was   , and tomorrow I'm going   which
should be   .

The food is really   and I drank some local
                    which tasted   .

Anyway, I'm looking forward to   .

Love,

8 Communication

Globetrotters

Who in your group ...

has used the greatest number of different forms of transport?   (100 points)   _____

has used the most unusual form of transport?   (100 points)   _____

has visited the most continents?   (100 points)   _____

has visited the most capital cities?   (100 points)   _____

can say 'Thank you' in the most languages?   (100 points)   _____

can count to ten in the most languages?   (100 points)   _____

has spent the least time in his/her own country in the last twelve months?   (100 points)   _____

has been on the longest journey?

(a) number of hours from start to finish   (100 points)   _____

(b) number of kilometres from start to finish   (100 points)   _____

has spent the most time in a foreign country?   (100 points)   _____

has eaten the most unusual food?   (100 points)   _____

Our

Globetrotter Extraordinaire

is _____

9 Grammar

Reported interviews

A

Read the interviews.

> **Ella**
>
> I'm a student so I don't have much money. I live in a shared house in London. I study fashion. I've just finished my second year at university. Next year I'm going to study in Milan.
>
> **José**
>
> I'm a manager in a company in Madrid, although I am originally from Seville. I'm married and I have two children. I love travelling. I've been to the USA ten times. I believe that one day I will be the head of my company.
>
> **Hiro and Erika**
>
> We're from Kyoto in Japan. We work very hard so we don't have much free time. We've just returned from our honeymoon in Hawaii. We loved it. We'll definitely go back again.

1 **Put a ✓ or a ✗ next to each statement. Then complete each reported statement.**

  1 Ella isn't rich. ✓
     She said that she *didn't have much money* .

  2 Ella is going to study in Rome. ✗
     She told me that *she was going to Milan* .

  3 José is from Madrid. ☐
     He told me _____ .

  4 José hasn't visited the USA. ☐
     He said _____ .

  5 Hiro and Erika are from Tokyo. ☐
     They told me _____ .

  6 Hiro and Erika are married. ☐
     They said _____ .

2 **Test Student B's memory. Read each (first) statement out. Student B says if the statement is true or false and then supports their answer with a reported statement.**

B

Read the interviews.

> **Ella**
>
> I'm a student so I don't have much money. I live in a shared house in London. I study fashion. I've just finished my second year at university. Next year I'm going to study in Milan.
>
> **José**
>
> I'm a manager in a company in Madrid, although I am originally from Seville. I'm married and I have two children. I love travelling. I've been to the USA ten times. I believe that one day I will be the head of my company.
>
> **Hiro and Erika**
>
> We're from Kyoto in Japan. We work very hard so we don't have much free time. We've just returned from our honeymoon in Hawaii. We loved it. We'll definitely go back again.

1 **Put a ✓ or a ✗ next to each statement. Then complete each reported statement.**

  1 Ella is living in the UK capital. ✓
     She said that she *was living in London* .

  2 Ella has one more year at university. ✗
     She told me that *she had just finished* .

  3 José has three children. ☐
     He told me _____ .

  4 José is ambitious. ☐
     He said _____ .

  5 Hiro and Erika are busy people. ☐
     They told me _____ .

  6 Hiro and Erika don't like Hawaii. ☐
     They said _____ .

2 **Read each (first) statement out. Student A says if the statement is true or false and then supports their answer with a reported statement.**

9 Vocabulary

Blockbuster

Choose at least three items from each column.

Location	Characters	Props	Events
A haunted house	A robot	A sword	An explosion
A museum	A model	A gun	A chase
A church	An inventor	A book	A party
A spaceship	A baby	Poison	A festival
A desert	A cowboy	A diamond	A trial
Australia	A soldier	A code	A race
Antarctica	A doctor	A bomb	A competition
Mars	An explorer	A key	An investigation
A farmhouse	A politician	A password	A fight
A swimming pool	A monster	A picture	A battle
A school	A giant	A clue	A discovery
A hotel	A cook	A maze	A phone call
A theatre	A policeman	A magic lamp	A test

 PHOTOCOPIABLE *New Inside Out* Intermediate Teacher's Book © Macmillan Publishers Limited 2009

9 Communication

Film, books and music

A

Write the **DOWN** clues:

1 _____

2 _____

3 _____

4 _____

6 _____

7 _____

8 _____

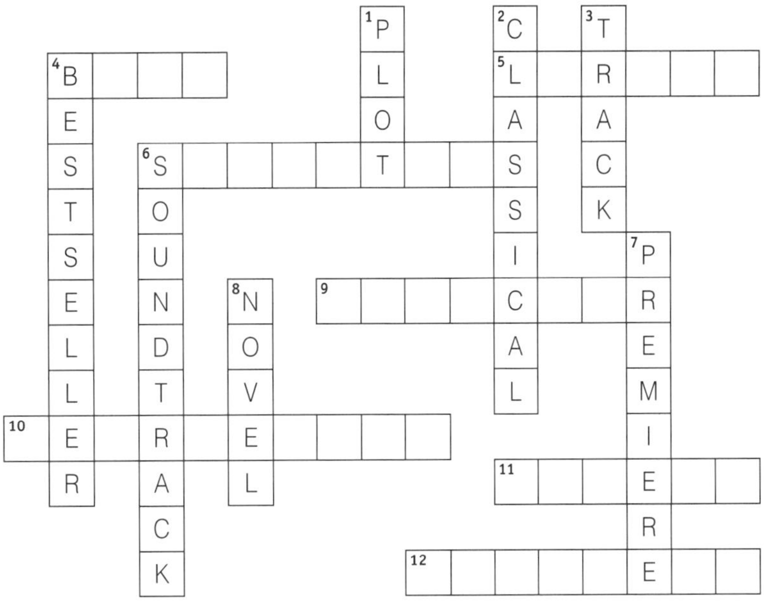

Crossword grid (A):

Down words: ¹P L O T, ²C L A S S I C A L, ³T R A C K, ⁴B E S T S E L L E R, ⁶S O U N D T R A C K, ⁷P R E M I E R E, ⁸N O V E L

Across answers filled: ⁵T R A C K, ⁹..., ¹⁰E...R...E L..., ¹¹..., ¹²...

B

Write the **ACROSS** clues:

4 _____

5 _____

6 _____

9 _____

10 _____

11 _____

12 _____

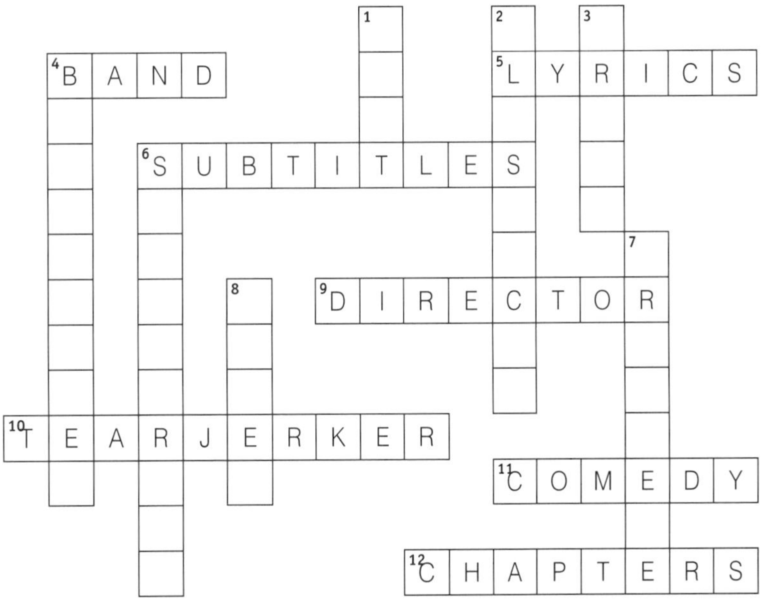

Crossword grid (B):

⁴B A N D ⁵L Y R I C S

⁶S U B T I T L E S

⁹D I R E C T O R

¹⁰T E A R J E R K E R

¹¹C O M E D Y

¹²C H A P T E R S

Review C

Somewhere Only We Know

Somewhere Only We Know was written and recorded by the British band Keane in 2004.

1 🎵 2.43 **Work with a partner. Listen to the song and choose the best summary.**

a) Someone describing an afternoon walk in the countryside with their dog. Both the singer and the dog are very familiar with this particular walk.

b) Someone describing walking through their city after a nuclear war and realising he is the only person left alive.

c) Someone thinking about how complicated and difficult their life has become and wanting to return to a familiar place with friends for some peace and relaxation.

I walked across an empty land.
I knew the pathway like the back of my hand.
I felt the earth beneath my feet,
Sat by the river, and it made me complete.
Oh simple thing where have you gone?
I'm getting old and I need something to rely on.
So tell me when you're gonna let me in.
I'm getting tired and I need somewhere to begin.

I came across a fallen tree.
I felt the branches of it looking at me.
Is this the place we used to love?
Is this the place that I've been dreaming of?
Oh, simple thing where have you gone?
I'm getting old and I need something to rely on.
So tell me when you're gonna let me in.
I'm getting tired and I need somewhere to begin.

And if you have a minute why don't we go,
Talk about it somewhere only we know?
This could be the end of everything
So why don't we go
Somewhere only we know?
Somewhere only we know?

2 **Find words and phrases in the song which mean the same.**

a) to know something very well.	d) loved at one time in the past	f) have time
b) under	e) think about something you hope to have	g) discuss
c) depend on		

3 **Think about the following and then describe each one to your partner.**

a) A place you know like the back of your hand.

b) A place you used to love that you don't go to anymore.

c) A type of place you dream of going to when you want a break.

d) A person, animal, or thing you rely on to cheer you up when you're feeling sad.

 PHOTOCOPIABLE *New Inside Out* Intermediate Teacher's Book © Macmillan Publishers Limited 2009

10 Grammar

When I was at school

START **1** I knew a girl who …	**2** I particularly used to enjoy subjects that …	**3** I didn't like a schoolmate who …
16 I like PE lessons in which …	**17** I had a very strange schoolmate who …	**4** There was a trouble-maker who …
15 The teacher's pet was a boy/girl that …	**18** The worst part of the school day was when …	**5** There was a bully who …
14 My very best friend was a boy/girl who lived …	**19** I had to get up …	**6** There was a schoolmate who was punished for …
13 I had a very good teacher who …	**20** There was a game that …	**7** I had a very nice teacher who …
12 I always got good marks …	**21** I liked a schoolboy/ schoolgirl who … **FINISH**	**8** I remember an occasion when, in front of the whole group, I had to …
11 The best part of the school day was when …	**10** I missed lessons when …	**9** I didn't like lessons that …

10 Vocabulary

Make and *let*

A good teacher should make his/her students ...

1 _____

_____

2 _____

_____

A good teacher should let his/her students ...

1 _____

_____

2 _____

_____

A good parent should make his/her children ...

1 _____

_____

2 _____

_____

A good parent should let his/her children ...

1 _____

_____

2 _____

_____

A good boss should make his/her employees ...

1 _____

_____

2 _____

_____

A good boss should let his/her employees ...

1 _____

_____

2 _____

_____

 PHOTOCOPIABLE *New Inside Out* Intermediate Teacher's Book © Macmillan Publishers Limited 2009

A knuckle is the part of the body where the finger joins the hand.

A winkle-picker is a 1950s style shoe which has a pointed toe.

A dumbwaiter is a person who serves food in expensive restaurants.

What am I bid? £4,000 ... £4,500 ... £5,000. Any advance on £5,000? Do I hear £5,500? Going ... going ... gone! For £5,000

A gargoyle is something you drink when you have a sore throat.

A pew is a seat where you sit in a church.

A quiff is a small animal that comes from North Africa, often kept as a pet.

A caretaker is a woman whose job is to look after young children.

Glue is something that you use to fix things to each other.

A miser is someone who doesn't like spending money.

A rib is something you wear when you eat.

If I were a bird, …

If I had magic powers, …

If I could speak perfect English, …

If I were the richest person in the world, …

If my parents hadn't met, …

If the world was going to end next week, …

If I could go anywhere in the world, …

If I had met Mahatma Gandhi, …

If I could go to the moon, …

If I were invisible, …

If I won the lottery next week, …

If aliens landed on Earth, …

If I could change sex for a day, …

If I'd been born a thousand years ago, …

If I could be any animal, …

11 Vocabulary

Then and now

A
- Remember what you were like as a child – how you felt about things, what your attitude to life was.
- Make notes about yourself and your ideas about the topics. Then, ask your partner how they felt about these things. Compare your responses.
- When you've finished, discuss how your ideas have changed since then. Who has changed the most – you or your partner?

Ideas about ...	You as a child	Your partner as a child
1 The perfect parents		
2 Your best friend		
3 Ideal holidays		
4 Your physical appearance		
5 The ideal job		
6 The greatest ambition in life		

- ✂

B
- Remember what you were like as a child – how you felt about things, what your attitude to life was.
- Make notes about yourself and your ideas about the topics. Then, ask your partner how they felt about these things. Compare your responses.
- When you've finished, discuss how your ideas have changed since then. Who has changed the most – you or your partner?

Ideas about ...	You as a child	Your partner as a child
1 School		
2 The ideal bedroom		
3 The best way of spending money		
4 Favourite food		
5 Favourite clothes		
6 Favourite type of music/books		

11 Communication

Unreal!

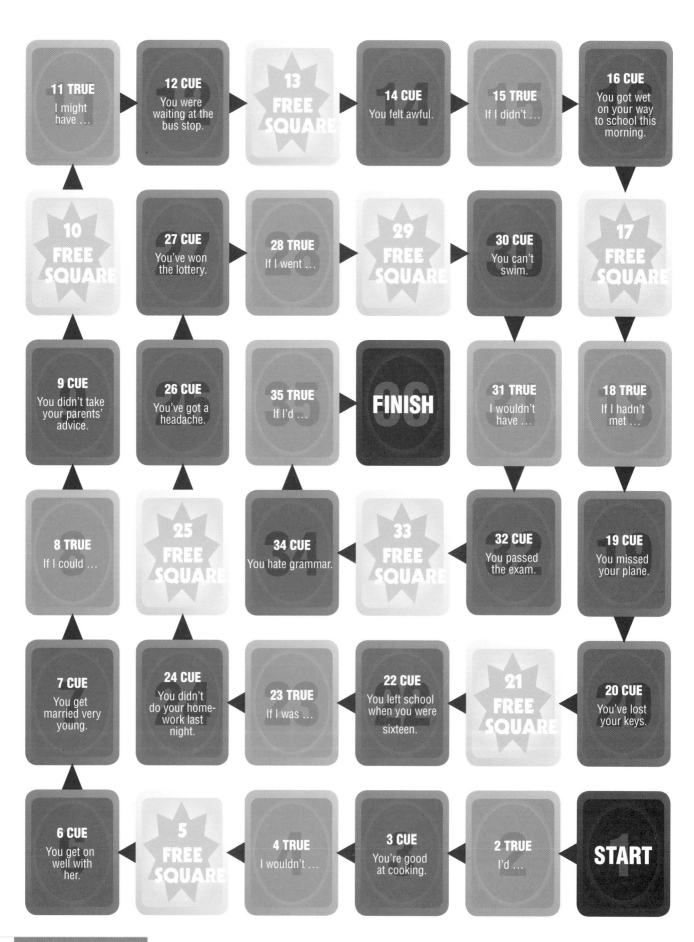

11 TRUE I might have …

12 CUE You were waiting at the bus stop.

13 FREE SQUARE

14 CUE You felt awful.

15 TRUE If I didn't …

16 CUE You got wet on your way to school this morning.

10 FREE SQUARE

27 CUE You've won the lottery.

28 TRUE If I went …

29 FREE SQUARE

30 CUE You can't swim.

17 FREE SQUARE

9 CUE You didn't take your parents' advice.

26 CUE You've got a headache.

35 TRUE If I'd …

FINISH

31 TRUE I wouldn't have …

18 TRUE If I hadn't met …

8 TRUE If I could …

25 FREE SQUARE

34 CUE You hate grammar.

33 FREE SQUARE

32 CUE You passed the exam.

19 CUE You missed your plane.

7 CUE You get married very young.

24 CUE You didn't do your homework last night.

23 TRUE If I was …

22 CUE You left school when you were sixteen.

21 FREE SQUARE

20 CUE You've lost your keys.

6 CUE You get on well with her.

5 FREE SQUARE

4 TRUE I wouldn't …

3 CUE You're good at cooking.

2 TRUE I'd …

START

New Inside Out Intermediate Teacher's Book © Macmillan Publishers Limited 2009

12 Grammar

Ever had it done?

is going to have his/her hair cut in the next few days.

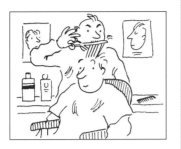

has had his/her photo taken in the last week.

has never had his/her nails done.

has had his/her portrait painted.

needs to have his/her car repaired.

regularly has his/her eyes tested.

has recently had some clothes dry-cleaned.

has had his/her fortune told at some time in his/her life.

will never have his/her ears pierced.

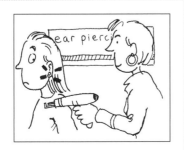

has had his/her temperature taken in the last month.

12 Vocabulary

First impressions

	DO	DON'T
Before the interview		
During the interview		

 PHOTOCOPIABLE *New Inside Out* Intermediate Teacher's Book © Macmillan Publishers Limited 2009

12 Communication

Phonetics guessing

START

1 A group of people who play together against another group. /iː/

2 Main city of a country. /æ/

3 Between the ceiling and the floor. /ɔː/

4 You feel like this when you have done something very well. /iː/

5 A relative. /ɑː/

6 You need one to practise surfing. /ɔː/

7 You leave one on someone's answering machine. /e/

8 Someone who works with you in class. /ɑː/

9 You spent much of your time here when you were a boy/girl. /uː/

10 You are like this when you have a lot of work and you don't have time to do anything else. /ɪ/

11 Part of the year. /ʌ/

12 It is not false. /uː/

13 You ask for one when you don't have a car and you don't feel like walking. /ɪ/

14 Opposite of 'go'. /ʌ/

15 They behave in a violent way, especially at football matches. /uː/

16 Someone – not a relative – who you like and spend much of your time with. /e/

17 Your mother's brother. /ʌ/

18 A modal verb you use for invitations. /ʊ/

19 Not very light. /e/

20 You have to do this when you want to practise skydiving. /ʌ/

21 The period of your life that comes before adolescence. /ʊ/

22 Past tense of 'sweep'. /e/

23 You can have it black or white. /ɒ/

24 You cannot speak without saying them. /ɜː/

25 Some people only read these in a newspaper. /e/

26 You must get one if you want to earn your living. /ɒ/

27 Your sister's daughter. /iː/

28 Many couples do this. /æ/

29 Verb that goes with another verb and shows tense or voice, or is used to make questions. /ɔː/

30 Some people go there on Sunday. /ɜː/

FINISH

Review D
Dedicated Follower of Fashion

Dedicated Follower of Fashion was written and recorded by British band The Kinks in 1966. The light-hearted song was aimed at the fashion-obsessed young people in the London of the 'Swinging Sixties'.

1 🎧 **3.27 Listen to the song. Which activity does the song *not* refer to:** *buying clothes; looking for new fashions; going to parties; catching butterflies?*

They **seek** him here, they seek him there,
His clothes are **loud**, but never **square**.
It will make or break him so he's got to buy the best,
'Cos he's A **Dedicated** Follower Of Fashion.

And when he does his little rounds,
Round the **boutiques** of London Town,
Eagerly pursuing all the latest **fads** and trends,
'Cos he's A Dedicated Follower Of Fashion.

Oh yes he is (oh yes he is), oh yes he is (oh yes he is).
There's one thing that he loves and that is **flattery**.
One week he's in polka-dots, the next week he's
    in stripes.
'Cos he's A Dedicated Follower Of Fashion.

They seek him here, they seek him there,
In Regent Street and Leicester Square.
Everywhere the Carnabetian army marches on,
Each one A Dedicated Follower Of Fashion.

Oh yes he is (oh yes he is), oh yes he is (oh yes he is).
His world is built round discotheques and parties.
This pleasure-seeking individual always looks his best
'Cos he's A Dedicated Follower Of Fashion.

Oh yes he is (oh yes he is), oh yes he is (oh yes he is).
He **flits** from shop to shop just like a butterfly.
In matters of the cloth he is as **fickle** as can be,
'Cos he's A Dedicated Follower Of Fashion.
He's A Dedicated Follower Of Fashion.
He's A Dedicated Follower Of Fashion.

Glossary: *Carnabetian army* refers to the many people who used to shop in Carnaby Street, London's fashion centre in the 1960s.

2 **Work with a partner. Match each emboldened word in the song with its synonym/definition in the box.**

always changing your mind about what you like   boring   enthusiastically
fashion shops   (insincere) praise   ~~look for~~   moves quickly from one place to another
spending a lot of time and effort on something   things that are fashionable for a short time
very brightly coloured

seek – look for

loud –

 PHOTOCOPIABLE   *New Inside Out* Intermediate Teacher's Book © Macmillan Publishers Limited 2009

Chocolate

Chocolate is a very special kind of food. Although certainly not a vital part of the human diet, it is loved for its delicious sweet taste and the way it melts in the mouth, and would be missed by many millions of people if it suddenly ceased to exist. Indeed, the global population of 'chocoholics' (people who find chocolate very difficult to resist) is very large. The most chocoholic countries in the world are in Europe; Switzerland and Austria top the list with an annual average consumption of around ten kilograms of chocolate per person, closely followed by Britain and Ireland.

Many people believe that eating chocolate has a mood-enhancing effect. There is disagreement, however, about whether this is due to the ingredients of chocolate or the significance attached to eating it. Some scientists have suggested that chocolate releases chemicals in the brain that create feelings of happiness, while others believe the happy feelings might only occur because people see eating chocolate as a way of being nice to themselves.

The vital ingredient in chocolate is the seeds of the cacao tree, which only grows in tropical countries. Cacao was first cultivated at least 2,500 years ago by the Maya and Aztec civilisations of Central America, which used the seeds to make a chocolate-flavoured drink. In the early sixteenth century, Spanish explorers who arrived in Central America recorded that the Aztec emperor, Montezuma, was particularly fond of this chocolate drink, although it was not mixed with sugar and therefore had a bitter rather than a sweet taste.

The Spanish took cacao seeds back to Europe, where the chocolate drink quickly became popular with very rich people, the only ones able to afford it. It wasn't until the nineteenth century that chocolate began to appear in the solid form that is so familiar today. The world's biggest producers of cacao today are the Ivory Coast and Ghana, both in western Africa.

The three main varieties of chocolate are dark, milk and white (which doesn't contain any solid part of the cacao seed, and perhaps therefore shouldn't be considered 'real' chocolate). No one would pretend that eating large amounts of any of these is good for you, but there is some evidence to suggest that regularly eating small quantities of dark chocolate might reduce the risk of heart disease.

This page has been downloaded from www.insideout.net.
It is photocopiable, but all copies must be complete pages. Copyright © Macmillan Publishers Limited 2009.

Chocolate

Exercise 1

Team A

Below are the answers to some questions about the text on Worksheet A. Work with your team and write the questions. When you have finished, Team B will have to answer them as part of a quiz.

1. They are both in western Africa.

2. The vital ingredient is the seeds of the cacao tree.

3. He was an Aztec emperor in Central America.

4. The Spanish first took cacao seeds from Central America to Europe.

5. About ten kilograms.

6. Very rich people.

7. Dark, milk and white.

8. A 'chocoholic' is a person who finds chocolate very difficult to resist.

....

Team B

Here are the answers to some questions about the text on Worksheet A. Work with your team and write the questions. When you have finished, Team A will have to answer them as part of a quiz.

1. It was first cultivated in Central America.

2. In tropical countries.

3. It had a bitter taste.

4. At least 2,500 years ago.

5. Dark chocolate might reduce the risk of heart disease.

6. In the nineteenth century.

7. It doesn't contain any solid part of the cacao seed.

8. Britain and Ireland.

This page has been downloaded from www.insideout.net.
It is photocopiable, but all copies must be complete pages. Copyright © Macmillan Publishers Limited 2009.

Chocolate

Exercise 2

Student A

You and your partner have the same crossword, but with different words completed. Take it in turns to describe the words to each other and fill in the gaps. When you have finished, the name of the chocolate objects traditionally given in the UK in March or April will be revealed.

1	I	N	G	R	E	D	I	E	N	T

2

| **3** | C | E | A | S | E |

4

| **5** | R | E | S | P | O | N | D |

6

| **7** | M | E | L | T |

8

| **9** | S | I | G | N | I | F | I | C | A | N | C | E |

10

· ·

Student B

You and your partner have the same crossword, but with different words completed. Take it in turns to describe the words to each other and fill in the gaps. When you have finished, the name of the chocolate objects traditionally given in the UK in March or April will be revealed.

1

| **2** | Q | U | A | N | T | I | T | Y |

3

| **4** | C | U | L | T | I | V | A | T | E |

5

| **6** | R | E | S | I | S | T |

7

| **8** | G | H | A | N | A |

9

| **10** | S | E | E | D |

This page has been downloaded from www.insideout.net.
It is photocopiable, but all copies must be complete pages. Copyright © Macmillan Publishers Limited 2009.

Chocolate – Glossary

afford verb
if you can afford something, you have enough money to be able to pay for it
We need a bigger house, but we just can't afford the rent.

bitter adjective
something that is bitter has a strong sharp taste that is not sweet

cacao noun [uncount]
a tropical tree, the seeds of which are used for making chocolate and cocoa

cease verb
stop happening or continuing
Conversation ceased when she entered the room.

civilisation noun [count/uncount]
a society that has developed its own culture and institutions
the ancient civilisations of Mesopotamia and Egypt

consumption noun [uncount]
the amount that someone eats, drinks, or smokes
Most people need to increase their daily consumption of fruit and vegetables.

cultivate verb
to grow crops or plants, especially in large quantities
Rice is cultivated throughout the coastal regions.

diet [count/uncount]
the food that a person or animal usually eats
Try to eat a balanced diet.

enhance verb
to improve something, or to make it more attractive or more valuable
The measures taken should considerably enhance the residents' quality of life.

explorer noun [count]
someone who travels to a place that other people do not know much about in order to find out what is there

familiar adjective
well known to you, or easily recognized by you
Harry Potter will be familiar to many readers.

fond adjective
getting enjoyment and satisfaction from something, especially often or over a long time
fond of music/poetry

global adjective
including or affecting the whole world
global changes in climate

ingredient noun [count]
one of the foods or liquids that you use in making a particular meal
The food is home cooked using fresh ingredients.

melt verb
to change a solid substance into a liquid
Melt the butter in a small saucepan.

mood [count/uncount]
the way that someone is feeling, for example whether they are happy, sad, or angry
medicines that affect mood and mental function

pretend verb
to claim that something is true when it is not
I don't pretend to have all the answers.

release verb
to let a substance or energy spread into the area or atmosphere around it, especially as part of a chemical reaction
Oxygen from the water is released into the atmosphere.

resist verb
to stop yourself from doing something that you would very much like to do
It's difficult to resist a challenge like that.

risk noun [count/uncount]
the possibility that something unpleasant or dangerous might happen
Most major changes involve some risk.

seed noun [count/uncount]
a small hard part produced by a plant that can grow into a new plant of the same type
a packet of seeds

significance noun [singular/uncount]
the meaning of something, usually a special meaning or a meaning that is not obvious
I didn't realize the true significance of this comment at the time.

solid adjective
a solid substance is firm and hard and is not a liquid or a gas

vital adjective
very important, necessary, or essential

This page has been downloaded from www.insideout.net. It is photocopiable, but all copies must be complete pages.
Copyright © Macmillan Publishers Limited 2009. Definitions from the Macmillan English Dictionary 2nd Edition © Macmillan Publishers Limited 2007 and the Macmillan Essential Dictionary © Macmillan Publishers Limited 2003

e-lesson

1. Chocolate
This week's lesson focuses on chocolate, which might not be the world's healthiest food but is certainly one of the most popular.

Level
Intermediate and above (equivalent to CEF level B1 and above)

How to use the lesson
1. Brainstorm on the subject of chocolate. What words do your students associate with chocolate? What are their favourite kinds of chocolate, and when do they eat them? Is there anyone in the class who *doesn't* eat chocolate, and if so, why?

2. Give each student in the class a copy of Worksheet A and give them five to ten minutes to read through it, encouraging them to look up new vocabulary. Tell the students it is important that they try to remember as much of the information as possible.

3. Tell the students they are going to prepare a quiz for each other. Then divide the class into two teams, A and B.

4. Cut Worksheet B in half and give each member of each team the corresponding half. Explain that each team has to work together to formulate the questions that produce the answers given, based on the text on Worksheet A. Note that it is possible for there to be slight variations of each question.

5. When both teams have finished preparing their questions, ask them to turn over Worksheet A and the glossary so that they can't see them.

6. The two teams now take it in turns to ask and answer the questions. Encourage the teams to confer before answering, but make it clear that once they have given their answer they cannot change it. You should only accept answers given in correct English. Keep the score on the board: the team with the most correct answers at the end of the quiz wins.

7. Before the next exercise you need to cut Worksheet C into two halves. Divide the students into pairs, Student A and Student B, and hand out the halves of the worksheet so that Student A's grid has the words that Student B's grid is missing, and vice versa. The idea is for the students to *describe* the words they have in their grids so that their partners can guess what they are, and then fill them in. It is therefore vital that they don't show their grids to their partners.
Give the students time to check that they understand all the words on their worksheet. Then tell them to describe the words to their partner one by one, and to take it in turns to speak. You could let the students carry on describing the words for as long as it takes for their partners to identify them, or as a fun alternative you could impose a time limit for the description of each word.
Before the students begin, point out that all the missing words feature in the text on Worksheet A.

8. Check answers in open class.

Answers:

Exercise 1

Team A
1. Where are the Ivory Coast and Ghana?
2. What is the vital ingredient in chocolate?
3. Who was Montezuma?
4. Who first took cacao seeds from Central America to Europe?
5. What is the annual average consumption of chocolate per person in Switzerland and Austria?
6. After cacao seeds arrived in Europe, who did the chocolate drink become popular with?
7. What are the three main varieties of chocolate?
8. What is a 'chocoholic'?

Team B
1. Where was cacao first cultivated?
2. Where can cacao trees grow?
3. What kind of taste did the Aztecs' chocolate drink have?
4. When was cacao first cultivated?
5. What kind of chocolate might reduce the risk of heart disease?
6. When did chocolate begin to appear in solid form?
7. What does white chocolate not contain?
8. After Switzerland and Austria, which are the most 'chocoholic' countries?

Exercise 2
1. ingredient 2. quantity 3. cease 4. cultivate 5. respond 6. resist 7. melt 8. Ghana 9. significance 10. seed

When the grid has been completed correctly, *Easter eggs* will read from top to bottom.

2. Related Websites
Send your students to these websites, or just take a look yourself.

http://news.bbc.co.uk/1/hi/sci/tech/6991289.stm
A BBC article (2007) investigating the roots of chocolate cravings. Intermediate level and above.

http://news.bbc.co.uk/1/hi/sci/tech/7087899.stm
A BBC article (2007) on the evidence that chocolate was part of the diet of the ancient civilisations of Central America. Challenging for intermediate level.

http://news.bbc.co.uk/cbbcnews/hi/chat/your_comments/newsid_2514000/2514843.stm
A BBC *Newsround* forum (2002), aimed primarily at children and younger teenagers, asking 'Would you pay more for fair trade chocolate?' Appropriate for intermediate level.

This page has been downloaded from www.insideout.net.
It is photocopiable, but all copies must be complete pages. Copyright © Macmillan Publishers Limited 2009.